JOURNAL

In memory of the CSS *Alabama* and her men:

"Heart must be keener, courage the greater,
Bolder the will as our band diminishes."

—from an Old English poem

The Journal of
GEORGE TOWNLEY FULLAM

Boarding Officer of
the Confederate Sea Raider
Alabama

EDITED AND ANNOTATED BY
Charles G. Summersell

*Published for
The Friends of the
Mobile Public Library*

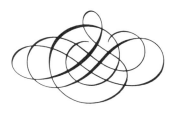

THE UNIVERSITY OF ALABAMA PRESS
University, Alabama

CONTENTS

INTRODUCTION

Few Civil War subjects, and certainly no other phase of the Civil War's naval history, have stirred up as much controversy as the career of the Confederate States Steamer *Alabama*, most successful of the Confederate commerce raiders. So it cannot be claimed that George Townley Fullam's Journal of the CSS *Alabama* will introduce the reader to an adventure hitherto unknown. Yet this is the first time this Journal has had obscure references clarified and, indeed, the first time the complete Journal has been edited with footnotes. The editing is done with regard to events which concerned Fullam. Related characters and actions are treated incidentally—the full focus being intentionally zeroed in on Fullam and his Journal.

The cruise of the CSS *Alabama* was a romantic episode, one of the most romantic in American sea warfare, as many books attest in detail. It was surely the high point in the American Civil War at sea, the least-known side of the "Lost Cause." Therefore, this story has many potential starting places. For the scholar seeking the significance of the past, the start could be with the payment from Great Britain to the United States of $15,500,000 for the *Alabama* Claims. This was highly significant, and at least one place to start the chronology of international arbitration settling major controversies between major powers. This broad significance is by no means new. Thirty-six years have passed since Allan Nevins' Pulitzer Prize winner, *Hamilton Fish: The Inner History of the Grant Administration,* was published, and 74 years since John Bassett Moore wrote the *History and Digest of the International Arbitrations to Which the United States Has Been a Party*. Fullam's actions, as recorded in his Journal, may be seen as one step in the events leading up to the international arbitrations between Great Britain and the United States.

Another possible start of the Fullam story could focus on Mobile, home of the commanding officer of the CSS *Alabama*, Rear Admiral Raphael Semmes, and could tell how the Fullam Journal found its way from Hull in Yorkshire to Mobile in Alabama. In a prominent place in the Mobile Public Library, the Fullam Journal is proudly displayed in a locked glass case. The neat, bound volume in a relatively legible nineteenth century handwriting consists of a Log as well as a Journal. The Log is one of several appendices and is limited to giving the dates and noontime locations by celestial observation. The total manuscript is now included in this edited work under the title, *The Journal of George Townley Fullam: Boarding Officer of the Confederate Sea Raider Alabama.* Like the Log, the Journal has almost daily entries. The Journal describes, often in picturesque language, the life, labor, and adventures aboard the Confederacy's most famous war cruiser. In the manuscript the reader looks through the eyes of this 21-year-old Englishman who was a dare-devil enough subject of Queen Victoria to join in a war not strictly his own. Yet the American Civil War became for Fullam, cruising in the CSS *Alabama*, a personal struggle to which he gave his whole enthusiasm and talent. That the great adventure ended in defeat no doubt enhanced the drama.

There were various paradoxes in the character of Fullam. For one example, he was very precise but by no means especially cautious. With a watch officer's combination of candor and precision, he wrote of many courts martial and of insubordinate sailors. Desertions were noted by Fullam and reckoned by the score as to when, where, and sometimes who. In contrast, Admiral Semmes and John McIntosh Kell, in narrating the cruise of the CSS *Alabama*, rarely gave the names of deserting sailors. In many cases, when Fullam himself lacked details identifying men and ships, the editor has supplied this information in footnotes. Footnotes and Introduction are designed to round out Fullam's narrative with details garnered from diverse sources and to present to the reader new perspectives.

George Townley Fullam was born 21 March 1841 at Kingston-upon-Hull, on the northeast coast of England. His birth certificate indicates that his parents lived at 37 English Street. The maiden name of his mother was Ann Parker and his father, a schoolmaster, was also named George Townley Fullam. The senior Fullam was a teacher of navigation and, in time, a writer on the subject. The book which he wrote in 1868 was entitled *Hand-Book to the Humber,* a navigational guide to the Humber River at Hull in Yorkshire. It is now rare, but may be found in the British Museum. It lists subjects taught at Fullam's Navigation School, including English, bookkeeping, and surveying, as well as mathematics and other subjects related closely to navigation. One of the names for the school over the years was "G. T. Fullam's Trade, Civil Service, and Naval School," and another was "G. T. Fullam's Nautical and Steam School," both located at 13 Osborne Street, Hull. There were other teachers in the Fullam family also. Thus it should not seem unusual that young Fullam would be well educated for his day, have a good background for navigation and the seagoing skills, and probably be familiar enough with the French language to use the French phrases which appear from time to time in the Journal.

When George Townley Fullam was 21 years of age, he joined the Confederate States Navy. He had already learned much of the mariner's trade before Confederate secret agents appeared in England with missions which included acquiring blockade runners and cruisers for the Confederacy. Fullam worked with the most successful agent of the South, James Dunwody Bulloch (that is to say, most successful if any man could be said to succeed in serving a losing side). Bulloch was certainly the chief promoter of the three most important of the Confederate commerce raiders: *Florida*, *Alabama*, and *Shenandoah*, named in the order in which Bulloch provided them.

In addition to Fullam, there were four other officers who served under Bulloch in Liverpool and later became officers in *Alabama*. These joined Bulloch in Savannah, Georgia, where he had gone on official Confederate business: E. M. Anderson, E. A. Maffitt, Clarence R. Yonge, and John Low. Yonge was the only officer in the CSS *Alabama* to desert, or to join forces with the Union, or to serve as a witness for Union diplomats. Lieutenant John Low, a Britisher transplanted to Georgia prior to the Civil War, played an important role on the *Alabama*, later becoming commanding officer of the CSS *Tuscaloosa* and frequently appearing in the Fullam Journal.

On 4 June 1861 Bulloch arrived in Liverpool and commenced the work which he graphically described in his two-volume publication, *Secret Service of the Confederate States in Europe, or How the Confederate Cruisers were Equipped*. On 1 August 1861 Bulloch let the contract with the already-celebrated shipbuilding firm, Laird Brothers of Birkenhead, for construction of the CSS *Alabama*. *Alabama* was earlier known by various names, such as *Enrica*, *Barcelona*, and also by her hull number *290* (the number in the list of vessels built by Lairds). While working with Bulloch, Fullam and Yonge saw the CSS *Alabama* long before Raphael Semmes set eyes on her because Bulloch had that ship built while Semmes was still cruising in the CSS *Sumter*. Other officers-to-be of *Alabama*, who had served in *Sumter* in addition to Semmes, were: John McIntosh Kell, Richard F. Armstrong, Joseph D. Wilson, Francis L. Galt, Miles J. Freeman, B. K. Howell, William B. Smith, William P. Brooks, Mathew O'Brien, Simeon W. Cummings, Benjamin P. Mecaskey, Thomas C. Cuddy, and William Robinson.

It was 29 July 1862 when Fullam signed on the CSS *Alabama*, then under the alias of *Enrica* and supposedly a merchant steamer. At the time, Fullam was a merchant mariner who was obligated only for the trial trip. When Bulloch learned on 26 July, obviously from sources high in the British government, that it would not be safe to detain *Enrica* in Liverpool another 48 hours, he hurriedly arranged the escape of the Confederate cruiser. To do this, Bulloch availed himself of a clause in the shipbuilding contract and requested of the Laird Company a second trial run, ostensibly to check the performance of the new cruiser with stores aboard but actually for the purpose of deceiving the Argus-eyed American consul in Liverpool, Thomas H. Dudley. If Dudley could be hoodwinked, there was no question that the British officials could also be deceived into permitting the escape of the cruiser. This Journal is not the place to consider the insanity of a British law officer who held up vital papers which would have delayed the sailing of *Enrica*. Of course, Bulloch had expert advice on British law and especially the germane Foreign Enlistment Act.

Captain Mathew J. Butcher was in command of *Enrica* and understood the deception before *Enrica* departed, ostensibly for her test but actually for her rendezvous with Captain Semmes and assorted Confederate officers. Butcher was thus captain of *Alabama* before that steamer was actually put into commission under her Confederate name. The first officer of *Enrica*, as an unarmed ship, was another Britisher, John Low, and the second officer was Fullam. All three officers were British.

Fullam's Journal, to which he gave the title: "Our Cruise in the Confederate States Steamer of War Alabama," begins 29 July 1862 (at 9:15 to be exact), the day and the hour when he became the second officer of *Enrica*. One might make the point that Fullam was an officer of *Alabama* before Captain Semmes ever laid eyes on the ship whose name was welded to his own throughout history.

A glimpse of the actors in the Journal is in order. John Low, *Enrica's* first officer, was born in Aberdeen, Scotland, lived for a time in Liverpool, and was living in Savannah, Georgia in 1861 when he was appointed to the Confederate States Navy. Low kept a Journal of the CSS *Tuscaloosa* (1862–1863) which proved very useful in understanding Fullam's Journal of the CSS *Alabama*. In time, Low became the subject of a biography by W. Stanley Hoole. The surgeon of *Enrica* was David Herbert Llewellyn, who later became assistant surgeon of *Alabama*, and the paymaster was Clarence R. Yonge, the previously mentioned traitor-to-be. Shortly before, Yonge had been secretary to Captain Bulloch, one of the best possible positions to gain intelligence of future value to the Union cause. When *Enrica* was slipping away from Liverpool, Yonge was the only one of her officers who was not a Britisher.

Other Confederate officers, including Semmes, Kell, and Arthur Sinclair, were embarked in another ship, *Bahama*, and headed for a meeting with *Enrica* in the Azores off the coast of Africa. In this group, and selected to be second in command of the new cruiser, was Lt. John McIntosh Kell, the subject of a recent biography by Norman

x

C. Delaney, published by The University of Alabama Press under the title *John McIntosh Kell of the Raider Alabama*. Kell was a man of impressive appearance and resolute bearing, six feet two, well-proportioned, lithe and straight. His fine, large head was enhanced with wavy hair and a magnificent mustache and beard. By nature he was forthright and affable, but on occasion his eye would flash and his anger become awesome. He believed in discipline and commanded great respect from his men, as well as loyalty and affection. Kell started his naval career and served 20 years in the Old Navy. During that time he was with American expeditions of peace and war, including the War with Mexico, the California coast (afloat and ashore), and Perry's expedition to Japan. As did others, Kell resigned his commission and cast his fortunes with his own people of Georgia.

Arthur Sinclair was an officer of the Old Navy, a native of Virginia, and a member of an old navy family. His father attained the rank of captain, then the highest grade the navy had to offer. Sinclair's grandfather had also been a navy captain. Young Sinclair had a robust sense of humor and an insight into the motives of men as well as the mores of mariners. On occasion he was one of the few in *Alabama's* ship's company who ventured an opinion different from that of Captain Semmes. Shortly before reporting aboard *Alabama*, Sinclair served in the CSS *Virginia (Merrimac)*, including the Battle of Hampton Roads with the USS *Monitor*. Thus Sinclair served in the two most famous ships of the Confederate Navy—*Merrimac* and *Alabama*. Just before *Alabama* was put into commission in the Azores, Sinclair, along with Semmes, Kell, and others, was embarked in *Bahama*, which was under command of Eugene L. Tessier (earlier Tessier commanded *Florida's* tender, *Bermuda*, sister ship of *Bahama)*. There was also a third ship headed for the rendezvous in the Azores, the collier *Agrippina*, Captain Alexander McQueen. McQueen and his ship were often mentioned in Fullam's Journal.

Choosing the Azores for the rendezvous was an inspired decision on the part of Captain Bulloch. The Azores had a history going back to the first voyage of Christopher Columbus, and earlier to Portuguese explorations. (Recently they were the site of a conference between President Nixon and the French president in 1971, nearly 110 years after serving as the birthplace of Fullam's *Alabama*.) The place of meeting for the Confederates was Terceira in the Azores, where in 1829–1830 had occurred the Terceira Affair, an episode which involved arming previously unarmed Portuguese vessels. The Terceira Affair may have suggested Terceira to Bulloch as a place for the *Enrica-Alabama* episode. Thus, in 1862 this Portuguese possession was about to witness the commissioning of the ship which became the most famous commerce raider of the Civil War. This was a cruiser which never entered any port of the Confederate States. *Enrica's* armament was on its way also to the prearranged meeting, secretly riding aboard the two vessels of British registry, *Bahama* and *Agrippina*.

At the start of the cruise, *Alabama's* crew were mostly Englishmen, and about the only objects that could be called Confederate about the ship, besides the flag, were her officers. The number of officers who joined the cruiser at Terceira was 27 and the number of men 87. Three officers and 99 men were recruited during the cruise. Altogether, many nationalities were represented among the crew of the raider. Most of the original crew were British and most of those recruited at sea were from Yankee merchantmen. It is true that not all seamen in American ships were United States citizens. Yet it may be estimated that of *Alabama's* crew at least 45 percent were British (including Irish), at least 10 percent were of other foreign origin, and at least 45 percent were recruited from Yankee merchant vessels. It is true that *Alabama* seldom had more than 120 men at one time, exclusive of the officers, but the difference in figures is largely accounted for by desertions. Although Semmes insisted that he did not want to enlist sailors of Yankee birth, Kell stated that there was a sprinkling of Yankee tars. At that time American sailors had an international reputation as the world's best. It would be interesting to find the places of birth of this last 45 percent. No doubt American seamen, like foreign seamen, were often attracted into Confederate service by the prospect of prize money and relatively high wages, about double prewar wages.

On 23 August 1862, George Townley Fullam was elevated from second officer of the merchantman *Enrica* to acting master's mate of the CSS *Alabama*. This was just the day before *Alabama* was formally put into commission. Fullam's appointment came from Captain Semmes, already a celebrated commerce raider because of his cruise in the CSS *Sumter*. After appointing Fullam, Semmes took command of *Alabama* in dramatic ceremonies, and made a forceful speech to the assembled ship's company. At the time, the British flag flew at the fore, the Confederate ensign at the peak, and the ship's pennant at the main. This act of commissioning, according to Semmes (based upon 7 Wheaton, 337), gave to the CSS *Alabama* in international law the standing of a man-of-war.

Arthur Sinclair, in his *Two Years on the Alabama,* described the raider as having "A long, trim, black hull, elliptic stern, fiddle-head cutwater, long raking lower masts...." He further wrote,

The Alabama was a screw steamer with full sail-power. She measured 235 ft. over all, beam 32 ft., tonnage 1,000. Her draft with full coal-bunkers was 15 ft. Her engines were two in number, horizontal, of 300 nominal, or 1,000 actual horse-power. She was barkentine-rigged, with very long lower masts, giving her principal sails an immense "drop" or surface. She was at the same time a perfect steamer and a perfect sailing-vessel, each entirely independent of the other. Her screw, which was a two-bladed one, hoisted in a propeller-well, and when triced up was quite clear of the water, hence no drag or impediment to her speed under sail-power alone. Kept constantly under banked fires, and with frequent hoisting and lowering of screw, her crew and engineers executed this manoeuvre with surprising alacrity and precision. Indeed, so rapidly could she be changed from sail to steam-power that no enemy, appearing on the horizon in clear weather, could surprise her under sail, nor could a sailing-vessel of superior speed escape her before getting her full steam-power.

After the commissioning ceremony, it was Fullam who commanded the small boat which transported both Captain Bulloch and Captain Butcher from the decks of the new Confederate commerce raider to the tender *Bahama* for their return voyage to England. Meantime, *Alabama,* fully loaded with guns, ammunition, sea stores, and all other supplies including coal, on 24 August 1862 commenced the cruise which the Fullam Journal recorded from day to day with detailed observations.

The purpose for which the raider was sent out and her ability to accomplish the mission had been meticulously calculated. The CSS *Alabama* was planned, built, and outfitted carefully and shrewdly with the object of annihilating American shipping on the high seas. Her commander was a man who had a genius for this particular assignment, and her officers were selected for toughness to endure the rigors of sea life plus a character to tolerate the isolation from home and the constant close association on shipboard. The raider was planned as a small but swift vessel that could hit the enemy suddenly, and quickly become lost in the vast ocean. Her route of destruction was according to design, not surprising to a person today familiar with modern operation plans. In the 1860's, however, there was much in *Alabama's* cruiser war which was innovative and different from earlier commerce raiding. New was the knowledge of the sea lanes of Matthew Fontaine Maury, which made the routes of seaborne commerce more predictable by the time of the Civil War. Because her movements were swift and mysterious, she became a terror to helpless enemy shipping and a challenge to Union warships, many of which had to roam the world, expensively seeking her out in that age before instant communication. Few, if any, men-of-war of the sixties could boast *Alabama's* resources for self-sufficiency. She could make all ordinary repairs on her engines, spars, and armament even while at sea or in remote and strange harbors where no dry docks were available. In her 22 months of cruising, only one time did she make major repairs, and then in an improvised dry dock at almost desolate Pulo Condore in the China Seas. *Alabama* necessarily had to be self-sufficient because for her no sympathetic hand was outstretched from other nations, except the British, and even that country was to a considerable extent limited by neutrality laws and diplomatic caution. The sea raider flew the flag of a blockaded nation and was alone in a world of vast oceans.

In his new ship Fullam's new job was really an ambiguous one. Although a very old grade, the rank of master's mate had been abolished in the United States Navy in 1847 because of the creation of the Naval Academy. It was supposed then that the Naval Academy would furnish a sufficient supply of officers without retaining the master's mates. [Tom H. Wells, *The Confederate Navy.*] The coming of the Civil War, however, created such a great shortage of junior officers that the position of master's mate was revived in the United States Navy and established also by the Confederate States Navy. The Confederate States Navy generally imitated the United States Navy, even as the latter copied the Royal Navy in a pattern of "like father, like son." To be eligible for appointment as a master's mate in the Confederate Navy, a man had to survive examinations in navigation, mathematics, and seamanship. He also had to pass a physical examination, to submit character references, and to be more than 21 years of age.

Fullam had just attained his twenty-first birthday when Semmes appointed him acting master's mate. As the son of a teacher of navigation, he had had ample training in the know-how needed by a merchant marine officer. In later life Fullam was to be recognized by Sir Walter Runciman, himself a fabulous mariner, as the "most distinguished of the Hull captains." [Sir Walter Runciman, Bart., *"Sunbeam II" in 1932, With Some Reminiscences of Sailing Ship Captains.*] After joining the Confederate States Navy, Fullam soon demonstrated that in the handling of small boats his skill was truly outstanding, and much the same could be said of his knowledge of deck duties in merchant ships. Among many of the 96 acting master's mates in the Confederate States Navy in 1864, some had been officers in the merchant marine, others had been bar pilots. A few master's mates came from a different navy, such as Baron Maximilian von Meulnier from the Prussian Navy. Although von Meulnier and Fullam do not illustrate this particular point, many of the master's mates of that period were merchant seamen of limited formal education.

Boarding a strange ship to see whether ship and cargo should be tried in the Confederate prize court (which Captain Semmes conducted aboard the CSS *Alabama)* was one of the chief duties of the master's mates. This required good judgment, self-control, and steady nerves in commanding armed men in an eyeball confrontation. The master's mate would be the first of the raider's personnel to board a hostile Union merchant ship, and sometimes the only one of *Alabama's* officers to face a neutral ship's captain, furious that his vessel had been stopped on the high seas. From the start of *Alabama's* cruise, the principal master's mate with whom Fullam shared boarding duties was James

Evans, a former bar pilot of Charleston. Evans was a "genuine salt" and a man of personal dignity, a great spinner of yarns when off duty. He was brave almost to recklessness, with steel-gray eyes suggesting intense concentration. Evans far surpassed all hands aboard ship in one particular. When a vessel was sighted, Evans could more quickly and more accurately tell whether the stranger was or was not Yankee. Despite his inclination to stammer, Evans' skill in identifying ships from a great distance became one of the legends of the cruise of *Alabama*. On the very few occasions when he failed, it was usually because the ship, although built in America, had been sold to a neutral owner. Evans was proud of his accomplishments and did not take well to the frequent ribbing on the subject. In general, however, Evans and Fullam were full of repartee, particularly with each other in the style of two very competent and work-oriented young men. Some of the joshing came from the fact that Evans' identification of an enemy speedily put Fullam into his cutter—off on another difficult but adventurous boarding duty. As to such assignments Arthur Sinclair, who was himself a boarding officer at times, wrote:

> ... we of the watch and boarding-party must be on hand always, and stand up to the calls at all times and hours. We get the weather with no back-out, answer the notice of the quartermaster at dead of night that a sail is to be boarded, frequently board a vessel in wet clothes, and remain in charge of her until time has made them dry and warm again; yet we are young, and full of warm blood, and pull through all right.... We are as tough as hickory, the truth of the assertion borne out by the fact we are never on the sick-list, pulling through with slight ailments always.

Among the boarding officers of the CSS *Alabama* (other than Sinclair, Evans, and Fullam) were Lieutenants Richard F. Armstrong, William Sinclair, and John Low. There were other officers who seldom boarded prizes. Sometimes a lieutenant and a master's mate were involved in boarding the same prize, or even two master's mates. For example, Lt. Joseph D. Wilson and Fullam both boarded the brig *Altamaha*. The California treasure ship *Ariel* was boarded by Low and William H. Sinclair. *Ortone* was a ship boarded together by Fullam and Master's Mate Max von Meulnier. The Dutch ship *Anna* was boarded by the same two master's mates. Examples of vessels boarded by John Low include *La Foi, Baron de Castine, Ocean Rover, Ariel, Virginia, Courser, Manchester,* and *Lamp Lighter.* Armstrong boarded *Ocmulgee, Crenshaw, Starlight, Weathergauge, Emily Farnum,* and *Lauretta.* Wilson, in addition to the ship *Altamaha,* boarded *Elisha Dunbar* and *Lauretta.* Arthur Sinclair boarded *Olive Jane,* and William Sinclair boarded *Dunkirk* and *Ariel.* Evans boarded *Brilliant* and *Nora.*

Most of the vessels boarded by someone other than Fullam were encountered in September or October 1862. During this time, *Alabama* cruised from the Azores northward to intercept ships, especially ships with cargoes of wheat bound to Europe from New York, which was even then the chief seaport of the United States. Lashed by a hurricane off New York, which Kell said equalled the worst storm he had seen in all his years at sea, *Alabama* had to abandon for the moment the strategy of appearing where she would be least expected. (Semmes was influenced by John Paul Jones, who during the American Revolution sought prizes just outside a British naval base.) Instead of harrying New York shipping, *Alabama* moved toward the Caribbean, traditional cruising ground of pirates, searching for a neutral harbor in which to make repairs. The repairs duly made, *Alabama* continued her increasingly famous cruise.

After October 1862, Fullam gradually replaced the other officers as the one principally responsible for going aboard strange ships in all conditions of light and weather to determine whether the master and his ship's papers should be taken aboard *Alabama*. Fullam became adept at this duty. Arthur Sinclair's description of Fullam was very revealing: "[Fullam], the prize-master, is a typical Englishman, five feet eight in height, broad-shouldered and muscular, with blue eyes, brown hair, and huge side whiskers. A typical sailor too, big hearted, full of animal spirits and fun. [Fullam] can spin the toughest yarn of any man on board; and with this quality, joined to his happy and magnetic disposition, he succeeded in keeping chipper even the captains of the prizes he calls upon in the way of duty. Withal, it may as well be said here, [Fullam] was a most competent officer, and would have graced a lieutenant's commission." His nickname was Hell-fire Jack Fullam.

Fullam's boarding procedure should be explained, and one of the best accounts of boarding came from the captain of the grain ship *Brilliant*. On 3 October 1862, while sailing from New York to London, *Brilliant* was burned by the CSS *Alabama*. *Brilliant's* captain, George Hagar, returned to New York and gave to the newspapers a detailed description of the Confederate raider and her boarding procedures. Although *Brilliant* was boarded by Evans rather than by Fullam, Captain Hagar described the same boarding procedures used by Fullam and the other boarding officers of *Alabama*. (While *Alabama* had a full bag of national and merchant flags, Fullam's Journal makes it clear that *Alabama* usually displayed the Red Ensign of the British merchant marine, the White Ensign of the Royal Navy, or the Stars and Stripes before demanding that the prospective prize lie to for boarding.) When Fullam, or another boarding officer, with a boatload of armed men by day or night, in fair weather or foul, climbed up the gangway of a suspected ship, the papers of the ship were examined and the merchant captain was questioned. If still suspect, the master and his papers were then taken aboard *Alabama*, escorted by one boat crew while another temporary prize crew remained in the merchantman. Sometimes the prize crew had a longer stay aboard the captured vessel. Once on board the rebel raider, the merchant master was ushered into the cabin of Captain Raphael Semmes. Semmes, from the background of his second profession, the law, interrogated the hapless mariner as to his ship, port of origin, destination, name of owners of ship and cargo, nationality of owners, and, above all, proof of the assertions. In reply to Semmes' question as to the nature of *Brilliant's* cargo, Captain Hagar said that some of it was British owned, and then he said that Semmes scowled and asked, "Do you take me for a d—d fool? Where are the proofs that part of your cargo is on English account?" [*Harper's Weekly,* 1 November 1862] Hagar did indeed have papers asserting the English claim, but his documents lacked a consular seal to verify the allegations. Therefore, Semmes condemned *Brilliant* and her cargo of grain, and set a mighty bonfire glowing over the Atlantic Ocean.

Only one of the suspected prizes was ever boarded by Captain Semmes. The episode occurred after Fullam had first boarded the ship and run into a unique problem. The case was that of *Martaban,* also known as *Texan Star,* a ship which was encountered 11 December 1863. When Fullam, in following his usual routine, took a party of armed men aboard *Martaban,* Captain Samuel B. Pike refused to take his official papers and go to the CSS *Alabama.* Fullam reported the facts to Captain Semmes, who thereupon called for his gig and boarded *Martaban.* Under the name *Texan Star, Martaban* was indeed an American-built vessel, and the transfer to neutral registry was spurious, as the case before the *Alabama* Claims Court finally showed. According to Semmes' quick decision, *Texan Star* was burned, being number 50 among the 55 ships destroyed by *Alabama.* By that time, the boarding procedure long since had been crystallized.

When the armed men under Fullam appeared on the deck of a merchantman, a ship which often was owned in part by her master, there was always a chance that the mariners would put up a fight despite the fact that they were under the guns of the raider. Actually, the merchant seamen encountered by *Alabama* never chose to fight the boarders. There was no shooting, even in the case of the California treasure steamer *Ariel,* although there were 140 marines on board that ship and these were drawn up in battle position on the deck.

There were good reasons for having Fullam serve as *Alabama's* boarding officer. His Yorkshire accent helped disguise the true nationality of the Confederate raider. When a prize was boarded and proved to be a true neutral, Fullam usually gave a false nationality and name to his ship. This was part of *Alabama's* elaborate cover plan to elude the numerous and constant Union warships which were aided in their pursuit by Union diplomats and consuls in many lands. Another reason for the choice of Fullam as boarding officer on most occasions (since there were other Englishmen on the raider) was his intimate familiarity with the ways of ships and seamen, added to his training, his natural qualities of keen observation, alertness, jovial disposition, and common sense. A further cause for Fullam's preoccupation with boarding was that, as various officers were tried out for important specialized duties, some were discovered to excel in vital work other than boarding. Master's Mate Evans' skill in spotting vessels has been mentioned. John Low, who was boarding officer more often than any other during the first two months, became involved as prize master of *Tonawanda, Baron de Castine*, and *Ariel*. Low, an officer whose skill ranked just after Kell's, was trained in the English merchant service. When *Alabama* was struck by a hurricane, Low's superb seamanship no doubt saved the vessel. He was officer of the deck during the watch, and on his own responsibility wore ship in the nick of time. If he had hesitated a moment in his quick and proper response, the story of *Alabama* might have ended then. Eventually Low became commanding officer of the CSS *Tuscaloosa*, formerly a merchant ship named *Conrad*, which was converted by Semmes into a Confederate cruiser.

There were others who served as prize masters. Richard F. Armstrong was prize master of *Emily Farnum* before that ship was released, and of the schooner *Crenshaw* before she was burned. Armstrong was straight and tall, fully six feet in height, with blue eyes. A man of intelligence and character, although of a somewhat impulsive and excitable nature, he had the ability to command with ease. Armstrong was a midshipman at Annapolis and a mere lad when the war started, but he resigned his commission and immediately went South. *Alabama's* third lieutenant, Joseph D. Wilson, was prize master of *Altamaha, Elisha Dunbar*, and *Lafayette* (the first of the two prizes named *Lafayette*). In addition, Wilson was designated to be in charge of the men who burned *Ocmulgee* and *Ocean Rover*. Lt. Wilson, who came from Florida, had a dark complexion with brown hair and eyes. He was somewhat quick of temper and described as a "most earnest fighter," but nevertheless a warm-hearted man of generous disposition. He had been a midshipman in the Old Navy at Annapolis.

The duties of officers other than Fullam are mentioned in this Introduction as a frame for discussion of the work which was performed by Fullam himself. Fullam was prize master of *Golden Rule, Louisa Hatch, Winged Racer*, and *Sea Bride*, which meant that he was temporarily captain of these vessels. An important point in establishing the Journal's authorship was the fact that Fullam, writing in the Journal, stated that he was prize master of these vessels, and Sinclair stated in his own book that Fullam was appointed prize master of *Sea Bride*,

Louisa Hatch, and *Golden Rule,* mentioning only that "our boarding officer" went on *Winged Racer.* The length of time he was prize master varied with the circumstances, but Fullam's responsibilities in *Sea Bride* were considerable. While there is no complete list of ships boarded for *Alabama* by Fullam, the editor has compiled a list from various sources. The list is entirely too long for reproduction here, but a sample is as follows: *Alexandra and Herculano, Ally, Alma, Aloinir, Alphonse Cezard, Alster, Amanda, Amazonian, Amy Douglas, Anna, Anna F. Schmidt,* and *Avalanche.* This is merely a list of the ships beginning with the letter A, and thus the names run through the alphabet. There were 76 ship names which were certain, and at least 15 more ships which were probably boarded by Fullam. In the case of the ships noted above, only *Anna F. Schmidt* was seized and burned. The other ships were neutral or had neutral cargoes. While the prizes destroyed by *Alabama* have been named in many places, there is no narrative of *Alabama's* cruise which approached Fullam's in identifying the neutrals boarded. Fullam's story of the neutrals gives insight into the decline of the Union merchant marine during the Civil War and a corresponding increase in the carrying trade of Great Britain and of other nations. This story is implicit in Fullam's Journal of the CSS *Alabama* and is made explicit in the footnote comments. In his article "The Alabama, 1862–64, A Crisis in Anglo-American Relations," in *History Today,* March 1955, Arnold Whitridge commented upon the sensational decline of the American merchant marine while British shipping in 1863 increased to some 14 million tons. At the same time, all other foreign nations had only half as much. In the mortal wounding of the American merchant marine, Fullam's *Alabama* scored more conspicuously than other ships and other causes.

Fullam's duties played a vital role in *Alabama's* cruiser war, and these duties of the master's mate are better understood if one observes the duties of the principal job immediately below him in the table of organization, that is, the boatswain, and that of the position just above him, the master (or sailing master). The boatswain was in charge of all the rigging over the mastheads and over the yards, and even the rigging in the storerooms. His routine required daily morning and evening inspections of the rigging throughout the whole vessel. Before breakfast he examined the standing and running rigging, the blocks and tackle, and reported his findings to the executive officer. The boatswain's mate held the senior position of all the navy's enlisted personnel. The position of boatswain has long been regarded as the most seagoing of all grades. A traditional symbol of the boatswain is his silver pipe, the whistle used for signaling, and in 1972 the subject of an interesting exhibit in the British National Naval Museum at Greenwich. Fullam sailed in the CSS *Alabama* during the time of crash transition from sail to steam. In retrospect it is interesting to see how the position of boatswain, immediately below Fullam's rank, has survived the changes from sail, to steam, to diesel, to nuclear power, and still remains the most seagoing rate in the navy.

Above Fullam's rank as master's mate was the ship's master, interchangeably known as the sailing-master. On the CSS *Alabama*, the sailing-master was Irvine S. Bulloch. It is amusing to note that Rapael Semmes, in this one matter at least, agreed with the United States State Department. The department and Semmes consistently misspelled Bulloch's name, a surprise, especially since Irvine Bulloch was a half brother of Captain James Dunwody Bulloch who built *Alabama*. As far as the Liverpool builders of *Alabama*, the Laird Brothers, were concerned, the senior Bulloch *was* the Confederate States Navy. Fullam thus was not the only Confederate seadog to have his name misspelled.

Irvine S. Bulloch was born in Georgia and was appointed acting midshipman in the Confederate States Navy on 24 August 1861. He served in the gunboat *Savannah* under John N. Maffitt, who later commanded the CSS *Florida*. During 1861–1862, Bulloch was stationed in the CSS *Nashville*, commanded by R. V. Pegram, and later in 1862 served in the CSS *Nansemond* under Sidney S. Lee. To join the CSS *Alabama*, Bulloch had proceeded from Liverpool to Terceira in *Bahama*, as had many other officers assigned to *Alabama*. Bulloch succeeded John Low in *Alabama* when Low became commanding officer of the CSS *Tuscaloosa*. It was 22 June 1863 when Bulloch was appointed acting master. Arthur Sinclair said that Bulloch was " . . . born and cut out for a sailor. . . . He was an indefatigable student of his profession, pursuing its study at every spare moment, and at the end of the cruise had little to learn of the duties of a sailor." Bulloch was a watch officer whose primary duty was navigating the CSS *Alabama*, a responsibility shared with Fullam under the observant eyes of the executive officer, John McIntosh Kell, and also of Captain Semmes himself. Later, after the loss of the CSS *Alabama*, Bulloch was ordered to the CSS *Shenandoah* as sailing-master under James I. Waddell. Thus Irvine Bulloch had the possibly unique experience of serving under the commanding officers of all three of the most successful Confederate cruisers, *Alabama*, *Florida*, and *Shenandoah*. Like others in *Shenandoah*, Bulloch did not learn definitely of the end of the Civil War until August 1865, four months after Lee's surrender. In *Shenandoah*, Bulloch proceeded to Liverpool, arriving 6 November 1865, at which time *Shenandoah* was turned over to the British government. It was at that late date that Bulloch received his commission as lieutenant in the Confederate States Navy, a document which had been awaiting his return! It is unlikely that anyone received a Confederate commission at a later date. Thereafter, Bulloch joined his brother, James Dunwody Bulloch, as a cotton broker in Liverpool. Not the least interesting fact about Fullam's shipmate was that Irvine S. Bulloch was the uncle of another lover of the sea, President Theodore Roosevelt. Roosevelt published *The Naval War of 1812*, in 1882, one year before James Dunwody Bulloch published his book, *The Secret Service of the Confederate States in Europe or, How the Confederate Cruisers were Equipped*. Thus uncle and nephew wrote two important early works in United States naval history, one of which was intimately concerned with Fullam's CSS *Alabama*.

The duties of Irvine S. Bulloch and other sailing masters in the Confederate States Navy generally were similar to the duties of a captain in the merchant marine, with the exception that the sailing master was a part of the naval chain of command, while the merchant captain, in the absence of the ship's owner, had the final responsibility for decisions when at sea.

As to Fullam's duties, one special responsibility concerned prisoners of war. Fullam was immediately in charge of the prisoners of war and shared this responsibility with the only marine aboard, Lt. Beckett K. Howell, brother of Mrs. Jefferson Davis. While the prisoners sometimes recorded strong complaints concerning their treatment by Howell and Fullam, such complaints were moderate in contrast with those concerning the treatment of army prisoners by both the Confederate and Union sides, a subject of voluminous writing. Comparisons might be made also with the treatment of prisoners by commerce raiders in other wars, for example, by German surface raiders in World War I and World War II. In these wars the treatment was apparently no better, and possibly worse, than on the CSS *Alabama*.

Fullam's prisoners of war, who were nearly all merchant seamen, were housed on the decks of the Confederate raider. There was no room for them on the berth deck, which accommodated some 120 men, the total of *Alabama's* crew. Indeed, in the balmy weather of a typical night in the tropics, the deck might well be preferred to the crowded hammock life of the berth deck. Tropical storms were another matter, and might flood the prisoners with buckets of rain. Awnings and tarpaulins were provided by the sailmakers and were spread for protection from rain, but were often inadequate. Food for prisoners was prepared by the captives' own cooks, taking turns in the galleys. Considering the compactness of the ship's galleys, this presented problems when prisoners were numerous. On the other hand, Fullam saw to it that he carried out his orders to give prisoners the full ration allowed the Confederate naval personnel, with the exception that the Confederate spirit ration was omitted for the prisoners, doubtless to the regret of many, but the cruise of *Alabama* developed too many problems with liquor aboard without giving a liquor ration to prisoners.

Women prisoners were another problem. They were not, of course, in those days of Lincoln, Jeff Davis, and good Queen Victoria, considered prisoners at all, and were entirely outside the custody of Howell, Fullam, or, indeed, other officers of *Alabama*. When women were on board, it was considered necessary to alter, often drastically, the Confederate billets, especially those of the wardroom officers. Fullam's Journal often referred to the women, passengers and wives of ships' captains, who came on board, and the footnotes sometimes elucidate the officers' reluctance to take women aboard, however much they otherwise may have welcomed female companions.

Fullam's Journal of the CSS *Alabama* reflects what his shipmates were doing from day to day, and especially Fullam's daily responsibilities. Particularly interesting are the appendices of the Journal. These contribute varied statistics and insights concerning Fullam himself and the cruise of *Alabama*. From the appendices emerge Fullam's quality of detail and precision in a measure even more marked than in the body of the Journal, no doubt conforming to the procedures taught a century or so ago in the navigation school of Fullam's father.

Why had this Englishman become such an ardent Confederate? At least one of the reasons is clearly reflected in some of the appendices. Fullam was interested in the prize money, an interest which largely accounted, no doubt, for the enrollment of nearly half of the crew of *Alabama* from Great Britain. Even more notable is the fact that approximately half of the crew came from the Union merchant marine (of whatever national origin). Few indeed were the personnel in *Alabama* who made their homes in the Confederate States. Fullam's appendices are very detailed on the subject of prize money. Had the Confederacy won the Civil War, the officers and men of *Alabama* would have been entitled to $5,344,261 credit for disposing of 66 Union vessels, according to Fullam's calculations. Of these 66 vessels, 53 were destroyed (52 were burned and one, the USS *Hatteras,* sunk by gunfire); nine were released on ransom bond; two others were released without bond (and Fullam was excessively optimistic in claiming $150,000 for the two); one *(Sea Bride)* was sold; and one *(Conrad)* commissioned as the CSS *Tuscaloosa. Sea Bride* was valued at $17,500, and *Conrad* at $100,936. In comparison with the value of the prize ships and cargoes, the data is not to be found elsewhere as to how one department of *Alabama* found more benefit than another. The department with the least valuable stores was the boatswain's, with $905. The department having the most was the purser's, with $16,848. By value of stores taken from prizes, the departments ranked as follows: 1. purser's, 2. gunner's, 3. sailmaker's, 4. engineer's, 5. carpenter's, and 6. boatswain's.

Fullam kept a record of *Alabama's* nautical miles at sea, daily positions by celestial navigation, and separate figures on hours spent cruising under steam, *Alabama's* only known record on this last-named subject. The raider started her cruise in the North Atlantic and shifted her scene of action frequently—the West Indies, the Gulf of Mexico, back again to the West Indies, Brazil, the Cape of Good Hope, the East Indies, the China Sea, Ceylon, the Arabian Gulf, Mozambique Channel, again Cape Town, St. Helena, Brazil, and the English Channel—her course for two years. *Alabama* thus prowled the Atlantic, Indian Oceans, and China Seas, from 55° north to 40° south. She consumed 1,786 tons of coal on her voyage halfway around the world and back (for a total distance of 2.7 times around the earth measured at the equator), and at the time she came to rest off Cherbourg her bunkers contained 133 tons.

Concerning each prize, Fullam noted the name of the ship, the date of capture, the place of capture, and the value set upon her by the Confederate officer designated to estimate the value for the purpose of prize money. The total number of prisoners captured during the cruise was 2,000. Of these, 1,010 were paroled and 990 were not paroled. About a tenth of those who were not paroled enlisted in the Confederate States Navy. *Alabama's* men were persuasive recruiters and evidently had much to offer poverty-stricken merchant seamen: prize money, plus double wages. The exact wage scale for all rates is presented in a footnote. New recruits also meant less work for the old hands.

In addition to all the appendices and the daily activities recorded in the Journal itself, the English master's mate also kept a true Log of the CSS *Alabama*. Fullam's Log of *Alabama* gave the position of the cruiser each day as reckoned by celestial navigation at noon, from 1 August 1862 until 11 June 1864. The last position (10 June) showed *Alabama* entering the English Channel (49.19 north and 6.08 west), approaching the Channel Islands, and finally meeting with her destiny, a duel to the death between *Alabama* and *Kearsarge*. The only other *combat d'outrance* on the high seas during the Civil War was *Alabama's* victory over *Hatteras*.

After the historic battle, described in a footnote at the end of the Journal, was over and *Alabama's* broken bones lay on the bottom of the English Channel, Fullam proceeded from Southampton, where *Deerhound* had landed the Confederates, to his home in Hull. The master's mate, despite his fast-moving adventures afloat in the Confederate States Navy, was a youthful 23 years old. The sailor "home from the sea" was persuaded to remain ashore for a while—in the language of his fellow mariners, "to swallow the anchor."

Meantime, the Civil War moved on toward cataclysmic events, including some closely related to the CSS *Alabama*. The raider's officers went to new naval duties, some to the CSS *Shenandoah*, in certain ways the second most successful of the cruisers. Captain Semmes ran the blockade back into the Confederacy and took command of the James River Squadron. Semmes finished the war in command of some land forces, thus serving afloat and ashore in the Civil War as he had in the Mexican War. On 7 October 1864, *Alabama's* sister ship, *Florida*, was captured by the USS *Wachusetts*, sister ship of *Kearsarge*. Not long after, occurred the presidential election of 1864 and the closing events of the Civil War: the evacuation of Richmond (2 April 1865), the surrender of Lee (9 April), the assassination of Lincoln (14 April), the surrender of Joseph E. Johnston (26 April), and the arrival of the CSS *Shenandoah* in Liverpool (6 November 1865).

About a year later (29 November 1866), Raphael Semmes, who had become a rear admiral, a brigadier general, and a paroled Confederate, from his home in Mobile wrote to Fullam:

> It gives me great pleasure to comply with your request to speak of your services and character whilst you were with me on the *Alabama*. You joined me, in that ship, at the commencement of her career, and continued with me until its close. I ever found you as one of my cleverest and most reliable officers. In my disastrous engagement off Cherbourg you exhibited the courageous and manly qualities of your race, and this is the highest compliment I could pay you. Wishing you every success in life, I am, very truly yours, etc. R. Semmes.

As Fullam's later life continued to unfold, it was learned that on 12 August 1867, two years after the sinking of the CSS *Alabama*, he married Caroline Matilda Burkitt, daughter of John Burkitt, a wine merchant. The marriage was "according to the Rites and Ceremonies of the Established Church" in Lancaster County. For a time Fullam lived in his wife's home county, and it was there that the couple's eldest child, Charles Townley Fullam, was born on 14 August 1869. By the birth date of the second child, Arthur Stanley Fullam, on 19 August 1871, the author of the Journal and his wife were making their home in Hull (at 12 Clarendon Street). Two years later, 3 September 1873, George Robson Fullam was born. The family had the same Hull address when, 17 October 1875, the fourth child was born, Ernest Beltran Fullam; and the family still made their home at this address when the fifth and last child—their only daughter—was born on 25 May 1877, Edith Annie Fullam. In time, Edith Annie Fullam proved to be the only member of the family to write her name in her father's Journal, and in bold letters at that. The child's signature was one of the exhibits first recognized by the editor as proof that the Journal was indeed written by George Townley Fullam. Later an independent sample of the handwriting of Captain Fullam supported the same conclusion as to Fullam's true authorship of the Journal.

While his family speedily increased, George Townley Fullam advanced in his profession and became a master mariner. After his steam experience in the CSS *Alabama,* it was understandable that he should seek berths in merchant steamships, a type of vessel which each year became more numerous, as attested by the files of *Lloyd's Register* in the Mariner's Museum Library (Newport News, Virginia).

The recollections of a kinsman, Peter Brewis of Gloucester, indicate that Captain Fullam developed into a man of strong character and forceful personality. Brewis wrote to this editor:

> From the ripe old age of six I spent a good deal of time at sea with my Skipper Father; a splendid seaman and navigator with a lifetime of adventurous stories to relate; and from this time on I was raised on a diet of "Hell Fire Jack Fullam," this being the nickname always used in reference to G.T.F. He must have been a man of quick anger at times, which possibly gives rise to his nickname. Grandfather told of a happening when he himself was a boy which illustrates the point. It would seem that G.T.F. was staying at their home, possibly between voyages, when one day at breakfast he became very angry. Unable to contain himself, he chased the maid from the dining room and threw his breakfast after her. To Grandfather at this time, George Fullam impressed as being a massive man, usually gentle and very kind, evidently sporting a red beard, piercing ice blue eyes, and a "presence" which could never be ignored.

When he was in port, Captain Fullam sometimes lectured on his adventures in the CSS *Alabama,* that Confederate raider being a subject of frequent publications during Fullam's lifetime and later. Of all the travel accounts published by men who served in the famed CSS *Alabama,* as well as those by adventure lovers who were not on board but who cruised vicariously and rewrote the narrative of *Alabama,* the first to be published (at least more than a short story) was the Journal of George Townley Fullam. When the CSS *Alabama* put into South Africa, where Fullam's Journal was partially published, the Confederate raider had covered some 30,000 nautical miles of her 67,367-mile cruise. This account first appeared in print on 19 September 1863 in A Supplement to the *South African Advertiser and Mail* as a narrative of 64 pages. Also in 1863 a 48-page edition of Fullam's Journal was published under a slightly different title by Lee and Nightingale in Liverpool, and probably in the same year a 64-page edition by A. Schulze in London. In 1864 a 56-page edition was published also. It is of interest that Fullam's name was not mentioned on the title page of any of these editions, even though the author's work was partially identified in one edition as "The Private Journal of an Officer," and for another edition "An Officer on Board," and for yet another "The Private Journal of the Boarding Officer."

The second detailed narrative of the cruise of *Alabama* appeared in 1864 from the "Private Journals and Other Papers of Commander R. Semmes, CSN," published under the title, *The Cruise of the Alabama and the Sumter,* and with other titles in both one-volume and two-volume editions in London and in New York. Semmes said of the 1864 title (preface to *Service Afloat,* 1869), "I did not write a line of it." This statement has been misunderstood by several writers despite the fact that Semmes quickly added that the publishers of 1864 had in their possession various papers and journals of *Alabama*, just as they had claimed. Semmes said that he did not mean that the documents were spurious; he meant that he was disappointed that the publishers and their editors were unable to make a literary production—a production which, with these *Alabama* sources, Semmes knew that he could make from the same sources. All editions of the 1864 work in fact carried considerable excerpts from Semmes' Journal of the CSS *Alabama*, and one edition was entitled, *Log of the Alabama*. Both English and French editions of the 1864 title contained brief portions of Fullam's Journal, as it related to the battle between *Alabama* and *Hatteras*.

Later in 1864, Frederick Milnes Edge wrote *The Alabama and the Kearsarge*, published both in London and in New York. Following the *Kearsarge-Alabama* battle, Edge had speedily interviewed people in Cherbourg who had witnessed the event, including Confederate prisoners, as well as *Kearsarge* personnel. Edge frankly disapproved of Confederates generally, and particularly the role played in the CSS *Alabama* by his fellow-Englishmen, and he excoriated everyone connected with the raider. In addition to Edge's work, another publication in 1864 was Bradley S. Osbon's title, *Hand Book of the United States Navy... from April 1861 to May 1864*, published by D. Van Nostrand in New York and simultaneously by Trubner and Company in London. The book was in press at the time of the *Kearsarge-Alabama* battle, and publication was stopped so that a 14-page account of the duel could be included, from current newspaper sources and some official records. Newspaper accounts contemporary with the battle were naturally numerous.

Meantime, the United States and Great Britain argued about the *Alabama* Claims, and Charles Francis Adams continued after the Civil War to play a major role regarding the CSS *Alabama*, as he had during the war. In 1867 the Dominion of Canada was created, an achievement not unrelated to the *Alabama* Claims. In 1869, efforts to settle the *Alabama* Claims resulted both in the signing and in the refusal to ratify the Johnson-Clarendon Convention. In the same year was published Raphael Semmes' title, *Memoirs of Service Afloat and Ashore During the War Between the States*. This work was republished many times, including an abbreviated version in English and editions in other languages.

It was 8 May 1871 when Grant's secretary of state, Hamilton Fish, and four other representatives of the United States, meeting jointly with Mountague Bernard and four commissioners representing Great Britain, reached long-sought agreement by completing the Treaty of Washington. Thus was established the Geneva Arbitration which finally set up the machinery to dispose of the *Alabama* Claims and other contemporary conflicts between Great Britain and the United States, five subjects in all, covered in 43 articles of the Treaty of Washington. Of the 43 articles in the treaty, the first 11 covered arbitration of the claims caused by the Confederate warships, including Fullam's CSS *Alabama*.

From early summer of 1871 until 4 September 1872, the five-man tribunal met in Geneva and applied the Treaty of Washington to those controversies between Great Britain and the United States "known generically as the *Alabama* Claims." Representing the United States among the five was the same Charles Francis Adams who had resourcefully kept well informed by hiring spies to watch the building of *Alabama* and who had tried vainly to prevent her departure from Liverpool. One of the earliest copies of Fullam's first edition of a portion of his Journal was obtained by Adams in London and mailed to Secretary of State William H. Seward. That document is now to be seen in the National Archives, and a Xeroxed copy of it is in the files of this editor.

On 14 September 1872, with Britain's Sir Alexander Cockburn dissenting, the Geneva Tribunal decreed that Great Britain should pay the United States $15,500,000 in gold to compensate for damages done by the CSS *Alabama* and certain other Confederate cruisers. Damages were also assessed against the United States to compensate British subjects in the amount of nearly $8,000,000 ($7,429,819), a phase of the *Alabama* arbitration known as the Counter Claims. The difference in the two claims proved an investment for Great Britain. The principles of international law there ratified, if not indeed created, aided Britain in the Boer War, in World War I, and in later Empire history as well. Meantime, in 1873, Caleb Cushing, one of the chief actors in the *Alabama* Claims, had published his brilliant book entitled, *The Treaty of Washington*.

At the start of the Civil War, when George Townley Fullam commenced working for James Dunwody Bulloch, few, if any, could have anticipated the connection Fullam's activities would have with the five American judges who, on 22 July 1874 at 1514 H Street, N. W., Washington, D. C., first organized the Court of Commissioners of the *Alabama* Claims. This was five years after the publication of *Service Afloat* and three years before the death of Admiral Semmes. The judges appointed by President U. S. Grant under an act of Congress of 1874 were headed by Hezekiah G. Wells of Michigan, presiding judge. This court of 1874 decreed for claimants $9,315,753 of the $15,500,000 of the whole *Alabama* Claims under the Geneva Award.

Later the second Court of Commissioners of the *Alabama* Claims proved to be the answer to a difficult and long-discussed question of what to do with the difference between the $15,500,000 of the Geneva

Award and the less than ten million dollars distributed by the first court. This became a political question with many lively facets. Delay resulted, for one thing, in yet more money through interest, as the years passed. What to do with the money was finally answered in 1882 when an act of Congress revived the Act of 1874 and provided for the creation of a new court to disburse the remaining money. The Act of 1882 recognized not only direct damage by the cruisers, which had been "exculpated" by the Geneva Tribunal, such as *Georgia* and *Sumter,* but also claims which had resulted from the payment of premiums for war risks created by the Confederate raiders. The second court heard 1,602 cases concerning the cruisers and rendered judgments for the claimants in 994 of them, with total awards and principal and interest at $3,346,016.32. Comparable figures for war premium claims were three or four times as great. None of the writers on the cruise of CSS *Alabama* have properly exploited the thousands of cases detailed in the *Alabama* Claims. The two courts of the *Alabama* Claims produced voluminous, detailed records concerning people, ships, and events related to Fullam's Journal of the CSS *Alabama.* Thus an obscure man like Fullam became involved with world-shaking events and their consequences extending beyond his lifetime.

One of the most important events in the later life of George Townley Fullam was taking command of a large new merchant steamer, *Marlborough.* The date was 31 December 1878 when *Marlborough's* first register was issued, and the ship was at Newcastle Upon Tyne.

The Public Records Office in London in Chancery Lane shows that in 1879 the steamer *Marlborough* was lost and that her captain was George Townley Fullam. *Marlborough* is described in the Transcript of Ship Registers (Number 88, Hull, 31 December 1878, in the Public Records Office BT 108/155). *Marlborough* was a giant steam screw propeller of 2,308 gross tons (1,498 registered tons), built in Sunderland by Bartram Haswell and Company in 1878. Fullam became the first captain and, as events proved, the only one of this large steamship. She had three masts, two decks, and a frame of iron. Other dimensions were 301 x 36 x 25. *Marlborough,* named for the street in Hull rather than directly for the duke, had two engines (compound surface condensing) of 250 horsepower. The engines were built in 1878 by John Dickinson of Sunderland. She had two owners with equal shares, David Parkinson Garbutt of Hull and George Haswell of Sunderland, the latter being the builder of the ship.

Marlborough carried coal from Newcastle and operated for nearly a year before being lost in the storm of December 1879. The exact date and place of the sinking was noted on the Transcript of Register in the Public Records Office (BT 108/155) as follows: "Supposed lost in Bay of Biscay 4-12-79." A slightly different date of 29 November

1879 appeared as the estimate of the Somerset House keepers of the death records of persons lost at sea (Death Certificate 7.9466).

A vivid account of this time in Fullam's life is contained in a book by the noted yachtsman, Sir Walter Runciman, Bart., entitled *"Sunbeam II" in 1932 With Some Reminiscences of Sailing Ship Captains*. Quotations from this book throw unique light on the later years and loss of Captain George Townley Fullam.

> Hull was distinguished for the many able captains it produced.... I must tell the story of my connection with Captain George [Fullam] ... I have referred briefly in my book "Before the Mast—And After," to this singularly gifted Hull captain of *Alabama* fame. He was by far the most distinguished of the Hull captains, and was "Master's Mate" of the notorious privateer.
>
> I think it was in 1875 that I first met the gallant "Master's Mate," A close friendship sprang up spontaneously, and at my urgent request he was drawn in to relating tales of his two years' experiences under the command of Captain Raphael Semmes, who was one of America's high class sea captains. At that period Americans competed fiercely with our own nautical quarter deck monarch in class of ships and those who relatively commanded and officered them. Indeed, America seems to have monopolized the blue ribbon in vessels that were fast sailers and easily handled, and in captains who were matchless in managing and fearless in driving force, and also in ruthless discipline that knew no pity. In my early days all seafaring men imitated their fiery unique slang and their drawling accent, and many British shipmasters copied their bullying and methods of chastising their crews by the free use of the belaying pin and six shooter. Our men never became so adept at this as the Yankees, and the habit of it to a large extent subsided on the advent of the tea clippers; and the American Civil War almost put an end to their fine mercantile sailing fleet of full riggers. English owners purchased many of those which were left and made large fortunes with them.

Runciman wrote of Fullam's stories and of his tone of hilarity or sympathy as the tales varied from amusing to deeply tragic. A detailed story was recited of the adventures of the two men on a trip overland on donkeys through the Sierras to see the lead and ore mines. The area was inhabited by bandits, and the two adventurers were well armed. The trip through the glorious mountains was interestingly recounted by Runciman. He wrote,

> The last time we were together was at Porman [Porman River in Spain] ..., he in the *Marlborough* and I in the *Coanwood*, both loading iron ore ... We spent our last evening together on his ship. I drew him on to relate to me more of his adventures during his cruise in the Alabama, because they fascinated me and they were always told with such fine natural modesty. I had no thought then that I would ever write of him, but the impelling thought of the rich hours we spent together in sweet converse leads me to record again that [Fullam] had the distinction of being selected to effect more captures and care for the proper treatment and disposal of their crews, than any other officer. He was unassumingly proud of the trust and praise bestowed upon him by Captain Semmes and his shipmates for his gallant services on the cruise during the tragic battle off Cherbourg, and for the saving of many lives. His connection with the indomitable Captain and his gallant comrades came to an end by the sinking of the delusive privateer that had destroyed and swept two-thirds of the Northern States' merchant vessels off the seas, and subsequently cost this country 5,000,000 sterling indemnity.

[Fullam's] fame spread, and he became much in demand at Hull as a popular lecturer of his *Alabama* experiences. He subsequently served as Chief Officer in steam. [Later he was given command of a ship,] . . . a new one called the Marlborough; a 2,500 tonner, which was considered a large size at that time. [The owner] . . . had a quick eye for selecting suitable men for his purpose, and he could not have selected a better man to command his largest and crack ship.

Poor [Fullam] was a manysided lovable creature. Our last days together are an enduring memory to me. He had the art of making and drawing mirth, but occasionally lapsed into invincible gravity, that was puzzling to me. We left Porman almost together, and after discharging the ore cargoes we sailed from the Tyne together with the *Joseph Ferens* and the *Prometheus*. The *Joseph Ferens* and the *Coanwood,* which I commanded, ran alongside each other for 24 hours before passing Ushant, and the *Marlborough* was on our starboard beam, a good distance off. We exchanged courtesies by signalling. She was steering a more westerly course than the *Joseph Ferens* and ourselves and was soon hull down, and we parted company with each other. A few hours before, we had been struck by the most devastating gale that ever blew. Never in the history of sea life can there have been anything so severe. Certainly in my long and varied experience, I have only once encountered anything resembling its fury. In twelve hours our boats were smashed to pieces, charthouse and compasses gone, iron bulwarks flattened to the deck, half of the upper and lower bridge carried away, sidelights lost, the lee fires out, and only with superhuman efforts these were set going, so that the vessel could be kept head on to the hurricane. As to the sea, it came raging along from all directions, jumping up and down in savage walls. . . . We were all tired out when the gale in the Bay of Biscay abated but soon resumed our usual state. We were fated to meet with shocking weather after passing Cape de Gat, which lasted all the way to Genoa.

On the day of our arrival, sixty guineas premium had been paid on our vessel, and an hour after it was written, the underwriter heard of our arrival. The other steamers had not arrived and were never heard of again. The loss of my friend [Fullam] was a great blow to me. I had assured myself that the *Marlborough,* which was a much larger vessel than mine, would pull through, and I would have the pleasure of meeting him at Genoa. Day after day passed without news, and at last all hope was abandoned.

So was lost an Englishman who knew and loved the sea. A legacy he left his wife and five young children was his Journal of the CSS *Alabama,* an account of the years of his youth and the time of an outstanding adventure that still stirs the imagination.

After Fullam's death, writings on the CSS *Alabama* continued to appear. In 1884 two volumes importantly related to the subject (and previously mentioned in this Introduction) were published under the title, *The Secret Service of the Confederate States in Europe* by James Dunwody Bulloch. Bulloch's work is useful in identifying Fullam's references, especially in the early part of the Fullam Journal. Within two years of Bulloch's publication, there appeared two articles which made definite contributions to the Fullam Journal of the CSS *Alabama,* and also one fraudulent article, all three in *The Century Magazine* for April 1886. One of the articles was written by the surgeon of *Kearsarge*, Dr. John M. Browne, entitled "The Duel Between the 'Alabama' and the 'Kearsarge'." The second article in *The Century Magazine* was authored by Kell himself with the title, "Cruise and Combats of the 'Alabama' by Her Executive Officer, John McIntosh Kell." Thus Kell became the third of *Alabama's* officers (after Fullam and Semmes) to publish an historical account of that ship. In 1888 the *Century* articles of Kell and Browne were republished in *Battles and Leaders of the Civil War,* edited by Robert U. Johnson and Clarence C. Buel.

The spurious article was written purportedly by "Philip Drayton Haywood," who said that he had been a sailor aboard the CSS *Alabama.* Within a year of "Haywood's" original article, *The Century Magazine* (volume 33, p. 805) published a repudiation of the article and a statement that "Haywood" admitted that he had never served aboard the CSS *Alabama.* "Haywood's" real name was James Young of Philadelphia, a man wanted for forgery! Even so, the fraudulent Young narrative was separately published under the title, *Cruise of the Alabama by One of Her Crew* in 1886.

While the "Haywood" story ran its course, a useful contribution to the cruise of the raider appeared as a small part of a thick book entitled, *History of the Confederate States Navy* by J. Thomas Scharf. True, it is easy enough to complain of Scharf's errors, but it may be more significant today that Scharf supplied many correct statements on hitherto little-known subjects, including many referred to by Fullam. Although Scharf had the advantage of personally having served in the Confederate States Navy, most of the records of that navy had been destroyed when Richmond was evacuated, and Scharf's work was published seven years before the beginning publication date of the *Official Records of the Union and Confederate Navies in the War of the Rebellion (hereinafter frequently cited as ORN).* Between 1894 and 1896 were published the first three volumes of Series I of *ORN,* the chief works relating directly to the Confederate cruisers, after ten years were spent in compilation. It was not until 1914 that volume 26 was published, bringing to an end Series I; Series II was not published until 1921–1922, but Series II is much scarcer than Series I. (The *Index* was published in 1927.) This series is by far the most extensive publication on the Confederate States Navy.

Up to the nineties only three officers of the CSS *Alabama* had published memoirs of their cruise: Fullam, Semmes, and Kell. Then in 1895 Arthur Sinclair published his brightly written, but by no means error free, *Two Years on the Alabama.* A year later appeared an English edition of Sinclair.

In 1897 Percy Cross Standing, in time a prolific writer of novels and magazine articles, was living in Yorkshire and working as a journalist on the Hull *Daily Mail.* Standing learned of the Fullam Journal and interviewed members of the Fullam family. As a result of this, some two decades after Fullam was lost at sea in the storm which destroyed the steamer *Marlborough*, Standing submitted to the distinguished British publication, *Cornhill Magazine*, an article entitled, "The Boarding Officer of the Alabama." The issue was that of May 1897. For some strange reason, Standing said (a statement later corrected in *Cornhill Magazine*) that the Fullam Journal had never been published. Perhaps Standing meant published *in toto*, but it may be that he was unaware of the partial previous publications because he, rapid writer that he was, does not appear to have dug deeply into the subject. Yet the article has value because Standing talked to Fullam's family and thus supplied previously missing biographical data.

Also, Standing evidently bought the Fullam manuscript Journal and later transmitted it to Sir Bruce Ingram, famed publisher of the *Illustrated London News*, collector of art and nautical lore, and an official of the Society for Nautical Research of Greenwich. He died in 1963. Mrs. Perpetua Ingram, niece of Sir Bruce, kindly supplied this editor with a sample of the handwriting of the late Sir Bruce so that notations in the Fullam manuscript could be tested as possible comments by that celebrated publisher and maritime collector. Sir Bruce's notations were identified as indicating that an earlier owner had been Percy Cross Standing. Standing in his time became a well-known free-lance writer, and therefore it was not difficult to discover that he had worked on the *Daily Mail* in Hull. No doubt he interviewed the Fullam family at some date between Captain Fullam's death in 1879 and the publication of the Standing article in *Cornhill Magazine* in 1897. Thus was identified Sir Bruce's handwriting in the Fullam Journal in relation to Percy Cross Standing.

In 1898 John Bassett Moore, occupying Columbia University's chair named for Hamilton Fish, published all six volumes of his *History and Digest of the International Arbitrations*. Moore utilized varied sources, including Fullam's Journal incidentally. Also in 1898, James R. Soley, a professor at the Naval Academy, wrote *The Blockade and the Cruisers*. This was volume I of the series *The Navy in the Civil War*.

In 1900, John McIntosh Kell became the last of *Alabama's* officers to bring into print a book-length autobiography, his title being *Recollections of a Naval Life*. Although Kell said, "The use of the pen has always been a burden to me . . . I thought Admiral Semmes' book was enough for history and the world," the fact that Kell had been persuaded to write the earlier *Century* (1886) article already referred to, apparently made it easier for him to embark upon his book-length autobiography. Kell's uncomplicated and precise narrative often showed surprising warmth. Indeed, on 3 April 1886, Walt Whitman wrote Kell that he had just completed reading the article in *Century* and other accounts of the battle with *Kearsarge* which together formed " . . . by far the best contribution I know to the literature of the Secession era, and are full of realism and thrill."

Although the voluminous literature of the Civil War contained far more on the Union than on the Confederate side, and although honors for *Kearsarge* and her commander, John A. Winslow, took many forms of preferment, it was not until 1905 that the *Life of John Ancrum Winslow* by John M. Ellicott was published. Even so, that was five years earlier than the first book-length biography of Raphael Semmes by Colyer Meriwether. A year later appeared the brief, but significantly ahead of its time, "Psychograph" of Semmes by Gamaliel Bradford in his *Confederate Portraits*. The *ORN* series came to an end in 1927 with publication of the *General Index*. The next Semmes biography came out in 1938 when W. Adolphe Roberts' book appeared, *Semmes of the Alabama*, with new material, especially from newspapers, concerning *Alabama*'s lively visit to Jamaica, but with a small fragment of sources which he could have used. In 1940 there was published an important critical study entitled *The Flight from the Flag* by George W. Dalzell, containing new archival material and treating the results of the destruction by Confederate cruisers, without especial focus on *Alabama*.

Some of the more significant book-length studies include: Joseph T. Durkin, *Stephen R. Mallory: Confederate Navy Chief* (1954); Edward Boykin, *The Ghost Ship of the Confederacy* (1957); W. Stanley Hoole, *Four Years in the Confederate Navy: The Career of Captain John Low* (1964); Frank L. Owsley, Jr., *The CSS Florida: Her Building and Operations* (1965); and Charles G. Summersell, *The Cruise of CSS Sumter* (1965). Just published in 1973 is Norman C. Delaney's *John McIntosh Kell of the Raider Alabama*. Also in recent years, writers of juveniles have continued to publish books regarding the CSS *Alabama*. The number of titles published on this subject marks a full turning of the wheel of time when this Journal of Fullam goes to press. Since Fullam wrote the first (fragmentary) narrative to be published on the CSS *Alabama*, it is fitting that this Journal should be the last publication—last, if only for a very brief time.

How the Mobile Public Library acquired this distinctive Fullam document is itself a story of lively interest. The date was 16 December 1963 when Mrs. Clara Stone Collins (at that time Mrs. Fields) received a cablegram from the distinguished London auctioneers, Messrs. Sotheby and Company. The cablegram notified Mrs. Collins that her bid for the Journal of George Townley Fullam, described in Sotheby's notice as "Lot 209," now belonged to her. Thus Fullam's Journal, which started out when the CSS *Alabama* was named *290*, came to the state of Alabama as "Lot 209." And Fullam's Journal, which had sailed every one of the 67,361 nautical miles in the total cruise of the CSS *Alabama*, added yet more mileage as it crossed from London to Mobile, Alabama. The winning bid on the Journal was for £1,300 ($3,640), although Sotheby had been informed that Mrs. Collins was prepared to pay more if necessary. The money was raised through newspaper advertising, news publicity, and public subscription. The total finally raised was $5,040, or £1800. Since much of this came at the last minute, it was an act of faith that prompted the maximum figure which was communicated to Sotheby. As late as three days before the sale, the amount raised had been $3,780, or £1,350, but on 13 December another $2,000 was contributed equally by the city and county governments of Mobile. Mrs. Collins had underwritten the difference with the hope of raising enough money if the bid proved successful. Thus, through the generous donations of many public-spirited people and the leadership of Clara Stone Collins, the Mobile Public Library came into possession of the Journal of George Townley Fullam. The Friends of the Mobile Public Library invited this historian to edit the Journal. A special Committee of the Friends, headed by Bill L. Roberson, has supported the work from the beginning idea to the publication of the Fullam Journal. Appreciation is expressed elsewhere in this volume to this Committee and to other Friends of the Mobile Public Library.

After the Friends of the Mobile Public Library invited this writer to edit the Fullam Journal, work was commenced at The University of Alabama and in libraries scattered over this country. Then, to learn more about the later career of George Townley Fullam, the editor journeyed to England in 1972 and visited Fullam's city of Hull in Yorkshire. In Hull, Fullam's grandson, Brian Townley Fullam, and Mrs. Fullam were most cordial and helpful, pointing out places of residence of the family and the location of the school run by his great grandfather. Since Brian Townley Fullam, a talented and personable young man, was a graduate of the ancient and justly famous Hull Trinity House Navigation School, he was able to arrange a tour for this editor, graciously conducted by the Superintendent of Trinity House, Mr. E. C. Evans. It was a tremendous experience to see the buildings and view the venerable documents belonging to Trinity House, signed by the kings and queens of England as each new monarch granted permission for the school to continue functioning. This editor is much indebted to Brian Townley Fullam for that privilege. It gave insight into the great seafaring background of George Townley Fullam's home town of Hull.

Other Fullam kinsmen, including Mrs. Emily Fullam, the daughter-in-law of Hull's famous Confederate, furnished interesting information. Particularly helpful was another kinswoman, Mrs. Monica Grant of Hull, who spent many hours in various record offices unearthing Fullam family data. Her work in the Holy Trinity Church records was rewarding, and the cooperation of the church officials appreciated. It was Mrs. Grant who finally secured a copy of the marriage record with the original signature of George Townley Fullam when he was a witness at the wedding of his sister. The signature showed the same handwriting as the Journal. Mrs. Grant's ability, interest, and tireless energy are highly appreciated. Other kinsmen were ready to give a hand, and this is recognized in the Acknowledgments. Unexpectedly, some members of the Fullam family became acquainted through the editor's inquiries.

Mike Thompson, otherwise known as "Peter Humber," of the Hull *Daily Mail* was generous in his comments in his newspaper column which enabled the editor to locate Fullam relatives after only one commercial ad sent from across the Atlantic to the Hull *Daily Mail*. After the editor met "Peter Humber" in the flesh, he was most liberal with his time and advice.

In addition to Hull, London yielded Fullam data, voluminous and significant. Some of this was gathered through microfilm before the search in England. Materials in the Public Record Office concerning the CSS *Alabama* and the *Alabama* Claims are extensive indeed. Chief among these for the CSS *Alabama* are FO 5, volumes 1318-1321 and BT 108/155. In London's Strand, not far from the Public Record Office, is Somerset House with records of births, deaths, and marriages which gave data on the Fullam family, supplemented by district records of Hull. The British Museum proved, not unexpectedly, a rewarding place to search for rare books and pamphlets.

Across the Atlantic, closer to home, the editor found that the National Archives had extraordinary quantities of official documents relating to the CSS *Alabama,* especially Record Group 45 (Naval Records), Record Group 56 (Treasury Records), Record Group 76 (Claims), and Record Group 84 (State Department).

Materials on Fullam's CSS *Alabama* continue to come to light, and the cards listing each related title in the Library of Congress take up several inches. Despite the different system of listing books, it could also be said that there are many titles to be found in the Catalogue of the British Museum. Other libraries and archives important in this study are listed in the Acknowledgments.

The bold italics and the unjustified margins used in this book hopefully suggest to the reader the physical appearance of the manuscript Journal. While it is too much to hope that Fullam's Journal has at last been published *in toto* without error, an effort has been made to present a full text, carefully edited.

CHARLES GRAYSON SUMMERSELL
THE UNIVERSITY OF ALABAMA

ACKNOWLEDGMENTS

Many collections in libraries and archives appear in the Introduction with descriptive comments, but thanks should be extended to others also. Libraries used in preparing footnotes and the Introduction for the Fullam Journal include the Hull Library in Fullam's Yorkshire home town with manuscripts, census records, and newspapers of that venerable seaport. In addition, the following libraries proved useful and, for the most part, essential to the search: Columbia University Library, Yale Library, Duke Library, The University of Alabama Library, the Alabama Department of Archives and History, the Maryland Historical Society, the Georgia Historical Society, the Library of Congress, the National Archives, the Confederate Museum (Richmond, Virginia), the Mariners Museum (Newport News, Virginia), the New York Public Library, the Rucker Agee Collection of maps and related publications in the Birmingham Public Library, the private library of James F. Sulzby, Jr. (Birmingham, Alabama), that of Clarence B. Hanson, Jr. (Birmingham), and the private library of Mrs. Clara Stone Collins (Mobile).

The staff of the Mobile Public Library assisted the editor, and it was the Friends of the Mobile Public Library who joined The University of Alabama Press in publishing this Journal. The names of these civic-minded Mobilians appear elsewhere in this book, as do the names of the generous contributors who joined Mrs. Clara Stone Collins in purchasing the Journal.

John Lochhead, librarian of the Mariners Museum (Newsport News, Virginia), over a period of time has repeatedly facilitated the editor's research. The chief sources of pictures have been the Mariners Museum, the National Archives, the Library of Congress, the Alabama Department of Archives and History, the Mobile Public Library, and the extensive files of the editor (the Summersell Collection). S. Andrew Russell, photographer of The University of Alabama, has rendered photographic services. The University of Alabama History Department secretaries and student assistants whose work is gratefully acknowledged are: Mrs. Carolyn C. Sassaman, Mrs. Ruth M. Kibbey, Patricia Patton, Mary Frazier, Paul A. Kusina, Ralph McMurphy, and Larry Black.

Appreciation is extended to Mrs. Frank Sturges III, Dr. Samuel Eichold, Lilian Sharpley, Norma Sims, the Fullam family, Col. M. N. Hardesty, Donald J. Sager, Frances S. Summersell, the staff of the Mobile Public Library, The University of Alabama Press, Mrs. Cherry Crawford, and Stephens G. Croom, Secretary of the USS Alabama Battleship Commission.

The Introduction contains additional acknowledgements. Elsewhere listed are the Sponsors, the Fullam Journal Committee, and Donors to the Bidding Fund for the Journal.

The manuscript was read critically by Dr. A. Russell Mortensen, Chief Historian of the National Park Service, whose skill as an author, editor, and publisher is widely known. Bill L. Roberson cast an alert and discerning eye on the page proof. Dr. Robert E. Johnson, Professor of History at The University of Alabama and author of books and articles on the American Civil War at sea, made perceptive and usable comments after reading the manuscript.

Fullam and some of his fellow officers of the CSS *Alabama*.

Captain, later Rear Admiral, Raphael Semmes, Commanding Officer of the CSS *Alabama*.

Private Journal of the Cruise of the Confederate States Steamer Alabama. 8 Guns. Capt. Raphael Semmes. With a list of her Officers. Prizes. &c &c.

Title Page of the neatly bound volume which gave details of one of the great sea adventures.

Positica each day at Noon of the
S.S. "290" "Enrica" "Barcelona"
Liverpool to Terceira.

Left the Mersey. 9.15 Am. 29th July 1862.
Left Anglesea. Aug. 2. Am. 31st July 1862.
Arrived at Porta Praya. Terceira. 10 Aug 1862.

Date.	Lat.	Long.	Cou.	Dist.
1862	N	W		
Aug 1	55 . 15	10 . 50		335
" 2	55 . 24	12 . 15		
" 3	51 . 28	14 . 52		
" 4	49 . 29	15 . 15		
" 5	47 . 52	15 . 54		
" 6	45 . 14	17 . 08		
" 7	42 . 57	18 . 59		
" 8	41 . 11	22 . 13		
" 9	39 . 33	25 . 24		
" 10	Anchored. 6. Am.			

A page of Fullam's Log of the CSS *Alabama* which is printed in an appendix of this Journal. It supplements Fullam's Journal.

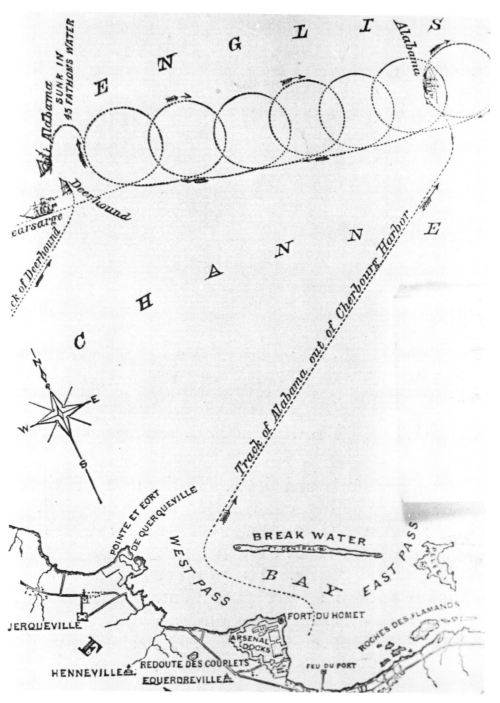

This chart diagrams the battle between *Alabama* and *Kearsarge* which brought death to the most successful Confederate sea raider.

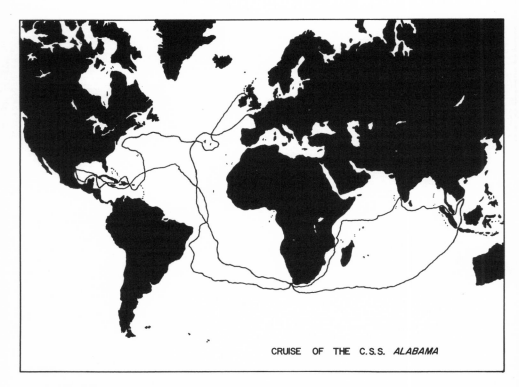

CRUISE OF THE C.S.S. *ALABAMA*

Chart of *Alabama's* cruise from England to Latin America, to South Africa, to Vietnam, and back to European waters.

John McIntosh Kell, Executive Officer of the CSS *Alabama*.

A merchant mariner fearfully identifies *Alabama* in the distance.

FRANK LESLIE'S ILLUSTRATED NEWS.PAPER

Entered according to the Act of Congress in the year 1863, by Frank Leslie, in the Clerk's Office of the District Court for the Southern District of New York.

No. 380—Vol. XV.]   NEW YORK, JANUARY 10, 1863.   [PRICE 8 CENTS.

UNAVOIDABLE DELAY.

In consequence of difficulty in obtaining paper, and the intervention of the holidays, our paper has been delayed in its delivery to News Agents and Subscribers. Arrangements have been made which will prevent a recurrence of this difficulty—more annoying to us than that it can be to our friends.

OUR SECOND PRIZE TALE.

We shall, next week, publish *complete*, our Second Prize Tale,

OLD PROUTMAN'S BOY.

By a Gentleman of Pennsylvania—a tale of equal interest, but of different character and moral. It is called a Tale, but it is really an episode of real life, of absorbing interest, no more disguised in its personalities than the necessities of the case require.

CAPTAIN RAPHAEL SEMMES,
Of the Pirate Ship Alabama.

Raphael Semmes, the notorious commander of the Sumter and the pirate Alabama, is also one of those officers now in rebellion against the flag who was educated at the Government expense, and developed his genius for battle under its auspices. He was born in Maryland, and must now be near 50 years old. He was educated at the Naval Academy, Annapolis, and became a midshipman in April, 1826. He was promoted to a lieutenancy in 1837, and lived the routine life of all naval officers until the period of the Mexican war, throughout which he distinguished himself both on sea and land.

Having served with the naval battery in March, 1847, at the siege of Vera Cruz, he was, at his own

request, we believe, detailed on the staff for services where he might have a chance to distinguish himself. In the position of aid to the gallant Gen. Worth, he participated in the battles of Cherubusco, El Molino del Rey, Chepultepec, Cosme Gate and at the capture of the City of Mexico. He has detailed many of his experiences of the war in a clever book, suitably entitled "Services Afloat and Ashore." He is of an excitable, energetic and daring nature, was a rabid Southern Rights man, intimate with the Southern conspirators, and on the breaking out of the rebellion immediately entered their service. His career since has been one of unexampled energy, and his track may be followed in the light of the burning vessels he has captured. In person he is slim, quick in his movements, and of the average height.

CAPTAIN RAPHAEL SEMMES, OF THE PIRATE SHIP ALABAMA.

THE CAPTURE OF THE CALIFOR
Steamer Ariel by the Rebel Pirate Steamer Alabama.

We are indebted to Mr. Thomas, first officer of the Ariel, for some very interesting sketches of the last and most audacious exploits of the pirate Alabama. The purser says:

"On the 7th of December, at 1.30 p.m., rounding Cape Maysi, the eastern point of Cuba, saw a vessel about four miles to the westward, under the high land of Cuba, bark-rigged and canvas. As there was nothing in her appearance dictating her to be a steamer, her smokepipe down, no suspicions were aroused, till in a short time we saw she had furled her sails, raised her stack, and was rapidly nearing us under steam. An American flag flying at her peak. Such was her speed in comparison to ours, that in about half an hour she had come up within half a mile of us. She fired a lee gun, hauled down the American and ran up the rebel flag. No attention was paid to the summons, and the Ariel was pushed to her most speed.

She then railed across our port quarter, about 600 yards distant, and two guns almost simultaneously, one shot pa...

THE CAPTURE OF THE U. S. MAIL STEAMER ARIEL, CAPT. JONES, OFF THE EAST END OF CUBA, BY THE PIRATE ALABAMA (290), CAPT. SEMMES, DECEMBER 7.—FROM A SKETCH BY MR. F. C. THOMAS, FIRST OFFICER OF THE ARIEL.

After the capture of the California treasure steamer *Ariel,* Captain Semmes and *Alabama* made the front page.

A good picture of the CSS *Alabama* which shows the symmetry of her beautiful lines.

Deck of the USS *Kearsarge* at the height of the battle.

The boat from *Alabama* in charge of Fullam announcing the surrender and asking for assistance.

Alabama captures a prize.

Two scenes of the famous Laird Brothers shipyards at Birkenhead.

Prisoners below deck were in Fullam's charge.

The sinking of *Alabama* by *Kearsarge*.

George Townley Fullam of Hull, Yorkshire, author of the Journal.

JOURNAL

S. S. "No 290" "Enrica" "Barcelona" [aliases of the CSS Alabama]. Capt. M. J. Butcher, Chief Officer Mr. J. Low (Eng) [England] Savannah, Second Officer Mr. G. T. Fullam, Hull, Eng., Surgeon Mr. D. Llewellyn, Easton, Wilts. Eng. [Wiltshire, England], Paymaster Mr. C. Yonge, Savannah, Chief Engineer Mr. J. McNair.

This is a list of officers who served in *Enrica* before she was commissioned as the CSS *Alabama*. The unnumbered manuscript page which begins the Journal was probably added later. Before September 1863, the introductory page had been added since it was included in the first printing of the first portion of the Fullam Journal in the Cape Town *South African Advertiser and Mail*, 19 September 1863. When, later in 1863, the first part of the Fullam Journal was published in Liverpool by Lee and Nightingale, the introductory page was omitted and in its place appeared the following paragraph: "PREFACE. However widely people may differ as to the merits of the contest between North and South, the adventures and performances of the Alabama will be read with eager interest by both parties. The following narrative is from the private journal of an officer. It may be thoroughly relied upon; and no account so complete has yet been published in England."

In other words, the insertion of new introductory matter was not of especial importance as it was done at an early time in the handwriting of this Fullam Journal.

C. S. Str. "Alabama"
8 Guns.

6 Thirty Twos, 1 sixty-eight pr [pounder] & 1 one hundred pr. Commander Raphael Semmes, Lieutenant J. M. Kell, Geo. [Georgia], R. F. Armstrong, Geo., J. D. Wilson, Fla., John Low (E) Geo. [native of England, appointed from Georgia], Master A. Sinclair, Vir. [Virginia], Surgeons F. L. Galt, Vir., & D. H. Llewellyn, Easton, Eng., Marine Lieut. B. K. Howell, La. [born in Mississippi, appointed from Louisiana], Paymaster C. R. Yonge, Geo., Engineers J. Freeman [Miles J. Freeman, Wales], W. P. Brooks, S. C., M. O'Brien [Ireland], S. W. Cummings, S. C. [born in New York, appointed from Louisiana], J. Pundt, S. C., Masters Mates G. T. Fullam, Hull, Eng., J. Evans, S. C., Midshipmen W. H. Sinclair, Vir., I. S. Bulloch, Geo., E. A. Maffitt, Md., E. M. Anderson, Geo., Captain's Clerk W. B. Smith, La., Boatswain B. P. Mecaskey, La., Gunner T. C. Cuddy, S. C., Carpenter W. Robinson, La. [born in Massachusetts, appointed from Louisiana], Sailmaker H. Alcott, Eng.

This is a list of officers who served in the CSS *Alabama* after she was commissioned.

The presidential election–the slave question–the slanderous tongues of Northern senators–the tone of the Northern press, and the unjust laws passed by a Northern congress, unjust because they acted, and were intended to act upon the Southern people–all these tended to produce a feeling of discontent and to foster minds, already embittered against the North–to withdraw from the Union and make for themselves a place among the nations of the earth.

To effect this object, negotiations were attempted to be entered into, which however, signally failed, and it was only after every exertion had been made to adjust the matter in a peaceful and proper manner (but without avail) that recourse was made to arms. After the outbreak of the war, the immense naval superiority of the North gave them considerable advantages over the South, who, lacking convenience and materials, were not able to build vessels with sufficient despatch [and the Confederate government] sent over Capt. J. D. Bulloch to England for that purpose [of obtaining war steamships]. Accordingly, the "No 290" was built and intended for a Confederate vessel of war.

The "No 290" was launched from the building yard of Messrs Laird of Birkenhead. She was a barque rigged wooden propellor of 1050 tons registered. Length of keel 210; length over all 220 ft; beam 32 ft; depth 17.

Fullam's statistics vary little from those of the U.S. Navy publications *ORN*, 2, I, and ND, *FS*, II, 494–495.

The variations are tabulated as follows:

	ND, *FS*, II, 494–495	*ORN*, 2, I, 247
Length Overall	220	Not stated
Length of keel	Not stated	211.6
Beam	31.8	31.8
Depth	17.8	17.8
Draft	14	14

Her engines, built by the same firm, were 2 horizontal ones, each of 300 horse power, with storage of 350 tons of coal. Her sails, carried at all times, were as follows: fore, foretopmast, staysail & jib; two large trysails; the usual squaresails on fore & main, with the exception of the mainsail, which was a flying one; spanker and gaff topsails;

all standing rigging wire. Double wheel with motto engraved
thereon—"Aide toi et Dieu l'aidera" placed just before the
mizenmast. Bridge in the centre just before the funnel.
Carried 5 boats, viz:—cutter and launch amidships, gig &
whale boat between the main and mizenmast, and dingey
astern. The main deck pierced for 12 guns; elliptic stern;
billet head; high bulwarks; cabin accommodations first class;
ward room furnished with a handsome suite of state rooms;
steerage; starboard for midshipmen; port for engineers; next
came engine room, coal bunkers, &c; then the berth deck,
capable of accommodating 120 men. Under the ward room
were store rooms; and under the steerage were shell rooms;
just forward of the fire rooms, came the hold; next the
magazines; and forward of all, the boatswains' and sailmakers'
store rooms; the hold &c being all under the berth deck.

At 9.15 a.m. of the 29th July 1862, we weighed anchor
and proceeded slowly down the [Mersey] river, anchoring
in Moelfra Bay—having on board relatives and friends of the
builders, both ladies and gentlemen.

The Mersey River is described for modern mariners in *Hydrographic*
Office Publication 145, pp. 245–260, and Moelfre Bay in the same
publication, on page 235, in a manner which would surely have
been welcome to Fullam had it been available at that time.

Our [ostensible] object in sailing was that we were going
"on a trial trip," and the presence of the ladies and gentlemen
gave a certain colour to the report. In the evening transferred
our visitors to a steam tug. We remained here, shipping
hands, &c, &c, until 2 a.m. of the 31st, when we got under
weigh, ostensibly bound to Nassau, Bahamas. A strong breeze
was blowing from the S. W. accompanied with heavy rain.
A boisterous sea running at the time, formed altogether a
most uninviting picture and one not at all calculated to
augur good luck. Our unceremonious departure was owing to
the fact of news being received to the effect that the Customs
authorities had orders to board and detain us that morning.

Passing successively the Isle of Man, Alsie [Ailsa] Craig,
&c., we hove to off the Giants Causeway, and landed Capt.
Bulloch and the pilot amid a drenching shower of rain.

The Isle of Man is described in *HO 145,* pp. 296–306. It is in the
Irish Sea. North of the Isle of Man, in the North Channel, is tiny Ailsa

Craig. Giant's Causeway is on the north coast of Northern Ireland. See *Britannica Atlas,* Plate 42. The pilot's name was George Bond.

Soon however it cleared up, and away we steered (to the westward) at the rate of 13 1/2 knots an hour. Soon after clearing the land, a strong S. W. wind with a heavy sea continued until our arrival at Porto Praya in the island of Terceira (Azores) on the 10th August.

Porto Praia is a later spelling for this port on the north side of Terceira Island. The port is also known as Praia da Vitoria. Terceira means "the third island." Some five years after the visit of Fullam's ship at Terceira, a volcanic eruption occurred there. The geography described by Fullam is found in *HO 134,* pp. 213–215; *HO Chart 1736;* and also in the British Navy publication, *BR 502C,* pp. 302–312. *Britannica Atlas,* Plate 138A.

The port bow port had been stove in, and a few minor damages done by the heavy sea we had encountered, notwithstanding which, she gave promise of being a good sea boat and also a swift one.
    The same afternoon the officials came off and in reply to their questions, we said that, we were the steamer "Barcelona" from London, 15 days out, bound to Havana and intended for the Spanish government, for the war with Mexico.

Before the CSS *Alabama* was commissioned, she already had other aliases, *290, Barcelona,* and *Enrica.* Later she had many more, used along with other disguises, to conceal *Alabama's* identity.

Were quarantined 3 days.
    The vessel was under command of Capt. M. J. Butcher, late of the Cunard service. The rest of the officers were as follows; viz;–Chief Officer, John Low (E.), Savannah, Geo. Second Officer, G. T. Fullam, Hull, Eng. Surgeon, D. H. Llewellyn, Easton, Wilts. Paymaster, C. R. Yonge, Savannah, Geo. Chief Engineer, J. McNair, England.

Mathew J. Butcher was very highly regarded by Captain Semmes and by the celebrated Confederate agent, Captain James Dunwody Bulloch. Bulloch wrote Butcher detailed orders, much along the lines summarized by Fullam. John Low was born in Aberdeen, Scotland, and was living in Savannah, Georgia, in 1861 when he was appointed to the Confederate States Navy. Low's Log is a *MS* (1862–1863) which is very useful in understanding Fullam's Journal of the CSS *Alabama.*

[6]

The E in Fullam's MS after Low's name means that Low was an Englishman. Since Fullam lived in Lincolnshire, not far from Scotland, it is interesting that he considered the Scottish-born Low to be English. However, Low lived for a time also in Liverpool. Concerning Low, W. S. Hoole wrote *Four Years in the Confederate Navy: The Career of Captain John Low.* See pp. 2–4, and *passim.*

For Hull, Fullam's home port, see *HO 150*, pp. 233–237.

The home of D. H. Llewellyn, Easton, Wiltshire, is in the south coastal area of England, west of Bournemouth. David Herbert Llewellyn was assistant surgeon in *Alabama.* The surgeon was Francis L. Galt.

Paymaster Clarence R. Yonge had earlier been private secretary to Captain James D. Bulloch while Bulloch served in England as a secret agent of the Confederate States. Yonge later became a spy and informer for the United States government. Fullam himself was one of Bulloch's selections, as were M. J. Butcher and John Low. Consideration of these four names notably improves Bulloch's record for good judgment. Clarence R. Yonge's defection was a weak point in the complex and generally successful career of Bulloch in England. Bulloch's orders to Yonge of 28 July 1862 were as follows:

Liverpool, *July 28, 1862.*

Sir: You will join the C.S.S. *Alabama,* temporarily under the orders of Captain M. J. Butcher, and proceed in her to sea. The *Alabama* may have to cruise several days in the British Channel and to touch at one or two ports. During this time you are strictly enjoined not to mention that you are in any way connected with the C. S. Navy, but you will simply act as the purser of a private ship. In this capacity you will keep account of all money paid, and you will assist Captain Butcher in any manner he may desire.

You have been provided with an invoice of everything now on board the *Alabama* as well as the cargo shipped on board the brig *Agrippina,* which vessel you will meet at the port to which the *Alabama* is bound.

The invoice of the *Agrippina's* cargo gives the mark and number of every case and bale, the contents of each, and the part of the vessel in which it is stowed. You will endeavor to make yourself fully acquainted with the invoices, and examine the storerooms so that you will be able to give efficient aid in getting everything in its proper place when the transfer of stores is made. When the *Alabama* is fairly at sea you will mix freely with the warrant and petty officers, show interest in their comfort and welfare, and endeavor to excite their interest in the approaching cruise of the ship. Talk to them of the Southern States, and how they are fighting against great odds for only what every Englishman enjoys— liberty. Tell them at the port of destination a distinguished officer of the C. S. Navy will take command of the ship for a cruise in which they will have the most active service and be well taken care of. I do not mean that you are to make the men set speeches or be constantly talking to them, but in your position you may frequently throw out to leading men hints of the above tenor which will be commented upon on the berth deck. Seamen are very impressionable, and can be easily influenced by a little tact and management. When Captain Semmes joins, you will at once report to him and act thereafter under his instructions. He will be a stranger to the ship and crew, and will be in a position of great responsibility and embarrassment. You have it in your power to smooth away some of his difficulties in advance, especially in having all the stores and cargo of the ship in an orderly state and the men settled and well disposed, and I confidently rely upon your exertions to bring about such a state of things.

You will consider yourself as temporarily under the orders of Captain Butcher, in whom I place great confidence, and by strict attention to your duties and the display of zeal and judgment in their execution, you will evince a just appreciation of the trust reposed in you, and will prove that your appointment to so important a post has been deserved.

Wishing you every success, I am, respectfully, your obedient servant,

JAMES D. BULLOCH,
Commander, Confederate Navy.

Acting Assistant Paymaster C. R. YONGE.

McNair and Captain Butcher were the only two of the officers mentioned by Fullam who did not remain aboard *Enrica* after she was put into commission as the CSS *Alabama*. The chief engineer of *Alabama* was Miles J. Freeman of Louisiana who had served as chief engineer of the CSS *Sumter* under Semmes. Fullam does not mention Freeman at this point, or any of the other officers of *Alabama,* including Semmes, who did not make the first leg of the cruise from Liverpool to the Azores.

The crew numbered about 70 men and boys.

The number of officers and men varied from time to time. Recruiting was done from the original crews of *Enrica, Agrippina,* and *Bahama*. The latter two vessels brought supplies and men to the Azores for the commissioning of *Enrica* as a Confederate cruiser. Fullam's figure of 70 doubtless refers to *Enrica* alone. The number of officers who joined *Alabama* at Terceira was 27, and the number of men 87. There were 27 officers at the start of *Alabama's* cruise and there were 26 officers the day *Alabama* sank. The total number of officers who served in *Alabama* after she became a commissioned warship was 30. The members of the crew the day *Alabama* sank were 122. The total number of names of men who served in the crew of *Alabama* at one time or another was 186. The number of officers and crew varied from month to month. Three officers and 99 men were recruited during the cruise.

Our object in going there, that is, to Terceira, was to obtain the necessary arms, ammunition, &c, requisite for a vessel

[8]

of war. England's proclamation of neutrality prevented the guns, &c, being placed on board in Liverpool. Skill and secrecy of no inconsiderable degree were required to escape the vigilance of the Yankees, who thro' the agency of their spies, were quite au fait *with regard to Confederate affairs in England.*

The building of the CSS *Alabama* attracted secret agents of the Union and of the Confederacy. The United States minister to London, Charles Francis Adams, was particularly alert to the usefulness of spies in obtaining detailed information concerning Confederate activities in England. Adams was vigorously supported by the United States consular service in general and in particular by the consul at Liverpool, Thomas H. Dudley. Dudley's chief spy was the experienced British detective, Matthew Maguire, who employed many agents to conduct surveillance of the Confederate shipbuilding by Laird Brothers at Birkenhead. Maguire obtained intelligence from shipbuilders and mariners, and hired various knowledgeable persons who already had jobs (or were to get jobs) in the actual building of that future scourge of Yankee commerce, the CSS *Alabama*. In other cases, Maguire bought information from mariners in the employ of the Confederates. The area of the Confederate cruisers became a hotbed of spies and agents. Some of Maguire's informants included Henry Redden (boatswain's mate), John de Costa (shipping master), William Passmore (mariner), Edward Roberts (ship carpenter), and George Temple Chapman. See *Correspondence Respecting the "Alabama" North America No. 3 Presented to Parliament 1863,* 4–11. The leading spy-master for the Union during the entire Civil War was John F. A. Sanford who operated out of Belgium. The secret mission of building the CSS *Alabama* and some other Confederate cruisers was in charge of James Dunwody Bulloch. See James D. Bulloch, *The Secret Service of the Confederate States in Europe or, How the Confederate Cruisers were Equipped.* Before arranging for the building of the CSS *Alabama,* Bulloch managed to conceal from Charles Francis Adams for some four months the fact that he was building the cruiser which became the CSS *Florida.* In general, the experience of Adams and Dudley regarding the CSS *Florida* alerted them to the need for more adequate espionage, and thus the surveillance on *Alabama* was relatively more effective. See the monograph by Frank L. Owsley, Jr., *The CSS Florida: Her Building and Operations,* 17–33, and Harriet C. Owsley, "Henry Shelton Sanford and Federal Surveillance Abroad, 1861–1865," *Mississippi Valley Historical Review,* vol. 48 (Sept. 1961), 211–228.

Fullam's use of French expressions, like *au fait,* was repeated with enough variation to indicate that he may have had a speaking knowledge of French. If so, it would not have been surprising in the son of a schoolmaster, and would have been of obvious value in a boarding officer. Two of the masters mates who joined the CSS *Alabama* at a later port of call were native Prussians and masters of several languages. Semmes spoke Spanish fluently and served as an official interpreter in the negotiations of the peace treaty at the end of the Mexican War (Guadalupe Hidalgo).

No sooner was our departure known than the U. S. Str. "Tuscarora" received, through the American consul at Liverpool, news of it.

The USS *Tuscarora* was a wooden steam sloop which, although completed after the start of the Civil War, had already had some important encounters with Confederate commerce raiders. *Tuscarora* had blockaded the CSS *Nashville* when that Confederate raider was in England. In 1862 during the blockade of the CSS *Sumter* in Cadiz, *Tuscarora* was in nearby Algeciras and thus was one of the Union warships which forced *Sumter* to end her career as a commerce raider. These activities, of course, preceded the attempt of *Tuscarora* to intercept *Alabama* upon her escape from Liverpool, as described above by Fullam. See, *MS* Log of *Tuscarora;* also *ORN,* 1, I, *passim;* Summersell, *The Cruise of CSS Sumter,* 158–159; A.B.C. Whipple, "The Hard-luck Frigate," *American Heritage,* II, 2, 16–19, 102–103 (Feb. 1956).

Every exertion was made by her Commander to seize us, but without avail, for by the time the Tuscarora arrived in Moelfra Bay, we had been gone two days.

Moelfre Bay is in North Wales not far from Liverpool. See, *HO 125,* p. 235.

Going on shore [at Terceira], I found the people both courteous and hospitable, every attention being paid by them. The Bay is a moderate sized one, with good holding ground, and protected from all, save easterly winds. Three or four forts (without guns), were built, but were nearly useless thro' decay. Beef has to be brought from Angra on the other side of the island. Fruit and vegetables are plentiful, but water is scarce.

Bahia Angra is the other chief bay at Terceira. It is on the southern coast. *HO 134,* p. 214; *BR 502C,* pp. 302–312; *Britannica Atlas,* 138a.

On the 13th, a sail was observed standing in the harbour; anchoring near us, she proved to be the American whaling schooner "Rising Sun" of Provincetown.

The doctor of the Portuguese port placed the schooner under quarantine and then released her.

Through the indiscretion of the Purser [Clarence R. Yonge], our real character became known, and considerable apprehension was felt for our safety, on her [Rising Sun's] departure a few days after.

On the 18th, a sail was observed making for the anchorage. In the evening she anchored near us, when we found her to be the barque "Aggripina" of London, Capt. McQueen, having on board 6 guns, with ammunition, coals, stores, &c. &c. for us.

Agrippina (under command of Captain Alexander McQueen, Britisher and active rebel agent) was *Alabama's* tender. This British bark of 258 tons burden was built by the Tindall Shipyard at Scarborough in 1834. She was engaged in the Mediterranean trade and otherwise in voyages between London and Ceylon before being acquired for the Confederates by Commander J. D. Bulloch in July 1862. While *Agrippina* was commanded by McQueen, *Alabama* (at that time known as *Enrica,* or *Barcelona,* or by her hull number *290)* was commanded by Captain Mathew J. Butcher. There was a rumor that *Alabama* was called *290* because she was paid for by 290 Englishmen. Charles B. Boynton, *The History of the Navy During the Rebellion,* II, 552, swallowed a tall tale of the sixties when he wrote, "Insultingly this vessel was named '290,' to show by the large number that had contributed to fit her out, how widespread was English sympathy for the rebel cause."

Alabama and *Agrippina* were to meet at the obscure anchorage of Terceira so that *Alabama* could safely be fitted out as a warship with stores from *Agrippina.* In this way the Confederate naval agent, James Dunwody Bulloch, sought to avoid the appearance of violating the British Foreign Enlistment Act. In the *Alabama* Claims award, Great Britain paid dearly for the Geneva Tribunal's judgment that the CSS *Alabama* and some other Confederate cruisers had violated the law in episodes such as that described by Fullam. Bulloch said that he had learned about the ideal rendezvous location quite by accident only a short time before he selected the spot for fitting out *Alabama.*

Bulloch was less than frank with Captain Alexander McQueen, skipper of the bark *Agrippina,* in his orders to McQueen dated 28 July 1862. Nowhere was the name *Enrica* or any of the aliases mentioned. Rather, McQueen was given the name of Captain Butcher and told the identification number of Butcher's ship. McQueen, of course, was assigned an identification number for himself and told to go to the Bay of Praia, Terceira.

[11]

Preparations were immediately made to transfer her cargo.
On the afternoon of the 20th, whilst employed discharging
the barque, the S. S. "Bahama,"

The third ship needed to help fit out *Alabama*, hopefully within the fictions of the law, was *Bahama*, which was bringing Raphael Semmes and many other Confederate naval officers for the first time to their new ship. *Bahama* continued thereafter to be a tender serving *Alabama* in many distant lands, and a description of her is in order. *Bahama* was only a few months old when Fullam first saw her; she had been built at Stockton-on-Tees and was a bark-rigged screw propeller of 888 tons. Painted black with a narrow red stripe, yellow houses and boats, with much filigree work and gilt about her bow and stern, she was a very fast and very distinctive vessel, a near-sister to *Bermuda*, tender to the CSS *Florida*. Perhaps the chief limitation of *Bahama* and *Bermuda* was that they looked too much like blockade runners. *Bahama's* dimensions were 226 x 29.2 x 20.8. Just shortly before Fullam commented upon *Bahama* in his Journal, the United States minister at Brussels had supplied the Union navy with a drawing of *Bahama* along with a considerable verbal description. In command of *Bahama* was Captain Eugene L. Tessier who had earlier commanded *Bermuda*.

Capt. [Eugene L.] Tessier, arrived, having on board Commr.
Raphael Semmes and officers of the C. S. Str. "Sumter."

There were 14 officers in *Alabama* who had served in *Sumter*: Raphael Semmes, John McIntosh Kell, Richard F. Armstrong, Joseph D. Wilson, Francis L. Galt, Miles J. Freeman, B. K. Howell, William Breedlove Smith, William P. Brooks, Mathew O'Brien, Simeon W. Cummings, Benjamin P. Mecaskey, Thomas C. Cuddy, and William Robinson.

All three [vessels] carefully went round to Angra on the
21st.

Bahia Angra had an anchorage of 30 fathoms. In Terceira were two harbors, West Angra and East Angra. Semmes' *290* moored in West Angra at first but was required by local authorities to move to East Angra because that was the port of entry for merchant ships and up to this time *290* was a merchant ship yet to be commissioned as the CSS *Alabama*.

Hauled steamer alongside, taking from her 2 thirty-two pdrs.,
with some stores &c., which took us until the following day.
21st. Got up steam, dodging slowly along the island, having
the barque fast alongside, taking from her a quantity of coal

&c., which took us until the evening of the 22nd, when we anchored in Angra Bay. About 9 p.m. we were startled by the report of a gun fired from a fort, and which was believed to have been a shot in. The "Bahama" immediately stood seaward, in order to draw the fire, from us towards her. At 11 p.m. another was fired. The explanation given by the authorities, the following morn, was that it was only a mail signal. We had however considerable reason to doubt it.

23rd. Was this day appointed "Acting Master's Mate" to the C. S. Str. "Alabama."

So it came about that on 23 August 1862, George Townley Fullam proudly accepted the appointment as acting master's mate. The duties of the master's mate are described in detail by F. A. Roe, *Naval Duties and Discipline with the Policy and Principles of Naval Organization*, 67–76, 107–116; Tom H. Wells, *The Confederate Navy*, 32. A master's mate ranked just behind a midshipman. With the creation of the United States Naval Academy, midshipmen less often sailed in warships. Both forecastle and quarter-deck often missed the "young gentlemen." To perform the duties of midshipmen at sea, the United States Navy created the grade of master's mates. They were assigned duties at divisional quarters, on the quarter-deck, and on the forecastle. At the start of the Civil War their position was ambiguous. They were the forerunners of warrant officers, but rarely enjoyed the respect which later sailors usually had for their warrant officers. Before the Civil War a master's mate had little chance of promotion, but the shortage of officers, particularly junior officers, which became acute with the start of the shooting war, changed speedily the status of master's mates. A master's mate could look forward to promotion to ensign or to master. By 1864, there were 96 acting master's mates in the Confederate Navy.

The master's mate on watch was an assistant to the officer of the deck. At the division of guns the master's mate was an assistant to the divisional officer. The master's mate was usually the mustering officer of the division and of the watch. He helped prepare the division for inspection and regularly conducted division drills. He posted lookouts and checked on their alertness. He was a channel of communications from the quarter-deck to any of the ship's officers. Often he actually served as a messenger, since the customs of the day presumed that official communications to an officer of any grade would ordinarily be carried by a junior officer and not by an enlisted messenger. On the other hand, enlisted messengers normally carried communications to petty officers and enlisted men. When the ship's boats were ordered to be ready for going ashore or for boarding prizes, it was the duty of the master's mate to see that they were properly fitted out and properly manned, that the boatswain's mates were doing their duties, and that all of this was properly reported to the officer of the deck.

Sunday 24th Aug. 1862. Strong N. W. wind. At 12.30 got under weigh in company with the Bahama, and stood along the Island of Terceira. At 2 p.m. Captain Semmes read his commission, and formally took command of the Confederate States Steamer "Alabama" 8 guns; hoisting the Confederate ensign at the peak, the English St. Georges at the fore, and the pendant at the main, firing a gun at the same time. Commr. Semmes made a most effective, spirited address, in which (after speaking of the relations existing between the North and the South) he said; "his principal object was to cripple the commerce of the enemy; that he was not going to fight a fifty-gun ship, but as soon as they had become proficient in the use of their weapons, he would give them an opportunity to show the world what they were made of." Three rousing cheers were given at its conclusion.

Semmes wrote of the occasion:

My speech, I was glad to find, had produced considerable effect with the crew. I informed them, in the opening, that they were all released from the contracts under which they had come thus far, and that such of them as preferred to return to England could do so in the *Bahama*, without prejudice to their interests, as they would have a free passage back, and their pay would go on until they were discharged in Liverpool. I then gave them a brief account of the war, and told them how the Southern States, being sovereign and independent, had dissolved the league which had bound them to the Northern States, and how they were threatened with subjugation by their late confederates, who were the stronger. They would be fighting, I told them, the battles of the oppressed against the oppressor, and this consideration alone should be enough to nerve the arm of every generous sailor. Coming nearer home, for it could not be supposed that English, Dutch, Irish, French, Italian, and Spanish sailors could understand much about the rights or wrongs of nations, I explained to them the individual advantages which they might expect to reap from an enlistment with me. The cruise would be one of excitement and adventure. We had a fine ship under us; one that they might fall in love with, as they would with their sweethearts about Wapping. We should visit many parts of the world, where they would have "liberty" given them on proper occasions; and we should, no doubt, destroy a great many of the enemy's ships, in spite of the enemy's cruisers. With regard to these last, though fighting was not to be our principal object, yet, if a favorable opportunity should offer of our laying ourselves alongside of a ship that was not too heavy for us, they would find me disposed to indulge them.

Finally I came to the finances, and like a skilful Secretary of the Treasury, I put the budget to them in its very best aspect. As I spoke of good pay, and payment in gold, "hear hear!" came up from several voices. I would give them, I said, about double the ordinary wages, to compensate them for the risks they would have to run, and I promised them, in case we should be successful, "lots of prize-money," to be voted to them by the Confederate Congress, for the ships of the enemy that they would be obliged to destroy. When we "piped down," that is to say, when the boatswain and his mates wound their "calls" three times, as a signal that the meeting was over, and the crew might disperse, I caused the word to be passed for all those who desired to sign the articles, to repair at once to the paymaster and sign. I was anxious to strike whilst the iron was hot. The *Alabama* had brought out from the Mersey about sixty men, and the *Bahama* had brought about thirty more. I got eighty of these ninety men, and felt very much relieved in consequence.

Having conveyed Capts. Bulloch & Butcher to the Bahama, I returned and at 11:30 p.m. we hoisted launch and parted, the Bahama returning to Liverpool and the Alabama proceeding on a cruise. (Including Cmr: 26 officers & 85 men.) 2.30 p.m. of the following day, hoisted up the propellor, and secured it, it being our intention to cruise under sail only, unless occasion demanded steam.

Semmes later wrote of this parting:

> It was eleven P. M. before my friend Bullock [Bulloch] was ready to return to the *Bahama*, on his way back to England. I took an affectionate leave of him. I had spent some days with him, at his quiet retreat, in the little village of Waterloo, near Liverpool, where I met his excellent wife, a charming Southern woman, with whom hospitality was a part of her religious faith. He was living in a very plain, simple style, though large sums of public money were passing through his hands, and he has had the honor to come out of the war poor. He paid out moneys in good faith, to the last, even when it was quite evident that the cause had gone under, and there would be no accounts to settle with an Auditor of the Treasury. I had not only had the pleasure of his society during a number of anxious days, but he had greatly assisted me, by his counsel and advice, given with that modesty and reserve which always mark true ability. As soon as the *Bahama* had steamed away, and left me alone, I turned my ship's head to the north-east, set the fore-and-aft sails, and directed the engineer to let his fires go down. The wind had freshened considerably, and there was some sea on. I now turned into an unquiet cot, perfectly exhausted, after the labors of the day, and slept as comfortably as the rolling of the ship, and a strong smell of bilge-water would permit.

29th. Gave chase to a brig, lost her in the darkness. The following day sighted another that showed French colours.

[15]

6.30 p.m. called all hands to muster, and stationed them at the great guns. Strong N.E. wind.

Reckoned by celestial navigation, *Alabama's* position on 29 August 1862 was 36.25 north and 21.24 west. Fullam omitted the entry for 30 August. On that afternoon another brig was chased and fired upon, but without yielding a prize.

31st. Sail reported on lee bow, gave chase, showed Portuguese colours.

Two ships were pursued on 31 August, a French brig and a Portuguese brig.

2nd. Sept. Chased a barque. On boarding she proved to be the "La Foi" from Timor to Nantes.

This was the first time a suspected prize was boarded by *Alabama*. John Low was the boarding officer. It is possible that Fullam was also in the boarding party. Low indicated that the destination of this French bark *La Foi* was Bordeaux, whereas Fullam said that it was Nantes. At the present time the point is important only as an indication of the independence of the journals kept by Fullam and by Low.

4th Exercised 1st and 2nd Divisions at great guns.

5th. Several vessels in sight. Gave chase to one. Discovering her to be a Portuguese brigantine, went about and chased a ship which showed American colours. On boarding she proved to be the "Ockmulgee" [Ocmulgee], a whaler, of Martha's Vineyard, with a valuable sperm whale fast alongside. Took possession, transferred her crew to the Alabama, and a quantity of stores. All prisoners American born were put in irons; the rest, if English &c, were not ironed.

6th. Burnt prize.

Ocmulgee was the first capture by *Alabama*. The prize was a 459-ton ship of Edgartown, Massachusetts, with Abraham Osborn as part owner and master. She was a whaling vessel which had been at sea only some two months and still had an ample supply of stores on board, having been fitted out for a 48-month cruise in the Atlantic, Pacific, and Arctic oceans. When stopped by *Alabama* on 5 September 1862, she was in the Azores near Pico Island, and was boarded by Lt. Richard F. Armstrong. In her short time at sea, *Ocmulgee* already had oil on board valued at more than the ship herself. Indeed, a large sperm whale was alongside her at the time of capture and all hands were at work "trying out the blubber." The ship was valued by her owners at $12,000. The stores and whaling gear were worth more than twice the value of the ship. Damages later sought by the owners of *Ocmulgee* and her outfit in the *Alabama* Claims reached $254,075. The total Confederate evaluation of the ship and her outfit by Lieutenants Armstrong and Kell was $50,000.

Harper's Weekly, 25 October 1862, reported the loss of *Ocmulgee* under the headline, "Another Pirate at Work." An English vessel *Cairngorm* arrived at Gravesend, England, from Sidney, Australia, and reported that, when at Flores, three whaleboat crews came alongside and said that *Ocmulgee* had been burned, together with 250 barrels of oil, and that her crew of 34 men had been made prisoners. *Harper's Weekly* also noted that the USS *St. Louis* departed Lisbon headed for the Azores as a result of *Alabama's* attack on *Ocmulgee* and other whaling vessels in that area. Record Group 76 of the National Archives has 38 cases of claims resulting from the loss of *Ocmulgee*. U. S. Minister to England C. F. Adams to Earl Russell (British Foreign Secretary), 20 November 1862, enclosed a letter of Captain Abraham Osborn, 13 September 1862, in *FA 1864,* pp. 5–8.

Lt. J. M. Kell said that Osborn was very much surprised at being captured, but accepted his fate with good grace. By the time *Alabama* had transferred from the well-stocked whaler supplies of pork, beef, and small stores, darkness had set in and Semmes decided to wait until morning to burn the vessel, lest a bonfire at night warn off other prospective prizes. Since *Ocmulgee* was *Alabama's* first prize, Lt. Arthur Sinclair described the burning procedures as follows:

> Perhaps the reader may imagine there is no art in it. Well, one way to do a thing well, another to bungle, there always seems to be. We have many more to send "where the woodbine twineth;" so listen to the *modus operandi* (though we were not put to the trouble with this whaler—inflammable enough without any preparation). First, you cut up with your broadaxe the cabin and forecastle bunks, generally of white pine lumber. You will find, doubtless, the mattresses stuffed with straw, and in the cabin pantry part at least of a keg of butter and lard. Make a foundation of the splinters and straw, pour on top the lard and butter. One pile in cabin, the other in forecastle. Get your men in the boats, all but the incendiaries, and at the given word—"fire!" shove off, and take it as truth, that before you have reached your own ship, the blaze is licking the topsails of the doomed ship.

In chase of a barque. Coming up with her, we found she was the French barque "Senegambia" of Marseilles. Made the islands of Flores and Corvo. Sent prisoners ashore off Flores. Chased and captured the schooner "Starlight" of Boston, with passengers, from Fayal to Flores. This was rather an exciting chase, for after firing a blank cartridge, still kept on his course (endeavouring to get shelter under the land). A shot was then fired across his bow but, without any effect.

[17]

So a shot was fired between his masts, which had the desired effect. Transferred prisoners, and hove to until daylight.

When *Alabama,* with the British flag flying in the breeze, came up to *Starlight,* the Confederates hesitated to fire at the schooner because women passengers could be seen on the deck, but when it appeared that the vessel would escape, *Alabama* fired a blank shot across the schooner's bow, ordering her to heave to. Instead, the captain chose to run for neutral waters about six miles away. Then *Alabama* showed the Confederate flag and fired solid shot from the bow gun just slightly ahead of the fleeing vessel. Still the valiant Yankee ran toward the shore, whereupon *Alabama* fired solid shot between the fore and mainmasts. Finally the schooner raised the United States ensign and hove to. A well-armed boarding party went on board and sent Captain Samuel H. Doane and his crew over to *Alabama,* while Lt. Armstrong himself served as prize master with a Confederate crew on board *Starlight.* Semmes put Doane and all seven of his crew in irons. Doane remonstrated that this was an indignity. Semmes agreed that it was, but explained that it was done in reprisal for the treatment inflicted by Union forces upon an officer who had served with Semmes aboard the CSS *Sumter,* Paymaster Henry Myers and another Confederate named Tom Tate Tunstall. The masters of the next several ships captured by Semmes were also put in irons.

The newly captured prize proved to be a schooner of Boston, bound from Fayal to Flores. She had passengers aboard and was about a month out. The morning after the capture, Lt. Low in the cutter with an armed boat's crew went out to *Starlight* and transported the passengers ashore. When Low reached the shore, he was greeted by so many men, women, and children that he thought the entire population of the island had gathered to observe the refugees from the commerce raider. After the passengers were landed, the remaining prisoners on board *Alabama* and their baggage were put in their own boats and sent ashore.

Semmes appointed Lt. Armstrong to appraise *Starlight* in order that the correct prize money could be recorded for the *Alabama* crew. The value set by the Confederates was $4,000. The owners asked $3,500 for this vessel in the *Alabama* Claims controversy. *Starlight* was from Deer Isle, Maine, owned by her captain, Samuel H. Doane, and four others. She had departed Boston 7 August 1862 and was captured by *Alabama* on 7 September. *American Lloyds, 1862,* p. 532; Adams to Russell, 20 November 1862, enclosed a deposition of Captain Samuel H. Doane; RG 76, eight cases. For navigational data concerning the area of capture of *Starlight,* see *BR 502C,* p. 67; *HO 134,* pp. 199–203; and *HO Chart 1373.* Flores is the westernmost of the Azores, while Corvo is the northernmost and smallest island of the archipelago.

7th. Saw a steamer on weather bow. Read Articles of War.

It was usual to read the Articles of War on the first Sunday of the month, and 7 September 1862 was the first Sunday. .

8th. Landed passengers and crew of "Starlight" at Flores. 7 sails in sight. Stood out from the land in chase of one, prize schooner following. Came up with her, and found her to be the barque "Ocean Rover" of New London with a valuable cargo of whale oil on board, having been out 40 months. Transferred prisoners, stores &c, and in the evening scuttled her; but, as it afterwards showed, ineffectually, owing to the buoyancy of the cargo.

The bark *Ocean Rover* was captured before *Starlight* was burned. While Armstrong was serving as prize master of *Starlight,* Lt. Wilson boarded *Ocean Rover.* Meantime, Semmes appointed Kell and Low to appraise *Ocean Rover.* This ship, the third destroyed by *Alabama,* was valued at $70,000 (including her cargo of oil). At this time, the value of the three ships destroyed by *Alabama,* according to Confederate statistics, totaled $124,000. The owners of *Ocean Rover* alone claimed $98,825 in damages, distributed as follows:

CLAIMS

Owners.

Loss on vessel	$25,000
Loss on outfits and appurtenances	25,000
Loss on 750 barrels sperm oil	47,250
Loss on 50 barrels whale oil	1,575
	$98,825

Losses claimed by the ship's 27 owners totaled $136,625, including damage accrued from breaking up the voyage ($37,800). Residences listed for the owners included New Bedford, Matapoisett, and Plymouth (all in Massachusetts). One of the owners, with a share of only 8/128, was *Ocean Rover's* captain, James M. Clark of Plymouth, who filed an additional claim for loss of personal effects in the amount of $750. Some of the owners had insurance against their losses. The claims of the insurors were filed by three insurance companies of New Bedford. The total claims filed for the burning of *Ocean Rover* amounted to $167,670. In addition to that of Clark, there were 16 individual cases presented to the *Alabama* Claims Commission for loss of personal effects in *Ocean Rover.*

9th. Captured barque "Alert" of New Bedford. Engaged all day transferring stores for ships use.

Alert proved to be one of the most memorable of *Alabama's* prizes.

This small vessel was the ship in which the celebrated author, Richard Henry Dana, Jr., served as a seaman in a voyage from San Diego to Boston during 1836 under Captain Francis A. Thompson. Thus *Alert* is identified as one of the two vessels which served as a center of the actions in the famous sea narrative *Two Years Before the Mast*. There is a picture of *Alert* facing page 296 in the edition edited by John H. Kemble. The same outstanding edition contains interesting descriptions of the vessel on pp. 175–179.

Lt. Armstrong was in command of the boarding party from *Alabama* which seized the bark *Alert* of New Bedford. *Alert*, although valued officially by Kell and Low at only $20,000, had supplies which were worth transferring to the Confederate raider despite the numerous prizes taken among the unsuspecting whaling vessels. *Alert* was well supplied with heavy underwear, something that the Confederates needed very much at that time. With the burning of *Alert*, the fourth prize destroyed, Confederate statistics totaled $144,000. Claims later filed by Richard H. Chapell, managing owner, and the bark's other owners, supported the Confederate estimate closely, with $21,358.91 set for the loss of ship and outfits. Thirteen cases were filed by owners of *Alert* before the *Alabama* Claims Commissioners. Cases claiming loss of personal effects totaled only 11. All claims amounted to $57,858.91.

At the time of her capture, *Alert* was on a voyage to Desolation Island, otherwise known as Kerguelan Land in the Indian Ocean, to obtain a cargo of sea-elephant oil. Evidence was presented that this type of oil came exclusively from Desolation Island and from Herd's Island, and that this business was entirely in the hands of *Alert's* owners. The normal operation was to have a bark like *Alert*, or a three-masted ship, working jointly with a schooner. At the time of *Alert's* voyage, the schooner *E. R. Sawyer* was sailing as a partner. *Sawyer* duly arrived at the destination. The owners of *Alert* claimed special losses because *Sawyer* reported that there were large numbers of sea-elephants on Desolation Island which would have been readily taken had *Alert* not been destroyed. When the owners of *Alert* heard of the loss of the bark, they sent out another vessel named *Arab* to Desolation Island where another cargo of sea-elephant oil was taken. In awarding damages, the first *Alabama* Claims Court disallowed the lost catch of sea-elephants, but did allow for the value of the ship and of the oil actually on board *Alert*. In view of *Alert's* value and mission, it is understandable why her master, Charles E. Church, would make an exceptional effort to escape the Confederate raider.

When *Alert* came into sight, *Alabama* was lying to with two other whalers, *Ocean Rover* and *Starlight*, standing by. It was the mid-watch. *Alabama's* crew had had very little sleep after a day of excitement. The Confederates started in pursuit of *Alert*, who got the wind of the raider. At daylight *Alabama* hoisted the British flag, and when *Alert* did not reply, fired a blank cartridge.

[20]

When *Alert* still did not respond, *Alabama* fired a shot astern of the bark while she was only about two miles distant. Then *Alert* showed United States colors and hove to.

Set on fire barques "Ocean Rover" "Alert" & schr. "Starlight."

It was about 9 a.m. on 7 September 1862 when the Confederates burned *Starlight*. About two hours later, they set fire to *Ocean Rover*. Some five hours later they fired *Alert*, so Dana's famous ship ended in flames her final voyage. Captain Church and the crew of *Alert* were sent ashore to Flores Island in four of their own boats. Similarly the crews of the other whalers were sent ashore. Thus the island had a sudden population explosion, and business rocketed.

Overhauled and captured schooner "Weather Gage" of Provincetown.

There are variant spellings of the name of this ship. *Weathergauge* appears to have somewhat better support than Fullam's spelling. *N. Y. Marine Register 1857*, p. 117. See also Edmund M. Blunt, *The American Coast Pilot*, p. 172; *HO 134*, p. 200; *BR 502C*, p. 67. The officer who boarded *Weathergauge* was Richard F. Armstrong. The Yankee master was Captain Samuel C. Small. Small was also one of the numerous owners of the vessel. The ship was valued at $9,853.84, and the total claims filed with the *Alabama* Claims in this connection were $11,545.54. *Weathergauge* was the fifth vessel destroyed by *Alabama*. The Confederate evaluation placed by Armstrong was $10,000.

Stood in chase of a barque, and which on boarding proved to be Danish.

This was the bark *Overman* proceeding from Bangkok, Siam, bound for Hamburg. This Danish vessel being neutral had no evident reason for fleeing the Confederate pursuer.

To this vessel we hoisted American colours, and passed as the U. S. Str. "Iroquois."

Some of the officers aboard *Alabama* had very good reason indeed to remember the USS *Iroquois*. In November 1861 this magnificent eight-gun ship, then under Commander James S. Palmer, had blockaded the first Confederate cruiser the CSS *Sumter*, but in a very dramatic episode the Confederate raider had escaped.

To all prizes we had captured we hoisted English colours, and exchanged them for Confederate as soon as the boarding officer gained the vessels deck.

10th. Burnt prize and shaped a course for Flores.

11th. Hove to off Flores and landed prisoners, the Governor paying us a visit. Filled away in chase of a barque, but owing to the darkness lost her.

12th. Fresh southerly wind, very pleasant. Made sail in chase of a vessel. Found her to be a Portuguese barque.

13th. A.M. Two vessels in sight. One proved to be a Spaniard, the other a Yankee brigantine, and which of course we captured, taking her crew on board our vessel, and setting her on fire, the "Altamaha" of Sippican.

Sippican Harbor, Massachusetts, was described by Blunt as it appeared a few years before *Altamaha* was destroyed by *Alabama. Altamaha* was a New Bedford whaling brig of 119 tons burden, commanded by Rufus Gray. She had been out five months and had had such generally bad luck that she was practically empty when she had the crowning blow of being captured by the Confederates. The boarding officer from *Alabama* was Lt. Joseph D. Wilson, accompanied by Fullam. There were many owners, as was usually the case with whaling vessels. The value claimed for *Altamaha* by her owners was $15,450. Additional claims brought the total to $48,000.60. Kell and Low appraised her at $3,000.

14th. 1.30 a.m. Gave chase, to a sail on lee bow. 2.30 a.m. Fired a gun for her to heave to. Darkness prevented us knowing who he was, so, I went on board to examine his papers, and which, if Yankee, I was to signal it and heave to until daylight. What I did on boarding this vessel was the course usually adopted in taking prizes. Pulling under his stern, I saw it was the whaling ship "Benj. Tucker" of and from New Bedford. Gaining the quarter-deck, I was welcomed with outstretched hands. In answer to my questions, the Capt. told me her name, port of registry, &c. &c. all of which I was previously aware. I then told him that he was a prize to the C. S. Str. "Alabama," ordering him to put his clothes in one trunk, allowing the mates and men one bag each, all navigation books and instruments being left behind. At daylight sent the Capt. and crew with the ships papers and their luggage to the "Alabama." I then examined the ship, and finding some cases of stores, they were transferred to our ship. The preparations to fire her were soon made, so that after seeing her well fired we pushed off and regained our vessel,

This was a night chase. Semmes, in discussing the pursuit of *Benjamin Tucker,* described his own habits under such circumstances. When there was no reason for doing otherwise, the lonely commanding officer would go to bed at nine o'clock. On the night of 14 September 1862, he went to bed at the usual hour. Two-and-a-half hours later, he was awakened by a quartermaster who told him about the prospective prize. Semmes jumped out of bed, dressed very rapidly, and was soon on deck giving the necessary orders to pursue the possible prize. *Alabama* had been proceeding leisurely under topsails only and headed in the opposite direction from the whaling vessel, and therefore it took some time to close the two or three mile gap which had been lost while the raider turned around. Within a couple of hours the distance had been shortened to one mile, when *Alabama* fired the usual blank cartridge to signal the stranger to heave to. The captain of the whaler, however, was not easily intimidated and kept running. *Alabama* fired a second time and, although this was again a blank, the whaler hove to. She was *Benjamin Tucker,* a ship-rigged, 349-ton whaler, under command of Captain William Childs. This New Bedford vessel was valued at $20,000 (in the claims of her owners), her cargo of oil from the five-month voyage was valued at $25,200, and her outfits and appurtenances at $25,000. The total claims filed were exceptionally large for a whaling vessel of her size, $178,495. Semmes appointed Lt. J. M. Kell to place a value upon *Tucker* for purposes of later prize money, and Kell set ship and cargo at $18,000.

the prisoners (Yankees) being placed in single irons.

As boarding officer of *Benjamin Tucker,* Fullam was carrying out the policy of reprisal for the imprisonment of Paymaster Henry Myers and T. T. Tunstall, an adventure in the CSS *Sumter.*

15th. Light breeze with heavy swell.
16th. Land in sight right ahead. 10.30 a.m. Sail reported right ahead. Chased, fired a gun, boarded and took possession of her, the schooner, "Courser" of Provincetown. We then stood to the land, sent prisoners ashore, stood out to sea, and made a target of prize. After some creditable shooting we burnt her.

This vessel illustrated the fact that *Alabama* worked early as well as late in capturing vessels. It was 5:15 a.m. when a sail was seen off the starboard bow heading toward the Isle of Flores, as was *Alabama* at the same time. *Alabama* moved to cut her off, and came in close enough to see that she had a fore-and-aft rig. After a two-hour chase, the Confederates fired a blank cartridge and brought her to. Lt. John Low headed the boarding party, and soon reported that the schooner was the 121-ton *Courser* of Provincetown, Massachusetts, commanded by Silas S. Young, one of nine owners of the vessel. *Courser* had been on a whaling voyage for six months when captured. The captain and his crew were made prisoners.

During *Alabama's* cruise, many men who served as seamen in captured prizes did an about-face in their allegiance and enlisted in the Confederate States Navy for duty in the raider. There is no precise record as to how many of these men were citizens of the United States. The first man to enlist in *Alabama* from a prize was Abram Nordhock. Nordhock had been serving in one of the following: *Weathergauge, Altamaha,* or *Benjamin Tucker,* most likely *Benjamin Tucker.* Nordhock enlisted with the Confederates on 15 September 1862. Another unusual thing about Nordhock was that he was an able-bodied seaman. Rarely did a man enlist from a prize who ranked higher than an ordinary seaman.

Because there were some 70 Yankee prisoners, who by virtue of their numbers offered some threat to the security of the rebel raider, Semmes decided to land the prisoners on nearby Flores Island. The crews of *Courser, Weathergauge, Altamaha,* and *Benjamin Tucker* were paroled and, along with their baggage, loaded into eight whaleboats belonging to their vessels. The Confederates also allowed the prisoners to help themselves to an assortment of the whalers' stores, including harpoons, coils of rope, salt pork and beef. Sinclair said that, "It was a royal present, and profuse were their thanks to Semmes. A sailor and a jackdaw hold equal honors in the art of pillaging." The prisoners used these supplies to trade with the natives on Flores. The whaleboats were towed toward the island by *Alabama* and when within sight of shore cast off. *Alabama* then went back to *Courser* and proceeded to transfer supplies. By four o'clock the loading was completed and for the next two hours *Alabama's* gun crews had target practice before burning *Courser,* the first time the gunners were exercised against an actual target.

In the *Alabama* Claims, *Courser* was valued at $10,233.84, and total losses for this vessel were set at $12,462.53. For the Confederates, Kell and Low valued *Courser* at $7,000.

Captain Silas S. Young made quite an impression upon Lt. Arthur Sinclair. Sinclair later wrote:

> We found the Courser's skipper quite a young sailor, frank and open under adversity. His cheerful, philosophical mien at once secured our admiration and sympathy. Standing aft on the quarter, Semmes, with the schooner's papers in his hand, informed him his vessel was a prize, and was about to be destroyed, with the addendum to return to his late command, get his men together, with bags and hammocks, and return. His "Aye, aye, sir," spoke volumes of don't care acquiescence and devil-may-care attention to the order.

17th. Whilst at quarters, two vessels were reported, bore down for the lee one. 11.20 Hove her to. She showed Yankee colours. Accordingly we took possession. Found her to be the barque "Virginia," whaler, of, and 21 days from New Bedford.

This prize was sighted by *Alabama's* lookout at 7:30 a.m. When Lt. Low boarded her, he learned that she was the 346-ton bark *Virginia,* commanded by Shadrach R. Tilton. She had sailed from New Bedford on 26 August 1862, and her destination was the Atlantic and also the Pacific. Captain Tilton was very much surprised to learn that he had been captured by the Confederate raider. Tilton commented on *Alabama's* great speed. Tilton said that *Virginia* was a fast vessel but was easily outrun by the speedy Confederate. The captain and his papers were sent aboard the cruiser for a prize hearing before Captain Semmes. It is of interest to note that John Low retained in his own keeping the log of *Virginia*.

When the ship was condemned, Kell and Low were appointed by Semmes to set a value upon her. This was done in the amount of $25,000. Later in the *Alabama* Claims, the vessel and her outfit were valued at $50,000. The two evaluations were not too much out of line since the outfit of a whaling vessel might be expected to double the value of a $25,000 ship. The total claims filed for the loss of *Virginia*, however, came to $167,500, including reimbursement of two insurance companies of New Bedford and one of Boston, and losses of personal effects of members of the crew. The largest item in the claims was some $103,000 based upon "loss of prospective profits."

Obtained late newspapers containing accounts of victories gained both by the Federals and Confederates, the former at Baton Rouge; the latter in Missouri. The news however was received with doubt on account of the source from which it emanated.

Two Confederate generals, Earl Van Dorn and Sterling Price, campaigned in Missouri during August 1862. Van Dorn attacked Baton Rouge on 5 August. Between the time of David G. Farragut's capture of New Orleans, 18–28, April 1862, and the attack on Donaldsonville, Louisiana, 10 August 1862, Union forces were involved at Baton Rouge.

4 p.m. Set fire to prize.

18th. Two vessels in sight. Chased one; proved to be a French brig. Bore away for the other. He evidently not liking our appearance, altered his course & made all sail. A fresh breeze was blowing at the time. His exertions however proved fruitless, for at 12.30 we came up with him, boarded and took possession of barque "Elisha Dunbar" from New Bedford, 25 days out. In the evening burnt her.

Elisha Dunbar was chased while *Alabama* sailed under British colors, but this did not slow down the alert whaler. The bark showed no colors herself until fired upon, when she broke out the Stars and Stripes. By that time the September weather was so rough that Semmes hesitated to send a boarding party to her, but finally decided that if he did not do so before dark, the prize would escape during the hours of darkness, soon to settle over the ships. Consequently, two of *Alabama's* best boats were put over the side under Lt. Joseph D. Wilson. Semmes said, "I had a set of gallant, and skillful young officers around me, who would dare anything I told them to dare, and some capital seamen, and . . . I thought the thing could be managed. . . ." Semmes told the boarding party to bring back from the prize nothing except the ship's chronometer, her flag, and the people aboard. Wilson was told to fire the prize before leaving her. As to the chronometer Wilson was to bring back, chronometers represented very compact value. No article was more important for the prize money which each of the officers and men expected to be paid by the Confederate government for prizes burned and for Union prizes which were released under ransom bond. Semmes kept the chronometers in his own cabin, although otherwise under the care of the navigator, Lt. Arthur Sinclair. Sinclair explained his duties in connection with the chronometers and the fact that he had to wind each one every day. After the burning of *Elisha Dunbar*, Sinclair wrote concerning the captured chronometers, "We had about fifteen of them, requiring half an hour to wind up, with the prospect of a steady all-day job at it in the near future, at the rate we were burning vessels. We had on hand at the end of the cruise, and landed at Cherbourg, seventy-five chronometers; and it need not be added *the winding-up* business soon came to an end, time being too valuable for expenditure on so many recording angels. The reason for saving these instruments was their portability as compared with their value." Semmes said that *Elisha Dunbar* was the only ship that he ever burned before examining her papers, and he added, "But as she was a whaler, and so could have no neutral cargo on board, the risk to be run was not very great."

Elisha Dunbar was a New Bedford bark of 257 tons. Under command of David R. Gifford, she departed New Bedford 25 August 1862, bound on a whaling voyage. In the approximate position 40.00 north and 40.00 west during a rain squall, *Elisha Dunbar* spoke the bark *Virginia* under command of Captain Shadrach R. Tilton. This meeting was 11 September 1862. One week later *Elisha Dunbar* was in position 39.50 north and 35.20 west when she was boarded by Lt. Wilson. When Captain Gifford, with his papers and his men, was taken aboard *Alabama* by Wilson, Gifford saw once more Captain Shadrach R. Tilton of the bark *Virginia* among the prisoners of war.

Later Captain Gifford testified:

> On the morning of the 18th of September, in latitude 39° 50', longitude 35° 20', with the wind from the south-west, and the bark heading south-east, saw a steamer on our port-quarter, standing to the north-west. Soon after, found she had altered her course, and was steering for the bark. We soon made all sail to get out of her reach, and were going ten knots at the time; but the steamer, gaining on us, under canvas alone, soon came up with us, and fired a gun under our stern, with the St. George's cross flying at the time. Our colors were set, when she displayed the Confederate flag. Being near us, we hove to,

and a boat, with armed officers and crew, came alongside, and upon coming on board, stated to me that my vessel was a prize to the Confederate steamer *Alabama,* Captain Semmes. I was then ordered on board the steamer with my papers, and the crew to follow me with a bag of clothing each. On getting on board, the captain claimed me as a prize, and said that my vessel would be burned. Not having any clothes with me, he allowed me to return for a small trunk of clothes;—the officer on board asked me what I was coming back for, and tried to prevent me from coming on board. I told him I came after a few clothes, which I took, and returned to the steamer. It blowing very hard at the time, and very squally, nothing but the chronometer, sextant, charts, &c., were taken, when the vessel was set fire to, and burnt; there were sixty-five barrels of sperm oil on deck, taken on the passage, which were consumed. We were all put in irons, and received the same treatment that Captain Tilton's officers and crew did, who had been taken the day before. While on board, we understood that the steamer would cruise off the Grand Banks, for a few weeks, to destroy the large American ships, to and from the Channel ports. They had knowledge of two ships being loaded with arms for the United States, and were in hopes to capture them. They were particularly anxious to fall in with the clippership *Dreadnought,* and destroy her, as she was celebrated for speed; and they were confident of their ability to capture, or run away from any vessel in the United States. The steamer being in the track of outward and homeward-bound vessels, and more or less being in sight, every day, she will make great havoc among them.

Elisha Dunbar, the tenth vessel destroyed by *Alabama* within two weeks, was also the tenth destroyed altogether by the raider. The evaluation placed upon her by Lt. Wilson was $25,000. This figure brought the Confederate statistics on all ten vessels destroyed by *Alabama* to $232,000. Since *Alabama* cost initially $228,000, in a very real sense *Elisha Dunbar* might be considered as being the last installment due on the Confederate commerce raider.

All the owners of *Elisha Dunbar,* except one, lived in New Bedford, and that one lived also in Massachusetts. Before the United States State Department concerning the *Alabama* Claims, the owners set a value of $12,000 on *Elisha Dunbar.* In addition, for the outfits and appurtenances, claims were set at $24,000, and damages accrued by breaking up the voyage at $88,200. At the time of her destruction, *Elisha Dunbar* had on board 65 barrels of sperm oil valued at $4,009. When fired, the ship and her oil made a spectacular blaze. The total claims filed for the loss of this ship amounted to $150,894.65, including losses of personal effects and supplies for a three-year cruise.

19th & 20th. Under double reefed topsails and trysails.
Sunday, 21st. Officers and men to muster. On the first Sunday in each month the Articles of War were read, and the ship and men inspected every Sunday.

[27]

A Sunday muster is here described:

With clean, white decks, with the brass and iron work glittering like so many mirrors in the sun, and with the sails neatly trimmed, and the Confederate States flag at our peak, we spread our awnings and read the Articles of War to the crew. A great change had taken place in the appearance of the men. . . . Their particolored garments had been cast aside, and they were all neatly arrayed in duck frocks and trousers, well-polished shoes, and straw hats. There was a visible improvement in their health, too. They had been long enough out of Liverpool to recover from the effects of their debauches, and regain their accustomed stamina . . . it was curious to observe the attention with which they listened to the reading [of the Articles of War], occasionally eying each other, as they were struck by particular portions of them. These Articles, which were copied from similar Articles, for the "better government of the Navy of the United States," were quite severe in their denunciations of crime. The penalty of death frequently occurred in them, and they placed the power of executing this penalty in the hands of the captain and a court-martial.

26th. Up to today cruising with fine weather. In the evening it became squally.

Fullam made no entry on 27 September, but this was the 53rd birthday of Raphael Semmes, an anniversary which is reflected in the papers of that Confederate captain.

28th. Sail reported, gave chase, proved to be a foreign brigantine. Not wishing our real character to be known, we kept on our course without speaking her. Fine with light winds.

30th. Gave chase to a vessel on lee bow, proved to be a French barque. Fresh breeze and heavy sea.

October 1st. Strong breeze, and occasionally rain. The crews of the Virginia and Elisha Dunbar still on board. A change of weather keenly felt, it being very cold.

In charge of these prisoners was Fullam himself and also Marine Lieutenant Beckett K. Howell. Howell was a brother of Mrs. Jefferson Davis. Arthur Sinclair said that the prisoners of war up to this time gave very little trouble to their captors. Thus far, all of *Alabama's* operations had been so near the Azores that it was possible to run in close to the shore and land the prisoners in their own boats. Later the problem for *Alabama* would become more difficult. The whaling captains in turn were very glad to get back their whaleboats, usually laden with provisions and gear. Captain David R. Gifford of *Elisha Dunbar* and Captain Shadrach R. Tilton of *Virginia* nevertheless complained bitterly about the treatment of prisoners of war aboard the raider. Inasmuch as Semmes said that their complaints were substantially correct, it is of interest to notice the statement of Captain Tilton.

I went on the quarter-deck, with my son, when they ordered me into the lee waist, with my crew, and all of us were put in irons, with the exception of the two boys, and the cook and steward. I asked if I was to be put in irons? The reply of Captain Semmes was, that his purser had been put in irons, and had his head shaved by us, and that he meant to retaliate. We were put in the lee waist, with an old sail over us, and a few planks to lie upon. The steamer was cruising to the west, and the next day, they took the *Elisha Dunbar,* her crew receiving the same treatment as ourselves. The steamer's guns being kept run out, the side ports could not be shut, and when the sea was a little rough, or the vessel rolled, the water was continually coming in on both sides, and washing across the deck where we were, so that our feet and clothing were wet all the time, either from the water below, or the rain above. We were obliged to sleep in the place where we were, and often waked up in the night nearly under water. Our fare consisted of beef and pork, rice, beans, tea, and coffee, and bread. Only one of my irons was allowed to be taken off at a time, and we had to wash in salt water. We kept on deck all the time, night and day, and a guard was placed over us.

3rd. Early in the morning the joyful cry of "Sail ho" was heard from the masthead; presently three sails were reported as being in sight. At 9.30 came up with one; hoisted the St. Georges ensign; boarded, hauled down, and hoisted the Stars & Bars, and took possession of the ship "Emily Farnum" of Portsmouth (N.H.). Made sail after another, prize following astern. On boarding she was found to be the ship "Brilliant" of and from New York, 12 days out, bound to Liverpool with a valuable cargo of grain and flour. The cargo of the Emily Farnum proving to be neutral, and the prisoners becoming irksome, it was deemed a favourable opportunity to get rid of them. All the prisoners were then placed on board her [Emily Farnum] and the ship allowed to proceed on her voyage, her Capt. promising to land them in Liverpool. It seemed a fearful thing to burn such a cargo as the Brilliant had, when I thought how the operatives in the cotton districts would have danced with joy had they shared it amongst them. I never saw a vessel burn with such brilliancy, the flames completely enveloping the masts, hull and rigging in a few minutes, making a sight as grand as it was appalling.

Emily Farnum and *Brilliant* were captured in rapid succession, but had quite different fates. *Emily Farnum* was a 1,119-ton, ship-rigged vessel, built in Portsmouth, New Hampshire in 1854. At the time of her capture she was on a voyage from New York to Liverpool under command of Captain N. P. Simes. *Alabama's* boarding officer was Lt. Richard F. Armstrong. The most important point about *Emily Farnum* in this situation was the fact that she had certificates proving her cargo of flour and grain to be neutral, and was the first American ship captured by *Alabama* with documents convincing Semmes that she carried neutral cargo. Therefore, this ship was spared and released as a cartel to carry away all of the prisoners whom Fullam and Howell had been guarding aboard *Alabama*, 68 in number. Unlike later ships released for cartel reasons, this one was not put under ransom bond.

In the first published account by a captured Yankee, Captain George Hagar of *Brilliant* described the procedure in prize-taking by *Alabama*. Captain Hagar, commander of the 839-ton, two-year-old *Brilliant*, reported that he was bound from New York to London in company with *Emily Farnum* when on 3 October 1862 a steamer proceeding under sail came over the horizon. The stranger on nearing *Brilliant* ran up at her peak the Cross of St. George. A few minutes later the steamer fired a gun across the bow of *Brilliant*, ran down the Cross of St. George and ran up the Confederate flag. Upon seeing the Confederate flag, Hagar hove his ship to and raised the Stars and Stripes. *Alabama*, for it was she, then sent one boat alongside with two officers and a boat's crew, all well armed. In charge was Master's Mate James Evans. When the Confederates boarded *Brilliant*, they instructed Hagar to report to Captain Semmes and to take all of his ship's papers. After a short wait aboard *Alabama*, Hagar was asked into the cabin to have his papers examined. Hagar claimed that his cargo of flour and grain was British owned, but had no document to prove this, consequently *Brilliant* and her cargo were condemned under Semmes' admiralty proceedings.

Hagar was sent back aboard *Brilliant* where the Yankee captain, his crew, and boats were then pressed into service in removing selected stores and cargo needed aboard the raider. Each of the officers and men of *Brilliant* was allowed a small bag of clothing. Hagar had to surrender some of his private possessions, including some of his clothing, along with charts, barometer, sextant, and his valuable chronometer. Hours passed while properties from *Brilliant* were removed to *Alabama*. At sunset *Brilliant* was set afire, and was blazing fore and aft by 7:00 p.m., continuing to burn all night long. A passing ship was attracted by the fire at sea and came up for rescue work, only to find herself stopped and boarded by the Confederates. The vessel which had been attracted to *Brilliant* while she burned in the night was overhauled by *Alabama* and boarded in the usual manner; this time the boarding party was under command of Lt. John Low. She proved to be a Russian bark with a cargo of grain from New York to Europe. The Russian captain said that he had come up to the burning ship with the thought of possible rescue operations. Another vessel that was also in sight at the time was identified by the Russian captain as one of his fellow countrymen, and therefore was not pursued by *Alabama*. Three of *Brilliant's* crew, all Englishmen, enlisted in the Confederate States Navy to serve aboard *Alabama*. All the others were loaded into *Emily Farnum* headed for England and for eventual return to the United States.

At the time of her capture, *Brilliant* was owned jointly by the New York firm of J. Atkins and Company and by Captain George Hagar, who owned one-third. The value of the ship, stated in the *Alabama* Claims, was $75,000, with an additional $16,531.03 for loss of freight, making the vessel and cargo valued at $91,531.03. The total claim filed by the owners amounted to $123,237.83. For Confederate prize purposes, Lt. Kell valued *Brilliant* at $164,000 for ship and cargo.

Brilliant was the first New York-owned vessel destroyed by *Alabama* and also the first of *Alabama's* prizes to provoke a great public outcry at the loss. No other captain or owners to that date had proved so articulate and knowledgeable as Hagar. On 21 October 1862, a special meeting of the Chamber of Commerce of the State of New York was held, ''To consider what action, if any, should be taken in consequence of the burning at sea, by the steamer Alabama, of the ship Brilliant and other vessels. . . .'' *Proceedings of the Chamber of Commerce . . . on the Burning of the Ship Brilliant by the Rebel Pirate Alabama. . . .* Concerning the ships other than *Brilliant,* little more than their names appeared, and that account was not without error. Most of *Alabama's* officers were correctly listed, except that Irvine S. Bulloch's name was misspelled and Fullam was represented as a corporal in the Confederate States Marine Corps. No doubt the reason for this error was the fact that Fullam shared with the Marine Corps' Lt. Beckett K. Howell responsibility for guarding the prisoners. Also published in the protest *Proceedings* was Captain Hagar's description of the CSS *Alabama*. The description was widely disseminated with the hope that this would help bring about the destruction of the Confederate raider. The protest *Proceedings* adopted stinging resolutions of rebuke for the Confederate ''pirate,'' for Semmes personally, and most particularly for Great Britain in allowing *Alabama* to be built. The treatment of prisoners by Semmes was scored in the following language:

> The conduct of the captain of the pirate to the crew of the captured vessels was most inhuman. The unfortunate men were clustered together on the deck, manacled, without room to lie down at night, or with only room for part of them, while the rest were compelled to stand; and in heavy weather they were continually washed by the sea—exposure and trials which only the stoutest and strongest men could endure. That is the way this pirate SEMMES treats the sailors of our captured ships.

It was not long after the resolutions were adopted that Secretary of State William H. Seward wrote to the American minister in London, Charles Francis Adams, 27 October 1862, and sent him a copy of the resolutions of the New York State Chamber of Commerce concerning *Brilliant*. Seward asked Adams to use his own judgment in the matter of presenting the protest to Earl Russell of the British Foreign Office. *Brilliant* was insured by the Atlantic Mutual Insurance Company of New York, and this company was soon joining the Chamber of Commerce of New York in protesting the burning of *Brilliant*. The protests of Seward and Adams regarding *Brilliant* were by no means the first received by the British Foreign Office against *Alabama*, but

Brilliant was evidently the first prize of *Alabama* to be protested in detail to the British Foreign Office in that long train of prizes that led eventually to the Geneva Arbitration of the *Alabama* Claims.

This evening, quite unexpectedly, we were called to general quarters, going through all the evolutions in quite a masterly manner. Sounded fire-alarm, manned pumps as for a leak, called away boarders, and went through everything expected to be done in action. After this, every Friday evening (when practicable) was set apart for general quarters. From the papers taken from the Brilliant, we read of the success of our brave troops in Virginia, and also of the successful escape of the C. S. Str. "Florida" into a Confederate port.

Frank L. Owsley, Jr., *The C.S.S. Florida: Her Building and Operations.* This monograph is an outstanding contribution of new information and interpretation.

5th. [October 1862] Boarded a French barque.

This was the French bark *Christophe* from New York bound for Cherbourg loaded with tallow.

In the evening chased a brigantine, who proved to be a Swede. Fresh breeze from the westward.
7th. Light winds. 4.30 a.m. Sail reported on starboard bow; chased, and at 6 fired a gun to heave her to, and hoisted the Confederate ensign. On boarding I found her to [be] the barque "Wave Crest," of and from New York to Cardiff, 8 days out. Her Capt., asserting that his cargo was English but not having any papers to prove it, of course he was made a prize. Cargo consisted of grain and flour. 2.30 p.m. Called all hands to quarters, port battery firing two rounds of shell at prize. Boarding to burn her, we found the two shells had struck, the rest passing over in good line firing.

As boarding officer, Fullam found that *Wave Crest, Alabama's* second prize from the port of New York, was of 409 tons burden with one deck, and dimensions of 128 x 31. This bark had been built in 1857 and, at the time of her capture, was commanded by John E. Harmon. Harmon was one-eighth owner and none of the other owners had quite as large a share of the vessel. Lt. Kell valued *Wave Crest* at $44,000. The total claims filed for this ship in the Civil War Claims was $59,264.10, of which the ship alone accounted for $26,000. Kell, who was usually accurate, here incorrectly named the vessel *Ocean Wave*, but there was no vessel of that name ever taken by *Ala-*

[32]

bama. *Wave Crest* was captured 7 October 1862. The Confederates moved considerable stores from the bark and then made further use of her as a target for the gunners. Finally, *Wave Crest* was fired, and was still burning when the next prize loomed over the horizon.

6.30 p.m. Sail reported on weather bow. 9.30 Brought her to with blank cartridge. Boarded and made a prize of the brigantine "Dunkirk" of and from New York to Lisbon, flour laden, 8 days out. By midnight had crew on board of us, and the vessel burnt.

Dunkirk was boarded by Fullam and by Midshipman William H. Sinclair. This vessel was a 293-ton brigantine, 113 x 27, under command of Samuel B. Johnson. Charles Peters and Edward J. Peters of New York owned 15/16ths of the vessel and Arthur F. Drinkwater of Maine owned the remaining 16th. Lt. Kell valued *Dunkirk* for the Confederates at $25,000. The owners made claims for this ship and cargo at $39,882.24. *Dunkirk* had sailed from New York 29 September 1862, bound for Lisbon, with flour and a general cargo which included tracts in the Portuguese language for distribution by the New York Bible Society and the American Tract Society of New York. On 7 October 1862, *Dunkirk* was captured in position 40.23 north and 54.30 west. Ship and cargo were burned at 11 a.m.

Examining the prisoners we found one of them to be a deserter from the C. S. Steamer "Sumter," he being one of seven deserting at Cadiz. Immediately upon arrival on board he was placed in double irons.

9th. Light westerly breeze. 10 a.m. Court Martial assembled in the ward room to try Geo. Forrest, A.B. [able-bodied seaman] for desertion from the Sumter. The court consisted of the following officers, viz; President, the First Lieutenant, and the Senior Second Lieutenant, Surgeon, Master, Chief Engineer and Lieutenant of Marines; Judge Advocate, the Captain's Clerk. 4.30 Captured the ship "Tonawanda" of and from Philadelphia to Liverpool, laden with grain, having also on board about 75 passengers. Took from her David White, a slave to one of the passengers. 8.15 p.m. Boarded the English brig "Ann Williams" from Cuba to Bristol.

When Fullam boarded the brig *Ann Williams* he was able to verify her British nationality and that she was bound from Manzanillo, Cuba for Bristol, carrying a cargo of cedar. For David White see page 35.

10th. Read sentence of court martial to prisoner, and discharged him. The sentence was "that all pay, prize money, &c. due him be forfeited, that he fulfill his term of service and forfeiting all pay,

[33]

excepting such as is sufficient to provide necessary clothing and liberty money.''

Semmes carefully refrained in his writings from mentioning the name of the deserter from *Sumter,* but otherwise discussed the recapture of this "worthless sailor." The deserter was George Forrest who jumped ship in Cadiz some months earlier from the CSS *Sumter* along with several other men apparently tired of their commerce-raiding adventures. Forrest was put in irons and tried by a court martial consisting of officers under whom he had served in *Sumter.* The court trying Forrest was composed of John McIntosh Kell, president of the court, Richard F. Armstrong, second lieutenant, Francis L. Galt, surgeon and acting paymaster, Beckett K. Howell, the ship's only lieutenant of marines, and William Breedlove Smith, the captain's secretary. In the midst of the court martial proceedings, *Alabama's* lookout reported a large sail on the weather bow. The time was 12:50 p.m. The court martial adjourned promptly, while *Alabama* chased a new target.

At 4 p.m. the court martial reassembled for another half hour of proceedings before a verdict was reached. Forrest was convicted of desertion from the CSS *Sumter,* a crime for which the maximum penalty at that time was death. Forrest was sentenced to serve for the remainder of *Alabama's* cruise without prize money and even without pay. This proved a singularly unwise decision, and Forrest awaited an opportunity to get even with the officers who had tried and sentenced him. Events proved that he was able to make a great deal of trouble, as Fullam noted later in his Journal of the CSS *Alabama.*

10.30 Made a sail on lee bow; after an hours chase fired a gun and brought her to. She proved to be a Mecklenburg ship, from New York to Dublin.

Low gave her name as *Johanna Hepler.* Half an hour after boarding and identifying this vessel, *Alabama's* position was 41.07 north and 55.29 west.

11th. Light easterly wind until evening. 5.45 a.m. Made a large sail on starboard bow; being far to windward and the wind light, did not chase. 3.30 p.m. Sail reported on weather bow. 5.30 Overhauled and hove her to. Upon boarding she proved to be the ship "Manchester" of and from New York bound to Liverpool, with wheat, cotton, &c. Transferred all prisoners to prize ship "Tonawanda,"

When the cry "Sail ho!" had come from the lookout on 11 October, it heralded the speedy appearance of a large ship over the horizon. *Alabama* gave chase and just before sunset overtook the stranger. John Low boarded the vessel and learned that she was the packet ship *Tonawanda,* under command of Captain Theodore Julius. It was not unusual for such a ship to be carrying grain from the United States to Europe in October, but it was unusual for her to have so many passengers. Thirty of the 75 passengers were women or children. *Tonawanda* was an exceptionally large (1,300 tons), three-deck, 12-year-old packet, with a draft of 21 feet, owned by Thomas P. and Francis R. Cope of Philadelphia. The Copes owned the cargo as well as the ship. Since *Alabama* had no facilities for caring for so many passengers, *Tonawanda* was released on ransom bond. Before making a final decision to release the vessel, however, Semmes made John Low prize master of *Tonawanda* and kept her cruising in company with *Alabama* for a couple of days. The Confederates hoped to fall in with some less valuable prize which could be released on ransom bond and used to take off *Tonawanda's* passengers. Although other prizes were soon discovered, none seemed suitable for so many passengers, and *Tonawanda* was finally released on ransom bond of $80,000, even though there was no claim of neutral cargo.

Two of *Tonawanda's* passengers, however, were taken from her. One of them was William Halford, an ordinary seaman who volunteered for duty in the Confederate States Navy. The other was David White, a 17-year-old slave who was traveling in company with his master *en route* to Europe. David White became a wardroom mess steward on the Confederate cruiser, and particularly the servant of Dr. Francis L. Galt, a Virginian, who was *Alabama's* surgeon and acting paymaster. Semmes devoted more than a page of his book to the story of the slave who was, ironically, emancipated by the Confederate sea raider on the ground that he was property of an enemy. David White served in *Alabama* for the remainder of the cruise. Like others in the ship's company, he repeatedly went ashore and it is interesting that he never sought to leave the Confederate States Navy.

and burnt the "Manchester."

Manchester, in the vital grain trade, was a New York ship of 1,062 tons, under command of John Landerskin. *Manchester* was owned largely by one man, Benjamin J. H. Trask, Jr. Other owners were Joseph Stewart and G. D. S. Trask. This large ship was only two years old. Ship and cargo were very valuable. Six insurance companies shared in her loss. In the *Alabama* Claims the value was set at $143,305.92. John Low was appointed by Captain Semmes to value the ship and cargo and he came up with a higher figure, $164,000 for ship and cargo. Low boarded *Manchester,* and the Confederate boats carried Captain Landerskin and his crew and baggage to the cartel ship *Tonawanda.* Water was transferred from *Manchester* to *Tonawanda* because of the large number of prisoners aboard the latter. At 9:30 p.m. *Manchester* was fired, and *Alabama* was once more underway with *Tonawanda* still being held as a prize.

Manchester also brought to the Confederates a new supply of the New York *Herald* with information as to the location of Union gunboats in pursuit of *Alabama.* Semmes said, "Perhaps this was the only war in which the newspapers ever explained, beforehand, all the movements of armies, and fleets, to the enemy."

The Captain of the "Tonawanda" being kept on board our ship as security. Strong variable winds up to the 13th. 10.50 a.m. Made a sail on weather bow. Made sail in chase. Suspecting her to be a disguised vessel of war: all hands were called to quarters, and the guns loaded with shell. Raining heavily at 5.50 p.m. Gave up the chase and secured the battery, the chase having shown Spanish colours. 6 p.m. Released the "Tonawanda," her master ransoming her at $80,000.

Tonawanda's ransom bond is an example of documents of this type.

Ransom bond of the ship Tonawanda, of Philadelphia, captured by the C.S.S. Alabama, Commander Semmes, C.S. Navy, commanding, October 9, 1862.

Know all men by these presents, that whereas the American ship *Tonawanda,* of Philadelphia, of which Thomas P. Cope and Francis R. Cope are the owners, together with her cargo, consisting of 47,500 bushels of wheat, etc., of which the said Thomas P. Cope and Francis R. Cope are the shippers and owners, under my command, was this day captured on the high seas by the C.S.S. *Alabama,* R. Semmes, commander; and whereas I, as the master of the said ship, am anxious to ransom the said ship and cargo for the benefit of the owners: Now, therefore, in consideration of the release of said ship and cargo by the said R. Semmes, the release whereof is hereby acknowledged, I am held and firmly bound, and I do hereby bind the said Thomas P. Cope and Francis R. Cope, owners of the aforesaid ship and cargo, their and my heirs, executors, and assigns, well and truly to pay unto the President of the Confederate States of America for the time being, at the conclusion of the present war between the said Confederate States and the United States, the sum of $80,000, current money of the said Confederate States, and the said ship *Tonawanda,* her tackle and apparel, are hereby mortgaged for the payment of this bond.

Done under my hand and seal this, the 9th day of October, in the year of our Lord 1862.

THEODORE JULIUS. [SEAL]

Witness:

W. B. SMITH,
    Commander's Clerk.

Her passengers testifying in rather a ludicrous manner (to me), their joy at their deliverance.

14th. Strong N.W. winds. A.M. Chased and overhauled the Danish ship "Judith."

Judith, despite her neutral protection, ignored two guns before heaving to.

[36]

Chased another, proved to be French. Another vessel in sight to windward. Coming up with her, she proved to be English. Her Capt. saluting our flag; which compliment we returned.

15th. Strong westerly winds accompanied with heavy rain. 6.45 a.m. Sail discovered on weather bow. Coming up with her, we fired a blank cartridge, hauling down the St. Georges ensign and hoisting the Confederate flag. No notice being taken of it; both bow guns were loaded with shot. Observing it, the chase hove to. On our boat returning with the Capt., it was found to be the barque "Lamplighter" of Boston, New York to Gibraltar, laden with tobacco. Brought crew on board our vessel, and burnt prize.

Lamplighter, an eight-year-old, 365-ton bark, was built in Boston but, as Fullam said, was operating out of New York. She had departed New York 9 October bound for Gibraltar. Her master was O. V. Harding and her owners (25 in all) were even more numerous than was usual in those days. Ship and cargo were valued at $27,500 by the owners. The Confederate evaluation by Low was a whopping $117,600. Such a wide descrepancy in evaluations by owners and Confederates was unusual. Neither side, however, wished to make the value too low.

The capture of *Lamplighter* was a dramatic sight. The wind was blowing half a gale, and increasing. It is not at all unlikely that *Lamplighter* could have escaped had Captain Harding chosen to do so, for Harding was very skillful in maneuvering his bark and his crew was as well drilled as the ship's company of a man-of-war, according to Sinclair. Harding was not one of those skippers who made a run for it, however. He seemed to believe that his ship was doomed, so he just downed helm, clewed up sails, and hove aback, awaiting *Alabama's* boarding party. The sea was so rough that the boarding party had difficulty in climbing on *Lamplighter.* Even so, *Alabama's* sailors managed to transfer some of the much-loved tobacco from the cargo of the prize. *Lamplighter* was captured early in the morning, and within a few hours the storm had increased to such a point that it would have been impossible to board her. Indeed, the storm raged for several days thereafter.

Midnight, blowing fresh.

16th. Commenced with a strong gale from the S. S. E. Towards daybreak it freshened considerably, a heavy sea running at the same time. 9.30 Blowing a perfect hurricane, the sea rising to a fearful height, and the ship labouring heavily. Shortly after, a squall of extraordinary violence struck us, we being under close reefed maintopsail, reefed maintrysail and foretopmast staysail. The heavy strain on the main braces, caused the weather bumkin to snap in two, the yard flew forward bending upwards until it was almost double, when with a sudden crash it broke in two, splitting the topsail with a noise equal to the loudest thunder. A sea striking immediately after smashed in the whale boat; it was soon cut away. No sooner had the maintopsail gone, then the foretopmast staysail was cut away by the Capt. of the forecastle, thereby preventing the ship falling off into the trough of the sea. A storm trysail was soon bent and the maintrysail lowered, splitting the sail during the operation. Various minor casualties occurred, but nothing of a very serious nature. Everybody was thoroughly wet by the salt spray. The vessels behaviour during the height of the storm was beautiful. A finer seaboat never floated. All the idlers, boys, &c. were placed under the weather bulwarks on the quarterdeck with a rope stretched before them to prevent them falling to leeward. Wind N. W. immediately after. Moderated towards evening, so that we were able to send down the wreck of the mainyard and bend new sails. The evening turned out with a heavy sea from the southward; the wind abating, causing the ship to roll heavily.

This cyclone in the North Atlantic struck as *Alabama* approached New York. It was the first really severe wind that Fullam's ship had encountered. In commenting upon this storm Semmes, in *Service Afloat,* launched a long discussion of hurricanes and other cyclones. The word bumkin means short boom.

17th. Opened with a moderate breeze and a heavy swell from the South. About noon the sea went down considerably. Sail was made and in about half an hour, a sail was reported on starboard bow. Went after her. Hoisted English colours, the chase hoisting English in return. The heavy sea and the amount of work requisite to be done prevented us following her up, so we hauled upon our course again. Hard squalls until Sunday.

19th. Commenced with fine weather. 4 p.m. Sent up mainyard and bent maintopsail.

In *Alabama's* crew list a number were designated simply as boys: H. Cosgrove, James Wilson, Robert Egan, Thomas L. Parker, and John Grady. All of these "powder monkeys" enlisted on 24 August 1862 and were among the first 80 recruits in *Alabama*. A boy's pay was $9.68 (£2) per month. These boys were often the center of entertainment and merriment aboard ship. There was, for example, the case of Egan and the cat. These young boys were products of the tough port life of Liverpool, and had smuggled themselves

[38]

aboard *Bahama* when that vessel was in Liverpool preparing to meet *290* in the Azores. While the Confederate cruiser was receiving her stores and supplies at Terceira, these boys appeared on deck and made themselves useful as powder monkeys and messenger-boys. They were signed up and put to work in the well-established pattern of the Union navy, the Royal Navy, and others of that day. One of the toughest of the boys was Robert Egan. He knew very well the attachment of sailors to their pets, no matter what kind or variety. Some of the sailors in *Alabama* had brought aboard a pet cat, and great affection had developed between the men and their cat. One day the cat was missing and a prodigious search was made for puss, but all in vain. Because of his reputation for mischief, Egan was suspected. He was hauled up to the mast and charged with knowing or abetting the disappearance of the cat. To further prod his memory, Egan was "spread eagled" in the mizzen rigging barefooted, a usual punishment for the powder monkeys. He seemed to hold out well under the punishment, and stoutly denied all knowledge of the cat's whereabouts. At this point, the lookout sighted a sail, and there was much scurrying about getting ready for the chase. The after pivot-gun was cleared away for use in making the suspected prize heave to. Just as the tampion was taken from the gun's muzzle, out jumped puss. The mystery was solved, and Egan confessed. Upon being questioned as to why he did it, his reply was, "Oh, to see what effect the firing would have on the cat!" To the joy of the animal lovers, Egan later deserted at the Cape of Good Hope.

20th. 4 a.m. Two lights, one ahead the other astern, were seen. Made all sail in chase of one. Coming within 2 miles of her, she hoisted English colours. Went about in chase of the other, who proved to be a brigantine under Dutch colours. Hauled up on our course again. Alternate sunshine and showers until noon when a heavy squall accompanied with rain struck us, the wind veering round to W. N. W. Double reefed topsails and trysails. Towards evening a sail hove in sight. She being so far to windward and darkness drawing on, we gave up the chase.

21st. Fine with a northerly wind. At daylight made a sail. Found her to be the barque "Heron" of Sunderland, from New York bound to Queenstown; we calling our ship H. M. Str. "Racehorse." Towards midnight the wind freshened considerably.

22nd. Blowing a fresh gale with a heavy sea. Hove to. 10 p.m. Cut away the dingey, it having been stove in by a sea striking her some time previously. Saw two vessels standing easterly.

23rd. 4 a.m. A light reported astern. Stood for her. Hoisted the English blue, to which chase answered by hoisting English also. Saw two vessels far to leeward, hauling up to the N.W. 3.40 p.m. "Sail ho" was heard again. Kept away for her. Called the 1st guns crew to quarters, fired a blank cartridge; hove her to, boarding and returning with her Captain and papers. She proved to be the ship "Lafayette" of New Haven, New York to Belfast, 3 days out with a large cargo of grain, &c. The Captain stated that his cargo was English, but not having papers to that effect, of course he was declared a prize. Transferred prisoners, chronometers, &c. not forgetting half a dozen porkers, &c. to our ship, and fired prize.

Alabama captured two prizes named *Lafayette*. This ship was the first of that name, and for clarity will be designated *Lafayette* #1. *Lafayette* #2 was a bark captured 15 April 1863, as later noted by Fullam. *Lafayette* #1 was a 945-ton ship, commanded by Alfred T. Small of Freeport, Maine. Small owned 1/16th of the ship and there were four other owners, all named Soule. *Lafayette* #1 had sailed from New Haven on 20 October 1862, bound for Belfast, Ireland, with a cargo of wheat, corn, and lard.

Captain Semmes, struck by the beauty of Lafayette #1, described her approach as follows:

> The ship which was now running down for us was, as I have said, a picture, with her masts yielding and swaying to a cloud of sail, her tapering poles shooting skyward, even above her royals, and her well-turned, *flaring* bows—the latter a distinctive feature of New York-built ships. She came on, rolling gracefully to the sea, and with the largest kind of a "bone in her mouth," . . . and was soon under our guns. A blank cartridge brought her to the wind. If the scene was beautiful before, it was still more so now. If she had been a ship of war, full of men, and with hands stationed at sheets, halliards, and braces, she could not have shortened sail much more rapidly, or have rounded more promptly and gracefully to the wind, with her main topsail aback. Her cloud of canvas seemed to shrivel and disappear, as though it had been a scroll rolled up by an invisible hand. It is true, nothing had been furled, and her light sails were all flying in the wind, confined to the yards only by their clew-lines, but the ship lay as snugly and conveniently for boarding, as I could desire. I frequently had occasion, during my cruises, to admire the seamanship of my enemies.

Lafayette #1 ushered in a new chapter in the struggle of the Union against the Confederate cruisers. Owners of neutral cargoes, now all too well aware of the depredations of *Alabama* hovering off Newfoundland Banks, henceforth would try to provide their cargoes with statements of neutral ownership. From *Lafayette* #1 onward, *Alabama* rarely seized an enemy ship that lacked legitimate or forged documents declaring the cargo to be neutral. All along, Semmes conducted a Confederate States Admiralty Court aboard *Alabama* to decide whether ship or cargo was neutral. It was easy to determine the nationality of a ship, but often difficult to say regarding cargo. When either ship or cargo was decided to be neutral, the ship would be released on ransom bond. Prior to the seizure of *Lafayette* #1 on 23 October 1862, only *Emily Farnum* had been released on ransom bond because of her neutral cargo and despite her enemy ownership. *(Tonawanda* had also been released on ransom bond but not because of the neutrality of ship or cargo but rather as a cartel ship for the convenience of the Confederate raiders in moving prisoners.) The second ship to be released on ransom bond because of a neutral cargo came within a week after *Lafayette* #1, and was duly noted by Fullam. See Fullam for *Baron de Castine.* In the case of *Lafayette* #1, there were sworn statements attested by consular seals declaring that the cargo was owned by British subjects and therefore could not be burned. Semmes convened the Confederate admiralty court, sat as admiralty judge, decided that *Lafayette* #1 statements were false, and that ship and cargo should be burned. *Lafayette* #1 was quickly fired, but the last had not been heard of the case. Protests were filed with the British government and aired in newspapers, saying that *Alabama* had committed acts of piracy against the British-owned cargo, and it was not long before additional ships resulted in additional charges.

The total claims filed in the *Alabama* Claims for *Lafayette* #1 and her cargo by the Union owners amounted to $113,290.42. This was not far from the evaluation officially set by Low for the Confederates of $100,337. *Lafayette* #1 was number 16 of the vessels destroyed by *Alabama.* After this ship was burned, Confederate statistics made the total $846,937.

The cold and weather generally being rather severe, the prisoners were put below in the forward fire room, it being vacated for that purpose, and the fires kindled in the after one instead. Hitherto they had lived on the main deck with a tent specially rigged for them.

24th. Fine with a strong northerly wind. Sail in sight. Coming up with her, she proved to be an English brigantine. From a stray newspaper, taken in the "Lafayette," we read that news had been received in New York of the capture of Yankee vessels by the "Alabama" in which it was stated that the treatment to which the prisoners were subjected was "worse than dogs." Such gross falsehoods annoyed us considerably, as all our prisoners had been treated with every kindness consistent with safety.

*25th. [October 1862]. Light winds. A sail in sight all day.
2 p.m. All hands to general quarters, going through all
naval evolutions.*

*Sunday, 26th. Fine, with a fresh breeze. Two vessels in sight.
Chased one for a short time, put about after the other. After
firing a blank cartridge, the first division was called to
quarters and two shots fired over her at a distance of 3 miles.
Hove to and made a prize of her, the schooner "Crenshaw" of
and from New York to Glasgow, 4 days out, grain laden. Burnt
prize and proceeded on our course.*

Crenshaw was a 279-ton schooner commanded by William Nelson and
owned by David B. Turner. This was a relatively unusual case in which
the vessel had only one owner. The prize crew from *Alabama* which boarded
and burned her was under command of Lt. Richard F. Armstrong who
valued the prize at $33,869, making the total value of ships burned $880,806.
Armstrong's evaluation compares with the claims filed for *Crenshaw* in
the *Alabama* Claims for $20,000. Total claims on this schooner amounted
to $27,474.49. *American Lloyds 1862*, p. 399.

*From this vessel we obtained papers in which we read the
infamous assertions made by the Captain of the "Brilliant"
[George Hagar] with respect to our treatment of prisoners. A
conviction was forced upon every mind that kindness extended
to them was completely thrown away.*

*27th. Weather assuming a threatening appearance. Reduced
sail accordingly. Sounded, but no bottom with 75 ftms.
[fathoms] Shipped 3 men, making a total of 11 men shipped
from prizes.*

The three men were: James Clements, Walter Vaness, and Martin Miditch.
Among the 11, in addition to the three foregoing men, were: John Allan,
William Clark, David Thurston, David Williams, Valentine Mesner, David
Leggett, Alfred Morris, and Abram Nordhock. Except for Miditch and Nord-
hock, all were ordinary seamen. Miditch was a drummer and Nordhock
was an able-bodied seaman.

*28th. Light westerly wind. Daylight, a vessel in sight.
Supposing her to be a foreign brigantine, did not chase her
long, another sail having been reported on lee bow. 11 a.m.
Fired a gun and hove her to. Boarded and took possession of
the barque "Laurietta" of Boston, New York bound to Gibraltar
and Messina.*

[42]

Lauretta (as correctly spelled) was a 284-ton bark (106 x 27 x 11), under command of Marshall M. Wells, and she raised a furor out of all proportion to her modest burden, dimensions, and value. Ship and cargo of grain were valued by *Alabama's* Lt. Joseph D. Wilson at $32,880, and by her owners in the *Alabama* Claims at $27,950. This bark was tried by Semmes' admiralty court in the usual manner, but with an unusual amount of attention to the case. *Lauretta* had a cargo of flour, nails, and pipe staves, shipped by two New York firms and consigned to "Gibraltar or Messina." Sworn and notarized affidavits attested neutral ownership of the cargo (belonging to subjects of England, Italy, and Portugal), but Semmes adjudged the claims fraudulent and burned her. When the New York *Commercial Advertiser* published a detailed and critical account of the *Lauretta* case, the narrative aroused Semmes' ire to the extent that when he wrote his book *Service Afloat* some six years later, he included the newspaper's criticism of him, as follows:

> But another case (that of the bark *Lauretta*) is about to be submitted for the consideration of the British authorities, as well as those of Italy and Portugal. The facts establish a clear case of piracy. The *Lauretta*, which had on board a cargo consisting principally of flour and staves, was burned by Semmes on the 28th of October. She was bound from this port for the island of Madeira and the port of Messina, in Italy. Nearly a thousand barrels of flour and also a large number of staves were shipped by Mr. H. J. Burden, a British subject residing in this city, to a relative in Funchal, Madeira. The bill of lading bore the British seal affixed by the Consul, to whom the shipper was personally known. The other part of the cargo was shipped by Chamberlain, Phelps & Co., to the order of parties in Messina, and this property was also covered by the Italian Consular certificates.
>
> The Portuguese Consul at this port also sent a package under seal, to the authorities at Madeira, besides giving a right to enter the port and sending an open bill of lading.
>
> Captain Wells' account of the manner in which Semmes disposed of these documents, and which he has verified under oath, is not only interesting, but gives an excellent idea of the piratical intentions of the commander of the *Alabama*.
>
> The papers of the bark were, at the command of Semmes, taken by Captain Wells on board the *Alabama*. There was no American cargo, and therefore no American papers, except those of the vessel. These, of course, were not inquired into. Semmes took first the packet which bore the Portuguese seal, and with an air which showed that he did not regard it as of the slightest consequence, ripped it open, and threw it upon the floor, with the remark that "he did not care a d—n for the Portuguese." The Italian bill of lading was treated in a similar manner, except that he considered it unworthy even of a remark.
>
> Taking up the British bill of lading and looking at the seal, Semmes called upon Captain Wells, with an oath, to explain. It was evidently the only one of the three he thought it worth his while to respect.

"Who is this Burden?" he inquired sneeringly. "Have you ever seen him?"

"I am not acquainted with him; but I have seen him once, when he came on board my vessel," replied Captain Welles.

"Is he an Englishman—does he look like an Englishman?"

"Yes," rejoined the captain.

"I'll tell you what," exclaimed the pirate, "this is a d—d pretty business—it's a d—d Yankee hash, and I'll settle it,"—whereupon he proceeded to rob the vessel of whatever he wanted, including Captain Wells' property to a considerable amount; put the crew in irons; removed them to the *Alabama;* and concluded by burning the vessel.

These facts will at once be brought before the British Consul. The preliminary steps have been taken. The facts will also be furnished the Portuguese Consul, who announces his intention of placing them before his Government; and besides whatever action the Italian Consul here may choose to take, the parties in Messina, to whom the property lost on the *Lauretta* was consigned, will of course do what they can to maintain their own rights. The case is likely to attract more attention than all the previous outrages of the *Alabama,* inasmuch as property rights of the subjects of other nations are involved, and the real character of Semmes and his crew becomes manifest.

Obtained news of a brilliant victory gained by our troops in Kentucky.

Major General Braxton Bragg's invasion of Kentucky against Union forces under Major General Don Carlos Buell produced some news stories to thrill a Confederate Englishman like Fullam, but the final outcome of Bragg's campaign was such as to disappoint all Confederates.

The excitement in the Northern States appeared to be intense, the papers acknowledging their inability to catch us. Much amused was I to read in a list of officers my name as corporal. I suppose it originated in the fact that in conjunction with Lieut. Howell and another officer, I kept watch and guard over prisoners.

George Hagar, master of the ship *Brilliant,* in protesting the burning of his vessel wrote to the New York *Journal of Commerce* a description of the "Confederate Steamer Propeller Alabama," including a list of the ship's officers. Seward to Adams, 27 October 1862, *FA 1862, 218,* forwarding data on *Brilliant.*

Shipped two men. Burnt prize.

29th. Got up steam and lowered propellor, with 8 lbs. of steam going 9 knots. 4 p.m. Sail in sight on starboard bow. 5 [p.m.] Came up with her, found her to be a barque under

Dutch colours. 5 vessels now in sight. Chased one. 6.30 p.m. Ordered him to heave to. Boarded and took possession of the brigantine "Baron de Castine," of and from Castine, bound to Cuba, with a cargo of lumber. Ransomed her on condition that he took all our prisoners and landed them. Sent them all on board and proceeded on our course. By this vessel Comr. Semmes sent his respects to the New York Chamber of Commerce, stating also that by the time this message reached them, he (Capt. Semmes) would be off that port.

Baron de Castine sailed from her home port on 20 October 1862 with a cargo of lumber, bound for Cardenas, Cuba. Within ten days, she was captured by *Alabama* and boarded by Lt. Low. The brigantine's captain, John Saunders, executed a ransom bond for the Jarvis family and other owners in the amount of $4,000 for the ship, and obligated the owners of the cargo (B. B. Farnsworth and Company of Bangor, Maine, and M. Cebellos of New York) for an additional $2,000. *Baron de Castine,* named for Castine, Maine, clearly was Union owned, with a Union-owned cargo, and had no claims to neutrality. As in the prior case of *Tonawanda,* however, the Confederates used *Baron de Castine* as a cartel ship to remove the danger to *Alabama* of 44 prisoners on board. Ransom bond of *Baron de Castine, ORN,* 1, I, 781. See also Moore, 4302–4303; *New York Marine Register 1857,* 125; *Harper's Weekly,* 15 November, 1862, 723. With the prisoners, *Baron de Castine* turned back in her tracks and headed for the nearest port, which was Boston, arriving there 2 November 1862. Turn-around time in Boston was about ten days, mostly taken up with making repairs, then the ship proceeded toward Cuba.

When captured by *Alabama, Baron de Castine* was operating under a charter which obligated the brigantine to transfer a shipload of lumber from Bangor to Cardenas and return to New York with West Indian cargo. The turn-around time in Cuba was planned at 30 "lay" days. Compensation sought under *Alabama* Claims for this charter was $2,250. Owners of ships sought compensation based on the value of the charter party, plus allowance for actual expenses resulting from *Alabama's* detention of the ships. The *Alabama* Claims court decided in favor of the complainants. When *Baron de Castine* arrived in Boston, she brought a summary of *Alabama's* cruise to that date, which was eagerly published in *Harper's Weekly,* 15 November 1862. The article noted that *Alabama* had already captured seven vessels in the past few weeks and had destroyed all of these except *Baron de Castine* and an earlier ransom-bond release of the ship *Tonawanda,* ransomed for $80,000. Altogether up to this time, *Alabama* had captured 21 vessels, released three, and destroyed 18. From newspapers noting the capture of *Baron de Castine* (in position 39.45 north and 69.0 west), Commodore Cadwalader Ringgold, commanding the USS *Sabine,* reported to Gideon

[45]

Welles that he was moving toward Semmes' cruising ground off the port of New York searching for *Alabama*. However, *Alabama* soon moved toward the southeast, as mentioned by Fullam, so Ringgold's hunt proved fruitless. Ringgold had sailed toward the Azores while *Alabama* had gone in a different direction.

The New York *Shipping and Commercial List* noted on 8 October 1862 "Vessels under foreign flags command higher rates, in consequence of the reported seizure and destruction of American vessels by the Rebel Steamer '290'." A week later the same publication noted, "Shipments making almost entire in foreign bottoms, American vessels being in disfavor." This publication gave freight rates for various commodities, especially wheat and flour, to London, to Liverpool, and to other foreign ports. This commercial journal showed that shipments of wheat and flour from New York to London and Liverpool continued to bring lower freight rates to American vessels while the higher-priced foreign transportation amassed the business; and these circumstances persisted into 1865. J. F. Manning, *Epitome of the Geneva Award Contest in the Congress of the United States,* 128–130. The effects of Confederate commerce raiders on the declining United States Merchant Marine has been mentioned in many books, particularly after Winthrop L. Marvin in 1902 published *The American Merchant Marine,* and even more particularly since George W. Dalzell in 1940 published *The Flight from the Flag the Continuing Effect of the Civil War Upon the American Carrying Trade.* It remains to be noted that *Alabama's* assault on the grain fleets operating out of New York in October 1862 was the turning point in the decline of the United States Merchant Marine. Writing in 1972, it might not be inappropriate to say, instead of decline, the virtual demise of the merchant marine. Fullam noted many details connected with this change.

30th. Strong N. wind. 8 a.m. Three vessels in sight. Passed a barque, evidently a foreigner, steering N. Wly. We were considerably startled and annoyed to find that only 4 days coal was on board. Such a discovery, however opportune as it was, annoyed us not a little. To astonish the enemy in New York harbour, to destroy their vessels in their own waters, had been the darling wish of all on board. It now being impracticable to continue our course, we reluctantly squared away and stood towards the S. E. 2 p.m. Hoisted up the screw and banked the fires. 3. Made sail in chase of a vessel. Found her to be the Dutchman we had spoken twice previously.

November 1st. Fine with light winds. Chased two vessels, one proved to be English, the other French. A third in sight.

Sunday, 2nd. Fine, light winds. 7 a.m. A sail descried steering to the N. E. This being the first Sunday in the month, the Articles of War were read as usual. 12.30 Hove the vessel to with blank cartridge. Took possession of ship "Levi Starbuck," whaler, of and from New Bedford, 5 days out. Obtained news of our successes in Kentucky. Employed until sunset transferring stores, &c. from prize. Then burnt her.

Levi Starbuck represented a return to the capture of whaling prizes. This vessel was a 376-ton whaler of New Bedford, under command of Thomas Mellen and owned by some six citizens of New Bedford. *Levi Starbuck* departed New Bedford bound for the Pacific Ocean, and she was captured and burned by *Alabama* in position 35.40 north and 66.00 west, in the North Atlantic Ocean. The vessel herself was valued by her owners at $15,000, outfits and appurtenances at $25,000, and the total claims filed were $236,672.50. Included in the claims were $75,000 for loss of whalebone. Three insurance companies shared in the losses and in the claims. *Levi Starbuck* was number 19 among the vessels destroyed by *Alabama*. The value placed upon her by Lt. Kell was $25,000. News of the loss of *Levi Starbuck* was published in *Harper's Weekly*, 27 December 1862, together with word that the USS *San Jacinto* had set off in search of *Alabama*.

For 70 days *Alabama* had been at sea and the diet of the Confederates had been chiefly salt pork, dried beef, navy beans, and similar standard items, but *Levi Starbuck*, only a few days out from New Bedford, yielded cabbages, turnips, and other antiscorbutic foods. While *Alabama* was pursuing *Levi Starbuck* on that Sunday, 2 November, the inspection and the reading of the Articles of War continued.

4 a.m. 6th. Two vessels hove in sight. Boarding one, I found her to be a French barque bound to Havre.

8th. 2 a.m. Made sail in chase of a schooner standing to the southward. Another vessel standing N. E. in sight shortly after. Went in chase of her. She showing Yankee colours, we answered by showing the same. In reply to his signal, we passed as the U. S. "Ticonderoga." His signal: "What is your longitude," we declined answering until we could verbally do it. Hove to until she neared us then fired a gun, and hoisting the Confederate ensign, sent a boat on board and took possession. Found her to be the "Thomas B. Wales" of Boston, from Calcutta with a general cargo; having as passengers the late U. S. Consul at Mauritius, with his wife and two children, the Captain having his wife with him also.

They were accommodated in the ward room, the officers vacating their room for that purpose.

The ex-consul was George H. Fairchild. In later years, John A. Bolles, solicitor of the United States Navy Department after the Civil War, conducted an official inquiry into the treatment of prisoners aboard the CSS *Alabama*. It is of interest to note that one of Fullam's major duties was looking after prisoners, and it was therefore revealing of Fullam's character when John Bolles found that charges of inhuman treatment were groundless. Some of the prisoners, including Fairchild, testified that they had been well treated.

Fairchild's wife, an Englishwoman, was bringing with her in *Thomas B. Wales* a number of handsome ebony chairs carved in the style of India. Mrs. Fairchild was greatly disappointed when told that she could not take those chairs with her into the small space of *Alabama's* wardroom. Sinclair said that one of the most unpleasant duties of boarding parties was the transfer of women from one ship to another at sea. He marveled that in all such transfers at sea of women into *Alabama* he never saw any of them betray fear, in spite of the fact that they were sometimes transported in boatswain's chairs, or with "whip-tackle and buckets" and often thoroughly drenched with sea water.

Many articles for ships use [were] taken from her, including a mainyard. Sunset, burnt her.

Some light is here cast on Fullam's accuracy concerning ships. *Thomas B. Wales* is correctly rendered by Fullam as the name of this ship, although most of the other sources less accurately abbreviated the name to *T. B. Wales*. *Thomas B. Wales* was a large, 599-ton Boston ship, commanded by Edgar Lincoln and owned by Thomas B. Wales and Company of Boston. She sailed from Calcutta for Boston on 19 June 1862 with a general cargo consisting principally of linseed, jute, and 1,700 bags of saltpeter. The saltpeter was obviously intended for gunpowder for the Union war effort. The jute was probably intended to replace cotton which was becoming scarcer in New England textile mills. The seizure of *Thomas B. Wales* with the 1,700 bags of saltpeter was one of the few captures by Raphael Semmes that spurred the Mobile *Advertiser and Register* to comment upon the sensational sea war of that home-town figure. The cargo was consigned to the house of Baring in Boston, connected with the famous firm in England. Before the *Alabama* Claims, there were seven insurance companies which shared in losses for this valuable cargo. The total amount claimed for the loss of *Thomas B. Wales* was $221,892.24, although the ship herself represented only a small part of this. Lt. Kell placed the Confederate evaluation upon this ship at $245,625. As a result of this figure, the value of ships destroyed by the CSS *Alabama* for the first time passed the million dollar mark. Captain Edgar Lincoln made quite an impression upon Semmes, who commented upon Lincoln's excellent English, pronunciation, and grammar.

[48]

Alabama had lost a main yard during the cyclone which Fullam had earlier described. The main yard of *Thomas B. Wales* was measured and found to be suitable for replacement on *Alabama*. Benjamin Mecaskey, the boatswain, and William Robinson, the carpenter, and their men worked diligently to fit the new main yard. To remove the old and install the new was a complex and difficult operation and became the principal topic of conversation on watch and at mess tables.

Shipped 11 hands.

At this time *Alabama* had 26 officers and 110 men. This was 10 short of the full personnel allowance. Thus the 11 members of the crew of *Thomas B. Wales* who, as Fullam noted, were persuaded to sign up in the Confederate States Navy, were welcome additions. The 11 men were: Henry Godson, James Williams, William Burns, Michael Shields, Charles Stetson, Joseph Martin, Samuel Brewer, James Raleigh, Joseph Neal, Louis Dupois, and Ivan Ochoa. All were ordinary seamen. Of the 11, three later deserted, but six served in *Alabama* until the end of the cruise, and one was transferred to the CSS *Tuscaloosa*. *Thomas B. Wales* established a record in the number of volunteers to the Confederate States Navy. On 10 November 1862 *Alabama's* position was 29.14 north and 57.57 west, as she approached the calm belt of the Tropic of Cancer.

11th. Light winds and showery. 6 a.m. Sail hove in sight. Boarding, found her to be the English brigantine [blank space], bound to Demerara.

This vessel is mentioned as being from New York but not named by Semmes either. Fullam boarded her but found neither news nor newspapers, and in his Journal omitted the ship's name.

He had heard of the "Alabama" destroying 6 vessels. Passed as the U. S. Str. "Wyoming." 4 p.m. Gave chase to a sail. Fired a blank cartridge, and sent a boat off to her. She not heaving to, a shot was fired at her, when to our astonishment 4 lights were seen. All hands were immediately called to quarters and every preparation made for battle. On our boat returning, we learnt that the vessel boarded was the English barque "Princess Royal" from Demerara, the crew having been afflicted with yellow fever, that she had shown two lights as a signal of being hove to, the third light being the brigantine previously boarded, and the fourth our boat's. Secured the battery.

13th. [November 1862]. After general quarters had been gone through with a celerity highly gratifying, the men were highly eulogized by the Cmmr. and officers.

[49]

15th. Moderate easterly wind. At daylight two vessels in sight, a three masted schooner being hull down to windward. Did not chase. The other proved to be a Spaniard from Cadiz to Habana, we passing as the U. S. Str. "Octorora."

The USS *Octorora* bore little resemblance to the CSS *Alabama*. *Octorora* was a sidewheel, double-ended steamer.

17th. 2.20 p.m. Island of Dominica in sight.

Dominica is in the Lesser Antilles, north of Martinique and separated from it by Dominica Channel. As *Alabama* cruised along the clean coast and heavily-wooded mountainous areas, Semmes was reminded of that night in October 1861 when he ran the CSS *Sumter* parallel to the shore of Dominica after *Sumter's* dramatic escape from Martinique. In 1861 *Sumter* was escaping from the USS *Iroquois*, then commanded by James S. Palmer. Now, a year after the *Iroquois* adventure, many of *Sumter's* officers, in newer and faster *Alabama*, were returning to the old cruising grounds off Dominica, Martinique, and other wide spaces of the Caribbean. *Alabama* rounded the northeast end of Dominica into Dominica Channel toward St. Pierre, the chief commercial port, which *Alabama* by-passed in favor of Fort-de-France.

18th. 9.30 Came to anchor in Fort Royal harbour, Martinique.

The seat of government, Fort Royal (now named Fort-de-France) was on the western side of the island, south of St. Pierre. The entire island was only some 36 miles in length.

Semmes seldom if ever told his officers his destination, giving even his navigator very short-range information, as he was more security conscious than most of his contemporaries. After *Alabama* had actually moved, however, the officers could often tell the captain's line of reasoning in planning the ship's cruise and strategy. The reason for Semmes going to Fort-de-France was to meet *Agrippina* which had a load of coal much needed for *Alabama's* bunkers. It was for this reason that, running along the shores of Dominica toward Fort-de-France, *Alabama* lowered her propeller and proceeded under steam. Being so close to the expected supply of coal, the Confederates felt that they could afford it. They were usually so economical with coal, however, that most prizes were chased under sail alone. Also sorely needed from Martinique were fresh foods and antiscorbutics. Sinclair said that the wardroom steward, Richard Parkinson, had served only "one square meal of fresh food" from Terceira to Martinique.

After the health officers had visited us, arrangements were made to lay in a stock of provisions.

[50]

Once the ship's company was no longer dependent upon "salt horse" and other sea stores, Richard Parkinson was given *carte blanche* to supply the wardroom with delectable food. This applied also to the other messes.

A most enthusiastic reception was given by the inhabitants, both civil & military. Invitations to the officers were given ad lib, the clubs being placed at our disposal. Our store ship "Aggripina" was being laden with coal for our use.

Fullam consistently misspelled *Agrippina*.

Letters were received by many on board. Landed all prisoners.

19th. 6.30a.m. A steamer was descried standing towards the harbour. On her coming nearer, we made her out to be a large barque rigged vessel. At 7.15 all doubt as to her nationality was set at rest, the Stars & Stripes being hoisted at her peak, and apparently a heavily armed vessel. On our communicating with the shore, it was found that the vessel (who was now within a mile of us) was the U. S. Str. "San Jacinto," 14 guns, viz;—12 sixty eight pounders and 2 eleven inch shell guns.

San Jacinto was commanded by William Ronckendorff. This was the same ship which, under command of Charles Wilkes, had become one of the best-known ships in the United States Navy because Wilkes in *San Jacinto* had triggered the *Trent* Affair in 1861 as the great diplomatic crisis with Great Britain. When the Civil War started, the USS *San Jacinto* was 11 years old. She was built at an original cost of $408,885. It is interesting to compare this with the original cost of *Alabama*. *Alabama* cost, when delivered by her builders, 47,500 pounds sterling, when the pound was worth about $4.80, or $228,000. *San Jacinto* went out of commission on 30 November 1861 at the Boston Navy Yard. However, she was overhauled and recommissioned in March 1862, and by April was at Hampton Roads facing the CSS *Virginia*. *San Jacinto* had been on her second career for only eight months when she appeared at Martinique, confronting the CSS *Alabama*.

San Jacinto was a screw steamer, sloop-rigged, of 1,567 tons, and two horizontal steam engines. Her battery, in 1862, consisted of one XI-inch Dahlgren, ten IX-inch Dahlgrens, and one light 12-pounder. At other dates, the armament was different. Statistical Data of U. S. Ships, *ORN*, 2, I, 200. See also, *Ordnance Instructions for the United States Navy*, 1866, 101–102. *Alabama's* characteristics were: tonnage 1050, speed 12.8 knots, armament one 110-pounder, one 68-pounder, six 32-pounders. None of *Alabama's* often repeated statistics give a speed greater than 12.8 knots, the official

[51]

speed on her trial run, except Fullam's notation below of 14 knots, when *Alabama* was under sail and steam.

Many commanders of Union warships pursued the Confederate raiders, especially *Alabama*. Such commanders included: T. A. M. Craven, Oliver S. Glisson, Charles W. Pickering, John A. Winslow, Cadwalader Ringgold, and Charles Wilkes. Also intent on pursuit of the raiders were United States ministers and consuls, journalists, and merchant captains. There were among all the pursuers only three ships which found *Alabama*, plus one other which barely missed. These were: the USS *Vanderbilt* (which barely missed), the USS *Kearsarge* (which finally sank *Alabama*), the USS *Hatteras* (which *Alabama* sank), and the USS *San Jacinto* (which *Alabama* playfully eluded). The reason *San Jacinto* arrived and blockaded *Alabama* at Martinique was perhaps due to the loose tongue of Captain Alexander McQueen, master of *Agrippina*, who was inclined to boast in the local bars that he was waiting for the already-famous Confederate cruiser.

San Jacinto had much heavier armament than *Alabama*, so there was no temptation for the Confederates to seek a fight with that blockader. On the other hand, *Alabama* was so much faster that Ronckendorff had no chance of catching her when she was ready to leave. Actually, a French naval officer assisted *Alabama* by supplying a detailed harbor chart showing the abundant choices of escape routes. The situation much resembled *Sumter's* escape from *Iroquois* in 1861, also at Martinique. Summersell, 132–137.

The Governor issued notices about the town forbidding any communication with her [San Jacinto], and prohibiting any supplies being sent to them.

The governor of Martinique was Maussion de Candé who had been governor also at the time of the *Sumter* episode. Summersell, 126–127.

He [the governor] also sent a communication to her Commander [William Ronckendorff] to the effect that "either he must come to an anchor, and if so remain 24 hours after our departure, or else go out to sea and remain outside of three miles." He [Ronckendorff] adopted the latter course.

The Governor stated that if we wanted to coal ship, it would be best for us to run down to St. Pierre and anchor under the forts. But it was deemed advisable to send the barque away to another rendezvous, she giving out that she was going to, and clearing for Trinidad.

Actually, the rendezvous was made at Blanquilla, between the islands of Margarita and Tortuga, off the coast of Venezuela.

[52]

The French gunboat "Fata" got up steam and anchored near us to prevent any demonstration being made by the enemy whilst we were at anchor, her Commander affording us every assistance, by showing us the best plan of escape the harbour afforded.

At first it had been our Captains intention to go out and give the enemy battle, but after deliberation he determined to wait until darkness set in. 1 p.m. The English mail boat passed the harbour. Before sundown every preparation had been made for battle, the enemy apparently pretty active in making preparations also. The broadside guns being loaded with shot and the pivot guns with shell. 7.15 p.m. "All hands up anchor." That was soon accomplished. All lights were then extinguished, and we steamed cautiously across the harbour along the shore. 8 [p.m.] Dismissed the pilot and called all hands to quarters and run out the guns, all expecting to hear a bang from the enemy. Signal lights were observed from a Yankee vessel in the harbour. The night was very favourable to us, the enemys vessel not having been seen since the last particle of daylight allowed us to see anything; she then being about the centre of the harbour evidently on the alert. After the pilot had left us, the engines were set agoing, and away we steamed at the rate of 14 knots an hour. At 9.20 all danger of interception being over, the guns were run in and secured, and all hands piped down. We then shaped our course towards Blanquilla, at which place we had made arrangements to meet the barque. We learnt afterwards that the "San Jacinto" had two boats on the lookout that evening, and had a set of signals instituted by which a Yankee vessel inside the harbour could afford him information of our movements. I believe the authorities arrested her Captain for signalling our departure; yet notwithstanding the facilities of the "San Jacinto's" command, they blockaded the port 4 days and nights after we left.

The preparations for battle with San Jacinto, described by Fullam, meant that Alabama would fight if necessary, not that she was seeking to fight it out with as formidable a ship as that Union warship.

The previous evening a drunken disturbance took place on board, by which it was found necessary to call the hands to quarters to quell it. It appeared that the deserter from the

"Sumter" (of whom mention has been made previously) had slipped down the cable, swam to a boat, and returned on board with a great quantity of spirits, and had handed it round to the crew, and all unknown to a single officer, he not tasting a drop himself, thus showing that his aim was to cause a mutiny on board. Those of the men that were inflated, or rather infuriated with liquor, were placed in double irons. With a few exceptions, these in addition to irons were gagged, and bucket after bucket of water thrown over them until they became partially sober. A short time previously one man had been stabbed severely in the arm. The officers and some of the petty officers were fully armed, the Captain having given orders to that effect, and to cut down the first man that hesitated to obey an order. The scoundrel Forrest was triced up in the mizen rigging, two hours on and two off.

On the way to Blanquilla, Fullam tells the story of a dramatic episode which happened before *Alabama* departed Fort-de-France. Semmes' account of the adventure follows:

Whilst I was below, a little after sunset, taking a cup of tea, and enjoying some of the delicious fruit which Bartelli had provided for me, I heard some confusion of voices, and a tramping of feet on the deck over my head, and soon afterward, the first lieutenant came into my cabin to tell me, that there was considerable disorder in the ship. I repaired on deck immediately, and saw at a glance that the crew was almost in a state of mutiny. It was evidently a drunken mutiny, however, and not very alarming. An officer had gone forward to quell some disturbance on the forecastle, when one of the sailors had thrown a belaying-pin at him, and others had abused him, and threatened him with personal violence. Some of the men, when directed to assist in seizing and confining their more disorderly comrades, had refused; and as I reached the deck, there was a surly, and sulky crowd of half-drunken sailors gathered near the foremast, using mutinous language, and defying the authorities of the ship. I immediately ordered the first lieutenant to "beat to quarters." The drum and fife were gotten up, and such was the effect of previous discipline upon the crew, that the moment they heard the well-known beat, and the shrill tones of the fife, they "fell in," mechanically, at their guns—some of them so drunk, that their efforts to appear sober were quite ludicrous.

This was what I had reckoned upon. At quarters, the officers always appeared armed, as if they were going into battle. There were very few arms about the deck, upon which the sailors could lay their hands—the cutlasses and pistols being kept locked up, in the arms-chests. Of course, I now had it all my own way—thirty armed officers being more than a match for 110 men armed with nothing but sheath-knifes and belaying-pins. I began now to quell the mutiny; or rather it was already quelled, and I began to bring Jack back to his senses.

[54]

In company with my first lieutenant and aide-de-camp, I passed along the platoons of men as they stood at their guns, and stopping wherever I observed a drunken man, I ordered his comrades to arrest him. This was immediately done, without demur in any instance, and the culprit was ironed. In this way I got as many as twenty disorderly fellows. These drunken men, the moment the attempt was made to arrest them, began to show fight, and to be abusive in their language. They were, however, soon overpowered, and rendered harmless. In this way I passed forward and aft, two or three times, eying the men as I passed, to be certain that I had gotten hold of all the rioters.

When I had done this, I directed the mutineers to be taken to the gangway, and calling two or three of the most active of the quartermasters, I made them provide themselves with draw-buckets, and commencing with the most noisy and drunken of the culprits, I ordered them to dash buckets of water over them in quick succession. The punishment was so evidently novel to the recipients, that they were at first disposed to deride it. With drunken gravity they would laugh and swear by turns, and tell the "bloody quartermasters" to "come on with their water, *they* were not afraid of it." But I was quite sure of my remedy, for I had tried it before; and as the drunken fellows would call for more water, in contempt and derision, I gratified them, and caused bucketsful to be dashed on them with such rapidity, that pretty soon they found it difficult to catch their breath, in the intervals between the showers. The more they would struggle and gasp for breath, the more rapidly the buckets would be emptied upon them.

The effect was almost electric. The maudlin fellows, somewhat sobered by the repeated shocks of the cold water, began now to swear less vociferously. In fact, they had no voice to swear with, for it was as much as they could do, to breathe. They no longer "bloodied" the quartermasters, or called for more water. Being reduced thus to silence, and still the water descending upon them as rapidly as ever, with half-sobered brain, and frames shivering with the cold, they would now become seriously alarmed. Did the captain mean to drown them? Was this the way he designed to punish them for mutiny, instead of hanging them at the yard-arm? They now turned to me, and begged me, for God's sake, to spare them. If I would only let them go this time, I should never have cause to complain of them again. I held off a little while, as if inexorable to their prayers and entreaties, the better to impress upon them the lesson I was teaching them, and then ordered them to be released. When their irons were taken off, they were sober enough to go below to their hammocks, without another word, and "turn in" like good boys! It took me some time to get through with this operation, for I had the delinquents—about a dozen of the most noisy—soused one at a time. The officers and crew were all this while—some two hours—standing at their guns, at quarters, and I could, now and then, overhear quite an audible titter from some of the sober men, as the drunken ones who were undergoing the shower-bath would now defy my authority, and now beg for mercy. When, at last, I had finished, I turned to my first lieutenant, and told him to "beat the retreat."

And this was the way, reader, in which I quelled my first, and only mutiny on board the *Alabama*. It became a saying afterward, among the sailors, that "Old Beeswax was h—ll upon watering a fellow's grog."

20th. Fine. No signs either of ships or land.

21st. Reduced sail to topsails, and hove maintopsail to the mast. 5.10 a.m. Filled away again. 10 a.m. Saw the "Aggripina" and signalled him to follow. Saw the land and a ship at 1 o'clock. At 3 got up steam and stood in towards Blanquilla. Drawing in towards the harbour, we observed a schooner at anchor. On coming within signal distance she hoisted the Stars and Stripes; we answered by hoisting the same. Shortly after, a boat put off from him. Coming on board (without undeceiving him) we asked him about the anchorage; after receiving satisfactory replies, we hauled down the Yankee flag and hoisted the Confederate ensign. Great indeed was the poor Yank's astonishment. Capt. Semmes told him that as he was at anchor we should not destroy his vessel, but, that for our safety we should detain him, ordering the Captain and mate to come on board every evening, and depart each morning to his own vessel. She proved to be the "Clara L. Sparks," whaler of Provincetown. At 4.30 anchored in 17 ftms. 5.30 "Aggripina" anchored.

As *Alabama* and *Agrippina* drew near to the Blanquilla anchorage, they saw that the whaler *Clara L. Sparks* was anchored very close to the beach. The whalers had pitched a tent on the beach and were operating some boilers to render blubber from a newly-struck whale. What followed was told with great gusto by Sinclair and Kell. Kell gave his version as follows: "As we were running under United States colors, the master of the whaler came out to us, delighted to see one of his own gunboats, and offered to pilot us in. He was quite carried away with our guns and battery; said he "thought we could give the Pirate Semmes fits if we met him, and hoped we would.' Imagine his state of collapse when he found we were the veritable pirate's ship!" Sinclair added his own little joke when he said that the young officers kidded the whaling captain in these words, " 'Say, Cap, did old Beeswax really tell you he should not burn your schooner?'—'Why, yes; of course he said so.'—'It may be all in good faith, Cap,' sighs the middy, as he shakes his head, 'but it's very like a joke of the old man.' And the skipper is again on the 'ragged edge,' and the youngster watching the anxious countenance is correspondingly happy."

Of course Semmes could not afford to allow the schooner to go find *San Jacinto* and report *Alabama's* presence, but it would have been out of character for a fussy practitioner of international law like Semmes to destroy an enemy in neutral waters. There were a few herdsmen on the island of Blanquilla and, had *Alabama* seized *Clara L. Sparks*, the Venezuelan government would have been justified in considering this an infringement

[56]

of neutrality, therefore Semmes decided not just to release her but not to capture her in the first place. *Clara L. Sparks* thus earned the distinction of joining that apparently select company of Union merchant vessels which were under the guns of *Alabama* and yet were allowed to go without signing a ransom bond.

22nd [November 1862, Saturday] At daylight commenced coaling ship, which operation was finished by Monday noon [24 November]. Blanquilla is nearly barren, producing absolutely nothing. The inhabitants, three in number, occupied themselves in rearing a few goats, &c. A small quantity of water is obtainable, but so brackish as to be nearly unfit for domestic purposes.

The island was six miles from north to south and three miles from east to west, flat and sterile, as described by Blunt. It was a good hideaway for *Alabama* to refit herself, to break out and whitewash the hold, to make all repairs possible outside of drydocking, and to give the crew liberty ashore. Among other entertainments on a nearly deserted island was the sight of another whale, and the chase and capture by *Clara L. Sparks* and her crew of friendly enemies of *Alabama*. The Confederates enjoyed watching the skill of the Yankee whalers.

25th. Whilst on shore observed a schooner standing in. She showed English colours, and on boarding stated that she was 4 days from Barbadoes & bound to Curacoa, and that the "San Jacinto" had left Barbadoes the day previous to her departure. The latter part of his story we credited, tho' believing him to be a Yankee scout. Exchanged three men with the barque.

Alabama exchanged three men with *Agrippina*. The new hands were all ordinary seamen: Martin Molk, William Robinson, and George Yeoman.

26th. 7.15 p.m. "All hands aft to muster." Sentence of naval general court martial read to prisoner, who had this day been tried for insubordination and inciting part of the men to mutiny, the men being in a state of intoxication at the time, and the prisoner perfectly sober. Said offences being committed in the harbour of Fort Royal, Martinique, on the evening of the 18th Nov. The sentence was that Geo. Forrest, A. B., forfeit all pay, prize money, &c. due him; that all wearing apparel (except what belonged [to] him when previously captured) be taken from him, and that he be ignominiously dismissed the ship and service, placed in the hands of the Master at Arms and conveyed on shore on the island of Blanquilla, with a stain of infamy upon him. A few appropriate remarks were then made by Capt. Semmes and the sentence carried out. 8.15 p.m. Got under weigh and hoisted propellor.

29th. Considerable excitement was caused by the lookout reporting a steamer on lee bow standing toward us; made her out to be a barque rigged sidewheel steamer. From, or rather in the direction she was steering, we concluded she was a French war steamer bound to Martinique. 10.30 a.m. Saw land on weather bow, the S. W. part of Porto Rico. Saw two vessels, one, a schooner hugging the shore, the other a barque standing to the northward. Shortened sail to allow her to come up to us, hoisting U. S. colours; the stranger hoisting English. Found her to be the "Barbadoes."

This bark was obviously named for the island of Barbados which is about 2 degrees south of Martinique and east by less than 2 degrees. No doubt, Fullam's spelling of the name of the English bark as *Barbadoes* was correct since Blunt indicates this spelling for 1850, twelve years before *Alabama's* encounter with *Barbadoes*. There is no doubt that Fullam himself boarded that ship.

30th. 6.10 Sail reported on starboard bow. 8.45 Another in sight two points on starboard bow. *Chased the latter. 10.30 Hove her to with blank cartridge; found her to be the Spanish schooner, "Neuveaux."*

It easily may be inferred that Fullam boarded the Spanish schooner *Neuveaux,* but there is no evidence beyond his own words written here. *Neuveaux* was told that the Confederate cruiser was the USS *Iroquois* (of 1,016 tons). *Alabama* obtained newspapers from *Neuveaux.*

12.45 Saw two more. Chased the one right ahead. 2 p.m. Brought her to. Boarded and took possession of the barque "Parker Cook" of Boston bound to Hayti. Engaged until 9 p.m. transferring stores, then set fire to her.

While Fullam spelled correctly the name of this bark, it is of interest to note that Semmes or his publishers made a typographical error and spelled the name *Parker Cooke.* Many later writers followed this error.

Correctly spelled, *Parker Cook* was a 136-ton bark, commanded by Thomas M. Fulton and owned by Edward Habich. It was relatively unusual for a vessel of this type, time, and place to have a sole owner. *Parker Cook* sailed from Boston 13 November 1862, bound for Aux Cayes on the south side of Santo Domingo, presently in Haiti. *List of Claims,* 62–63; Blunt, 351. When off the east coast of Santo Domingo, *Parker Cook* was sighted by *Alabama*. Fullam boarded and took possession of the ship and her papers. Later Semmes conducted his admiralty hearing.

When *Parker Cook* was captured, *Alabama* was searching for one of the returning California treasure steamers. The Confederate cruiser was transiting Mona Passage. Of course, there was considerable chance that *Alabama* would encounter a Union warship at one of the gateways to the Caribbean since several warships were chasing her. Instead of such an encounter, however, *Parker Cook* provided the Confederate raiders opportune provisions. The bark was provision-laden and could not have done better by *Alabama's* commissariat if it had been chartered and sent out for her special benefit. Semmes wrote: "We had found ... that our Boston friends put up the very best crackers, and ship-bread, and sent excellent butter, and cheese, salted beef and pork, and dried fruits to the West India markets; nor were we disappointed on the present occasion." Many hours were required to transfer provisions, and it was twilight before *Parker Cook* was set ablaze off Cape Raphael.

Lt. Kell gave the official Confederate estimate of the value of *Parker Cook* as $10,000. This brought the total value in Confederate figures of Union ships destroyed by *Alabama* up to $1,194,311. Total Union claims filed on *Parker Cook* amounted to $26,064.56. *Parker Cook* contained newspapers of New York and Boston denouncing "the privateer steamer *Alabama*," and lamenting the increased insurance rates and diminished Union cargoes. The New York Chamber of Commerce had drawn up new resolutions denouncing the British for their role in building *Alabama* and other Confederate commerce raiders. *Harper's Weekly,* 31 January 1863.

Filled away and stood N. Wly. Shipped 1 man.

1st Dec. 2.30 a.m. Hove to. Filled [away] in chase of a vessel on starboard beam. 7 a.m. Made another astern. Found both to be foreign. 9.30 p.m. Made a vessel under sail and steam on port quarter. Called all hands to quarters, and loaded the battery with shell, expecting every minute to hear a shot, a broadside whizzing over or into us. The stranger showed two signal lights. Receiving no answer he quietly steamed past us. Conjecture was busy as to his nationality, and as to his being a vessel of war or not. 10.15 Piped down and secured the battery. We now man 6 guns on a broadside, transporting one of the midship thirty twos to a porthole near the bridge. The state of efficiency the men have arrived at reflects the highest credit upon both officers and men.

2nd. Saw the land, and several vessels.

3rd. 7.45 p.m. Sail discovered on starboard bow, gave chase. At 9.10 fired a blank cartridge. No notice being taken of it, a shot was fired at him. This produced the desired effect. On boarding I found it to be the French barque "Feu Sacré" of Nantes from Port au Prince to Falmouth, we passing as the U. S. Str. "Wynona," her Captain protesting against the U. S. vessels annoying him.

The USS *Winona* (so spelled) was a screw steamer like the CSS *Alabama*, but was a much smaller warship.

4th. Light winds and fine. Cruising in the Windward passage, hoping to meet one of the Californian Mail Steamers, one being expected about this date.

California treasure steamers, on their homeward voyage laden with gold, emerged from the Caribbean Sea either through Yucatan Channel or through the Windward Passage. Sinclair graphically recounted the excitement of all hands in contemplating the capture of a treasure steamer. Writing in 1972, it is difficult to capture the fever for prize money which was well-nigh universal among the sailors of the Confederate as well as the Union navies. In November 1862, had the prize money been divided evenly (not that it would have been evenly divided) among *Alabama's* ship's company, the average share would have been more than $8,000. Sinclair wrote: "There is no gossip or conversation, either forward or aft, that interests but of the California treasure-steamer. Whether convoyed or no; amount of bullion; speed we may expect of her. And every soul on board of us has become a self-appointed lookout." Such was the excited speculation as *Alabama* transited the haunts of the buccaneers, sighting many sails but finding few additional prizes. Union ship owners had not been slow to learn that there were rebel raiders to be expected at the gates of the Caribbean. For buccaneers, *piratos*, privateers, and cruisers, whatever the age, the language, and the law, the love of gold and silver proved a common denominator.

5th. Still cruising in the passage between Cuba and St. Domingo. Saw several vessels, amongst which was a schooner showing Yankee colours. Boarded and took possession. The "Union" of and from Baltimore to Jamaica. His cargo being English, he was ransomed, the crew of "Parker Cook" being transferred to him.

Union was under command of Joseph H. Young and owned by three members of the Lamdin family and by Thomas E. Waddy. As *Alabama*

[60]

came in sight of her, *Union* made no effort to escape. When Fullam boarded *Union,* he learned that her cargo was neutral and that ship and cargo were not very valuable, being miscellaneous merchandise suitable for the trade with Port Maria, which is still so named and on the north side of Jamaica. Therefore, when *Alabama's* admiralty court passed upon her, she was released in consideration of a ransom bond of $1,500 and required to transport the prisoners from *Parker Cook. Union* arrived at Jamaica three days after her release by *Alabama.* When *Harper's Weekly,* 31 January 1863, published the news about *Union's* seizure and release, that "Journal of Civilization" noted that the USS *Vanderbilt* had returned to Fortress Monroe, Virginia, after an unsuccessful cruise in pursuit of *Alabama.* *Vanderbilt,* under command of Lt. C. H. Baldwin, was more persistent than any other unsuccessful pursuer of *Alabama.* See Baldwin's report of his search in *ORN,* 1,II, 37. The ransom bond of *Union* was published in ORN, 1, I, 781–2. See also *American Lloyds, 1862,* 541. It might be noted concerning Semmes' release of *Union* that the schooner was from Maryland and that this state was Semmes' birthplace. *Union* was the first Maryland vessel ransomed by *Alabama* and also the first one captured by that sea raider. Semmes said, "My original orders were not to capture Maryland vessels, but that good old State had long since ceased to occupy the category in which our Congress, and the Executive had placed her. She was now ranged under the enemy's flag, and I could make no discrimination in her favor."

Received news of Bragg's successful capture of baggage waggons, &c. And also that 7 U. S. vessels of war were off the Northern ports, expecting that we were going to attack their seaports.

Formby, 167–169. In *ORN,* 1, I–III, *passim,* are numerous references to fears that Confederates were going to attack northern seaports, and the reaction of the United States Navy Department to such unrealistic fears.

6th. 9 a.m. Hoisted up the propellor.
7th. Several sails seen. At 2.15 p.m. a sail descried on starboard bow. In a short time made her out to be a brigantine rigged side wheel steamer. Steam was immediately got up, the propellor lowered, sails taken in and furled. All hands called to quarters, the battery loaded with shell and run out, and every preparation made for a "mill." Everybody in the best possible spirits and eager for a fray. The celerity of the men in the preparations for battle was remarkable, giving proof of the spirit that actuated them. The steamer kept heading for us until 2.45 when we fired a blank cartridge

and hoisted the Confederate flag. No notice being taken of it, a broadside of 6 guns were trained on him awaiting the order to fire. We recognized him as the U. S. mail boat "Ariel" of and from New York to Aspinwall. The steamer turned and made for off. The order was then given to train and fire the pivot guns at him; a second order was given to fire at his smokestack. In the position she then was, her foremast was in a line with the smokestack. Both guns were then fired, one shot of which struck the foremast about 10 feet from the deck, taking away two thirds of it, the stick still standing; fortunately they did not explode at the time, else the carnage amongst the passengers would have been frightful. She then hove to. A boat was sent on board, and the Captain brought on board us with his papers. Three boxes of specie, a 24 lb. rifled port gun, 125 new rifles, 16 swords, and about 1000 rounds of ammunition were quickly transferred to our vessel. There being on board 140 officers and men (marines) going out to join the U. S. Pacific Squadron and about 500 passengers, men, women and children; several naval and military officers being also on board.

Dr. George Willis Read published an illuminating account narrating his adventures as a passenger aboard Cornelius Vanderbilt's mail steamer *Ariel* when, on 7 December 1862, she encountered *Alabama*. George W. Read, *A Pioneer of 1850*, 130–138. The account was, of course, entirely independent of Fullam's, but corroborated his words and added details, besides narrating a capture from the standpoint of the captured instead of the captor.

Read was at dinner on board the Panama packet *Ariel,* eating a "plain cooked potato," that Sunday at 3:30 p.m. when *Alabama* fired a blank shot across the bow of the mail steamer. When Read went on the hurricane deck, he saw a ship coming up about a mile and a half behind *Ariel.* He could see that she was a speedy craft that could very easily sail around *Ariel.* Indeed, Dr. Read was in no mood to admire *Ariel* because he had been suffering from seasickness and, except for his potato, had gone for two days without eating or drinking. Cooking aboard the Panama steamer was filthy beyond belief, according to Dr. Read. The filth, the smells, the discomfort and confusion aboard *Ariel* surpassed anything that the doctor could remember, even though he had been in the California Gold Rush a decade earlier. He was just now returning via San Francisco to his ranch in the Sacramento Valley after a visit with his mother in the East. (A year later, Artemus Ward made the same voyage in *Ariel,* New York to Aspinwall, and confirmed Read's worst criticisms of the ship and her owner, Cornelius Vanderbilt. Charles F. Browne, *Artemus Ward: His Travels*.)

In spite of his discomfort, Dr. Read took a lively interest in the drama unfolding before him. So did R. C. Thomas, the first officer of *Ariel*, who wrote an account of the capture which appeared in *Frank Leslie's Illustrated Newspaper*, 10 January 1863. This account corroborated and supplemented both Read and Fullam. An hour and a half earlier than had Dr. Read, Thomas first saw *Alabama* about four miles distant, as *Ariel* rounded Cape Maysi (now Maisi). The identity of *Alabama* was not immediately apparent to Thomas. She was obviously a bark-rigged vessel under sail. There was nothing in her appearance showing that she was a steamer, such was the ability of the sea raider to disguise herself, including a smokepipe that could be lowered out of sight. While Thomas watched, the approaching ship removed her disguise and raised her smokestack, but was still wearing the Stars and Stripes at her peak. Within half an hour, *Alabama* was close enough to fire a gun demanding that *Ariel* lie to, meantime raising the rebel flag. *Ariel*, instead of stopping, put on all speed. *Alabama* then closed the distance and fired two guns in rapid succession. One projectile missed *Ariel*, but the other crashed into her foremast and nearly severed it. Meantime, Dr. Read, standing on the after end of the deck, could see the projectiles as they hurtled past him. He observed the hole made by the projectile and noted that it was eight inches in diameter. When the firing had started, *Ariel's* deck was crowded, but when the vessel was hit the crowd scurried away. Captain Albert J. Jones, master of *Ariel*, decided to stop his engines and lower the Stars and Stripes in token of surrender because there was not much resistance he could offer to the naval ordnance bearing down upon them. See the perceptive monograph by Robert E. Johnson, *Thence Round Cape Horn*, 118–119. Note how closely Fullam's account is corroborated by the diverse sources of Johnson, Thomas, and Read.

As soon as *Ariel* hove to, Lt. Richard F. Armstrong, Coxswain George Freemantle, and a boarding party from *Alabama* came alongside the treasure steamer. Dr. Read noted that Armstrong assured the passengers that none of them would lose their baggage, private property, or in any way be molested. Then Armstrong demanded the keys of the special locker along with the ship's official papers. Furthermore, Armstrong took Captain Jones and his papers to *Alabama* for action by Semmes' admiralty proceedings. Thomas stated that the money taken from *Ariel* totaled $9,500, and Read said that the value of the 200 Enfield rifles, swords, pistols, and money confiscated came to $45,000. Read's estimate was high. The entire claims filed for *Ariel's* losses before the *Alabama* Claims totaled $10,041.86.

When Captain Jones went aboard *Alabama*, some 20 Confederates, all well armed and under command of Lt. Low, became the prize crew of *Ariel* and held her while her case was being considered. That night *Alabama* temporarily parted company with *Ariel* in order to chase a suspicious sail. When the ship proved to be neutral, *Alabama* rejoined her prize, but suddenly was confronted with another crisis. *Alabama's* engine broke down and altogether prevented the ship from moving with her steam screw. Had the enemy known this, they could have overpowered the prize crew stationed aboard them and escaped. Semmes and his officers kept this crisis a secret. After two or three days' cruising under sail in company with *Ariel,* Semmes still had not found a less valuable prize to use as a cartel in moving *Ariel's* passengers and crew to neutral waters. It became clear that *Ariel* would have to be released on ransom bond. Captain Jones and his passengers were delighted to execute a ransom bond to be paid at war's end by Cornelius Vanderbilt and the various owners of the cargo. Indeed, Kell said that some of the ladies on *Ariel,* " . . . called for 'three cheers for Captain Semmes and the Alabama,' which were heartily given, with a waving of handkerchiefs, and adieus." The ransom bond valued *Ariel,* plus her freight money, at $138,000, and the value of her cargo was set at $123,000. As with other ransom bonds, these sums were to be paid to the Confederate States government within 30 days of the end of the war, presuming that the Confederacy would be successful. *Ariel's* ransom bond for ship and cargo totaled $261,000, or $10,694.56 more than *Alabama* herself had originally cost to build.

Upon release, *Ariel* continued toward her destination, Aspinwall on the Atlantic side of the Panama route to California. Aspinwall (now Colón) was named for William Henry Aspinwall, tycoon of the Pacific Mail and Steamship Company. *Ariel* arrived in Aspinwall 22 December 1862 (17 days after her departure from New York) and Captain Jones requested Admiral Theodorus Bailey, stationed at Key West, to furnish an escort for the next California treasure steamer proceeding out of Aspinwall. Bailey complied with this request, the USS *Augusta* being at hand. Bailey to Welles, 24 December 1862, *ORN*, 1, XVII, 336. As far as *Alabama* was concerned, and also the Confederate States Navy, the future operations of California treasure steamers could proceed in safety. The really important point was that *Alabama* had not had the good fortune to bag a steamer coming from California carrying gold. *Ariel* continued, nevertheless, to fetch money for Cornelius Vanderbilt. In due time, *Ariel* was the subject of claims filed before the Court of Commissioners of the *Alabama* Claims, and the decision was made that the type of losses sustained were not direct losses and hence not collectable under the act creating the Court of Commissioners of the *Alabama* Claims. *Moses Hyneman v. United States,* Case 643, Moore, 4292.

The military were paroled. On boarding, the marines were found drawn up in fighting order.

Moses Hyneman v. U. S., Case 643, Moore, 4292, indicated that there were in *Ariel* 667 passengers, including 140 marines and their officers, under command of Captain David Cohen, USMC. Rear Admiral Charles H. Bell, USN, had requested that the marines be sent to Mare Island in San Francisco Bay to replace soldiers who had been stationed there to guard the Mare Island Navy Yard.

From the Captain of the steamer I learnt that the marine officers first advised the surrender of the vessel.

In consequence of their paroles, the marines were exchanged as prisoners of war after they reached the Mare Island Navy Yard. There is a chapter entitled, "Guarding the Gold Steamers," in Johnson, 113–123. Captain Albert J. Jones wisely followed the advice of the marines. When *Ariel* was first attacked, the marines were armed and drawn up in formation, but it was soon evident that there was not much resistance they could offer to the CSS *Alabama*.

The Yankees said that they had not the remotest idea we should dare show ourselves in that part of the world. Received newspapers up to the 1st Dec. In the evening, 2 officers, 2 engineers and 10 men were sent on board [Ariel] as a prize crew, her Captain remaining on board our vessel.

Lt. Armstrong was the boarding officer. After the admiralty proceedings, Lt. Low was made prize master of *Ariel*.

8th. Still cruising in the same passage, on the look out for the homeward bound steamer due about this time.

This was the Windward Passage between Cuba and Santo Domingo, one of the chief gateways to the Caribbean used by the gold steamers.

Prize [Ariel] being near us. 1 p.m. Our chief engineer [Miles J. Freeman] went on board [Ariel] to disable her machinery, orders also being sent to throw overboard her sails, so that, in the event of our being engaged with any other vessel she could not escape. It was our intention to tow her into some port and land the passengers, then to destroy [her], first replenishing our stock of coal, provisions, &c.

Fullam apparently was deceived by what was commonly believed on board *Alabama* at that time. However, Semmes indicated that his intention was, if possible, to find a ship less valuable than *Ariel* so that he could turn her into a cartel and then destroy *Ariel* on the high seas. Had *Alabama* taken *Ariel* into neutral waters to discharge passengers or for any other purpose, *Ariel* could have been seized under international law, and a diplomatic dispute with a foreign nation might have ensued.

[65]

*At 7.15 p.m. on account of the women and children we deter-
mined to run for Jamaica. Accordingly the "bonnet of the
steam chest, and a steam valve" were sent on board the
"Ariel" again, with orders to get up steam and follow us as
quickly as possible. Whilst doing the above, a steamer was
reported on starboard quarter. All hands to quarters, making
toward her. Nearing her it was found to be a barque. On
boarding found her to be a German. Secured the battery and
stood for prize. 11 p.m. Stood on course.*

*9th [December 1862]. In the evening Morant light was
distant about 5 miles.*

Morant Light was located at Morant Point on the eastern end of Jamaica.
In 1862 the light was presumably similar to that of 1850, described in part
by Blunt as a white tower rising 103 feet above sea level and visible in
clear weather for some 21 miles.

*7.15 p.m. Slowed the engines intending to run in on the
morrow. 8.15 p.m. A sail hove in sight. Got ready for action.
Coming up with her and boarding, we found she was a
foreigner from Kingston, Ja. bound to Europe. Understood
from him that the yellow fever was breaking out, so it was
determined to ransom the "Ariel" and let her go. Just however
as the order was given to go ahead, the chief engineer reported that "the brackets and guides of the valve" [of
Alabama's engine] were broken. The utmost caution was
observed to prevent any one on board the "Ariel" knowing the
disaster that had fallen upon us.
Whilst the boat was despatched to bring off the engineers
(who had been on board the "Ariel" to take charge of her
engines) and the Captain to make arrangements relative to
a bond; the propellor was hoisted up and sail made upon
our vessel. Shortly after, she [Ariel] was ransomed and the
prize officers and crew returned on board [Alabama]. The
"Ariel" when last seen was steering S. S. W. The passengers,
civil and military, highly eulogized our prize crew for their
quiet, orderly, and respectful conduct. From the papers taken
we read some important news, foremost of which was, the
proposal of France and the rejection by England of the intervention question. Its rejection we supposed arose through
the discord that was known to exist, upon this question in
the British Cabinet.*

Frank L. Owsley, *King Cotton Diplomacy,* covers the "climax of intervention," 337–359. The turning point in the intervention effort came when
news reached Europe of the Union success in the Battle of Antietam,
causing the withdrawal of Lee from his Maryland invasion. See also James
A. Rawley, *Turning Points of the Civil War,* 114, and *passim.*

*Then again the immense navy possessed by the U. S. caused
us to feel considerable uneasiness for our seaboard cities.*

Events proved this fear more justified than similar fears voiced by people
in Northern seaports of the small Confederate States Navy.

*The fearful disadvantages under which we labour compared
with the vast resources of the U. States is in itself fearfully
alarming. Our only trust is in God and our strong arms.
"Dieu et mon droit." Soon after the departure of the "Ariel"
we steered to the N. & E., standing off and on the island of
Jamaica, close under the land keeping as much as possible
out of the track of vessels. The whole staff of engineers had,
up to about midnight of the 11th, been working night and
day repairing the machinery. Great indeed was our joy on
its completion.*

Had not the engineering department made these repairs, *Alabama* would
have ceased to function immediately as a commerce raider. The fact
that her engines continued to operate on the long cruise was a great tribute
to Miles J. Freeman, the chief engineer, William P. Brooks, the first assistant
engineer, Mathew O'Brien, second assistant engineer, William Robertson,
the fourth assistant engineer, and others who served in the engineering
department.

*Steering to the N. & Wd., nothing to vary the monotony of
a sea life, cruising under small sail.*

*15th. Noon. Hauled up towards Cape St. Antonio on the
western extremity of the island of Cuba.*

Thus *Alabama* approached Yucatan Channel, the western gateway of
the Caribbean, one of the customary routes of homeward-bound California
gold steamers, a type of prize still on the minds of Fullam and his shipmates.

*16th. 8 a.m. Hove to on port tack. Wind E. N. E. Quietly
awaiting the arrival of anything in the shape of a homeward
bound California Mail Steamer, or in fact any little thing that
might turn up in our way. Until the 19th strong gales with
heavy sea from the N. E. heading N. Wly.*

[67]

21st. A steamer descried on starboard bow steering East, supposed to be a French vessel of war. [Alabama was] Making for an anchorage or rendezvous.

22nd. Moderate breeze. On account of the many dangerous reefs it was deemed advisable to let go the kedge anchor. A breeze springing up, we let go the port anchor.

23rd. About 10 a.m. hove up and got under weigh. Moderate breeze. 2.30 p.m. Sail discovered on port bow. It proved to be the "Aggripina."

Before *Agrippina* parted company with *Alabama* at Blanquilla, Semmes had instructed Captain Alexander McQueen to meet him at Las Arcas.

3 [p.m.] Land descried on starboard bow, our course being S. Wly. At 5.15 came to an anchor in 10 fthms. Las Arcas rocks bearing N. N. W., being about 100 miles W. N. W. of Campeche.

Blunt, 285, set the distance from Campeche to Las Arcas at 83 miles, as contrasted with Fullam's 100 miles.

6.30 The Aggripina anchored near us.

24th. Being desirous of being protected from the strong Northerly winds that blow here, an expedition consisting of the cutter, gig, and whale boat, under the immediate command of Capt. Semmes, sailed to discover the best anchorage. 12.30 The boats returned, having successfully accomplished the desired object. 1.45 Got under weigh and anchored at 2.35 in 9¼ fthms. between the three islands of Las Arcas, the barque following and anchoring near us. The propellor being kept down in case of any emergency.

25th. Christmas Day. Nothing to mark the difference between this and any other day, save the men being exempt from work, and in the evening all hands spliced the main brace. O for a good old English Christmas with its merry associations and innocent pleasures. The three islands were of coral formation, and with the exception of a few gulls, no signs of life either animal or vegetable were seen.

The island waters, however, abounded in fish. The island itself, with a bay in the center and a very narrow connection with the open sea, was a veritable fish trap, as the tide brought in fish and many failed to escape before the tide went out. It was there that Coxswain Michael Mars, armed only with a knife, successfully attacked a shark. Once more the crew of

Alabama, seeking to relieve the monotony of the diet of a ship underway, caught fish and ate the eggs of sea gulls.

Employed coaling and caulking ship.

Alabama was careened, after the fashion of ships unable to go into dry dock, in order to clean as well as possible the barnacles which grew so rapidly on a ship's hull in the tropical waters of the Caribbean.

Sunday [28 December 1862]. Mustered as usual.

30th. 2 p.m. Finished coaling. A sail discovered, on starboard bow. Made her out to be a brig beating to windward. Fresh easterly wind. Nothing unusual showed that 1862 had passed away!

1863. Came in with bright clear weather. An omen I trust of our future career. May this fearful war cease, that peace and prosperity be seen again. Still coaling and refitting ship generally.

4th. Jan. Sunday. Expecting a gale from the S. E., and being in a dangerous position; it was deemed advisable to make every preparation for sea. Hands receiving coal [on board], and supplying the barque with water.

5th. Jan. 6.30 a.m. In anticipation of news being received of Lincoln's proclamation,

Fullam referred to President Lincoln's Emancipation Proclamation of 1 January 1863 which declared free the slaves held in states which were then waging war against the United States. It is noteworthy that Fullam, who was a Confederate strictly by adoption, should have had such strong opinions on the subject. Since Fullam and his shipmates, officers and men, eagerly read (or had read to them) newspapers from prizes, they had every opportunity to know that in September 1862 Lincoln had issued his Preliminary Emancipation Proclamation which warned of the future Emancipation Proclamation of 1 January 1863. Therefore, on 5 January 1863 Fullam was expecting to hear shortly that the threatened proclamation of January had indeed been issued. See E. Merton Coulter, *The Confederate States of America, 264,* and Henry S. Commager, editor, "Extracts from Lincoln's Messages to Congress Recommending Compensated Emancipation," in *Documents of American History,* 402–405.

—a tombstone, consisting of a board about 4 feet in length and two in breadth, was sent on shore and placed in the most prominent position the largest island afforded. In black letters on a white ground was the following: "In memory of Abraham

*Lincoln, President of the late United States, who died of Nigger
on the brain. 1st January 1863." "290." Upon a piece of paper,
protected from the weather, was written in Spanish the following: "Will the finder kindly favor me, by forwarding this
tablet to the U. S. Consul at the first port he touches at."
This affair originated and was executed by the Steerage
Officers. 10.40 a.m. Got under weigh, leaving the barque
at anchor. 11 Made sail and hoisted propellor. Fine E. S. E.
wind. Making towards Galveston, Texas. Pretty certain of
falling [in] with something, either a merchantman or a vessel
of war.*

Despite the isolation, or perhaps because of it, all hands read newspapers, obtained when friendly vessels were boarded. After the officers had read the newspapers, the men took their turn, as the papers circulated among the crew. With a new batch of newspapers at hand, small groups of sailors were to be seen sitting around the deck with one person reading aloud to each group.

Usually *Alabama's* next destination was a secret locked in the mind of the commanding officer, but as *Alabama* drew northward toward Galveston many guessed that the move was toward the coast of Texas. From newspapers obtained as long ago as those from *Thomas B. Wales,* the Confederate raiders learned of the preparation in Boston of the Nathaniel P. Banks Expedition to assail Galveston. It is true that often the information was out of date before the Confederates were able to act on it. Unknown to Semmes and his men was the fact that on 1 January Confederate warships under Major Leon Smith successfully surprised Union ships and soldiers who were investing Galveston. When *Alabama* reached the vicinity of Galveston on 11 January 1863, the city itself, contrary to expectations, was once more in Confederate hands. ND, *Civil War Naval Chronology,* III, 3–4. Since Semmes knew that the controlling depth of water on the Galveston bar was 12 feet, he had expected troop transports and other auxiliaries (with few or no warships) to be awaiting *Alabama's* attack like sitting ducks. With the changed situation, however, and Confederates once more in possession, warships would be blockading, and it was mere chance that *Alabama* encountered *Hatteras* instead of a more formidable vessel.

*Sunday. 11th. [January 1863] Fine moderate breeze from
the eastward. Read Articles of War. Noon. 18 miles from
Galveston. As I write this, some are discussing the probabilities
of a fight before morning. 2.25 p.m. Light breeze. Sail discovered by the lookout on lee bow shortly after three, and at
last five vessels were seen, two of which were reported to
be steamers. Everyone delighted at the prospect of a fight.*

[70]

No doubt whatever existing as to their being war vessels.
Blockaders, we supposed. The watch below came on deck,
and of their own accord commenced preparing the guns, &c.
for action. Those whose watch it was on deck were employed
in getting the propellor ready for lowering, others were
bending a cable to a kedge and putting it over the bow, the
engineers firing up for steam. Officers looking to their side
arms, &c. and discussing the size of their expected adversary
or adversaries. At 2.30 shortened sail and tacked to the south-
ward. 4 p.m. A steamer reported standing out from the fleet
towards us. Backed maintopsail and lowered propellor. 4.50
Everything reported ready for action. Chase bearing N. N. E.
dist. 10 miles. Twilight set in about 5.45. Took in all sails.
At 6.20 beat to quarters, manned the starboard battery, and
loaded with five-second shell,–turned round and stood for
the steamer, having previously made her out to be a two
masted side wheel steamer of apparently 1200 tons, tho at
the distance she was just before dark, we could not form
any correct estimate of her size, &c. At 6.30 the strange
steamer hailed and asked "What steamer is that?" We replied,
(in order to be certain who he was)–Her Majestys Steamer
"Petrel!" "What steamer is that?" Two or three times we
asked the question, until we heard "This is the United States
Steamer_____, not hearing the name. However,
United States was sufficient. As no doubt existed as to his
character, we said at 6.35 that this was the "Confederate
States Steamer 'Alabama' " accompanying the last syllable
of our name with a shell fired over him. The signal being
given, the other guns took up the refrain, and a tremendous
volley from our whole broadside given to him, every shell
striking his side, it, the shot, striking being distinctly heard
on board our vessel, and thus found that she was iron.

The enemy replied, and the action became general. A most
sharp spirited firing was kept up on both sides, our fellows
peppering away as though the action depended upon each
individual. And so it did. Pistols & rifles were continually
firing from our quarter deck, messengers most deadly. The
distance during the hottest of the fight, not being more than
40 yards! Twas a grand though fearful sight to see the guns
belching forth, in the darkness of the night, sheets of living
flame, the deadly missiles striking the enemy with a force

that we could feel. Then, when the shells struck her side, and especially the percussion ones, her whole side was lit up and showing rents of five or six feet in length. One shot had just struck our smokestack and wounding one man in the cheek, when the enemy eased his firing, and fired a lee gun, then a second, and a third, the order was then given to "Cease firing." This was at 6.52. A tremendous cheering commenced and it was not until everybody had cleared his throat to his own satisfaction that silence could be obtained. We then hailed him, and in reply, he stated that he had surrendered, was on fire and also that he was in a sinking condition. He then sent a boat on board and surrendered the U. S. Gunboat "Hatteras," 9 guns, Lieut. Commr. Blake, 140 men.

Thus commenced the engagement of *Alabama* with the USS *Hatteras* which resulted in the first sinking of a steam warship in battle with another steam warship. There were two U. S. naval vessels so named for the Hatteras Inlet on the North Carolina coast. The one innocently steaming toward *Alabama* on 11 January 1863 was the first United States warship of that name, doing blockade duty off Galveston. Although her hull was iron, the USS *Hatteras* was one of the least formidable of the warships on duty there which *Alabama* might have encountered, and indeed she had been built as a merchant steamer named *St. Mary*. She had operated as a passenger vessel on the Delaware River before Admiral S. F. Dupont on behalf of the navy purchased her for $110,000 from Harland and Hollingsworth of Wilmington, Delaware, 25 September 1861. Fitted out at the nearby Philadelphia Navy Yard, *Hatteras* was commissioned in October 1861, with Commander George F. Emmons as commanding officer. Although of slightly more tonnage (1,126) than *Alabama* (1,050), *Hatteras* was only a sidewheel steamer with her propulsion at the mercy of any projectiles in her vicinity and a battery that was limited to four 32-pounder smooth bore guns plus one 20-pounder rifled gun. This was very little with which to oppose *Alabama's* eight Blakely guns, including one 68-pounder and one 110-pounder on pivots, which was double *Hatteras'* firepower. To the unpracticed eye, *Hatteras* and *Alabama* might appear to be evenly matched, since *Hatteras'* dimensions were: 210 x 34 x 18, (depth) while *Alabama's* were: 220 x 31.8 x 17.8 (depth). On that fateful 11 January, *Hatteras* approached *Alabama* apparently presuming the stranger to be a merchant vessel attempting to run the blockade into Galveston. *Alabama* did indeed turn around and deceptively flee the approaching *Hatteras* for the purpose of luring her beyond the support of Commodore Bell's flagship, the USS *Brooklyn,* or any other formidable Union blockaders in the vicinity.

In 1861, within a month after the commissioning of *Hatteras,* that sidewheeler proceeded to Key West for Florida blockading duty off Apalachicola, Cedar Keys, and Sea Horse Keys. At Cedar Keys, *Hatteras* captured and burned seven small vessels that were planning to run the blockade and were already loaded with cotton and turpentine. Later, *Hatteras* operated off Berwick, Louisiana, and fought the CSS *Mobile* until that light-draft Confederate retreated to shallow water. While George F. Emmons continued as commanding officer, *Hatteras* captured an additional seven blockade runners and some 534 bales of cotton. One captured vessel, the 20-ton sloop *Poody,* was renamed *Hatteras Jr.* and converted into a Yankee blockader. Emmons (1811–1884) had a remarkable career in the United States Navy. While in his twenties, he served in Charles Wilkes' explorations which discovered the Antarctic Continent, and had an interesting career otherwise before his Civil War adventures in Florida and Louisiana. Shortly after his service in *Hatteras,* Emmons published a book entitled, *The Navy of the United States, from the Commencement, 1775 to 1853,* which was in fact much concerned with the history of prize money in the navy before 1853, an interest no doubt generated by Emmons' own great success in taking Confederate prizes in Florida and Louisiana. After the Civil War, Emmons became a rear admiral, and a World War II destroyer was named for him, a destroyer which appropriately had a very successful career in World War II.

It was November 1862 when George F. Emmons was relieved of his duties in *Hatteras* by Lieutenant Commander Homer C. Blake. *Hatteras* was off Mobile at that time. On 6 January 1863, Blake carried out his orders to take *Hatteras* into the duty of blockading Galveston, Texas. The blockade at Galveston was being conducted by Commodore Henry H. Bell, not to be confused with Commodore Charles H. Bell who has been mentioned in connection with the *Ariel* episode and who commanded the Pacific Squadron. Henry H. Bell was Fleet Captain of the West Gulf Blockading Squadron. His superior was David G. Farragut, the first admiral in the United States Navy. In short, up to the time 11 January 1863 when *Hatteras* under Blake's command seemed to mistake the CSS *Alabama* for a merchantman trying to run the blockade, the Union warship, even though a converted merchantman and a sidewheeler at that, had been unusually successful. Reports of George F. Emmons and related documents in *ORN*, 1, XVII, 48–50; *ORA*, 1, VI, 74–77; New York *Herald,* 25 and 30 January and 14 February 1862; W. W. Davis, *Civil War and Reconstruction in Florida*, 152–153.

Hatteras sighted *Alabama* about 3 p.m. on 11 January and obeyed a signal from Commodore Bell's flagship the USS *Brooklyn* to investigate the strange vessel. For the following four hours *Alabama* moved closer and closer to the Texas shore, with *Hatteras* in pursuit and gaining. Finally in hailing distance, Commander Blake demanded that the stranger give her name. It was then that *Alabama* identified herself as Her Majesty's Steamer *Petrel.* To verify this claim, Blake ordered a boat lowered to board the stranger, the same pattern followed so many times by *Alabama*. Blake, in his official report, stated that prior to this time he suspected that he was pursuing the rebel steamer *Alabama*. With *Hatteras'* boarding vessel in the water, Kell, speaking with his powerful voice through his trumpet, sang out, "This is the Confederate States Steamer *Alabama!*" At the same time, *Alabama* raised the Confederate flag. For a very few minutes (reports vary from 13 to 17 minutes), the two ships exchanged fire from cannon and even from small arms at ranges from 25 to 200 yards, as the distance between the ships alternately closed and widened. Besides other damage, *Hatteras* sustained two big holes at the water line. Whole sheets of her iron hull were ripped off. It was not long after that *Hatteras* caught fire, and started to sink. Blake flooded his powder magazines to prevent an explosion and surrendered. *Alabama* sent boats to join the boats of *Hatteras* in rescuing the crew of the sinking Union vessel. Forty-five minutes after the start of the action, *Hatteras* (in position 28.53 north and 94.22 west) sank below the waves. Every living person aboard *Hatteras* was rescued and made prisoners of war aboard *Alabama*, 118 in all. Two *Hatteras* men were killed in the engagement, five were wounded, and the six men who were in the already-lowered boat escaped. Blake and the remainder of his crew were paroled and put ashore at Port Royal, Jamaica. *Alabama* had only one man wounded, and her hull was intact. The Union warships *Brooklyn*, *Cayuga*, and *Sciota* searched all night for the missing *Hatteras*. Next day, *Brooklyn* belatedly discovered *Hatteras*. She had sunk in 9½ fathoms and her masts were still above water with the ship's pennant flying.

Fullam's statement that *Alabama* identified herself as the British steamer *Petrel* is confirmed by Low, by Kell, and by Semmes. In view of this it is of interest that Blake thought that the identification was for HMS *Vixen*, and another Union account said HBMS *Spitfire*.

Fullam's account of the battle with *Hatteras* was published as an appendix in *The Cruise of the Alabama and the Sumter*, 272–275. This limited publication of Fullam's Journal is, of course, in addition to the other partial publications of this Journal. As usual, the publishers used Fullam's material and did not bother to mention his name. For prize purposes the Confederates valued *Hatteras* at $160,000, but the Union cost figures amounted to $110,000.

Boats were immediately lowered and sent to her assistance, when an alarm was given that another steamer was bearing down for us. The boats were recalled and hoisted up, when it was found to be a false alarm. The order was then given, and the boatswain and his mates piped "All hands out boats to save life," and soon the prisoners were transferred to our ship, the officers under guard on the quarter deck and the men in single irons.

[74]

There were only 126 men in *Hatteras* at the time of the battle, but Fullam thought that the number was 129. ND, *FS*, III, 270. Lieutenant Commander Homer C. Blake and his ship's company, after debarking from *Alabama* at Kingston, Jamaica, returned to the United States in a merchant ship and were exchanged as prisoners of war. At the Brooklyn Navy Yard, a Court of Inquiry investigated the loss of *Hatteras* and exonerated Blake, saying that his actions and those of his officers and men in *Hatteras,* except for one officer and one man, were commendable. Blake was ordered to the command of the USS *Eutaw,* and later to the USS *Onondaga* and other commands before the end of the Civil War. *Onondaga* was a twin-screw, double-turreted ironclad steamer and a much more prestigious command than *Hatteras* or *Eutaw.*

The boats were then hoisted up, the battery run in and
secured, the main brace spliced–all hands piped down–
the enemy's vessel sunk–and we steaming quietly away,–
by 8.30. All having been done in less than two hours.

Frank Townshend, an Irish fiddler and wit, entertained his shipmates in the CSS *Alabama* with the following song which he wrote:

THE FIGHT OF THE "HATTERAS" AND "ALABAMA."

Off Galveston, the Yankee fleet secure at anchor lay,
Preparing for a heavy fight they were to have next day;
Down came the Alabama, like an eagle o'er the wave,
And soon their gunboat Hatteras had found a watery grave.

'Twas in the month of January; the day was bright and clear;
The Alabama she bore down; no Yankee did we fear:
Their Commodore he spied us; to take us long he burned;
So he sent the smartest boat he had, but she never back returned!

The sun had sunk far in the West when down to us she came;
Our Captain quickly hailed her, and asked them for her name;
Then spoke our First Lieutenant,—for her name had roused his ire,—
"This is the Alabama—now, Alabamas, fire."

Then flew a rattling broadside, that made her timbers shake;
And through the holes made in her side the angry waves did break;
We then blew up her engine, that she could steam no more—
They fired a gun to leeward, and so the fight was o'er.

So thirteen minutes passed away before they gave in beat;
A boat had left the Yankee's side, and pulled in for their fleet;
The rest we took on board of us, as prisoners to stay;
Then stopped and saw their ship go down, and then we bore away.

And now, to give our foes their due, they fought with all their might;
But yet they could not conquer us, for God defends the right;
One at a time the ships they have to fight us they may come,
And rest assured that our good ship from them will never run.

*In fact had it not been for the fact of having prisoners on board
we would have sworn nothing unusual had taken place, the
watch below quietly sleeping in their hammocks.*

*The conduct of our men, was truly remarkable. No flurry,
no noise, all calm and determined. The coolness displayed
by them could not be surpassed by any old veterans. Our
chief boatswains mate apparently in his glory. "Sponge" "Load
with cartridge" "Shell five seconds" "Run out" "Well, down
compressors" "Left traverse" "Well" "Ready 'X' Fire" "Thats
into you" "Damn you, that kills your pig." "That stops your
wind" &c. &c. was uttered as each shot was heard to strike
with a crash that nearly deafened you.*

Fullam's enthusiastic account of firing naval guns may be compared with
the official instructions in *Ordnance Instructions for the United States Navy,*
1866.

The other boatswains mate equally enjoying the affair.

The battle station of a boatswain's mate at that time in the United States
Navy was on the forecastle. Since such matters in the Confederate States
Navy were generally modeled upon the "Old Navy," this was very likely
the battle station of the boatswain mentioned by Fullam.

*As he got his gun to bear upon the enemy, he would take
aim and bang it would plug her. He exclaiming as each shot
told "Thats from the scum of England" "Thats a British pill
for you to swallow." The New York papers having once stated
that our men were the "scum of England."*

In addition to Fullam, there were only three Britishers among *Alabama's*
officers: John Low, Dr. David H. Llewellyn, and Henry Alcott. There was,
of course, some ground for the charge that *Alabama's* crew was recruited
chiefly from British subjects. For a new view of this, see the Introduction
of this book.

*All the other guns were served with equal precision. We were
struck seven times.*

Semmes said that not one of the shot holes in *Alabama* required plugging.

[76]

*Only one man being hurt during the engagement, and he
receiving only a slight flesh wound in the cheek. One shot
struck under the counter, penetrating as far as a timber, then
glancing off. A second struck the funnel, a third going through
the side, across the berth deck and into the opposite side,
another raising the deuce in the lamp room, the others lodging
in the coal bunkers. Taking a shell up and examining it, we
found it filled with sand instead of powder. The enemys fire
being directed chiefly toward our stern, the shots flying pretty
thick over the quarter deck near to where our Captain was
standing. As they came whizzing over him, he with usual
coolness, would exclaim "Give it to the rascals" "Aim low
men" "Dont be all night sinking that fellow." When for all
anything we knew, she might have been an iron clad or a ram.*

*On Commander Blake surrendering his sword he said that
"it was with deep regret he did it." Captain Semmes smacked
his lips, and invited him down in his cabin on Blake giving
his rank to Captain Semmes, who gave up his stateroom for
Blakes special use. The rest of the officers being accommodated according to their rank, in the ward room and steerages,
all having previously been paroled; the crew being placed
on the berth deck, our men sleeping anywhere so that the
prisoners might take their places.*

*Of the enemys loss we could obtain no correct accounts,
a difference of 17 being in their number of killed, the "Hatteras" having on board men she was going to transfer to
other ships. Their acknowledged loss was only two killed
and 7 wounded.*

LCDR. H. C. Blake to Gideon Welles, 21 January 1863, reported that
two men of *Hatteras'* crew were killed and five wounded. Sinclair gave
the same figures. There were only 126 men assigned to *Hatteras* at the
time of the battle, according to the official source. Fullam, however, said
mistakenly that *Hatteras* had 129 men.

*A boat had been lowered, just before the action, to board us;
as we anticipated and learnt afterwards, it pulled in for the
fleet and reached Galveston.*

The six men in the boat, who were preparing to board *Alabama*, escaped
capture and returned to their squadron.

From conversation with her first Lieut. I learnt that, as soon as we gave our name and fired our first broadside, the whole after division on board her left the guns, apparently paralyzed– it was some time before they recovered themselves.

The two ships were sometimes so close that a slight turn could have locked yardarm with yardarm. At such close range there was hardly a chance for the gunfire of either side to miss. The big difference was that *Hatteras'* projectiles struck only in *Alabama's* upper works, while *Alabama's* guns were depressed so that the projectiles crashed into *Hatteras'* hull and machinery.

The conduct of one of her officers was cowardly and disgraceful in the extreme. Some of our shells went completely through her before exploding; others burst inside, and set her on fire in three places. One went through her engines completely disabling her, another exploding in her steam chest, scalding all within reach. Thus was fought 28 miles from Galveston a battle,–though small, yet, the first yard arm action between two steamers at sea. She [Hatteras] was only inferior in weight of metal. Her guns being, 9 in number, viz:–4 thirty-two pdrs., 2 rifled thirty pdrs., carrying 68 lb shot (conical), 1 rifled twenty pdr. and a couple of small twelve pdrs.

As to *Hatteras'* battery, for conflicting evidence, see *ORN*, 2, I, 100; Boykin, 269; Soley, 196; ND, *FS*, III, 270–271. *Alabama* was much more formidable than *Hatteras*.

On account of the conflicting statements made by her officers we could never arrive at a correct estimate of her crew. Our prisoners numbered 17 officers and 101 seamen.

Low also said that *Alabama* took aboard from *Hatteras* 17 officers and 101 men, 118 in all. See also Blake's report. Two were killed in the engagement. Five were wounded and taken aboard *Alabama*. The six men in the lowered boat escaped and were never in *Alabama*. At the time of the action, there were 126 men in *Hatteras*, or 118 after the shooting began. *Alabama* suffered only one casualty, a man wounded in the cheek by a shell splinter.

We further learnt that the "Hatteras" was one of seven vessels sent to recapture Galveston, it being (although unknown to us) in the possession of our troops. We also

*found that the flag ship "Brooklyn" 22 guns, and the "Oneida"
9 guns, sailed in search of us; by their account of the course
they steered, the[y] could not fail to have seen us.*

The USS *Brooklyn* was a ship which in 1861 had pursued Semmes when he daringly took *Sumter* past the blockaders at the mouth of the Mississippi River, as recounted in Summersell, *The Cruise of CSS Sumter. Brooklyn* was larger, more costly, and more heavily armed than *Alabama,* but much slower. At the time of the *Sumter* episode, *Brooklyn's* commanding officer was Charles H. Poor, USN. When *Brooklyn* was first commissioned, 26 January 1859, her commanding officer was David G. Farragut, a captain at the time. The original cost of *Brooklyn* was $417,921. Fullam listed *Brooklyn* with 22 guns when she actually had 21.

The USS *Oneida* was a screw steamer with the rig of a three-masted schooner, and of 1,032 tons. She was brand-new, having been commissioned 28 February 1862. Union records agree with Fullam's nine guns, but add to it one inconsequential 12-pounder boat howitzer.

*13th. Strong S. E. breeze, and heavy sea. At 1.20 a sail was
reported right ahead. Made sail. On nearing her we hoisted
Yankee colours . She replied by hoisting English. We soon
recognized her to be the "Aggripina" homeward bound to
England. Fearing she would destroy our mail bag, we hauled
down, hoisting our own flag. Saluted and kept on our course.*

Since *Agrippina* was carrying mail from the CSS *Alabama,* it was feared that the mail would be destroyed if *Alabama* were mistaken for a Union warship. Sinclair said that the officers and men of *Alabama* tried to conceal from the *Hatteras* prisoners the past connection between *Agrippina* and *Alabama.*

*14th. [January 1863] Fresh gale and head seas. 5 p.m.
Sail reported on port bow. 6 p.m. Blew off steam, and set
reefed fore and aft sails.
15th. Gale continuing. 6 a.m. Hove to. With a heavy squall,
the wind chopped round to the westward. 2 p.m. Made sail
again.
16th. Blowing heavily. A frightful sea running. 3 a.m. Hove
to. 6.30 Made sail on her, keeping the screw turning with
2 lbs. of steam, and going a comfortable 14 knots. Wind and
sea moderating towards evening.
17th. Strong breeze from the Nd. [northward]. Took in
all square sails, increasing steam. 2.50 p.m. Two sails reported,*

one ahead, the other on lee bow; both steering to the north-
ward. At 3.30 came up with one, who on our hoisting Spanish
colours, replied with English. Wind freshening.

18th. Fresh gales. Squally with rain, E. N. E.

20th. Land right ahead, the western part of Jamaica. Pris-
oners overjoyed at the prospect of being released so soon.
Passed two or three vessels, we showing French and Spanish
colours. 5. Stood towards Port Royal. 5.55 Hoisted French
colours, and received the pilot on board. 7. Anchored in Port
Royal harbour. Received an official visit from the flagship.

21st. Our Commander waited upon the Governor, for
permission to land prisoners, and effect the necessary repairs
after our conflict. Permission was readily granted. As soon
as our arrival became known, the most intense excitement
prevailed. It is impossible to describe the hospitable welcome
we received. Every one placing their houses at our disposal.
Up to 9 p.m., visitors were constantly received, all expressing
a most hearty encouraging sympathy for our cause; and
speaking hopefully of our prospects.

In no earlier country was *Alabama* received with more enthusiasm than
in Jamaica. Yet there were special problems. Sinclair said that "At no time
during the cruise was our ship in such a state of confusion as during our
stay in Kingston." One problem was the hospitable islanders who tried
to ride every available boat that would take them for a visit aboard *Alabama.*
Also, setting ashore the officers and crew of the USS *Hatteras* was certainly
no routine procedure, and it was in Kingston that Clarence Randolph
Yonge defected to the enemy.

Still the same enthusiasm prevails. Visitors, of each sex and
every class coming on board. Officers and men going on shore
and receiving the most flattering attention. Hauled the brig
"Reindeer" of London alongside and commenced coaling;
repairing damages, caulking, &c. &c. 11 a.m. Paroled prisoners
and landed them ashore.

24th. Still coaling, receiving provisions, &c. A report is
circulating that two Federal cruisers are in the offing. Reported
to be the "San Jacinto" and the "Iroquois."

The CSS *Sumter* under Semmes had quite an adventure with CDR. James
S. Palmer and his three-year-old, 8-gun USS *Iroquois* in November 1861.
Palmer was blockading Semmes at Martinique and *Sumter* escaped with

an adroit ruse. Admiral David D. Porter, USN, later wrote of this episode, "Semmes . . . was too clever for Palmer. . . ."

25th. Sunday. 7.30 The English mail steamer left for St. Thomas. Fine light northerly air. Found that on the evening previous our Commander held a levee, when he made a speech that made a most favorable impression, and correcting many erroneous ones that had been circulating here. The conduct of our men was anything but what it should be, towards each other. One watch going on shore on the 21st and not returning until the police lent their assistance, thus causing considerable discontent amongst the rest of the men, some of whom had to be put in irons. The chief petty officer in irons also for being absent without leave.

According to Sinclair, members of the crew were having such a good time in Kingston that it was difficult to get personnel back on board to relieve the watch so that they could take their turn at shore leave. He added,

One is reminded of the old problem of ferrying over the river the goose, the fox, and the bag of corn; for no sooner is one lot delivered at the boat and another raid made up-town, than the prisoners break guard somehow and are up-town again. The writer, visiting a dance-hall after dark with a boat's crew, in quest of delinquents, was met at the threshold by a body of men from the English squadron backed by the lady participants in the ball, and good-naturedly but firmly informed that he could not come in, the visit being quite *mal à propos*. One of the ladies remarked, "Say, middy, come some other time. The tickets are limited at this ball; and besides, the company is select!" "Tell old 'Beeswax,'" said another persuasive maiden, "your old piratical skipper, to go to sea, burn some more Yankee ships, and come back. We'll give up the boys then, and you shall have your turn."

Semmes observed of this situation, "They . . . made heroes of all my fellows, and plied them with an unconscionable number of drinks. . . . given in their honor by the beaux and belles of Water Street."

7 hands left here.

The seven hands were the first of the many men who deserted the CSS *Alabama*. Besides Yonge, there were nine hands who deserted at Kingston: William Halford, Joseph Neal, David Roche (also spelled Roach in some of the records), Thomas Potter, Thomas Welch, John McAttee, Gustave Schwalbe, John Latham, and Valentine Mesner. Latham supplied the Union government with information on individual crew members which proved useful in editing the Fullam Journal.

[81]

*Circumstances of a painful nature compelled our Commander,
though reluctantly, to dismiss the paymaster from the ship
and service. After depriving him of his sword, &c., he was
sent from the vessel on shore. The alternative of remaining
on board, confined to his room, until the ship reached a
Confederate port was left him.*

In contrast with the many sailors who defected from *Alabama,* Clarence R. Yonge was the only officer who did so. Yonge was paymaster and had served under Captain James D. Bulloch in England before accompanying Bulloch to the commissioning of *Alabama.* Thus Yonge was handling papers for *Alabama* even before Semmes took command. Because of his defection, Yonge's name was carefully avoided by Semmes who seemed to think that to mention Yonge was to honor him. Yonge was the only one of *Alabama's* officers who was not verbally sketched by Sinclair, but Sinclair did comment on Yonge by name. Abundant information is available concerning Yonge because he was very active in serving as an informer to the United States State Department. What actually happened in Kingston was that Yonge was openly consorting with *Hatteras'* personnel after they had been released ashore and he also had been communicating with the United States consul in Kingston. Apparently Yonge decided to defect immediately upon arrival in Jamaica, or perhaps before *Alabama* reached Kingston.

*Until darkness set in we were delayed with visitors. At
9.25 p.m. got under weigh, and steamed slowly out of the
harbour. 9.20 Discharged pilot and steamed away to the
E. S. E.*

*26th. Fine. Moderate breeze. At noon saw a vessel on port
bow, at 1.30 came up with her; fired a blank cartridge and
hove her to. On boarding, she proved to be the barque
"Golden Rule" of and from New York to Aspinwall.*

Golden Rule was a 255-ton bark owned by the Panama Railroad Company. She sailed from New York 17 January 1863, and was captured nine days later off the coast of Haiti. *Golden Rule* had moved southward through the Windward Passage into Jamaica Channel while *Alabama* was moving eastward from the shores of Jamaica to the point off Haiti where Confederate lookouts saw the valuable prize. *Golden Rule* carried supplies of foodstuffs, patent medicines, and ships' rigging. The cargo of this bark was owned by the Pacific Mail Steamship Company and many others. Ship and cargo were insured by some ten different companies. No doubt some of the cargo was of neutral ownership, but the Confederate admiralty court found no consular certificates or other legal proof, and therefore *Golden Rule* and her cargo were condemned and burned. This burning in the

[82]

Jamaica Channel was in sight of the shores of Jamaica, and Haiti as well. Captain Peter H. Whiteberry of *Golden Rule* and his crew were duly turned over to Fullam's charge. The claims filed for the loss of this ship and cargo totaled $82,036.47. Kell valued *Golden Rule* at $112,000. The ship was eight years old at time of capture. She was bound for Aspinwall (Colón) with cargo for transhipment to California. Loss of *Golden Rule* resulted in vigorous protest by the owners and by Secretary of State William H. Seward via Charles Francis Adams to Earl Russell and the British government. *Foreign Affairs,* 1864, 1, 200, 250–251; *American Lloyds,* 1862, 162.

Having on board in addition to a general cargo,–the spars, standing and running rigging belonging to the U. S. brig of War "Bainbridge," she having lost them in a recent gale off Aspinwall. Some of the running rigging, besides some stores, we took from her, then set fire to her.

The USS *Bainbridge* was in the neutral waters of Aspinwall, Panama (Colòn) awaiting the arrival of spars and a full set of sails. A severe storm had assailed *Bainbridge* from 22 to 24 November 1862. This was the storm earlier mentioned by Fullam. *Bainbridge* lost all of her gun carriages, guns, powder and shot, as well as her sails and spars. *Golden Rule* was the ship that was taking materials for refitting *Bainbridge.* The fact that *Golden Rule* was burned, along with the refitting materials, delayed the operations of *Bainbridge* for some additional months. *Bainbridge* was finally refitted in Aspinwall and arrived in New York in May 1863. Only three months later (21 August 1863), *Bainbridge* capsized off Cape Hatteras and, except for one man, lost all hands.

From newspapers we learnt that the **Florida** *had run out of Mobile;*

While the CSS *Alabama* never entered a Confederate port, the CSS *Florida* under command of John Newland Maffitt was in Mobile Bay from 4 September 1862 until 17 January 1863. This was one of the most dramatic episodes in the Civil War, and was carefully recounted in Owsley, *Florida,* 34–49. ND, *FS,* distinguishes among the various Confederate vessels named *Florida,* which is useful because some other writers have confused the CSS *Florida* with other vessels of that name. For example, the CSS *Selma,* had earlier been named the CSS *Florida,* but was not much more than half the size.

of the sinking during a gale of the **Monitor,**

The USS *Monitor* under Commander J. P. Bankhead foundered off Cape Hatteras on 31 December 1862. This was the same vessel that fought the

[83]

CSS *Virginia* in Hampton Roads 9 March 1862 in the world's first battle of ironclads.

and of an unsuccessful attack by the enemy upon Vicksburg. Such a collection of good news gratified us exceedingly. Disrated the Master at Arms to seaman, by sentence of court martial. (For being absent without leave.)

27th. At 1.30 p.m. a schooner reported on port bow. 7.45 p.m. A sail discovered steering to the westward. On boarding she proved to be Spanish; reported having seen a fleet of seven U. S. vessels of war, a day or two previously, to the northward of Hayti. At 9.15 another sail seen; on her heaving to I boarded and took possession of the brigantine Chastelain *of Boston, from Guadaloupe to Cienfuegos, in ballast. Transferred prisoners, and set fire to the ship.*

The 293-ton brig *Chastelain* was commanded by James Warren and was owned by John S. Emery and eight others. In presenting claims after the Civil War, *Chastelain* was valued at $10,000, and the total claims presented amounted to $11,670.55. This included the ship's chronometer, valued at $150, and some $700 in gold. It is evident from these figures that *Chastelain* was sailing in ballast at the time of her capture. The Confederate prize evaluation was set upon *Chastelain* at $10,000 by Lt. John Low, making a total value of all of *Alabama's* prizes destroyed of $1,476,311. *Chastelain* had sailed 22 January 1863 from Basse-Terra, Guadelupe, headed for Cienfuegos, Cuba. Five days later, she was just off the coast of Santo Domingo near the mountainous little island of Alta Vela (meaning tall sail) when she came under the guns of *Alabama*. At the time of her capture, *Chastelain* was engaged in New England's historic triangular trade. She had just delivered a cargo of staves in Guadelupe and was on her way to Cuba to pick up a cargo of sugar and rum.

28th. [January 1863] Hugging the land pretty closely. 6 p.m. Anchored off the city of St. Domingo.

Historic Santo Domingo, present capital of the Dominican Republic, was the one-time home of Christopher Columbus and seat of the viceroyalty of Diego Columbus. Various narratives of the CSS *Alabama* give the reader a guided tour through the venerable city. *Alabama's* reason for making that port was to dispose of prisoners from *Chastelain* and *Golden Rule*. Kell misspelled *Chastelain*. So did Semmes. However, Semmes' mistake was typographical, as it is correctly spelled on another page. Other sources leave no doubt as to the proper spelling of *Chastelain*. Since Semmes' *Service Afloat* was first published in 1868 and Kell's book in 1900, the evidence here is one more straw indicating that Kell leaned heavily upon *Service Afloat* in prodding his own memory.

[84]

*A Yankee brigantine at anchor. Paroled and sent all prisoners
on shore. At 8 p.m. prisoners returned, stating that after dark
people were not allowed to land. By this time the port officials
came off, went on shore again and returned, and said that
under the peculiar circumstances in which we were placed,
our prisoners might be sent on board the government vessel
that night, undertaking to land them next morning.*

As *Alabama* stood in toward Santo Domingo, the pilot as usual came
aboard to take the ship into the shallow coastal waters and Semmes was surprised to discover that the pilot was an old acquaintance. When in 1846, the
USS *Porpoise* had stood in to Santo Domingo, Semmes was her first lieutenant
and this was the same pilot. Via the pilot, Semmes sent an official request
to the Spanish military governor ashore asking permission to land the
prisoners. This was the first time the Confederate flag had been flown in
Santo Domingo.

*29th. Received fresh provisions on board. At 9 a.m. got
under weigh, steering to the eastward. Previous to leaving
we heard that a Yankee fleet was cruising in the Mona
Passage, so everybody expected a brush before morning.*

Despite the rumor, *Alabama* headed for Mona Passage, between Santo
Domingo and Puerto Rico.

*Gunners mate disrated to seaman for quitting ship without
leave, pursuant to sentence of court martial.*
*30th. Fine. Moderate easterly breeze. Our usual good luck.
Passed through the passage without seeing a single vessel.
Gave [chase] at daylight to a schooner. Our Long. [19.30
north and 67.40 west]. Saw a large barque standing to the
westward. Carpenter's mate disrated to seaman, forfeiting all
pay and emoluments due him; for insolence and insubordination. Three seamen disrated for leaving the ship without
permission, all the offences having been committed at
Kingston. 3.30 p.m. Made all plain sail and triced up propellor.*
*Sunday. 1st. Feb. [1863] Fine fresh breeze. Read as usual
the Articles of War. Saw a sail from the masthead.*
*2nd. Saw a brigantine, which on boarding I found to be the
"Ida Abbott' of Tartola, from Bathurst, W. C. A. [West Coast
of Africa, presently Gambia], bound to New York. Passed as
the U. S. Str. Iroquois. In the afternoon some excitement
was caused by the appearance of a long low-masted rakish
looking craft. She hoisted what I took to be our private signal,*

[85]

*we answered it; she then hauled down and displayed their
flag, a Hamburgh one. On boarding we found her to be 46
days from Cardiff to New York. This noon an affair occurred,
which, so far as it resulted in itself, was comparatively a trifle;
–yet, might have entailed the most serious and disastrous
consequences upon us took place. It appears that through the
carelessness of those engaged in the Spirit room some liquor
was spilt upon a nearly naked light; which of course ignited
instantly. A timely application of blankets soon stopped it,
else the fire would have soon enveloped the whole after part
of the ship. As soon as the Captain was acquainted with it
he ordered all hands to be called to quarters, but ordered
the retreat as soon as he heard of it being extinguished.
The captain of the hold was placed in irons.*

James Higgs was captain of the hold. He enlisted 24 August 1862 as
one of the original crew. The captain of the hold was in charge of the space
below decks used for stowage of ballast, stores, and cargo.

*3rd. Fresh southerly wind. At 2.30 p.m. saw a vessel coming
towards us. We hoisted the Yankee flag, the stranger hoisting
the same. Hove her to. Boarded and took possession of the
schooner* Palmetto *of and from New York to Porto Rico, 10
days out, with lumber, provisions, &c. Took from her a
considerable quantity of crackers, cheese, &c. Removed
prisoners and set fire to prize.*

Palmetto was the first capture since leaving Santo Domingo. She was built
in Trenton, Maine, in 1860 by the King Brothers, and was a 172-ton schooner,
90 x 24.3 x 8.11. Claims filed for the loss of this vessel totaled $12,400.
The Confederates valued the schooner at $18,430. Under command of
Oren H. Leland, *Palmetto,* with a cargo of provisions, departed New York
23 January 1863. She was bound for San Juan, Puerto Rico. On 3 February
she was in position 27.20 north and 66.9 west, when the schooner unhappily
was sighted by *Alabama's* lookouts. *Palmetto* had more spirit and more
speed than many of the prizes. She showed her heels to the agile Confederate
for several hours. It is true that *Alabama* pursued her under sail alone,
having a fine breeze and being confident of overtaking the little schooner
without spending precious coal. When *Palmetto* was finally overtaken about
half after one o'clock, Fullam was the boarding officer. In admiralty proceedings aboard *Alabama*, Captain Oren H. Leland testified that he did not know
who owned the cargo, despite the written evidence that he was the charterer
of the vessel as well as the master. There was no documentation proving
neutral cargo. In support of his decision, Semmes cited 3 Phillimore, 605, and

[86]

1 Robinson, 1, 14, 19, 255, then condemned *Palmetto,* removed some of her supplies, and burned the remaining cargo along with the ship. In his tabulation of Maine ships destroyed by Confederate cruisers, Rowe (315–316) overlooked *Palmetto.*

Previous to the capture of Ariel, *the captains of prizes were in irons on deck, but after her capture they were allowed to feed in the steerages.*

4th. Chased a brigantine, proved to be a Spaniard.

5th. Cold N. E. winds. Saw two vessels towards evening; darkness coming on, no attempt was made to chase.

11th. Have only seen one vessel up to today. P.M. Boarded the schooner Hero *of and from Yarmouth, N. S. [Nova Scotia] to Barbadoes. Gave our name as the U. S. Str.* Dakotah.

The USS *Dacotah* is the correct, albeit old fashioned spelling of that warship which was named for the Dakota Indians. The ship was almost as large as *Alabama,* had been built in 1859 and, a short time before Fullam's reference to her, had been patrolling the West Indies in search of the CSS *Florida* and the CSS *Alabama.*

13th. Light S. S. W. breeze. 2 p.m. Sail reported standing to the S. E. To her we showed U. S. colours. She showing English ones, continued our course without speaking her. Strong northerly winds until the morning of the 17th when a succession of light winds [blew].

21st. [February 1863] At 7 a.m. the inspiriting and welcome cry of Sail ho *was heard from the masthead. All sail was made in chase. Chase bearing 1½ points on weather bow. By 10.30 two more vessels were seen. We then tacked ship and stood towards the other two. 11.30 Observed them signalling to each other, then, part company, each on a separate tack. We then stood for the ship hoisting Yankee colours. 12.30 Fired a blank cartridge. No notice being taken of it, another was fired, hoisting our own colours. Still no notice was taken of it. Steam was got up and the propellor lowered. The rifled gun crew were called to quarters, and a shot fired over her. The gun was loaded a second [time] and trained upon him, and its captain just going to pull the lockstring when she hove to. A boat was despatched with an officer and five men with instructions to make all sail and follow the Alabama, who immediately went after the other one. Coming near her, we fired a blank cartridge, which*

[87]

caused her at 3.30 to heave to. Boarded and on her Captain coming on board with his papers we found her to be the barque "Olive Jane" of Boston, 30 days from Bordeaux with a general cargo of wines, brandy, &c. &c. His crew and one passenger were sent on board our ship, and the barque set on fire.

The first of the two vessels boarded was *Golden Eagle,* and Fullam was the boarding officer and was made prize master of this vessel and instructed to remain nearby while *Alabama* turned to chase *Olive Jane. Olive Jane* was quickly overtaken and the usual admiralty proceedings were completed before the Confederates returned to *Golden Eagle* where Fullam was in control.

Olive Jane was a small bark of only 360 tons burden. Under command of Robert Kallock, she had sailed from Bordeaux 24 January 1863 bound for New York. She was in position 29.17 north and 45.15 west when on Saturday, 21 February, she was captured by *Alabama,* condemned, and burned. She made a grand blaze because of her inflammable cargo. The owners' claims were $66,110.41. The Confederates valued *Olive Jane* at $43,208. *Olive Jane* had a cargo of canned meats, olives, *pates de foi gras,* fruits, various delicasies and, most important, brandies and French wines. Semmes sent Sinclair aboard *Olive Jane* with very strict orders to see that not one bottle of liquor was slipped aboard *Alabama* by any of the crew. The crew ordinarily had a grog issue, but the supply was strictly in the hands of the officers. It has been noted that in Martinique and Jamaica drunken men sometimes got out of control, and drinking versus discipline was a common complaint made by the ship's officers. Sinclair was very proud of the fact that this did not happen with the cargo of *Olive Jane.* Kell said that not a basket of champagne nor yet a bottle of brandy was brought aboard *Alabama* from that particular ship. Had there been only five bottles of liquor, no doubt these would have been confiscated with alacrity, but a whole cargo of booze in the hands of *Alabama's* crew was a frightening prospect.

Stood for the other prize. He proved to be the ship "Golden Eagle" of New Bedford, from Chinchas to Cork, laden with guano. Removed the prisoners and applied the match.

Golden Eagle was a very large and important ship. This prize was of 1,121 tons and the cargo of guano was needed for the wartime growing of wheat in the North. The owners' total claims presented for the loss of this vessel amounted to $113,522.50. Kell placed the Confederate prize value of $61,000 on *Golden Eagle.* This vessel was numbered 27 of the ships destroyed by *Alabama.*

When *Alabama* confronted *Golden Eagle,* it was evident that the commerce raider had moved deeply enough into the South Atlantic Ocean to encounter ships cruising between New England and the ports of the Pacific. Under command of Edward A. Swift, *Golden Eagle* had departed Chincha Islands, off the coast of Peru, bound for Cork, Ireland. When confronted by *Alabama,* she had been at sea for a longer time than most of *Alabama's* prizes. *Golden Eagle* was built in Kennebunk, Maine, by J. and G. P. Titcomb in 1852, according to *American Lloyds, 1862,* and the fact is mentioned here because the vessel was omitted by Rowe, 315–316, in his generally accurate list of Maine-built vessels which were destroyed by Confederate raiders. *Golden Eagle* was the specific subject of complaint in letters passing among William H. Seward, Charles Francis Adams, and Earl Russell.

Having put the torch to *Olive Jane, Alabama* returned to her other prize *Golden Eagle,* then under command of Fullam who had instructions to stay nearby. Finding *Golden Eagle* a lawful prize by admiralty decision, the crew of the prize was transferred, along with her flag and chronometers, and she was fired. As *Alabama* left the scene of her captures, on one side lay *Olive Jane* and on the other was *Golden Eagle,* both wrapped in flames that cast a lurid red glow over the heavens and across the waters, while officers and crew aboard the raider watched in solemn silence.

Shipped 2 men.

The two men shipped were Jacob Verbot and Jean Veal, both ordinary seamen.

8.55 p.m. Blew off steam and hoisted the propellor.
23rd. This morn. three vessels in sight ahead. Made all sail in chase. Light northerly airs. 11.15 There being no wind got up steam and lowered propellor, giving chase to a large ship right ahead. At 12 came up with her, hoisting Yankee colours, the chase hoisting English, dipping it to us. We then hoisted the Confederate ensign, the ship dipping to it also, the male passengers cheering and ladies waving handkerchiefs. On boarding she proved to be the ship "Prince of Wales" from Melbourne to London, 80 days out.

Prince of Wales was the largest of the English vessels referred to at this time by Fullam. She was an Australia-to-England packet. *Alabama* received from her an Australian newspaper that told of the proceedings in the parliament of Australia and also about the Gold Rush down under, but had little or no news of the American Civil War.

Gave her steam again and chased another, who on

boarding proved to be the English barque "Charles Lambert" from Chile to Swansea. Chased another who on boarding proved to be the French barque "Gil Blas" from Buenos Ayres to Havre.

That Fullam's spelling of Buenos Aires was correct in his day is attested by Blunt, 556.

Sent on board her two men, natives of France, taken prisoners on board the "Olive Jane." Exchanged colours with another English vessel. At 3 [p.m.] hoisted propellor. Made sail and at 3.30 hove to. 10 p.m. Made sail.

24th. 2.45 p.m. Sail reported on weather bow. In reply she showed French colours. Chased another who on boarding was found to be a Portuguese brig, bound to Lisbon.

This brig led *Alabama* a merry chase for several hours. When finally she was overtaken and boarded, she proved to be the Portuguese brig *Oporto* en route from Pernambuco to Lisbon with a cargo of sugar and hides.

This day, Boatswains Mate Harwood and fireman McFadgens term of service expired.

These two were the only members of the crew who were paid off and sent home when their enlistments expired at sea, being honorably discharged. George Harwood had earlier served in the British Navy and later enlisted as one of the first members of *Alabama's* crew, 24 August 1862. He was paid off and discharged, 27 February 1863. Later he served as boatswain in the CSS *Shenandoah,* the Confederate cruiser which finally ranked among the three highest in damage to Union commerce. James McFadgen was, like Harwood, an Englishman from Liverpool who had enlisted the same day as Harwood and had served from the start of *Alabama's* cruise.

25th. Fresh S. W. breeze. Two sails reported, one ahead and the other abeam. Coming up with one, she showed Dutch colours. Made for the other fellow. Coming up and boarding her I found she was the English brig "Cedar," Guayaquil to London. Reduced sail to topsails and jib. At midnight a large sail was reported running before the wind. Made her out to be a fourmaster. Called all hands to quarters, got the guns ready for loading and hailed him, his answer however being scarcely audible; we announced our name, and ordered him to heave to. On boarding it was found to [be] the steamship "Sarah Sands" from India to England, 140 days out.

Sarah Sands was boarded by Fullam. She proved to be a four-masted steamship of British registry on a voyage to Falmouth. She refused to transport to England the two sailors, George Harwood and James McFadgen, whose enlistments had expired.

Secured the battery and piped down.

26th. Moderate W. S. W. breeze. Two vessels in sight. Stood towards one. By 11 six vessels in sight. Saw 4 more towards evening. Boarded one who proved to be a Hamburgher. Exchanged colours with many vessels. All English and French.

27th. Eight vessels in sight. Exchanged colours with a Portuguese brig. Saw a ship and a brig exchanging signals. Coming up with the ship, we found by signal that she was the "Henry" of St. John, N. B. [New Brunswick] In answer to our signal we found that the ship ahead was the "Washington" of New York, Callao to Cork. Made sail in chase. Fired a blank cartridge, and hoisting our own colours, no notice being taken of it, a shot was dropped within five feet of his stern. She then hove to. Boarding, we found our information respecting her to be true. Her cargo proving neutral she was ransomed, on agreeing to take our prisoners. After paroling them they were transferred and the vessel allowed to proceed on her course.

Washington, a ship under command of Joseph G. White, and owned by William T. Frost and other Northern merchants, was fair game except for one fact: her cargo of guano from the Chincha Islands belonged to the Peruvian government and was consigned to an agent in Antwerp. The neutral cargo saved the ship. Captain White signed a ransom bond for $50,000 and agreed to transport the prisoners aboard *Alabama*.

The "Henry" being a suspicious looking craft was boarded and found to be what they represented themselves to be. Evening. Two vessels in sight. 10.30 Another seen on lee bow. 11.15 Hailed and ordered him to heave to. On boarding I found her to be the English ship "Glendover," Foo Choo to London, with a valuable cargo of tea, silks, &c. Discharged and transferred the two men whose term of service had expired, to the "Glendover," her Captain agreeing to land them in England.

28th. Light airs. Two vessels seen to the S. E. Signalled one, the English ship "Schomberg," Sourabaya [Surabaya in

Indonesia] to Amsterdam. Passed as the U. S. Str. "Dacotah."
Signalled the other, the English barque "Three Bells," South
Australia to London. Gave our name to her as the U. S. Str.
"Iroquois."

The USS *Iroquois* ranked with the USS *Dacotah* as a favorite alias of *Alabama*.

5 p.m. Two more in sight. 7 p.m. I boarded the French ship
"Alphonse Cezard," Batavia to Nantes. During the night saw
two vessels.
1st. March [1863]. 6.30 a.m. Hove to, boarded, and took
possession of the Yankee ship "Berthia Thayer" of Rockland,
[from] Callao to Cork. Having a neutral cargo on board, she
was ransomed and allowed to proceed on her voyage.

Bethiah Thayer was an 890-ton ship of Rockland, Maine, built in Thomaston, Maine, by McLoon and Williams in 1856. At the time of her capture by *Alabama,* 1 March 1863, her commanding officer was Thomas Mitchell Cartney. Owners of the ship were William McLoon and Horace Williams. The cargo was documented as being owned by neutrals, so *Bethiah Thayer* was released on ransom bond for $40,000. *Bethiah Thayer,* like *Washington,* was loaded with guano owned by the Peruvian government. Thus far, *Alabama* had boarded three ships having cargoes of guano from Chincha Islands via Callao: *Golden Eagle, Washington,* and *Bethiah Thayer.* Of the three, only *Golden Eagle* was burned and the other two released on ransom bonds.

A suspicious looking barque with the English flag at her peak,
hove in sight. Fresh S. W. breeze. Set our flying mainsail,
both vessels crowding every stitch [of canvas] upon them.
At 4.30 p.m., after a most exciting chase we came up with
her. By signal we found her to be the "William Edward,"
Bahia to Liverpool. At first we called our vessel the U. S. Str.
"Ticonderoga."

The USS *Ticonderoga* was then a brand-new ship, having been launched in October 1862. Larger than *Alabama, Ticonderoga* was a screw steamer with the following characteristics: tonnage of 1,533, dimensions: 237 x 38.2 x 17.10, and a maximum speed of 11 knots.

After obtaining some slight information from her, we an-
nounced our real name. 5.30 Passed an Oldenburg brig. 8 p.m.
A large barque hove in sight. After an hours chase fired a gun,
she not heaving to, came down to him and hailed him; after

repeated hailings, she hove to. On boarding I found her to be the barque "Nile" of London, from Akyab to London, 109 days out. He corroborated a statement made by a ship, some days ago, to the effect that a U. S. vessel of war was in the South Atlantic. Supposed to be the "Ino" by us.

The USS *Ino* retained the name which she bore as a merchant vessel. She was a clipper ship acquired by the United States Navy in 1861 and was no match for the CSS *Alabama*. Earlier *Ino* had, however, more success than most Union vessels in several encounters with Semmes in the CSS *Sumter*. At the time when Fullam supposed *Ino* to be in the South Atlantic, however, she was en route from St. Helena for New York, under command of Acting Master James M. Williams, and was indeed searching for the CSS *Alabama* and the CSS *Florida*.

2nd. Light winds. Daylight, sighted a large ship steering toward us. At 6 boarded and took possession of the ship "John A. Parks" of Hallowell, New York to Buenos Ayres, with a cargo of lumber, &c. Transferred [to Alabama] her Captain, his wife, and crew, also some stores, and set fire to prize.

John A. Parks, under Captain John S. Cooper, was a ship of 1,047 tons of Hallowell, Maine, owned by Henry Cooper and others. She had sailed from New York with a cargo of lumber, 11 February 1863, bound for Montevideo. On 2 March she was boarded, condemned, and burned by *Alabama* (position 29.15 north and 38.20 west). The case of *John A. Parks* was a knotty one for Semmes' admiralty proceedings because there was considerable documentation claiming that the cargo was neutral. Semmes finally decided that the documents were fraudulent, and ordered the ship and cargo burned. She was number 28 of the ships destroyed by *Alabama*. Lt. Kell valued her at $66,157. The total claims filed in the *Alabama* Claims amounted to $126,517.50.

4 p.m. chased another. Hoisted the U. S. ensign to her, she replying with English. At 6.30 I boarded and found her to be the barque "Miss Nightingale" of Sunderland, Columbo to London, her Captain agreeing to take, the Captain, wife, and two boys, and land them in England.

Miss Nightingale was probably named for Florence Nightingale (1820–1910) who had become famous during the Crimean War. The reference to the captain was to the master of *John A. Parks,* J. S. Cooper.

From this vessel received information that a Yankee barque had passed them a few hours previously.

3rd. Light westerly winds. Saw four vessels but did not chase any. Hoisted U. S. colours to a brigantine, who, however, did not reply. Steering to the S. & Ed.

6th. [March 1863] Light E. S. E. wind. Cloudy. 10 a.m. Sail discovered on weather bow. Tacked ship in chase. Boarded and found her to be a Spaniard from Santander. Gave our name as the U. S. Str. "Dacotah."

7th. Light E. S. E. wind. 10 a.m. Sail reported to windward running. Hoisted U. S. colours, chase showed English. Hove her to by signal. On boarding found it to be the English brig "Elleanor," London to Bermuda with government stores. Our name, the Yankee steamer "Dacotah." Her crew rather jocose at our Yankee losses.

The boarding party brought back from *Eleanor* some English newspapers reporting that the British parliament was proceeding quietly and keeping aloof from the American Civil War.

8th. Sunday. Mustered as usual. Strong E. winds. Exchanged colours (Yankee) with an English barque, and a Norwegian barque and schooner. Very strong winds to the 14th.

Under reefed topsails, &c. We were considerably startled at 11.30 by the lookout singing out, "Sail ho, close aboard us Sir." Our helm was immediately placed aport, and we just sheered clear of a large ship, running to the northd. Ere, however, it had been done, the fact had been communicated to the Captain, who ordered, "All hands to quarters." All sail was made, and the ship bore round in chase. Beat the retreat at 12. At 3 a.m. of the 15th came up with the chase, fired a blank cartridge, and ordered him to heave to. On boarding, and her Captain coming on board with his papers, she was found to be the ship "Punjaub" of Boston, with a general cargo, from Calcutta to London. Her cargo being English owned, she was ransomed, taking with her the prisoners taken from the "John A. Parks."

In the log of *Punjaub* for Friday, 12 December 1862, Captain Lewis F. Miller stated, " . . . having all the Cargo on board—unmoored Ship and dropped down to Garden Reach—just below Botanical Gardens Landing—within the bounds of Calcutta." On 14 March 1863 as *Punjaub* continued on her voyage to London, her log entry prosaically recorded a dramatic event as follows, " . . . were hove to by C. S. Alabama—R. Semmes—At 3 AM were Captured—At 5 AM Released on Ransom Bond $55,000 dollars—20 Passengers sent Onboard—Boarded in Lat. 8.40 & Long. 31.45 West." Captain

Miller's remarks on the subject, at least in *Punjaub's* log, did not extend beyond the few words quoted in this footnote. On other subjects the remarks were more extensive. During the week prior to contact with *Alabama*, *Punjaub* had been boarded by a boat from the Portuguese brig *Relampago*, and spoken by the American bark *Lucy A. Nickels* and the British bark *Bride of the Seas*. After Captain Miller executed the ransom bond to his Confederate captors, witnessed in the usual manner by *Alabama's* clerk, W. Breedlove Smith, *Punjaub* continued on her way to England, arriving at Gravesend Dock, 23 April 1863. A fact of interest about *Punjaub* was that one of her owners was Thomas B. Wales and another was Thomas B. Wales, Jr., members of a family who had already suffered loss when *Alabama* burned as a prize the vessel *Thomas B. Wales*. Yet more remarkable was the fact that *Punjaub* on 3 September 1863, for a second time was captured by *Alabama*, was boarded by Fullam, identified, and released. Most of the Yankee ships seized by *Alabama* did not survive to be caught again. On her first seizure when the ransom bond was signed, 15 March 1863, *Punjaub* was the seventh ship to be ransomed: *Tonawanda* ($80,000), *Baron de Castine* ($6,000), *Union* ($1,500), *Ariel* ($261,000), *Washington* ($50,000), and *Bethiah Thayer* ($40,000). *Punjaub*, plus the six preceding ships ransomed, totaled $493,500.

16th. Light N. E. [breeze]: Fine. 6.30 a.m. Descried a sail on weather bow, hauled up for her. At 8 [a.m.] by signal, found her to be the ship "Hermione" of Liverpool, from Mauritius to Cork.

Hermione confirmed the growing suspicion aboard *Alabama* that Union merchantmen were avoiding the paths of the sea previously taken by ships, according to the charts of Matthew Fontaine Maury, the great pathfinder in oceanography. Instead, Yankee ships were seeking routes which were more time-consuming but also less threatened by Confederate raiders.

Passed as the "Dacotah."

21st. Until noon this day we had a succession of light moderate N.E. winds. At 11.30 a.m., three sails in sight steering to the southward. Made sail in chase, one showed Dutch colours; darkness prevented us making out the others.

22nd. Heavy rains and light winds until noon, when it cleared up. Three vessels in sight. Exchanged colours with one; an English barque.

23rd. Heavy rains. At 10.30 a.m. hoisted Dutch colours to a large ship standing northerly. She replied with the Stars and Stripes. Of course we invited her Captain on board with his papers, by which we found that she was the ship "Morning

Star" of Boston, Calcutta to London, with a general cargo. The cargo proving neutral; she was ransomed.

Morning Star was carrying a neutral cargo from one British port to another, and therefore had to be released on ransom bond in a situation directly parallel to that of *Punjaub*. *Morning Star* was captured in position 2.8.10 north and 26.8.5 west. The ransom bond was signed for $61,750, making the total for all ransom bonds exacted by *Alabama* to this date $555,250.

1 p.m. Four vessels in sight. Exchanged Yankee colours with an English barque. Bore away for a schooner. At 5 [p.m.] chase answered with U. S. colours. Boarded and took possession of the schooner "Kingfisher," whaler, of New Bedford with 20 bls. of oil, having (fortunately for them) transferred two cargoes of oil to neutral vessels, for shipment home, a short time previously.

Kingfisher was a small (120-ton) whaling schooner of Fairhaven, Massachusetts, commanded and in part owned by Thomas F. Lambert. She was built in Kingston, Massachusetts with dimensions of 78.9 x 21.2 x 8.1. *Kingfisher* sailed from Fairhaven, 21 July 1861, bound on a whaling voyage. Concerning the capture of *Kingfisher*, Captain Thomas F. Lambert gave a detailed account. About 2:00 p.m. on 23 March 1863, a lookout in *Kingfisher* reported a sail. She was soon recognized as a steamer flying the Stars and Stripes, and apparently an American warship. Four and a half hours later, the warship had closed the distance to about half a mile, and sent a boat alongside the whaler. This was the boarding party presumably under command of Fullam, but Lambert did not mention the name of the boarding officer. The boarding officer told Lambert that he should take his papers and repair to the CSS *Alabama*. In Confederate admiralty proceedings, *Kingfisher* was condemned.

Lt. Kell was ordered to remove from the whaler whatever supplies were needed by *Alabama*. Kell's men took nine barrels of beef and pork, some flour, and a few other things. Meantime, the members of *Kingfisher's* crew (all Portuguese except Captain Lambert) were taken aboard the raider and placed in irons. Kell took a party of men and set fire to the whaler, then in position 1.26 north and 26.30 west. *Kingfisher*, number 29 of the ships destroyed by *Alabama*, was valued at $2,400 by Lt. Kell, making a new total of $1,667,506 for vessels destroyed. In the *Alabama* Claims proceedings, owners of the vessel valued her at $7,000, and the claims filed totaled $31,952.17.

Kingfisher was burned very close to the equator at nightfall during an exceptionally severe thunderstorm. Of the scene, Sinclair wrote,

> The little craft, though oil-soaked, blazed by fits and starts. In the lull of passing rainsqualls, the flames would shoot mast-head high, seeming to play at hide-and-seek with the vivid lightning, anon shrinking beneath a drenching shower, leaving nature to keep up the pyrotechnic display,—a weird-like spectacle.

[96]

[Kingfisher] *Reported having left the U. S. Ship of War "Ino" at Ascension a fortnight ago. Our fellows delighted at the prospect of a brush with her.*

Bahia de la Ascension is on the Caribbean side of the Yucatan Peninsula not far south of Yucatan Channel.

25th. Light airs. Saw several vessels yesterday. Seven in sight today. At 11 a.m. boarded the English ship "Pizzaro" [Pizarro], Liverpool to Valparaiso, 37 days out. At 2.30 I boarded the English brig "Isabella," Liverpool to Melbourne. A large double top-sail yard ship being to leeward, the Captain of the "Isabella" told me he thought it was the Yankee ship "Eastern State." We immediately made all sail in chase. Soon three vessels, two ships and a barque, were seen. At 5 [p.m.] we hoisted Yankee colours, both ships hoisted the same. Boats were lowered, one under M. M. Evans,

Fullam knew very well that Evans' name was James, but he used M. M. to indicate his grade. Master's Mate James Evans ranked just junior to Fullam. Evans was a bar pilot from South Carolina who had been appointed acting master's mate on 29 July 1862. His ability to recognize the nationality of vessels from extreme distances was legendary among the ship's company of *Alabama*. It was most unusual for a steerage officer like Evans to spend so much time as a lookout, but it was because of his unusual skill in distinguishing between Yankee and foreign vessels. Evans took great pride in his ability to speak with authority in selecting legitimate prizes at a time when there was a premium to a predator sailing under false colors.

boarding and taking possession of the ship "Nora" of Boston, Liverpool to Calcutta, laden with salt.

William H. Seward wrote a position paper to Charles Francis Adams 6 October 1863, concerning specifically *Alabama's* burning of *Nora*. In Seward's *Diplomatic History*, he showed the case of *Nora* and asserted that his position paper on the case was a foundation of the *Alabama* Claims. Protests had been made earlier to Seward and Adams, and through them to Lord John Russell, but in the position letter of 6 October 1863 Seward was instructing Adams how to reply to Russell's request to Adams that no more claims concerning commerce raiders be presented to him. Seward said that the "building, armament and equipment, and expedition" of the CSS *Alabama* "was one single criminal intent." The United States secretary of state said further that the British government was given adequate notice of the building of the CSS *Alabama*, and Seward held, " . . . that the British government is justly responsible for the damages which the peaceful, law-abiding citizens of the United States sustain by the depredations of the Alabama.

[97]

I cannot, therefore, instruct you to refrain from presenting the claims which you have now in your hands of the character indicated." The claims in Adams' hands were for the burning of the schooner *Nora*.

Lt. Kell's evaluation of *Nora* for the purpose of prize payments to the ship's company of *Alabama* was $76,636, and the claims later presented by the owners of the schooner in the *Alabama* Claims amounted to $83,500. The *Alabama* Claims Court allowed claims for $74,603.10, including legal interest from the date that *Nora* was burned until the date of the payment of the claims. The cost of *Nora* when new was $60,000, and the judgment rendered added to this figure payments for freight,producing the figure $74,603.10. This figure did not include insurance payments previously received by the owners. The explanation is given here because it represents the problems involved in 1972 in determining the value of a ship in 1863.

The commanding officer of *Nora* was Charles E. Adams and the ship was owned by George B. Upton and George B. Upton, Jr. *Nora's* cargo of salt, mentioned by Fullam, was really neutral, in the frank opinion of Captain Semmes. There were also documents among the ship's papers indicating neutral ownership of the salt and declaring it to be the property of a British subject, W. N. de Mattos of London. The certificate, however, was not signed by any consul in the usual manner, was not sworn to by anyone, and was in the opinion of Semmes, who was a punctilious practitioner of international law, " . . . a more awkward attempt to cover a cargo than any of my Yankee friends of New York or Boston had ever made." Among the papers of the prize *Charles Hill,* captured at the same time as *Nora,* was a letter from Franklin Percival, captain of the ship, to the owners (one of whom was Charles Hill) requesting that Hill and his partners, " . . . have your bills of lading endorsed as English property, and have your cargo certified by the British Consul." Thus the judgment of the Confederate admiralty court to burn was held despite the fact that both ships carried neutral cargoes from one neutral port to another neutral port, and the decision turned upon a technicality.

The other on boarding I found to be the ship "Charles Hill" of Boston, Liverpool to Monte Video, laden with salt. The barque showed Spanish colours, but suspecting he was a Yankee we made sail in chase, prizes [Nora and Charles Hill] following. Boarding her, she was found to be bona fide Spanish. About 35 tons of coal besides a quantity of provisions was taken from both ships. This occupied us until the evening of the 26th, when both were set fire to. The Captains of each asserting that their cargoes were English owned, but having no papers to prove it, they of course said no more about it.

Fullam's boarding party brought the master and crew of *Charles Hill* to *Alabama* as usual, and the case ran parallel to that of *Nora,* as indeed both ships, as noted by Fullam, were in company carrying cargoes of salt from Liverpool to Montevideo. (Monte Video may seem to be semi-literate spelling, yet let it be said for Fullam that his spelling was standard for the day, as witness Blunt, 551–562, who used the same spelling in his 1850 edition.) *Charles Hill* was built in Newburyport, Massachusetts, by John Currier, Jr. Dimensions of this 699-ton ship were: 150 x 31.10 x 23. She was a smaller and less valuable vessel than *Nora*. *Charles Hill* was valued by Lt. Kell at $28,450. The owners of the ship (*Charles Hill* and others) filed claims for the vessel at $32,000.

Fullam's work as boarding officer was described in detail by Franklin Percival who was captain of *Charles Hill*.

Statement of Franklin Percival, late master of the ship Charles Hill.

On this 27th day of April, A. D. 1863, before me, the undersigned consul of the United States of America for Pernambuco and the dependencies thereof, personally appeared Franklin Percival, late master of the ship *Charles Hill*, who, being by me duly sworn according to law, doth depose and state as follows:

The ship *Charles Hill*, of Boston, of which I was master, was a vessel of 699 tons registered measurement. She was owned by Charles H. Tripp and others, of Boston, and was built at Newburyport in the year 1850. I sailed from Liverpool in command of the said ship on the 12th day of February last past, bound for Montevideo. The ship's cargo consisted of 699 tons of salt, shipped by H. E. Falk, of Liverpool, and consigned to Green, Montevideo. My crew on leaving Liverpool consisted of 17 persons, officers and seamen. One of the seamen, viz, John Ryan, fell from aloft and died about nine days after leaving Liverpool; besides this, nothing of importance occurred until the 25th day of March last past. On that day, being then in latitude 1° 23' N. and longitude 26° 30' W., at 2 o'clock p.m. a steamship was discovered making toward us. At this time the ship *Nora*, of Boston, was near us; we knew her, having exchanged signals the previous day. About 4:30 o'clock p.m. the steamship was between the ship *Charles Hill* and the ship *Nora*, and only about a quarter of a mile distant from either. We had previously discovered that it was an armed vessel, and now when near us, he ran up the American ensign, and at the same [time] I set my colors. He then sent a boat to my ship in charge of a master's mate, whose name I afterwards learned was Fullam. This person informed me that my ship was a prize to the Confederate steamship *Alabama*, and ordered me to report myself, with my papers, on board that vessel. On my arrival on board of the *Alabama* I was shown to the cabin and exhibited my papers to Captain Semmes. Captain Semmes said to me, "I suppose that you know enough of the rules of warfare to know that you are a prize." My papers showed that one-third of the freight money had been paid in advance. The captain's clerk asked if I had any of the freight money on board, to which I answered in the negative. He then asked me if I really believed the cargo to be British property. I told him that I had no doubt that it was. He wrote down his questions and my answers, and administered to

[99]

me an oath, in which I declared my answers to be true to the best of my knowledge and belief, and to which I subscribed my name. I was then permitted to return to my ship, where I remained during the night. On the morning of the 26th of March I was sent on board the *Alabama,* with my trunk, which was at once searched. During that and the following day the ship's crew, the small stores, and about 10 tons of coal were taken on board the *Alabama* from my ship. On the evening of the 27th of March, at about 8 o'clock, my ship was set on fire by order of Captain Semmes, the order being given in my hearing. About this time I saw that the ship *Nora* was also on fire. From this time we were prisoners on board the *Alabama.*

On the 4th day of April the *Alabama* captured the ship *Louisa Hatch.* A prize crew was put on board of her, and she sailed in company with the *Alabama* toward the island of Fernando de Noronha, where we arrived on the 10th instant, and both of the vessels were anchored within a mile of the land. A part of the prisoners were then employed in taking coal from the *Louisa Hatch* to the *Alabama.* This occupied about four days. On the 15th instant two whaling vessels hove in sight and laid off the island, the captains of which came on shore in their boats for provisions. Upon this, Captain Semmes weighed anchor in the *Alabama* and stood out under steam and captured both vessels within two hours after leaving the anchorage and at a distance of, to the best of my judgment, about 3 miles from the land. One of the vessels was immediately set on fire, the other, namely, the brig *Kate Cory,* was towed by the *Alabama* to the anchorage within 1 mile of the land. On the 16th all the prisoners and their baggage were searched, and were then sent on board the brig *Kate Cory* and were told that they would be allowed to go whither they might choose. We had not been on board more than two hours when the captain's clerk came on board and gave us the alternative of signing a parole, promising not to take up arms against the Confederate States unless first regularly exchanged, or to go back on board the *Alabama.* All signed the parole, and then were ordered on shore with their baggage. The prisoners, to the number of about 109 persons, went to the house of the commandante of the island where we were provided for. On the 17th of the present month the ship *Louisa Hatch* and brig *Kate Cory* were put under sail and taken to the distance of about 4 miles from the land and set on fire. This occurred in the evening, and I can not speak positively as to the distance. Both vessels continued burning through the night and next morning nothing was seen of them. On the 21st instant the crews of the ships *Charles Hill, Nora, Louisa Hatch,* and schooner *Kingfisher,* as well as the masters of said vessels, were put on board the Brazilian schooner *Tergipano,* for the purpose, as we were told, of being sent to Pernambuco. The order to go on board this vessel came through a Portuguese sailor, who acted as interpreter, and who said it was the order of the commandante of Fernando de Noronha. About 6 o'clock p.m. of the 21st instant we set sail and proceeded in the said schooner *Tergipano* for Pernambuco, where we arrived on the 26th of the present month, after a voyage necessarily attended with the greatest discomforts, as we were 61 in number and the schooner had no conveniences for carrying so many persons, being only 61 tons measurement. The consul of the United States residing at Pernambuco came on board the schooner soon after our arrival and at once accorded his protection. And further this deponent said not.

FRANKLIN PERCIVAL.

10 hands shipped.

The ten men were recruited from the combined crews of *Nora* and *Charles Hill*. They were: Joseph F. Minor, John Hughes, Christian Olsen, William H. McClennan, Albert Hyer, Peter Jackson, William Nordstrom, Fred Myers, John Benson, and Charles Coles. All of these men were ordinary seamen. Five of the ten later deserted, four of them after six months and one after a year. Four (Olsen, McClennan, Myers, and Benson) served in *Alabama* to the final sinking of the ship in 1864 by the USS *Kearsarge*. The one remaining recruit from the salt ships, Joseph F. Minor, became third officer aboard the CSS *Tuscaloosa*, *Alabama's* commerce-raiding daughter whose adventures will be described later.

At the time of the ten enlistments into the Confederate States Navy from the two Yankee ships, *Alabama* was much in need of recruits. The actual recruiting was largely done by *Alabama's* enlisted men, eager to add more sailors to help with the work load. Bearing in mind that seafaring men, then and now, have a more international attitude than most landsmen, the rebel recruiters had enticing facts to dangle before the eyes of impoverished and usually improvident mariners. Pay in *Alabama* was double. The pay was in gold. Grog was issued twice a day and in generous quantities. Tobacco was abundant and the smoking lamp was often lighted (sometimes dangerously). Rations were generous. Above all, there was the glittering prospect of prize money, the share of each man possibly running into thousands of dollars. Even at this point *Alabama* had quite a bag of prizes. *Nora* was number 30 of the ships destroyed by *Alabama,* and *Charles Hill* was number 31. With the destruction of *Charles Hill,* exclusive of the ransom bonds (which were supposed obviously to add to the amount), the total value placed by the Confederates on prizes destroyed by *Alabama* to this date was $1,772,592. Only half of the value of a prize was to be awarded by the Confederate government. The number of officers and men varied from time to time and the amount of prize money that was supposed to go to each recipient varied by rank and other circumstances. Nevertheless, if we take 26 officers and 122 men and divide this equally into one-half of the official Confederate value of the prizes destroyed (although, of course, the money was not to be divided equally), the average would have been $5,988, and this was exclusive of the money from ransom bonds. The whole of the ransom bond money was allowable for prize money. Actually, as events proved, the Union lost 55 vessels to the CSS *Alabama* and of these 53 were destroyed. Also, there were nine that were ransomed. Confederate value placed upon Union ships destroyed was $4,613,914. When to this the ransom bond money was added, the value was $5,176,164. Eager salesmen could have taken the facts at hand in March 1863, added some wishful thinking, and presented enthusiastic inducements to Yankees and assorted foreigners who might become rebel raiders.

28th. Many vessels seen, both yesterday and today. 10 a.m. Boarded the English barque "Chili," Cardiff to Coquimbo [Peru], 33 days out.

At this time Fullam's boarding duties were becoming more frequent, or he had started referring to his own role more often. Fullam and James Evans were the only two master's mates aboard until *Alabama* later reached South Africa and acquired two more master's mates: Julius Schroeder and Baron Max. von Meulnier.

We as usual passed ourselves off as Yankees. She reported that the "Alabama" had whipped a vessel twice her size, and strongly recommended us not to attempt fighting her should we meet. Made sail in chase of vessel right ahead.

29th. Light variable winds. In chase of three vessels right ahead, At 5.30 crossed the Equator.

This proved to be the first of only two occasions when *Alabama* crossed the equator. The second time was after the return from the China Seas. Lt. Arthur Sinclair enjoyed poking fun at the midshipmen who had trouble with their sextants in finding the latitude when they were actually crossing the equator at twelve noon. Apparently their navigation was more by rote than by understanding.

30th. A.M. Showery. Boarded the English barque "Sinope," Cardiff to Rio Janeiro.

Only two days after he boarded the bark *Chili,* Fullam boarded the bark *Sinope,* bound for Rio de Janeiro. Fullam's spelling of that city was standard in his day, as attested by Blunt, edition 1850.

Found that one of the vessels ahead was a Frenchman.

1st. April. A.M. Variable winds with occasional rain. P. M. Fresh N. N. W. wind. Two vessels in sight.

2nd. Variable S. E. winds with squalls. The same vessels still seen.

3rd. Squally. Chased a suspicious looking ship. Called all hands to quarters. On boarding we found her to be the French ship "Mathilde," Havre to Rio Janeiro. S. E. trade wind. P.M.

4th. Light S. E. wind. Seven vessels in sight. Chased one who towards evening showed what we supposed to be Yankee

colours. 8 p.m. Wind growing light, lowered a boat and sent
M. M. Evans in chase 10 [p.m.] Chase stood down for us.
Her Captain coming on board with his papers, we found that
she was the ship "Louisa Hatch," of Rockland, 28 days from
Cardiff to Point de Galle, laden with coal.

5th. I was sent on board to take charge. (I remained on
board until the 17th inst.)

Master's Mate James Evans was in command of the boarding party on
4 April. When this prize was identified as *Louisa Hatch,* with a cargo of
coal, Fullam was appointed prize master of *Louisa Hatch* and relieved
Evans on 5 April.

Louisa Hatch was built in Rockland, Maine, in 1855. She was an 853-ton
ship, with two decks and a draft of 19 feet. Her owners, Charles W. McLoon
(owner of seven-eighths of the ship) and William McLoon (owner of one
eighth) were both New Yorkers and *Louisa Hatch* ordinarily operated out of
New York. The ship alone was valued by her owners at $65,000, and the total
claims submitted, after she became number 32 in the list of prizes destroyed
by *Alabama,* amounted to $85,380. There was a wider than usual breach
between the owners' figures and the Confederate figures, for Kell placed
the value on *Louisa Hatch* at $38,315.

On 5 March 1863 *Louisa Hatch,* under command of William Grant
departed Cardiff, Wales, bound for Point de Galle, Ceylon. *Louisa Hatch,*
like *Chili* and *Sinope,* was carrying a load of Welsh coal. Unlike the two
barks, *Louisa Hatch* was definitely a Union merchantman. This settled
her fate when, on 4 April in position 3.13 south and 26.12 west, she encountered *Alabama.* The reason *Louisa Hatch* was not burned speedily, and
instead Fullam was made prize master and instructed to stay nearby, was
that *Alabama* needed for her own bunkers the coal in the Yankee vessel.
Not only was *Alabama's* supply of coal running low, but the quality of the
nearly smokeless Welsh coal was just the kind needed by a commerce
raider seeking to escape detection.

6 a.m. Four sails reported to be in sight. Chased one, proved
by signal to be an English barque.

6th. At 6 a.m. made a schooner on port bow. Hauled up
and made sail in chase. 7.40 Sail reported two points on lee
bow. 9.30 Got up steam and lowered propellor and stood for
schooner. 12. Came up with her, found to be Portuguese.
Chased another, fired a blank cartridge, she not heeding it,
fired a shot across his bow. She then hove to. Proved to be
a Brazillian. Kept away for prize ship "Louisa Hatch." 1.45

Came up with [her]. Blew off steam and hoisted propellor. Made sail and stood on course [Louisa Hatch keeping nearby].

7th. Made sail in chase of a vessel ahead. 5.30 p.m. Reduced sail. Whole sheets of water pouring down, in fact the heaviest rain ever seen by any on board.

8th. I came on board [Alabama] and received further instructions.

It was necessary for Fullam to learn enough of the plans of Captain Semmes so that he could properly command *Louisa Hatch*.

Pressed the Captain of the schooner "Kingfisher" into the service to pilot prize in to harbour. Sent him and the steward and his wife, of the "Nora" on board the "Louisa Hatch." Received the mates on board. 7 vessels in sight.

9th. Two vessels in sight. 9.30 a.m. Land reported in sight. 9 p.m. Got up steam, lowered propellor, took in all sail and took prize in tow. Coaling ship in boats.

10th. Prize still in tow. Coaling ship. Tow line parted twice so knocked off coaling, and stood for the anchorage off the Island of Fernando de Noronha.

Alabama and *Louisa Hatch* were moving in the equatorial current which was running at about 1½ knots, when *Alabama* got up steam, took *Louisa Hatch* in tow, and headed for Fernando de Noronha, a Portuguese island not far from Cape São Roque, the eastern tip of Brazil. Blunt called it Fernando Noronha, without the de. Fernando de Noronha is at the western end of the chain of Brazilian volcanic islands. See also *HO 172*, p. 180. Blunt gives a remarkable description of Fernando de Noronha, including the southwest point named Hole-in-the-Wall, and the tricky tides and currents. Hole-in-the-Wall is so called because the sea with tidal changes ran through a narrow opening into an inland lake. It was a time and place that called for an experienced pilot, and Fullam was fortunate in being able to get the piloting services of Thomas F. Lambert, master of the recently destroyed *Kingfisher*, prize number 29.

Both vessels under Confederate colours. 2.45 p.m. Came to an anchor in 13 fthms. Hauled prize alongside and commenced coaling.

Alabama and *Louisa Hatch* anchored in a depth of 78 feet.

11th. On account of heavy swells, cast off prize at 7.30 a.m. Coaled by the boats.

[104]

Louisa Hatch had a cargo of 1,133 tons of Welsh coal valued at $12,958.69. The coal was a godsend because *Alabama* was very much in need of coal and had been looking in vain for the regular collier, *Agrippina*. Later it was learned that Captain James D. Bulloch had, as usual, sent out the collier, but Captain Alexander McQueen had failed to find *Alabama* and so he sold his coal and went back to England. Never again did *Alabama* and *Agrippina* meet. *Alabama's* bunkers could hold only 300 tons of coal and that left 833 tons to be burned along with *Louisa Hatch*. *Louisa Hatch*, however, had extra sails, spars, bolts of canvas, and other gear, as well as food supplies, because the ship was fitted out to spend two years in the Orient after delivering her coal to Point de Galle, Ceylon.

12th. 2 a.m. Saw a steamers lights. Called all hands to quarters. Finding she stood on her course, piped down. During the day saw a vessel. Coaling.

13th. Expecting a strong breeze, took all people on board [Alabama] *from prize.*

14th. A.M. Despatched officer and crew to prize again. Still coaling.

15th. This morning finished coaling. Two vessels seen standing off and on the land. Two boats from vessels observed going to the "Louisa Hatch."

Fullam had scarcely finished lightering as much coal as *Alabama's* bunkers could hold, when the two Yankee whalers came in sight. The vessels lay five miles offshore while their captains in the small boats came to the island to make inquiries. Although the ships were wearing no colors, they were easily recognized as American. Whens the small boats pulled alongside *Louisa Hatch,* Fullam, in his shirt sleeves and without any uniform by which he could be recognized as a Confederate, went to the gangway and invited the captains of the two whaling ships to come aboard. The two masters came up close in their small boats and were interested in conversation, but declined the invitation to come aboard. Meantime Fullam, despite his Lincolnshire accent, tried to pass as a Yank. The real Yanks identified their ships as *Lafayette* of New Bedford and *Kate Cory* of Westport. The whaling captains asked the name of the other ship at Fernando de Noronha, and pointed to *Alabama*. Fullam replied that the steamer was a Brazilian packet which had come from the mainland bringing convicts to the penal colony on Fernando de Noronha. In turn, Fullam asked why they had come in and learned that one of the ships had sprung a considerable leak in a storm and had put into port to make repairs. While the two masters were talking with Fullam, one of them chanced to see a small Confederate ensign that had been left out to dry and, suddenly realizing their danger, commenced immediately to pull for their vessels lying five miles off shore.

1.15 p.m. [Alabama] *started under steam after the two vessels. 2.30 Boarded and took possession of the whaling brigantine "Kate Cory" of Westport. At 3 came up with barque "Lafayette" of New Bedford, whaling. Set fire to the barque.*

Alabama had finished her coaling, and seeing the situation hurriedly steamed toward the vessels lying quietly outside the marine league (according to the Confederates) waiting for their captains. *Alabama* threw her Confederate flag to the breeze and took possession of the two whalers.

Kate Cory was a small brigantine of only 132 tons burden, commanded by Stephen Flanders, and belonging to Alexander H. Cory of Westport and others. *Cory* had sailed 13 October 1862 on a whaling voyage and therefore was loaded with the usual whaling stores. The vessel and outfit were valued at only $20,000, but the total claims came to $47,562. The Confederate evaluation placed upon *Kate Cory* by Lt. Kell was $10,568.

Lafayette was the second ship of that name to run afoul of *Alabama*. *Lafayette* #1 has already been discussed. *Lafayette* #2 was commanded by William Lewis and operated by J. H. Bartlett and Sons, agents and managing owners. *Lafayette* #2 had departed New Bedford 20 May 1862 on a whaling voyage, and fell into the hands of Fullam while he was prize master of *Louisa Hatch*. *Lafayette* #2 had no official papers aboard, the first mate having thrown them over the side upon being confronted by *Alabama*. She was condemned and burned after Lt. Kell had valued her at $20,908, approximately twice the value placed upon *Kate Cory*. The total filed with the *Alabama* Claims in the case of *Lafayette* #2 amounted to $88,946. *Lafayette* #2 was burned before *Kate Cory,* and the two prizes proved to be numbers 33 and 34 of the vessels destroyed by *Alabama*. When *Lafayette* #2 was burned, this brought the official Confederate reckoning of the value of Union vessels destroyed by *Alabama* to $1,842,383.

5 [p.m.] Took brigantine in tow and stood for the anchorage. 7.30 Anchored in 14 fthms. Pyramid bearing S. W. ¼W. Eastern part of island E. N. E.

The Pyramid is a very barren high rocky peak on the north side of Fernando de Noronha. It was commonly used by mariners to get a bearing, as Fullam did in this case. See Blunt.

16th. Paroled all prisoners and sent them on shore. Provisioning from prizes. Sent 21 days provisions on shore for use of prisoners–140 in all.

The number of prisoners of war (140) was approximately equal to the size of *Alabama's* crew. The number of men aboard *Alabama* changed from ship to ship and port to port. In April 1863 there were 24 officers and some 116 men.

[106]

17th. 5.30 p.m. Ship "Louisa Hatch" and brig "Kate Cory" slipped cables, and proceeded seaward. 7 p.m. Both vessels being 5 miles from land were set on fire, Mr. Evans and myself returning on board [Alabama] *by 9 p.m. Shipped 4 men.*

From the whaling ships, *Alabama* enlisted four seamen: George Getsinger, Robert Owens, James Wallace, and Maurice Britt. Getsinger was discharged as an invalid four months later when *Alabama* was in South Africa. Wallace deserted at Saldanha on 1 August 1863. Owens was transferred to the CSS *Tuscaloosa,* 21 January 1863, and Britt served in *Alabama* through the engagement with *Kearsarge.*

Fernando de Noronha is a Brazilian penal settlement.

Publishing in 1850, Blunt noted that Fernando de Noronha (which he spelled without the de) was very largely used by the Brazilian government "as a place of exile for their vilest criminals." There were some small forts defending bays and anchorages. Sinclair pointed out that the governor of the whole establishment was a very amiable fellow, but according to that officer of the CSS *Alabama,* "International law don't bother him—indeed, it is doubtful if he has ever given it a thought."

There is an abundance of live stock, but vegetables are rather scarce. There is good water, but owing to the surf it is at times difficult to be obtained. The anchorage is unprotected from north westerly winds.

Fresh water was obtainable from a well near the governor's house located on Water Bay, but water casks had to be rolled over some rocks and moved through the surf. Blunt described the situation much as did Fullam.

18th. Several vessels in sight. Awaiting the arrival of our store ship.
21st. 6 p.m. A small schooner got under weigh and proceeded to sea, her destination being Pernambuco [present-day Recife], conveying as many of the crews of our prizes as she could carry.
22nd. At 9.30 a.m. we got under weigh, steering to the eastward. 4.30 p.m. Hoisted propellor. Steering S. Westerly.
24th. Saw a vessel yesterday. 2 a.m. A vessel hove in sight. Chased, hailed, and ordered him to heave to. On boarding she proved to be the barque "Nye" of New Bedford, whaling, having on board 500 bls. of oil. Transferred prisoners [from Nye] and burnt prize.

On 25 July 1862, *Nye* under command of Joseph B. Baker sailed from St. Helena off the coast of Africa homeward bound for New Bedford with a cargo of oil and whalebone. Her crew of 24 persons had been at sea for 11 months. On 24 April 1863, *Nye* was off the coast of Brazil (5.45 south and 31.53 west), when she was captured and burned by *Alabama*.

Nye proved to be number 35 among the vessels destroyed by *Alabama*. She was valued by Kell at $31,127, making a total to this date (24 April 1863) of $1,873,510. In the *Alabama* Claims the owners valued the vessel at $20,000 and the whaling outfit at $10,000, a figure which was remarkably close to the Confederate evaluation. To this, the numerous owners added claims for the loss of 565 barrels of sperm oil and other claims, making a total of $104,936. This was high value associated with a 211-ton bark. No attempt was made to conceal the identity of *Nye* with false documents. This was always the case with whaling ships encountered by *Alabama*. The ownership of the cargo was never in doubt.

P.M. Saw another vessel.

26th [April 1863]. Fresh wind. 2.30 p.m. Sail in sight, standing southerly. 4 [p.m.] Hoisted Yankee colours to her, chase not replying, fired a blank cartridge. He then hove to. Boarded and took possession–the ship "Dorcas Prince" of New York, from there to Shanghai, 44 days out, with coals, bread, &c. Took from her a quantity of stores. 11.30 p.m. Burnt her.

Dorcas Prince was a 699-ton ship, built in 1850 at Yarmouth by S. Lapham. In 1863 she was owned by N. L. and G. Griswold. On 13 March 1863 *Dorcas Prince*, under command of Frank B. Melcher, departed New York. On 26 April off the coast of Brazil (7.35 south and 31.30 west), she was captured, tried, and burned by *Alabama*. Kell placed the Confederate evaluation on her at $44,108. Up to this date, the official Confederate reckoning of the value of ships destroyed by *Alabama* was $1,917,618.

The Captain having his wife with him, was, as usual in such cases, accommodated in the ward room.

There were 20 prisoners in all. The fact that Captain Frank B. Melcher had his wife on board was not so unusual in the sailing ships of that day. More unusual was the amount of loss which he presented in the *Alabama* Claims of personal property destroyed with *Corcas Prince* totaling $3,038.60.

29th. Fine moderate breeze. 2.30 p.m. Gave chase to a sail on weather bow. 5 [p.m.]. Brought her to with blank

[108]

*cartridge. On boarding I found her to be the Hanoverian
brigantine "Elsie," Rio Grande, 30 days to England.*

*1st. May [1863]. Fine light winds. 5.45 a.m. Made a sail
on weather bow. Chased. On boarding she was found to be
the English brig "Hound," St. John (N.B.) to Mauritius.
Obtained news up to the 1st of April.*

The brig *Hound*, on 24 September 1864, became the center of a diplomatic controversy between the United States and Great Britain when
Lieutenant W. B. Cushing, commanding the USS *Monticello*, had *Hound*
boarded and detained in proceedings somewhat like those that Fullam
often went through. But the case of *Hound* resulted in protest by the
British minister, Lord Lyons, and related correspondence with Gideon
Welles and William H. Seward. Cushing was reprimanded.

Mauritius is in the Indian Ocean east of Madagascar and is very
close to the intersection of 20.0 south and 57.5 east. Port Luis still has
this name.

*Saw and chased several vessels during the day. All had neutral
colours. Exchanged signals with the brig "Geerdina," Trieste
to Bahia.*

*3rd. Fresh breeze. Two vessels in sight, gave chase. 12.15
Came up with her. On boarding she proved to be the barque
"Union Jack" of and from New York to Shanghai, 35 days out,
having on board as passengers a U. S. Consul for Chee Foo;
a gentleman and his wife; the Captain having his wife, servant,
and two children. A general cargo.*

After a long succession of foreign vessels plowing the sea lanes off
Brazil, *Union Jack* was the first prospective prize to be identified by Master's
Mate James Evans. In the case of *Union Jack*, the officer of the deck in
Alabama sent Evans to board the bark and also to serve as prize master
because another Yankee came up over the horizon within a few minutes
of *Union Jack*. *Union Jack*, a 483-ton bark commanded by Charles P. Weaver,
sailed from New York on 28 March 1863. Her position at the time of
her capture was 9.40 south and 32.30 west, in the South Atlantic. She
was valued by Kell at $77,000. The owners claimed $35,000 for the loss
of the vessel and had total claims connected with this ship of $161,513.70.

As a passenger aboard *Union Jack*, the Reverend Franklin Wright was
on his way to a United States consulate in China. At the time, Wright
was carrying with him his commission as consul and his consular seal.
Wright later claimed personal damages of $10,015. Shortly before this
frustrating adventure, Wright entered the services of the United States
State Department. Earlier he had edited a religious publication for some

[109]

years. The captain of *Union Jack,* Charles P. Weaver, also sued in the Court of Commissioners of the *Alabama* Claims. His claims covered loss of personal property and ship's stores: $2,400, expense of homeward passage, $320, and other losses of $5,000, for a total of $7,720.

Altogether there were three women taken aboard *Alabama* from *Union Jack.* The servant mentioned by Fullam was an Irish stewardess who was so reluctant to go aboard the Confederate raider that it was necessary to tie her into a "whip," similar to a boatswain's chair, and hoist her up on the yardarm. Later the protesting woman faced Semmes down and gave him a tongue-lashing. She publicly denounced him to his face as a pirate and rebel. To cool her temper, Semmes had her doused with water.

Gave chase to the other [vessel]. At 2.45 p.m. came up with her. On boarding I found her to be the ship "Sea Lark" of and from Boston to San Francisco with a general cargo. Transferred prisoners and stores, and set fire to them [Union Jack and Sea Lark]. Both vessels report having seen a vessel burning in Lat. 0.50 S. Long. 32.00 W.

Sea Lark was considered by the Confederates as the most valuable prize destroyed by *Alabama.* Kell placed her value at $550,000. The claims presented by the owners totaled $342,917.27, including $51,000 for the ship and her outfit. Using Confederate figures, *Sea Lark* ranked third in value of ship plus cargo among all prizes destroyed by all Confederate cruisers. In first place was *Jacob Bell* destroyed by the CSS *Florida* and valued at $1,500,000, and in second place was another prize of the CSS *Florida* named *Oneida,* valued at $760,000. The reason for the high evaluation of *Sea Lark* was primarily her very valuable and varied cargo.

After *Sea Lark's* captain, W. F. Peck, had been brought aboard *Alabama* by Fullam and after *Sea Lark* had been condemned in the admiralty proceedings, she was brought alongside *Alabama* and some hours were spent in breaking out cargo and selecting articles needed by the sea raider. Many valuable articles were cast over the side as being mere hindrances in the systematic despoiling. Dr. Francis L. Galt, who had replaced Yonge as paymaster, gave a list to Fullam of articles needed in particular departments of *Alabama.* Sometimes the articles were soap, candles, or other necessities of little value. Some apparel was taken, as were charts, nautical instruments, and inevitably the ship's chronometer. Most of the equipment and cargo, however, was consigned to the flames. By the time *Alabama* added the crew and passengers of *Sea Lark,* the prisoners of war aboard the raider numbered 108. Once again, the prisoners nearly equaled *Alabama's* crew. Thus the safety as well as the comfort of all hands required *Alabama* to head for port. Such were the pressing reasons for putting into Bahia.

Sea Lark was by no means a very large vessel at 973 tons, although larger than the average *Alabama* prize. She was a clipper ship. It was unusual that such a valuable ship was owned by only three persons: Edward Mott Robinson of New York, Lyman Grimes of Brooklyn, and Samuel G. Reed of Roxbury, Massachusetts. *Sea Lark* was built at Trescott, Maine, in 1852, and subsequently operated out of Boston. Under command of W. F. Peck, *Sea Lark* had departed Boston on 28 March 1863, bound for San Francisco. She unhappily came under the guns of the CSS *Alabama* 3 May in the sea lanes off the coast of Brazil (9.35 south and 31.20 west).

4th. Boarded a French brig, Monte Video to Havre.

5th. Saw and boarded several vessels, all English and Foreign.

10th. P.M. Two vessels in sight. Boarded one, a Norwegian, 36 hours from Bahia. No American war vessel there when she left.

11th. Exchanged colours with a foreign brig. Saw several vessels. 12. Got up steam and lowered propellor. 5.30 p.m. Anchored in Bahia harbour. Health officers visited us; stated that three American war vessels were off the coast.

12th. The most intense excitement was created by our appearance. The U. S. Consul officially demanded that the "Alabama" should be detained, to be delivered up to the U. S. government, to answer for the ravages committed upon their commerce. [We] Obtained (rather reluctantly given) permission to land prisoners and obtain supplies.

In Fullam's day, Bahia was the name of the city and of the province. Today the province is still named Bahia, but the city is named Salvador. During the reign of Dom Pedro II as emperor of Brazil there was considerable involvement with Confederate cruisers, the Union navy, and the United States State Department. This was complicated by the fact that the presidents of Brazilian provinces exercised excessive authority, sometimes to the embarrassment of the central government, in dealing with foreign powers. In September 1861, Semmes had coaled the CSS *Sumter* in São Luis and had become involved in complex diplomatic negotiations. A few days after the departure of the CSS *Sumter,* David D. Porter, commanding the USS *Powhatan,* arrived in São Luis pursuing *Sumter.* As to Semmes' initial success in Brazilian diplomacy, Porter wrote:

... [In Brazil,] during their stay, Commander Semmes and his officers were the lions of the hour, and brought a good deal of odium on the head of the United States consul, who did all in his power to prevent the "Sumter" from proceeding on her work of destruction. His small pay had prevented him attaining such social consideration, so that he had but little influence.

Another character in the struggle raging around *Sumter* was the eccentric United States minister to Brazil and erstwhile editor of the New York *Courier and Inquirer,* James Watson Webb. Webb's opposite number, representing Brazil in the argument, was B. A. Magalhaes Taques, Brazil's talented secretary of state for foreign affairs. The diplomatic storms which swirled around the earlier Confederate raider concerned questions as to whether coal was contraband of war and whether Confederate warships and Union warships sould be allowed equal coaling facilities. Brazil supported the Confederate contention in this matter.

Twenty months later, with the CSS *Alabama* now in Brazil, coal was no longer the main question, although some coal was taken aboard, but coal lingered on in another controversy in Brazil. This time it concerned the argument in Salvador regarding *Alabama's* coaling in Fernando de Noronha, and more particularly the fact that *Alabama* had brought into Brazil's neutral waters a prize ship, had coaled from her, and subsequently had taken the ship (*Louisa Hatch* with Fullam as prize master) out and burned her. This was clearly a violation of international law, but it was a violation on the part of the governor of Fernando de Noronha and not on the part of the Confederates, since the governor gave his permission. Later on, there would be a more dramatic violation of international law involving Brazil and the American Civil War at sea when the CSS *Florida* on a later visit to Salvador was rammed by the USS *Wachusett,* under command of Napoleon Collins, and towed out to sea. Thus the United States government kidnapped *Florida* in neutral waters and took her to Hampton Roads, Virginia, where the CSS *Florida* was sunk. From the time of the *Sumter* episode to that of the CSS *Florida,* J. Watson Webb was the United States minister to Brazil and had a considerable hand in this violation of Brazilian neutrality.

Visitors innumerable coming on board. The most unbounded hospitality and kindness shown, with every mark of sympathy by all. Per the English mail boat Capt. Semmes sent a message to the Commr. of the U. S. Str. "Mohican" to the effect "that if the 'Mohican' would come where Capt. Semmes could conveniently meet her, he would have great pleasure in paying some attention to her. Circumstances not permitting Capt. Semmes to go out of his course to meet anything."

As the mail boat passed, both passengers and crew cheered us.

The USS *Mohican* was smaller, slower, and less well armed than the CSS *Alabama.* Yet she was a screw steamer of 994 tons, launched 15 February 1859, and therefore was by no means old. O. S. Glisson, commanding officer of *Mohican,* had the mission of searching for Confederate cruisers, while Semmes' mission was to search for merchant vessels and not for Union warships. Glisson did come fairly close in his search for *Alabama* in the spring of 1863. On 20 May 1863, Glisson wrote Secretary of the Navy Gideon Welles the following pathetic words:

> I have to inform you the honorable Secretary of the Navy that I arrived at this port this day and am taking in coal and shall be off in chase as soon as possible. The *Florida* is cruising in this vicinity. The *Alabama* and *Virginia (Georgia),* formerly called the *Japan,* are at Bahia. The *Lapwing,* a bark with 8 guns, and a brig called the *Clarence,* with 6 guns, are also cruising on this coast. You will see that this is quite a formidable fleet for me to encounter, but the Department may rest assured that we will do our duty, and it will not be many days before we have a battle. I would earnestly urge that more vessels be sent to this coast.

13th. At 3 a.m. a steamer was observed to anchor about two miles distant. At daylight saw it was a brig rigged screw steamer, presenting unmistakable signs of being a war vessel. 8 a.m. Great was our astonishment to see the Stars and Bars hoisted at her peak. Private signals were exchanged. She then got up steam and anchored near us. Soon after, sent a boat on board when it was found to be the C. S. Str. "Georgia," 5 guns, Lieut. Commr. Maury. Had captured one vessel. Crowded with visitors. Bahia has a very pretty appearance from the bay; which is not altogether lost on landing. Victoria, the place where the English residents live, is a charming spot.

14th. The officials (nearly all English) connected with the Railway gave an excursion to the officers of the "Alabama" and "Georgia." A most numerous assembly joined it. An exceedingly pleasant day was spent.

15th. A ball in connection with the above was given. Both commanders with a numerous staff of officers went and enjoyed themselves. After supper was served; in reply to a toast Capt. Semmes made a suitable return which on its conclusion was most enthusiastically applauded.

The host was an English merchant named Ogilvie. Although the elite of Bahia (Salvador) attended the ball and the Confederates had an excellent time, both Sinclair, from the *Alabama,* and James M. Morgan, from the CSS *Georgia,* noted that the populace at large showed no very great enthusiasm for the visiting Confederates. The situation was quite different from that in Kingston, Jamaica.

17th. Sunday. 3.30 p.m. According to an invitation given by Capt. Semmes, a party of ladies and gentlemen (chiefly English) came on board. After a minute inspection, they sat down with the Captain and officers on the quarter deck and partook of a slight refreshment. 5.30 p.m. Visitors left the ship. An official came on board with an order for us to leave in 24 hours, after receipt of the message. Capt. Semmes' reply was that if he had 30 tons of coal on board by that time he would willingly comply, otherwise he would not.

19th. Received an intimation from the authorities to the effect, that as they had strong suspicion that the barque "Castor" of Liverpool, lying there with coal for the "Georgia," had also a quantity of arms, &c. to be transferred to the "Alabama," they could not permit us to coal from her. So took coal from the shore.

The CSS *Georgia,* a short while before, had been placed in commission (19 April 1863) and had set out on a commerce raid under Commander William Lewis Maury. Like *Alabama,* she was armed at sea, cruised against Union merchant ships, and arrived at Bahia 13 May 1863. Meeting old shipmates was a joyful occasion on both cruisers. An officer, Robert T. Chapman, who had served under Semmes in the CSS *Sumter,* was at this time an officer aboard *Georgia.* Semmes, in his book *Service Afloat,* wrote of Chapman's distinctive services in *Sumter.* Chapman was the officer who had the highly secret mission of transporting the Great Seal of the Confederacy from London, where it was made, into the Confederate States.

Before the arrival of the CSS *Georgia* at Bahia, the master of the English bark *Castor* came aboard *Alabama* and informed Semmes that *Castor* carried coal and provisions for *Georgia* (which vessel he still called by her old name *Japan*). Brazilian authorities refused *Alabama* permission to coal from *Castor,* but she was permitted to coal from a lighter operating from the shore. While in Bahia, *Alabama* also received 528 pounds of gunpowder from *Georgia.* There is a tradition that a copper kettle, on display in the battleship USS *Alabama* (now permanently moored in Mobile Bay), was transferred from the CSS *Alabama* to the CSS *Georgia* while the two ships were in Bahia. The two ships were never together at any other time, nor did either one of them ever enter the Confederate

[114]

States. United States Minister J. Watson Webb and the United States consul at Bahia, Thomas H. Wilson, vigorously protested Brazil's treatment of *Alabama* and *Georgia*. Connected with this was the arrival of the CSS *Florida,* under command of John Newland Maffitt, at Pernambuco (now Recife).

20th. Considerable surprise was manifested by the desertion of the Master-at-Arms James King of Savannah. His antecedents proving his devotion to the Southern cause. He was a pilot of considerable standing in his native place. Another deserted.

James King was also listed by Latham and Sinclair. The other deserter was Peter Henry, an ordinary seaman who had enlisted 24 August 1862 before *Alabama* started on her cruise. Sinclair noted that Henry deserted 17 May 1863.

21st. 1 a.m. Finished coaling. Received farewell visits. 12. Got under weigh, and proceeded seaward. The "Georgia" expecting to sail the following day. 3 p.m. Showed Yankee colours to a Hamburgh brig. 4. Hoisted propellor and made sail
22nd. A.M. Passed a large frigate. Standing towards Bahia. 6 a.m. Two vessels in sight.
23rd. [May 1863]. Moderate S. S. E. wind. Steering easterly. Saw a large ship. On boarding I found to be the English ship "Virginia," Liverpool, 42 days to Sidney. Her passengers and crew giving us three cheers as we left them.
24th. Fresh S E. wind. 4.30 p.m. Sail in sight. On boarding she proved to be a Dutch barque, Amsterdam to Batavia. Told them we were the U. S. Str. "Sacramento."
25th. Srong S. S. E. wind with a heavy sea. 10.30 a.m. Two vessels in sight. Gave chase. Another vessel seen. Hoisted U. S. colours to a ship; she not replying, [Alabama] *signalled: "I want to speak you," upon which she stood towards us and hoisted Yankee colours also. On boarding, took possession. The ship "S. Gildersleeve" of New York, Sunderland to Calcutta, laden with coal.*

S. *Gildersleeve* was an 848-ton ship, owned in New York. J. H. Brower and Company, New York, was part owner and also managing owner. Under command of John McCallum, S. *Gildersleeve* took on a cargo of coal in Sunderland, England, and headed for Calcutta. The coal was owned by the Peninsular and Oriental Steam Navigation Company, a British concern, but there was no proof of neutral ownership. On 25

[115]

May 1863 *Gildersleeve* had reached position 12.14 south and 35.11 west where she was boarded by Fullam, tried by Semmes, condemned, and burned. She was number 39 among the Union vessels destroyed by *Alabama*. The Confederate evaluation placed upon *Gildersleeve* by Lt. Kell was $60,000 for the ship, and $2,783 for the cargo, making a total value placed by the Confederates upon all prizes destroyed by *Alabama* up to this point of $2,607,401. The owners of the ship and the insurance companies altogether claimed only $35,000 for *Gildersleeve* and no claims were made for the cargo. It is likely that the cargo was British owned, since it was proceeding from one British port to another. This would certainly be a reason that the owners could not collect damages under the *Alabama* Claims. As to why there was so much discrepancy in the evaluation placed upon the ship by Union and Confederate sources is difficult to determine. It might be noted, however, that both sources had an economic motive in making the value high rather than low. The Confederate government provided that each commerce raider was entitled to one-half the value of each vessel destroyed and the full value of ships released on ransom bond.

Chased a barque which on boarding I found to be the "Justina" of Baltimore, Rio Janeiro to Baltimore, in ballast. Chased another vessel who proved to be Dutch. The "Justina" was ransomed and allowed to proceed on her voyage, taking with her the crews of the just captured ship [S. Gildersleeve].

Justina was a bark in ballast on a return voyage from Rio de Janeiro to Baltimore when captured by *Alabama* and placed under ransom bond for $7,000, executed by her acting master, Charles Miller. *Justina* brought the Confederate ransom bond total to $562,250. Semmes placed 19 of *Alabama's* prisoners aboard *Justina* and told Miller to take them to Baltimore without making an intermediate stop. Ordinarily *Justina* would have stopped in the West Indies for cargo, but Captain Miller carried out his promise. The owner, John M. Bandle, later filed claims for passage money of each of the 19 men at $100 in gold each, totaling $2,750.25. The owner also sought payment for freights that were lost for 36 days at a claim of $75 a day. The total claim in this case was $5,475.25. Included in the amount was the loss of one crate of bananas taken by *Alabama* and valued at $25. The actual award made in this case was less than one-half of the claim. The award of the court was only $1,425, representing $2 per day per man for passage money plus $25 for the crate of bananas. The *Justina* case illustrates the type of claim which was allowed as well as the type which was denied in the case of the vessels released by Semmes on ransom bond.

26th. Strong breeze. Gave chase to a barque, but eventually lost sight of her.

Kell, most terse of all the writers who tell the tale of the CSS *Alabama*, was stirred by the all-night chase of a ship which Fullam mentioned here and which proved after all to be neutral. This was *Arnheim*. Sinclair said that she was probably the fastest ship encountered by *Alabama*.

Saw a vessel to which we showed U. S. colours, she answered by showing, on the 27th, Dutch colours.
28th. Fresh breeze. Saw several vessels. 6 p.m. Fired a blank cartridge, and hove to a large ship. On boarding I found her to be the English ship "Lady Octavia," London, 28 days to Calcutta. Obtained papers to 30th April.

Alabama was able to glean valuable military intelligence from New York newspapers in the most unsecurity-conscious, large-scale war of modern times. Other newspapers were only slightly less valuable. Had Evans been able to tell Fullam that it was not necessary to go aboard *Lady Octavia* because she was British, it might still have been worth *Alabama's* time just to get those newspapers which, Fullam said, were as late as 30 April.

29th [May 1863]. 2.30 a.m. Sail discovered on starboard bow. Set all sail in chase. 6 a.m. Fired a blank cartridge and hoisted our own flag. No notice being taken of it, another was fired and a feint made with coal.

Perhaps Fullam meant that *Alabama* pretended to get up steam by suddenly putting out a quantity of smoke to show the stranger that there was no chance for his sails to outrun the warship's steam-propelled screw.

She hoisted Yankee colours and hove to. On boarding she was found to be the ship "Jabez Snow" of Bucksport [Maine, from] Cardiff, 35 days to Calcutta. Took prisoners and provisions from prize, and set her on fire. In consequence of the gross false-hoods made by released prisoners about the treatment they were subjected to, the Captain of her was placed on deck.

Jabez Snow triggered disputes running beyond treatment of prisoners, here referred to by Fullam. Questions of what claims were allowable with regard to charter parties made this a pilot case. The facts were well documented. *Jabez Snow* was a 1,074-ton ship which was built in Newburyport in 1853. Most of her owners lived in Bucksport, or elsewhere in Maine, and the ship operated out of Bucksport. Under command of George W. Guin, *Jabez Snow* was in Liverpool when charter parties were signed by Captain Guin providing that the ship should sail from Liverpool to Cardiff, Wales, pick up a cargo of Welsh coal, take it to Montevideo, there discharge the coal and, under the second charter party, proceed to the west coast of South America to Callao. In Callao, *Jabez Snow* would report to agents of the Peruvian government, load guano, and thence return to Europe, landing in Havre. Part of this contract was fulfilled. *Jabez Snow* sailed from Liverpool to Cardiff and loaded coal. She departed Cardiff on 16 April 1863. On 29 May, while headed for the Straits of Magellan (in position 12.35 south and 35.33 west) she encountered *Alabama,* was boarded by Fullam and his men, and enmeshed in admiralty proceedings aboard the raider. She was then burned, number 40 among the ships destroyed by *Alabama.* The Confederate evaluation of the ship was made by Kell at $68,672 and the cargo at $4,109. The *Alabama* Claims Court allowed net freight on the cargo for the charter party to Peru and disallowed claims based upon the charter party from Peru. The name of this case was *Buck and Spofford, et al. v. United States.* The claims filed for the loss of "ship and appurtenances" amounted to $70,000, and total claims filed in connection with this valuable vessel came to $140,008.

2nd. June. 3.20 a.m. A sail discovered on weather bow. Made sail, and at daylight hoisted U. S. colours to her. 6.15 Fired two blank cartridges, chase showing U. S. colours. No notice being taken of it, at 11.30 a.m. fired a shot from rifle gun, she being about 4 miles distant. She then hove to. Boarded and took possession of the barque "Amazonian" of Boston, New York to Monte Video, with a general cargo. Removed prisoners and set fire to her.

Amazonian was a 480-ton bark. She sailed from New York on 22 April 1863, bound for Montevideo. She was captured and burned by *Alabama* on 2 June 1863. At the time of the capture the master was Winslow Loveland. Not long before this he had relieved Captain D. E. Mayo of command of *Amazonian.* When Fullam took Captain Loveland aboard *Alabama,* the captain came without his ship's papers. In the absence of papers it did not require much time for Semmes' admiralty proceedings to decide to set the torch. Meantime, Lt. Armstrong placed a value of $97,665 on the vessel. She became number 41 among the ships destroyed. The total Union claims that were later filed came to $126,902.82. Of this amount, the vessel plus the charter party came to $43,000.

The Confederates as usual expected to take some articles from the prize. *Amazonian* had a considerable supply of candles, soap, and a variety of small stores. The first mate of the bark accommodatingly pointed out to the Confederates the location of this article and that, requested by various departments of *Alabama.* This was no disloyalty to the owners, as all the merchandise in the condemned vessel not taken by the Confederates was burned with the ship. Willingness to aid the Confederate war effort was another matter, but not really surprising when one considers the international outlook of many sailors. To reach the needed minor articles, the boarding party tossed over the side cases of shoes and boots, pianos, and other valuable items. But it made little difference, it was all about to be burned anyhow, and a length of rope or a whale oil lamp might be needed much more aboard the Confederate raider than a case of boots, and presumably there was no need for a piano.

3rd. 10 a.m. Chased a brigantine, which on boarding was found to be the "Widna" of Hanover, London to Rio Janeiro. Sent 10 days provisions and all prisoners on board her, her Captain being presented with a chronometer for his kindness in taking them.

An estimated value of a chronometer was about $200 in the currency of a hundred years ago.

4th. 9.30 a.m. Saw a large ship with foretopgallantmast gone, dead to windward. Chased until sundown. 6.35 p.m. Saw a burning vessel bearing W. S. W. Stood towards it. 9.30 Saw a flash, then darkness. Supposed it to be a prize captured by some Confederate vessel.

Fullam's surmise was probably incorrect. Scharf lists by date each prize of each Confederate cruiser and none is shown for 4 June 1863 in the South Atlantic or elsewhere.

5th. 3 a.m. Brought to with blank cartridge a large ship standing southerly. On boarding she proved to be the ship "Talisman" of and from New York, 32 days to Shanghai, laden with coal.

While Mathew Brady, and his numerous photographic employees, were doing so much to make the American Civil War the most photographed war to that date, one lone American photographer was making his way from New York to Shanghai to take his new skills to that teeming Chinese city. It just happened that he embarked as a passenger in *Talisman,* together with his cameras, photographic supplies, and such equipment as one might take on a distant voyage. Thereon hangs a tale that is distinctive among the multitudinous claimants. This passenger aboard *Talisman* was Lorenzo F. Fisler. Some interesting facts concerning him appeared when he brought his claims before the *Alabama* Claims Court, Case 404: *Lorenzo F. Fisler* v. *United States.* Fisler had a contract with a business firm in Shanghai, according to which he would work as a photographer and receive his expenses paid plus 100 Mexican dollars per month. The contract provided that, instead of that amount of money, under an alternate provision, Fisler would receive one-fourth of the profits of the business. Fisler elected the one-fourth of the profits feature. Before the *Alabama* Claims Commission his lawyers argued that, because he was delayed 13 months in setting up in business as a result of the capture of *Talisman* by *Alabama,* Fisler was due $2,600 in gold. This was in addition to the value of his clothing, equipment, etc., destroyed when *Talisman* was burned. The claim for delay was not allowed by the court, but Fisler was awarded $1,722.80 as the value of his photographic equipment, supplies, and clothing which he lost in the *Talisman* fire.

Talisman was a valuable ship, carrying an exceptionally valuable cargo. Lt. Armstrong set a value of $139,195 on *Talisman,* which proved to be number 47 of the ships destroyed by *Alabama.* The total claims presented by the owners of the ship and her contents amounted to $187,405. *Talisman,* a ship of 1,238 tons, was owned by George Warren, Eben B. Crocker, and William A. Sales. Under command of D. H. Howard, *Talisman* departed New York on 2 May 1863 with general cargo, in addition to the coal mentioned by Fullam. En route to Shanghai, she was captured by *Alabama* on 5 June 1863 at the point 14.47 south and 34.7 west.

Took 5 passengers (one, a lady), the crew, stores, and two brass rifled 12 pounders. 5 p.m. Set fire to her.

Among the five people were Fisler, the photographer, and a Mr. and Mrs. Murphy. The two brass cannon from *Talisman* were later used to arm the CSS *Tuscaloosa,* together with some small arms from the same merchantman.

6th. 2.30 p.m. Saw a large ship to windward. On boarding she proved to be the (late Yankee) ship "St. Leonard," Hull to Calcutta. Transferred a passenger and lady to her.

Fullam, like *St. Leonard,* called Hull, Lincolnshire, his home port. Mr. and Mrs. Murphy were en route to Calcutta.

7th. Chased a barque, until lost her in a rain squall.
8th. 4 a.m. Gave chase to a brigantine, that turned out to be Hanoverian.
9th. Fresh gales. Saw a ship to windward.
11th. 2 a.m. Saw a very brilliant meteor.
13th. 6 a.m. Made a sail on lee bow, which on boarding was found to be English.
14th. In the evening saw two vessels.
15th. Saw a vessel on lee bow.
16th. Chased a barque. "G. Azzopadi," Boston to St. Louis, Mauritius. Proved to be French.

G. Azzopadi was a bark operating out of Port Louis, Mauritius. This was a very good example of the flight from the American flag as a result of the commerce raiding by the CSS *Alabama* and other Confederate cruisers. Dalzell noted transfers from United States to British registry as: 41 ships in 1860 with a tonnage of 13,638; 126 ships in 1861 with a tonnage of 71,673; 135 ships in 1862 with a tonnage of 64,578; and 348 ships in 1863 with a tonnage of 252,579. Booth gives even larger figures for 1863.

[120]

G. *Azzopadi* had acquired her new name and new nationality in October 1862. Built in Portland, Maine, the original name was *Joseph Hale*. Under command of Frederick Thorndyke, *Joseph Hale* was damaged and in distress when she put in to Port Louis, Mauritius. There she was sold to a British owner who sent her on a voyage to Boston. At the time of her encounter with *Alabama*, this vessel, under her new name of *G. Azzopadi*, was on her return voyage from Boston to Port Louis. Confederate admiralty proceedings adjudged this American-built ship to be a bona fide transfer to British registry (rather than French) and, as such, neutral property.

17th. Saw several vessels. In the evening saw a suspicious looking ship. Beat to quarters, fired two blank cartridges and a shot, upon which she hove to. On boarding she was found to be the ship "Queen of Beauty" from London, 35 days to Melbourne, with passengers.

Fullam's Journal stated in a footnote, "The gun captured from the 'Ariel' was thrown overboard some time ago."

Queen of Beauty represented another change of name and nationality. As an American ship, she was named *Challenger*. As *Queen of Beauty*, she was operating as an Australian packet. When Fullam boarded her, he not only found proof of her current British identity, but also learned that she had 300 passengers on board. Fullam informed Semmes that there was much excitement among the passengers and crew of *Queen of Beauty* created by the halting of the ship. Fullam further told Semmes that when the passengers learned that they had been boarded by the rebel raider *Alabama*, the passengers surprised him by giving three cheers. It is significant to note that, with *Queen of Beauty*, the last four ships boarded by Fullam were all neutrals, although two of the vessels were of American build.

18th. Made a light on port bow. Chased, and hove her to with a blank cartridge. Proved to be the Norwegian brig "Iduma," Rio Grande to Bahia.

19th. 4 a.m. Saw a sail, gave chase. On boarding I found her to be the Bremen barque "Brema," Buenos Ayres, 13 days to New York. Called ourselves the U. S. Str. "Dacotah."

20th. Two vessels in sight. Gave chase to a barque. The wind being light, and the darkness coming on, got up steam and lowered propellor. At 7.50 p.m. I boarded and took possession of the barque "Conrad" of Philadelphia, Buenos Ayres to New York, laden with wool. Sent Captain and mates on board the Alabama. Prize hove to (received written instructions).

The 348-ton bark *Conrad* of Philadelphia was a slim bark with a "very Yankee" look about her. She was owned by J. W. Field and commanded by

William H. Salsbury. She was built in 1844. With a cargo of Argentinian wool and 277 bales of goatskins, *Conrad* departed Buenos Aires 7 June 1863. Thirteen days later she was in position 25.44 south and 39.51 west when she was confronted by *Alabama* in a beginning series of remarkable adventures. Fullam boarded the prize and took Captain Salsbury aboard the raider for the usual admiralty proceedings. There was no question that *Conrad* was under the American flag and with an American register. There was considerable evidence that the cargo was neutral property, belonging in part to a British subject, Thomas Armstrong, and to Dr. Frederico Elortondo, a citizen of Argentina. On technical grounds the Confederate admiralty court condemned the ship and cargo. Accordingly, 22 people were moved from *Conrad* to *Alabama:* Captain Salsbury, a crew of 20 men and one passenger, a woman. The bark was valued by Lt. Kell at $15,000 and her cargo at $85,936, for a total value of $100,936. Claims filed by Northern merchants were $94,241. *Conrad* was officially reckoned number 43 of vessels seized by *Alabama.* Actually, she was not destroyed during the Civil War. Instead, she was converted into the CSS *Tuscaloosa,* as explained by Fullam, and had adventures of her own. She was subsequently seized by the British, later ordered released after John Low and his ship's company were no longer around to receive her and, after the Civil War was over, turned over to the United States government.

Stood after the other vessel. Lost her in the darkness, so stood again for prize. 11.30 Hove to 'till daylight.

21st [June 1863]. Sunday Preparing the prize for commissioning as a Confederate vessel of war. Sent on board her provisions, coal, and the two brass guns taken from the "Talisman" with a quantity of small arms.

The two brass cannon were 12-pounder rifled guns and the small arms included 20 rifles, 6 revolvers, and a quantity of ammunition.

At 5 p.m. she fired a gun, hoisted the Confederate flag and pendant; both ships crews manning the rigging and giving three cheers. She was then formally declared commissioned as the Confederate States Barque "Tuscaloosa," Lieut. Commanding Low, late junior lieutenant of the Alabama. Actg. Master Sinclair, Executive Officer, late midshipman, Masters Mate J. F. Minor, late seaman, and H. Marmelstein as quartermaster. The vessels saluted each other and parted company.

The officers and crew of *Tuscaloosa* totaled 15, enough for a 348-ton bark, but few for a commerce raider. These were: John Low, William H. Sinclair,

[122]

Henry Marmelstein, Joseph F. Minor, Martin Molk, Robert Owens, Edwin Jones, Henry Legris, Samuel Brewer, William Rinton, John Duggan, Robert P. Williams, Thomas J. Allman, Thomas Williams, and Sam Brown.

[Alabama] *Went after a vessel. She looking suspicious,* [we] *went to quarters. On firing a blank cartridge, she hove to. Boarding, it was found to be the English ship "Mary Kendall," Shields to Point de Galle. Her crew had refused to work her any longer unless her master made for a port, she leaking badly. A boy having fallen from aloft hurt himself severely, Dr. Llewellyn went on board and rendered the needful assistance.*

Dr. David H. Llewellyn, assistant surgeon in *Alabama,* was a native of Wiltshire, England. A year after his services to the injured lad, Dr. Llewellyn was one of the ten men in the CSS *Alabama* who lost his life in the action with the USS *Kearsarge.*

Her master agreeing to take our prisoners, was rewarded with a chronometer. Shipped 6 men from prizes.

The six men shipped were: William Wilson, George Percy, George Thomas, John Williams (the first of the name), John Miller, and James Wilson. All of these were ordinary seamen recruited from recent prizes. Three deserted some three months later: George Thomas, John Miller, and James Wilson. The other three served continuously in *Alabama* to the end of the cruise, including the battle with *Kearsarge* in June 1864.

22nd. Saw several ships. Light winds and calms. The following promotions were made. Master A. Sinclair to be lieutenant, vice Low promoted, Midshipman I. S. Bulloch to be Master, vice Sinclair promoted.

In the CSS *Alabama,* Arthur Sinclair was promoted to take the place of John Low, who had become commanding officer of the CSS *Tuscaloosa.* Midshipman Irvine S. Bulloch (younger brother of James D. Bulloch who had arranged for the building of *Alabama)* was promoted to replace Arthur Sinclair. William H. Sinclair had been detached from *Alabama* to become first lieutenant (master) of the CSS *Tuscaloosa.*

26th. Seeing a suspicious looking craft, went to quarters. Proved, however, to be a Frenchman.
27th. Since leaving the "Tuscaloosa," we have been steering to the Cape of Good Hope; but, discovering our bread to be bad, turned back this morning.

Alabama had on board about a month's supply of bread, or so it was thought until it was discovered that almost the entire supply had been destroyed by weevils. When Fullam said that *Alabama* turned back, he meant that she put about, turning away from the Cape of Good Hope, which had been her destination, and heading instead for Rio de Janeiro, some 825 miles away. Fullam neglected to say that on Sunday, 28 June, he or some other officer of *Alabama* had boarded *Vernon,* a frigate-built Melbourne packet. *Alabama* had identified herself as the USS *Dacotah* and presumably the English ship accepted the identification. The captain of *Vernon,* however, refused the boarding officer's request to see the ship's papers. This case illustrates the responsibility of the boarding officer in making an on-the-spot decision which might prove difficult to reverse. By the time Captain Semmes had received the report of the boarding officer, *Vernon* was already too great a distance away to warrant another pursuit, particularly under the circumstances. Under international law a belligerent had a right to capture a neutral who refused to identify herself. *Alabama* could have seized *Vernon,* but since Semmes was satisfied that the ship was in fact the Melbourne packet as professed, the boarding officer's decision was upheld. This boarding officer was very likely Fullam. There were, however, still some cases in which, because Fullam was tied up with other duties, the boarding party was headed by Evans or some other officer.

29th. Saw a large ship standing southerly, proved to be an English barque.— Chased another, found her to be by signals, the barque "Asshur" of London. Strong S. E. wind.

30th. In the evening boarded the English barque "Medora."

The bark *Medora* was from Cardiff to Shanghai with a cargo of Welsh coal. The latest newspaper aboard *Medora* was nearly two months old.

1st July [1863]. *Chased a sail until 9 p.m. Saw another, chased her until* [Fullam never completed this thought.].

2nd. When on boarding she was found to be the ship "Anna F. Schmidt" of Boston, from St. Thomas last, to San Francisco. General cargo. Transferred prisoners and stores, and burnt prize.

On this Thursday, 2 July, *Alabama* sighted 11 ships and caught only one Yankee, but this was a prize indeed. *Anna F. Schmidt* had just the cargo that enabled the rebel raider once more to turn in her tracks away from Rio and toward Cape Town. Also, this prize proved to be the second most valuable of *Alabama's* prizes, ranking just behind *Sea Lark*. The official Confederate evaluation of *Anna F. Schmidt,* placed by Kell, was $350,000, and she was number 44 of the ships destroyed by the raider, as compared with Kell's evaluation of $550,000 for *Sea Lark,* number 37 of the ships destroyed, as previously discussed.

[124]

Anna F. Schmidt had much to defend, and she made an earnest effort to escape the pursuing Confederate. The 784-ton Yankee crowded on all canvas. A blank cartridge failed to bring her to, but *Alabama* closed the range and, when within three miles, fired a shell from the 100-pounder rifled Blakely gun. The projectile gave the Yankee the message. *Anna F. Schmidt* luffed to the wind, raised the Stars and Stripes to her peak, and waited for Fullam and his boarding party to climb the ship's ladder. Captain Henry B. Twombly and his ship's papers were soon aboard *Alabama*, enmeshed in the Confederate admiralty court. The ship was built in 1854 in Kennebunk, Maine. Her several owners included two men from Maine and six from Massachusetts. The ship's register showed that her home port was Boston. She sailed from Boston 17 January on a voyage to San Francisco, and put in to St. Thomas, Virgin Islands, in distress. At the time of her capture, she was deep in the South Atlantic (25.27 south and 37.56 west).

There was no attempt to claim neutral property in *Anna F. Schmidt*. Confederate condemnation proceedings took only a short while, but many hours were required to break open holds and case after case of "Boston notions," food, clothing, medicines, ship's bread, boots and shoes, and such a variety of cargo as Boston merchants in 1863 may have believed to be in demand in California. Some of the most valuable items from a monetary standpoint were of no more use to the raiding rebels than so much seaweed. Valuables encountered by rummaging hands and all kinds of goodies were thrown over the side. Indeed, the ocean was a true litter when the British warship HMS *Diomede* came upon the scene shortly after *Alabama's* departure. Meantime, Confederate looters were searching for specific items. They showed much more restraint than the Germans of World War II in their commerce raider *Atlantis* under Captain Bernhard Rogge, according to Rogge's own account. In the CSS *Alabama* individuals were never allowed to loot for their own enrichment. Instead, the looting of prizes was systematic and disciplined. Requests passed through channels of military communications. A prize was looted to find articles on the official want list. Ordinarily articles were not taken because of their cost, except for some things of small size and high value, such as chronometers. In the case of *Anna F. Schmidt*, among the articles needed were boots and shoes, and in this regard *Alabama's* needs were more than filled. When the Sunday muster was held on 5 July, there was no reason for any member of the ship's company not to have shiny new shoes of the proper size. Of course, the chief significance of *Anna F. Schmidt* was that her cargo yielded ample supplies of the hard ship's bread which was considered so necessary in the diet of seadogs of that day.

7 vessels in sight. On boarding I found [her] to be the (late Yankee) ship "Thorndeer" of Greenock bound to Calcutta.

When Fullam boarded *Thorndeer*, he learned that this American-built ship's home port was Greenock, Scotland, and that she was carrying coal

[125]

from Cardiff, Wales, to Calcutta. *Thorndeer* was operating under British registry with a Scottish captain and an English crew.

8 p.m. Made a sail on lee quarter, wore ship in chase, fired a blank cartridge to which chase replied with another. Called all hands to quarters, lowered propellor, and stood in chase, under steam. Loaded port battery with five second shell, and issued arms. Everyone certain of a brush. Overhauled chase. Upon speaking, she proved to be H. M. Frigate "Clio," or "Diomede." Secured the battery and piped down. Made sail.

Fullam first called the ship HM Frigate *Clio* and later corrected it to *Diomede*. Semmes and Sinclair both identified her as *Diomede*. *Diomede* was a beautiful ship that from a distance looked like an American clipper. *Alabama* took after her and had fairly to fly, even with steam plus sail. The chase was exciting, a race between two greyhounds of the sea. HMS *Diomede* was homeward bound to Plymouth when she and *Alabama* exchanged signals at sea. *Diomede* had just passed close to the flaming wreck of *Anna F. Schmidt,* and the quartermaster of the British frigate commented through his trumpet upon the flotsam around the burning ship, saying "I suppose this is some of your work."

4th. Made a sail on weather quarter.

6th. 2.30 a.m. Sail descried one point on weather bow. Gave chase. Paying no attention to the two blank cartridges, fired a shot which had the desired effect. On boarding I found her to be the ship "Express" of Portsmouth. N. H., Valparaiso to Antwerp, laden with guano. Removed prisoners, bread, provisions, &c., and fired her.

When Fullam boarded *Express,* he learned that she was a Boston ship of 1,072 tons. Among the owners was William S. Frost, who was also master of the vessel. Mrs. Frost was aboard ship with her husband. With Mrs. Frost was her maid-companion. Women passengers were always a special problem for the Confederate sea raiders because of the cramped quarters of ships and the uncertain control over a crew of predators. *Express* was in the guano trade out of Peru. She had sailed from the Chincha Islands on 5 March 1863, with a cargo of guano, bound for Antwerp. When Fullam boarded *Express,* the date was 6 July and the place was 28.28 south and 30.07 west. As Captain Frost and his ship's papers went through the usual admiralty proceedings aboard *Alabama,* there was evidence that this undoubtedly American vessel was carrying guano owned by neutrals, but on technical points the Confederate admiralty court decided that the claims of neutral ownership were fraudulent, and therefore condemned ship and cargo. While there were many claims submitted to the United States Department of State and the *Alabama* Claims court, the evidence would seem that the Confederate admiralty proceedings in this case indeed resulted in the burning of neutral cargo. The total claims filed in connection with the loss of *Express* amounted to $76,108.75. The Confederate evaluation, placed by Kell upon this vessel number 45 destroyed by *Alabama,* was $57,000 for the ship and $64,300 for the cargo. *Alabama's* own statistics of the value of destroyed vessels (including *Express*) totaled $3,489,278.

From the crews of *Express* and *Anna F. Schmidt, Alabama* shipped five new seamen. These were: Fred Columbia, William Bradford, H. Saunders, James Broderick, and John Williams (2nd of this name). Saunders and Williams served in *Alabama* little more than two months before deserting. All the others served through the remainder of the cruise, including the battle with *Kearsarge.* These five additional men brought the total complement of *Alabama* on 7 July 1863 to 120 men and 23 officers.

The Captain's wife and servant were accommodated as usual in the ward room. Proceeded again to the eastward.

17th. Fresh westerly breeze. Noon. Crossed the Meridian of Greenwich.

22nd. 11 a.m. Made a sail, chased. On boarding I found her to be the ship "Star of Erin" of Belfast, Calcutta to London. Transferred the Captain and lady of prize ship "Express" and the Captain of "Anna F. Schmidt."

When Fullam boarded *Star of Erin* and learned the facts that he stated here, the vessel was speedily released after her captain agreed to embark as passengers Captain William S. Frost, his wife, and the maid. As a rule, when a neutral ship was persuaded to take passengers after being stopped at sea, it was customary for *Alabama* to pay for the passage with presents.

26th. Sunday. Saw a suspicious looking sail, gave chase. On boarding I found her to be the ship "Lillian" of St. John, cotton laden, Bombay to Liverpool. Passing as the U. S. Str. "Dacotah."

Actually, in July 1863, the USS *Dacotah* was in Baltimore, Maryland, having her boilers repaired.

Boarded a Dutchman, Batavia to Amsterdam. Chased another ship. He paying no attention to a blank cartridge, a shot was fired over her. She then showed her colours and hove to. She proved to be the English ship "Havelock," Bombay to Liverpool, her Captain corroborating a report made previously to the effect that a steamer was observed under steam steering easterly.

[127]

*27th. A.M. Saw a schooner. Signalled him to "heave to."
Boarding I found her to be the schooner "Rover" of Cape
Town, Walwich Bay to Cape Town. [She] Had exchanged
signals with a barque rigged steamer the day previous. Large
ship reported at sundown bearing south. Three vessels seen
during the night. Fresh S. S. W. gale. The Lions Rump, C. G.
Hope [Cape of Good Hope] in sight.*
   28th. Dassen Island on starboard beam, dist. 10 miles.

Lion's Rump is a very distinctive feature of the Table Bay area, a
land of picturesque place names. On Table Mountain a ridge extends
about a mile and a quarter from Lion's Rump to Lion's Head. *HO 105,* p.
347; *BA Chart 2091; Britannica Atlas,* Plate 148; *HO Chart 2393.*
Dassen Island has dangerous reefs on three sides and mariners have
been warned of these reefs. Dassen Island today has a circular iron
tower with a light used for navigation, and even in Fullam's day Dassen
Island was used for navigation because of the reefs.

*29th. Saw a schooner on port bow. I brought her Master
off to pilot us in. 2.40 p.m. Anchored in Saldanha Bay. Splendid bay. Fresh provisions abundant, but water scarce. A
splendid harbour for a capital.*

Saldanha Bay was the first area in South Africa visited by the CSS
Alabama and was the first British port of call reached by *Alabama* after
Kingston, Jamaica. Saldanha Bay lies north and west of Cape Town.
There is approximately one degree of latitude (60 miles) between the
two. Saldanha Bay lies 55 miles north of Table Bay. *Alabama* put into the
safe harbor of Saldanha Bay to make repairs.

*3rd [August 1863]. This day proved the most melancholy
one since we have been out. Four officers left the ship in the
dingey to go shooting. Whilst in the act of drawing a gun
towards himself (in the boat), it went off, at a distance of
three inches from his breast, and its contents entered his
breast, going through the lungs, and causing instantaneous
death. The deceased was Third Assistant Engineer S. W.
Cummings. His death caused universal sorrow. 5.15 p.m.
Passed his body on deck.*

Simeon W. Cummings, like other members of *Alabama's* company, was
impressed by the abundant game in the wilds of Saldanha Bay: deer,
pheasant, antelope, quail, hare, curlew, snipe, plover, ducks, geese,
and other wildlife. On 3 August 1863 while *Alabama* was moored in the
bay calking and painting, Cummings, Irvine Bulloch, and Arthur Sinclair

[128]

formed a party and spent the day at the head of Saldanha Bay shooting ducks. Late in the afternoon while still hunting ducks from the boat, Cummings accidentally shot himself. Sinclair, who was an eye witness, wrote, " . . . Cummings shot himself through the heart in an effort to pull the gun to himself by the muzzle. The hammer of the gun caught the thwart. Without an outcry or groan, but with a look of despair and appeal never to be forgotten, he sank into the bottom of the boat, his body coming together limp as a rag." Cummings was taken back aboard *Alabama* and treated by Dr. Llewellyn, but died shortly after.

4th. 2.45 p.m. Called all hands: "Bury the dead." Passed the body over the side into a boat. Everything being prepared, the funeral party accompanied by a guard left the ship for the shore. On landing, the body with 4 men was placed in a waggon. The guard also in a waggon. The officers in uniform on horseback. The pallbearers were Engineers Freeman, O'Brien, & Pundt, and myself. Arrived at the grave, the First Lieut. read the service, and after three volleys had been fired over the grave and a temporary headstone placed, we returned on board.

For the first time on the cruise of the CSS *Alabama,* the Confederate flag flew at half-mast. This was in mourning for the much-beloved assistant engineer, whose death was the first aboard the warship—Simeon W. Cummings. Miles J. Freeman was chief engineer and Mathew O'Brien was third assistant engineer, as was John M. Pundt. Since Cummings himself was also a third assistant engineer, Fullam was honored by being the only one of the pallbearers who was not in the engineering department. Kell had been a shipmate of Cummings in the CSS *Sumter,* as had Freeman and O'Brien. Pundt and Fullam were the only ones mentioned in connection with the funeral who had not been in *Sumter.* Captain Semmes later wrote, " . . . the next morning, the colors of the ship were half-masted, and all the boats—each with its colors also at half-mast—formed in line, and as many of the officers and crew as could be spared from duty, followed the deceased to his last resting place. There were six boats in the procession, and as they pulled in for the shore, with the well-known funeral stroke and drooping flags, the spectacle was one to sadden the heart. A young life had been suddenly cut short in a far distant land."

Cummings was buried in the family burial ground of a Dutch farmer at Saldanha Bay. The officers of the Royal Navy attached to the squadron operating out of Cape Town, later replaced the temporary headstone. Edna and Frank Bradlow, writing of their home area, said that Cummings' tombstone is the only monument to a citizen of the onetime Confederate States that they know of in all of South Africa.

[129]

At the time of his death, Cummings was about 28 years of age. He was born in the North, but moved with his family to New Orleans. He had lived in Louisiana for about 12 years prior to the Civil War and had served a regular apprenticeship as a machinist in the large machine shop of Leeds and Company in New Orleans. He had also worked for the Coastline Steamship Company. He was a friend of Chief Engineer Miles J. Freeman, of the CSS *Sumter,* and it was Freeman who recommended that Semmes appoint Cummings as a third assistant engineer in *Sumter.* After *Sumter* was blockaded at Gibraltar and, under orders, abandoned by her officers and men, Cummings was one of *Sumter's* people who embarked on the Spanish steamship *Euphrosyne,* bound for London. Off Vigo, Spain, *Euphrosyne* was wrecked, but Cummings finally made his way to London in time to join the CSS *Alabama* at the start of her cruise.

5th. 6 a.m. Got under weigh and stood out of the bay along the land in chase of a sail. Nearing her, it was found to be the C. S. barque "Tuscaloosa," Lieut. Commg. Low. I boarded and brought him off to communicate with Captain Semmes. Took him off [to the CSS Tuscaloosa] again and parted company.

On the morning of 5 August 1863 *Alabama* departed Saldanha Bay after a week of repairing and refitting. She headed for Table Bay and Cape Town, some 60 miles south of Saldanha, hugging the coast. The weather was fine and the wind light when suddenly there came into sight the CSS *Tuscaloosa,* from whom they had parted 46 days before (21 June). Great was the astonishment of all on board, except Semmes who had ordered Lt. Low to bring *Tuscaloosa* for a rendezvous with *Alabama* and a report on Low's commerce-raiding operations. Semmes sent Fullam in one of the small boats to pick up Low and bring him aboard *Alabama* for his report. Details of this part of the cruise of the CSS *Tuscaloosa* are available in Low's Journal. In brief, the cruise of the CSS *Tuscaloosa* was a story of boarding one neutral ship after another of various nationalities, as the converted commerce raider sailed across the South Atlantic. Never in the entire cruise was a single United States merchantman destroyed in the 46 days, although *Tuscaloosa* encountered an average of one ship a day, and boarded many. Sinclair said that the cruise of *Tuscaloosa* was a failure. Bradlow accepted the judgment of Sinclair. Yet there was almost as much reason for *Tuscaloosa* to continue showing the Confederate flag as there was for *Alabama* to continue her cruise (admittedly with diminishing results), or for *Shenandoah* at a later time to fit out. Had the Confederate flag not been shown repeatedly in 1863, the figures for the decline of the United States merchant marine in ships and tonnage might have been different. Dalzell showed that 348 American ships with a tonnage of 252,579 in 1863 shifted to British registry. The tonnage in 1864 mounted to 400,865. Thus Confederate commerce raiders had become effective in persuading shrewd Yankee capitalists that it was better to sell their ships to British or other foreign registry and instead put their money into the burgeoning interior economy of the North.

The CSS *Tuscaloosa* continued her dogged tracking of enemy ships. It was midnight on 31 July 1863 when a lookout on *Tuscaloosa* cried, "Sail ho!" The raider hoisted additional canvas and turned to chase the newcomer. Within an hour *Tuscaloosa* closed the range, customary before firing a blank cartridge as a signal to lie to. The chase had no idea of giving in so easily, and *Tuscaloosa* followed this with a shot across the bow of the merchantman, but she still did not respond until two more shots were fired. When at last she shortened sail and hove to, Midshipman William H. Sinclair, serving as the lieutenant of *Tuscaloosa*, went on board and learned the identity of this prize, the ship *Santee*. Low's Journal showed that of some four dozen contacts, only *Santee* was found to be enemy owned, and even in this case the ship was proceeding from Akyab, Burma, where presumably less was known of Confederate commerce raiding than in Atlantic ports.

Santee was built in 1860 in Portsmouth, New Hampshire, with the following characteristics: 898 tons, and dimensions of 172 x 33.5 x 24, according to *American Lloyds, 1862*. After *Santee* was seized by the boarding officer, the captain of the vessel, William Parker, with his ship's documents was taken aboard *Tuscaloosa* and presented to Low and the Confederate admiralty court, acting after the manner of Semmes in the CSS *Alabama*. It was learned that *Santee* was owned by Jonathan M. Frederick and Son but the cargo, consisting exclusively of 1,500 tons of rice, was owned by Halliday, Fox and Company of London. Because of the neutral cargo, Captain Parker was allowed to sign a ransom bond for $150,000 for the release of *Santee*. The whole proceeding, from first sighting *Santee* to release of the ship, had transpired between twelve midnight and three a.m., some 750 miles west of Cape Town.

After Lt. Low's report to Semmes was made on 5 August, Low returned to the CSS *Tuscaloosa*, in accordance with Semmes' orders, to take that merchantman-cruiser to Simon's Bay, while *Alabama* continued on her course toward Cape Town. Simon's Bay is located south and east of Cape Town, between Table Bay and False Bay. Located there also was a naval station, a circumstance which seemed to offer more security to the CSS *Tuscaloosa*, as Union diplomats had opportunity to protest the metamorphosis of *Conrad* into the CSS *Tuscaloosa*. Simon's Bay is described in *HO 156*, pp. 59–60, and *HO Chart 2387*.

On 13 September the CSS *Tuscaloosa* captured *Living Age*, a Maine vessel proceeding from Akyab to Falmouth with a cargo of rice. Low's admiralty court decided that the ship was enemy but the cargo was neutral, consequently *Living Age* was released on a $160,000 ransom bond.

At 1.30 p.m. stood in chase of a sail. 3 p.m. Overhauled him, we being under English colours. She then showed U. S. colours. Fired a blank cartridge, hauled down the English, and hoisted the Stars and Bars. Ran alongside and ordered him to heave to, or we would fire into him. Showing no disposition to heave to, a musket shot was fired over him. After some delay, she hove to. Sent Mr. Evans on board. Found her to be the barque "Sea Bride" of Boston, from New York to Cape Town. We being five miles distant from land by cross bearing. I was sent on board as prize master with eight men. The Captain, mates, and crew sent on board from prize.

A short while after twelve noon on 5 August, *Alabama's* lookout aloft cried, "Sail ho!" and thus began one of the most exciting and controversial pursuits by the raider. Soon after the officers and men of the watch were alerted by the lookout, they could see the white canvas, the tapered spars, and the fresh paint on an American bark. She was running before a light breeze toward Table Bay. It was fortunate for *Alabama* that there was no brisk wind, otherwise the chase probably would have been able to run to safety inside the three-mile limit before the commerce raider could have reached her. As usual, *Alabama* at first raised false colors, this time British. It was not usual, however, for the fast-sailing cruiser to use up some of her precious coal in a routine chase, but it was done in this pursuit. Fullam determined by cross bearing, as he stated, the exact distance from the shore of the point of capture to be five miles. Later there were some to affirm and others to deny that this vessel was captured outside the three-mile limit.

Master's Mate Evans boarded the new prize, and soon brought her captain, Charles F. White, and the ship's papers back to *Alabama*. The bark was *Sea Bride,* a 447-ton Boston-owned, Newburyport-built vessel, valued at $30,000. Captain White shared ownership of *Sea Bride* with some dozen other proprietors—21/64th of the bark being in his own name and the same number of shares in the name of William Currier of Newburyport. *Sea Bride* departed New York 28 May 1863 with a cargo of notions, provisions, and other general items selected for trade on the East Coast of Africa, with the intermediate destination of Table Bay. On 5 August, *Sea Bride* was close to Cape Town when boarded by Master's Mate Evans. Soon Fullam was sent to relieve Evans and to become prize master of *Sea Bride.*

As prize master of *Sea Bride,* Fullam received orders from Semmes to stand off and on Table Bay without actually entering the waters of any

South African port. This was for the purpose of avoiding legal complications over the expected Union claims that *Sea Bride* had been illegally seized inside the three-mile limit. Semmes, however, modified his orders to Fullam by saying that, in case a gale blew Fullam's command out to sea, he was to bring *Sea Bride* into Saldanha Bay for rendezvous with *Alabama* by 15 August 1863. Semmes knew that to take a captured ship into a neutral harbor would be a clear violation of international law. A different principle was involved with *Tuscaloosa* at Fernando de Noronha because there was evidence, which was finally accepted by the British, that *Tuscaloosa* was a Confederate warship. See Wheaton, *Elements of International Law*, 11, 88.

3.30 "Alabama" came to an anchor in 7 fthms water in Table Bay.

HO 105, p. 345, indicates that most of Table Bay is 10 fathoms or more in depth. The South African newspaper *Cape Argus* of 6 August 1863 reported in detail the arrival of *Alabama* at Cape Town and the enthusiastic reception.

Banked fires. Lieut. Wilson sent on shore to visit the governor.

Lt. Joseph D. Wilson was third lieutenant in the CSS *Alabama,* ranking just after Richard F. Armstrong. Wilson was a native of the then sparsely populated state of Florida and a veteran of brief service in the "Old Navy," commencing in 1857. Wilson served with Semmes in the CSS *Sumter* before the cruise of *Alabama*. Before Wilson's visit to Governor P. E. Wodehouse (progenitor of the author P. G. Wodehouse), Semmes had exchanged letters with the governor. Semmes had written the governor, while *Alabama* was in Saldanha Bay, requesting permission to land 33 prisoners in Cape Town and also requesting permission to obtain supplies and ship repairs. Actually, *Alabama's* greatest need at the moment, although Semmes did not mention this in his letters to the governor, was coal, for *Alabama* had been waiting in vain in Saldanha Bay for a Confederate coal tender which never arrived.

Visitors coming on board in numbers. 5.15 English mail steamer "Lady Jocelyn" anchored near us, her crew cheering us as they passed. 10.30 p.m. H.B.M. sloop of war "Valorous" anchored near us.
6th. The enthusiasm displayed by the inhabitants of the Cape, amounted almost to a frenzy. All day, crowded with visitors.

Captain Semmes' letters to Governor Wodehouse had caused great excitement in Cape Town. The people were intensely stirred over the announcement that the celebrated Confederate cruiser was expected. Also expected at about the same time was the *Lady Jocelyn* from England and the *Hydaspes* from India. When the news came in that the Confederate steamer had been seen coming from the northwest, crowds of citizens began gathering on the streets. Another announcement that a Union bark could be seen coming in from the southeast was tremendously stimulating because everyone felt sure they were going to be able to watch the rare sport of the stalking and capturing of a Union ship by the famous raider.

People by cab and on foot rushed up on the surrounding heights to view the drama. The newspaper *Cape Argus* of 6 August reported, " . . . as we reached the corner [around the height], there lay the *Alabama* within fifty yards of the unfortunate Yankee. As the Yankee came around from the southeast, and about five miles from the Bay, the steamer came down upon her. The Yankee evidently taken by surprise. . . . Like a cat, watching and playing with a victimized mouse, Captain Semmes permitted his prize to draw off a few yards, and then he up steam again, and pounced upon her. She first sailed round the Yankee from stem to stern, and stern to stem again. The way that fine, saucy, rakish craft was handled was worth riding a hundred miles to see. She went round the bark like a toy, making a complete circle, and leaving an even margin of water between herself and her prize, of not more than twenty yards. . . . This done, she sent a boat with a prize crew off, took possession in the name of the Confederate States, and sent the bark off to sea. The *Alabama* then made for the port. . . . We found the heights overlooking Table Bay covered with people . . . and ladies waved their handkerchiefs . . . nothing but a sea of heads as far as the eye could reach. [After the capture] Nearly all the city was upon the bay; the rowing clubs in uniform. . . . On getting alongside the *Alabama,* we found . . . about a dozen boats before us . . .and as boat after boat arrived, three hearty cheers were given for Captain Semmes and his gallant privateer . . . in admiration of the skill, pluck, and daring of the *Alabama,* her captain, and her crew. . . ."

The protesting role of the United States consul was made difficult, but Consul Walter Graham waged a vigorous battle for his side by his claims that *Sea Bride* was seized within the marine league. Captain Charles G. Forsyth of the ship *Valorous* reported to Governor Wodehouse his official opinion that *Alabama* was about six or six and a half miles offshore when *Sea Bride* was captured. The port captain of Table Bay (Captain H. Wilson) concurred with that official opinion. Frederick Carter, who had observed the capture from atop Lion's Rump, an excellent vantage point above Cape Town, gave a report similar to Wilson's.

Sent on shore all prisoners. Sent the cutter with instructions to the prize barque "Sea Bride." She was observed to stand out to sea.

Semmes instructed Fullam to keep *Sea Bride* outside the marine league off Table Bay, sailing back and forth if weather permitted. To have taken this prize, which had not been condemned by any court other than *Alabama's* admiralty court, into a South African port would have been a clear violation of international law.

8 p.m. Cloudy threatening weather. Strong northerly breeze.
7th [August 1863]. Strong gales. Veered out 90 fthms. of
cable and let go the other anchor.

As a nautical term, veered means paid out, or let out, as in the case of an anchor chain, cable, or rope. Fullam was speaking of a gale that wrecked a Brazilian brig which was moored in the bay, but all of her crew were saved by local boats.

Evening blowing strong with heavy sea. Contradictory rumours respecting the "Sea Bride."

It is not strange that, afloat and ashore, rumors should grow, considering that the status of *Sea Bride* was the subject of correspondence among important men: Governor Philip E. Wodehouse, Captain Charles F. White of *Sea Bride*, and United States Consul Walter Graham. An examination into the status of *Sea Bride* was conducted by the senior officer of the Royal Navy at Simon's Bay, Rear Admiral Baldwin W. Walker, resulting in reports from telegraph signalmen, lighthouse keepers, and Captain Charles C. Forsyth, Royal Navy, commanding officer of HBMS *Valorous*.

It is noteworthy that while the official fur was flying over *Sea Bride*, Semmes and his officers were royally entertained by British officialdom. At the same time, United States Consul Graham was free to protest and to reflect upon the significance of the contrast in treatment between the United States consul and the Confederates. Graham's letters to the British were answered officially but coolly. There is no question that articulate South Africa was pro-Confederate. Not a little of the admiration for *Alabama* stemmed from her British origin and partly British crew. The widespread interest of South Africans in the CSS *Alabama* is attested by the Malay folksong, "Here Comes the Alabama," which supplied the title in 1959 for the Bradlow publication. Edna and Frank Bradlow in that year published their interesting story of a ship and a folksong under the title, *Here Comes the Alabama*. People who knew little of the politics or the history of the Confederate warship expressed with music and words their feeling of excitement over the coming to South Africa of the great warship. More evidence of the stir which *Alabama* created in South Africa became apparent when the title by George Townley Fullam "Our Cruise in the Confederate States' War Steamer Alabama. The Private Journal of an Officer" was published for the first time on 19 September 1863. The Journal was a supplement to the *South African Advertiser and Mail*.

8th. Moderate breeze from N. W. Hove up starboard anchor.
9th. 6 a.m. Steamed out of Table Bay along the land. Saw
a vessel on starboard bow. 8.35 a.m. Made a sail right ahead.
11 a.m. Overhauled and boarded the barque "Martha Wen-
zell" of Boston, rice laden, from Akyab to Falmouth. She being
at time of capture within three miles of a line drawn from
headland to headland of False Bay, was in British waters, and
therefore not liable to capture. Consequently she was released.

Rear Admiral Baldwin W. Walker lost no time in pointing out to Semmes that *Martha Wenzell* was captured in neutral waters, as Walker wrote to the Secretary of the British Admiralty. Walker reported also that Semmes gave the British assurance that capturing *Martha Wenzell* inside the three-mile limit was quite unintentional, and that as soon as the Confederates discovered the error, the vessel was released. This explanation Walker considered sufficient, and so reported to the Admiralty.

Martha Wenzell was one of three prizes taken in or near South African waters by the CSS *Alabama* which produced unique solutions. The fact that *Martha Wenzell* was captured and released, although a Union-owned vessel, was unusual but not unique. The uniqueness came from her being released without a ransom bond. She was also the only prize which Semmes admitted officially that he captured illegally. Another of the three prizes taken in the area whose case resulted in a unique solution was *Conrad,* which was tried and condemned as a prize and then commissioned as a Confederate cruiser under the new name CSS *Tuscaloosa.* No other prize was so treated by *Alabama* (although there were other such cases by the CSS *Florida).* The uniqueness of *Sea Bride* came from circumstances yet to be narrated by Fullam. In essence, *Sea Bride* was unique in that she was the only prize that was sold and the cash put into the coffers of the CSS *Alabama,* although there were other cases, of course, of cash money being taken from condemned prizes. The *Sea Bride* procedure was an avenue that could have been followed with other prizes conceivably, but Semmes was doubtless correct in saying that the procedure was too time-consuming and that *Alabama* was in the business of waging war and not of making money. In any case, *Alabama's* coffers were still full. Sinclair said that businessmen in all the ports of the cruise were quite willing to accept Confederate drafts in place of hard money and that *Alabama* still had hard money upon arrival in Cherbourg before the 19 June duel with *Kearsarge.*

2.30 p.m. Came to an anchor in Simons Bay with both cables
in seven fathoms. Official visits paid and received.

11th. Caulking, &c. Lost three hands by desertion.

The three men who deserted were Thomas James, Alfred Morris, and an unidentified third man possibly, like Morris and James, an ordinary seaman. There were two additional men discharged 12 August 1863 at Simon's Bay, both as invalids and both as seamen. In addition to the three men whom Fullam mentioned as deserters, *Alabama* lost many other seamen by desertion during the stay in South Africa. Indeed, Consul Walter Graham exerted himself to persuade *Alabama's* men when they were ashore to remain ashore. In this Graham had considerable success. This is mentioned in several official reports of both Union and Confederate sources. Between the dates of the arrival of *Alabama* in Saldanha Bay, 28 July 1863, and her departure, 24 September, for Sunda Straits and the China Seas, there were the following desertions from that rebel raider: Albert Gillman (31 July), William Nordstrom (1 August), James Wallace (1 August), Thomas James (12 August), Alfred Morris (12 August), George Ross (17 September), John Veal (17 September), John Hughes (18 September), John Jack (18 September), Charles Coles (19 September), Peter Jackson (19 September), George Thomas (19 September), James Raleigh (19 September), Robert Egan (21 September), Nicholas Maling (21 September), John Miller (21 September), Richard Ray (21 September), Henry Saunders (21 September), Samuel Volans (21 September), John Williams (21 September), and James Wilson (21 September).

If *Alabama* and her crew were popular with the people of South Africa, it cannot be denied that South Africa was popular with *Alabama's* deserting seamen. Many of the deserters had doubtless become so tired of the discipline and the monotony of being at sea much of the time that not even the prospect of thousands of dollars in prize money and routine pay that was twice as much as they could make in a merchant ship could hold them aboard *Alabama* and away from a lively liberty port like Cape Town. Also the efforts of Walter Graham should not be overlooked. The day before *Alabama* sailed from South Africa, headed for Sunda Strait, there were 20 men still absent from the raider. Rewards were offered for their apprehension and a few were brought back to the ship for the reward by the Simonstown police. Shortly before *Alabama* sailed, 24 September, there were numerous sailor landlords coming on board presenting bills against members of the crew. In these cases, Semmes refused to pay such bills on the ground that the landlords were extortioners. The rates of pay aboard the CSS *Alabama* were as follows:

		£	S	Dollars.
Master-at-arms	per month	6	0 —	29.04
Yeoman	''	6	0 —	29.04
Ship's steward	''	6	0 —	29.04
Ship's corporal	''	5	10 —	26.62
Armorer	''	6	0 —	29.04

Ship's cook	''	5	10 — 26.62
Chief boatswain's mate	''	6	0 — 29.04
Second ditto	''	5	10 — 26.62
Gunner's mate	''	6	0 — 29.04
Carpenter's mate	''	6	0 — 29.04
Sailmaker's mate	''	5	10 — 26.62
Quartermaster	''	5	10 — 26.62
Quarter gunners	''	5	10 — 26.62
Coxswain	''	5	10 — 26.62
Capt. of forecastle	''	5	10 — 26.62
Capt. of top	''	5	0 — 24.20
Capt. of aftguard	''	5	0 — 24.20
Capt. of hold	''	5	0 — 24.20
Cabin steward	''	5	0 — 24.20
Ward-room steward	''	5	0 — 24.20
Seamen	''	4	10 — 21.78
O. seamen	''	4	0 — 19.36
Landsmen	''	3	10 — 14.94
Boys	''	2	0 — 9.68
Firemen	''	7	0 — 33.88
Trimmers	''	5	0 — 24.20

14th. The Chinese gunboat "Kwantung" steamed out at sea.

On 10 August 1863, Semmes dined on board the Chinese gunboat *Kwantung* in company with the ship's captain, Commander Young, and Captain Joseph G. Bickford, commanding officer of HBMS *Narcissus,* besides other British naval officers. The side-wheel steamer *Kwantung* was constructed at Birkenhead, England, by Laird Shipbuilders, as a British gunboat serving in Chinese waters. In August 1863 she was in Simon's Bay having her engines repaired at the naval dry dock. When she made her trial run after the repairs, Admiral Walker's family were on board as guests.

[Kwantung] Reported having met the U. S. Str. "Mohican" off the Cape de Verde. 6 a.m. The C. S. barque "Tuscaloosa" got under weigh. Visitors ad lib. Repairing ship. Mr. Max Meulnier and Mr. Jul. Schroeder appointed masters mates.

Baron Maximilian von Meulnier was an officer in the Prussian Navy on leave of absence and making a world tour with Julius Schroeder who was also on leave from his post with the Prussian Navy. Meulnier and Schroeder had been shipwrecked near Table Bay. The two were in Cape Town when the CSS *Alabama* arrived there, and both eagerly applied for billets in the cruiser. Semmes interviewed both men and closely questioned them as to their skill and motives. To recruit in an English port was a violation of the Foreign Enlistment Act, but it was a law violated by both sides in the American Civil War. Along with nine enlisted men, Meulnier and Schroeder were added to the Confederate rolls. Thus *Alabama* had 13 replacements for the 21 men she lost during the stay in South Africa. The 13 more than made up for the 21, especially because Meulnier and Schroeder rendered outstanding service when *Alabama* fought *Kearsarge*. Long before that engagement on 19 June 1864, these experienced officers were put to good use as master's mates in *Alabama*. Before the addition of the two Prussians, Fullam and Evans were the only master's mates, and they had their hands more than full. It is true that the duties of master's mates slackened off somewhat as *Alabama* moved from Cape Town toward the China Sea, there being fewer prizes, and yet there was not so much slackening as it was necessary to board many of the vessels they encountered even though they were identified as neutrals. Of course, for a time James Evans was the only master's mate because Fullam was prize master of *Sea Bride,* being careful not to take that Union merchantman into South African waters.

15th. 11 a.m. Got up anchor and steamed out of Simons Bay.

The departure from Simon's Bay was made in threatening weather. It was raining and the barometer was falling.

2.30 Two sails reported on port bow. Boarded the English barque "Saxon," Algoa Bay to Cape Town. 3. Blew off steam and hoisted propellor. Shipped 9 hands, stowaways from an American ship in Simons Bay.

The names of eight of the nine hands shipped are available. They were ordinary seamen, listed on the muster rolls as James Welsh, P. Wharton, F. Mahoney, Richard Ray, Nicholas Maling, John Russell, John Adams, and Samuel Volans. Three of these men deserted after some five weeks' duty in the Confederate Navy. Another served for four months before deserting. Four others served for the entire remainder of the cruise, including the battle with *Kearsarge*. These four were: Welsh, Wharton, Russell, and Adams. Three of these nine men were in *Alabama* such a short time that Fullam's reference to their enlistments falls in the note beyond the reference to their desertions: Nicholas Maling, Richard Ray, and Samuel Volans.

11 p.m. Made a steamer on lee bow, steering S. E.
  16th. Saw two vessels to windward.
  17th. Made a large ship on lee quarter. Stood in chase. 7.10 Hove her to by signal. Proved to be the ship "Broughton Hall" of Belfast, Bombay to Liverpool. Medical aid being required, Dr. Llewellyn was sent on board.

The medical aid was needed by the captain's wife. Therefore, Dr. Llewellyn went on board *Broughton Hall* and prescribed medicine. Although Dr. Llewellyn was junior to Dr. Francis L. Galt, much of Galt's time appears to have been taken up with his duties as acting paymaster, replacing *Alabama's* unmentionable Clarence R. Yonge.

8.15 Boat returned and [we] stood on course. Three vessels in sight before dark.

18th. Made a large sail on weather quarter. Beat to quarters. Hove her to by signal. Proved to be the English ship "Camper- down," Madras to London. Seven vessels in sight.

19th. Chased and boarded the English barque "Durban," Natal to London.

21st. Chased a vessel. Found to be Dutch.

22nd. Chased and boarded the English ship "Sarawak," Bombay to Liverpool, with cotton, &c. &c.

Sarawak was boarded about 3 p.m. in a moderate gale. It may be inferred that Fullam was the boarding officer. The cotton cargo merits comment. The London *Economist* gave statistics showing the great increases made by India in the growing of cotton because of the cotton shortages in English textile mills during the American Civil War. At the end of the Civil War, England was obtaining from India 85 percent of all British cotton imports. Owsley, *King Cotton Diplomacy*. When Fullam boarded *Sarawak*, the position was approximately 32.13.9 south and 16.8.30 east.

Saw another sail.

23rd. Court Martial sentenced chief boatswains mate, Johnston [Brent Johnson], to lose all pay and prize money due him, be confined in irons three months, and disgraced by a discharge from the ship. In a general order the Captain expressed his regret at having to confirm the above sentence, and stated further that the plea of drunkenness should not protect any offender from punishment; he, believing that intoxication was a crime in itself. The charge was resisting, and drawing a knife upon his superior officer, whilst in the execution of his duty.

Brent Johnson had had experience in the Royal Naval Reserves and was in Liverpool when he first decided to sign up in the CSS *Alabama*. He enlisted 24 August 1862 in the Confederate States Navy, and was one of the three boatswain's mates who put *Alabama* into commission. It is plain from remarks of his shipmates and particularly of Sinclair that Johnson was a very salty seaman, one of *Alabama's* seniors in the rate most senior of all enlisted men in the navy. He was a pastmaster of scrimshaw. Concerning Johnson, Sinclair wrote, "He is engaged in embroidering, with silks of many colors, the collar of a frock for his 'chicken,' the sobriquet of the messenger-boy time out of mind. This old salt has taken him under his wing, acting the part of foster-father, and proud he is of his charge." The name of this "powder monkey" was Robert Egan who had enlisted 24 August 1862 at the start of *Alabama's* cruise. A month after Brent Johnson's court martial, in other words, at the earliest opportunity, on 21 September 1863, Egan deserted at Simon's Bay.

The sentence of the court martial disrated Brent Johnson to seaman and also sentenced him to three months solitary confinement, and at the end of that time to be discharged in disgrace with forfeiture of all pay and prize money. This sentence was modified on 24 September, three days after Egan's desertion, although possibly not connected with it, to remission of the remainder of Johnson's confinement and his return to duty as a seaman. Three months later, Johnson became a petty officer again, and on 24 December 1863 was rated quartermaster.

24th. Tacked ship in chase of a sail to windward. Boarding she proved to be the Dutch barque "Minister Van Hall" of and to Amsterdam from Batavia, with sugar and tobacco.

The newspaper *Cape Argus,* 18 September 1863, reported that the vessel *Maria Elizabeth* was boarded and found to be en route from Batavia to Amsterdam. The same source also mentioned the ship *Minister Van Hall,* giving the same facts as Fullam. Fullam made it plain that he boarded *Minister Van Hall.* If the two vessels were boarded in rapid succession, it is likely that Master's Mate James Evans boarded *Maria Elizabeth.* This might explain the fact that Fullam omitted the name of that vessel. For Fullam to be less specific than some other writer in recording the name and nationality of a vessel boarded was unusual, but the statement is not without exception. *Alabama* was on her way (unknown, as usual, to her ship's company) to Angra Pequeña and the path of trade from the Netherlands East Indies to the Netherlands.

27th. 5 a.m. Stood in towards the land. Sounded at 10. Sandy bottom in 15 fthms. Boarded a schooner, the "Flower of Yarrow" of Cape Town, from Ichaboe to Cape Town. Took her Master on board to pilot us in.

Cape Argus, 18 September 1863, confirms the boarding of *Flower of Yarrow* by *Alabama.* It is plain that Fullam was the boarding officer.

Ichabo Island was so spelled then and now. It was a place of somewhat uncertain sovereignty then, and the same thing could be said of it since the United Nations in 1966 announced that the mandate of South Africa over Southwest Africa was ended. Ichabo Island is located between Hottentot Bay and Luderitz Bay. Luderitz Bay is also called Angra Pequeña. This land of uncertain sovereignty was the destination of *Alabama* for reasons which will soon appear from Fullam's narrative. *HO 105,* pp. 315–318; *HO Chart 2320; Britannica Atlas,* 146.

28th. At 1 p.m. came to an anchor in 15 fthms. in Angra Pequeña. 2 p.m. Got under weigh and anchored in the inner harbour. Found the C. S. barque "Tuscaloosa" and prize barque "Sea Bride" at anchor. Officers and prize crew of *"Sea Bride" returned. (*By orders I delivered the "Sea Bride" up to Capt. Loete, a purchaser.)

Back in the days of 1861 when Semmes commanded the CSS *Sumter* and had captured his first string of prizes, he took the ships into Cuba to sell. When the Spanish government returned the prizes to their owners, *Sumter* initiated the procedure of burning and scuttling which became the pattern for the CSS *Florida, Georgia, Alabama,* and other Confederate cruisers. Since it was impossible to take prizes into the blockaded Confederacy and since the Cuban experience was fair warning of the international law as administered by neutrals, the Confederate alternative was to burn. But now in South Africa a new idea emerged. Why could not *Alabama* take her prizes into one of the nearby areas, such as the land of the Hottentots, and sell them to South African merchants who might be persuaded to be present to make the purchase. After such arrangements were made at the Cape, it was no surprise to Semmes to find *Sea Bride* and *Tuscaloosa* in Luderitz Bay, and also to find there his business friend from the Cape, Captain Thomas Elmstone representing Robert Granger and Company of Cape Town and London. Elmstone employed Captain Loete to take command of *Sea Bride.* It is possible that Semmes explained to Elmstone that, during the time interval between *Alabama's* departure from Simonstown and arrival at Luderitz Bay, the raider had been cruising in the stormy seas south of the Cape and had found no prizes. Of this part of the cruise, Sinclair said that it was the most dangerous and uncomfortable part of the entire cruise of *Alabama.* The most regrettable phase of it to Semmes was that it had yeilded no prizes and the only merchandise Semmes had to sell to Elmstone was *Sea Bride* and her cargo and the cargo which was still aboard the CSS *Tuscaloosa. Sea Bride* and her cargo were worth over $75,000 and Semmes sold them for $16,940. This appeared to be a very great bargain for the purchaser, but it was not without considerable risk. Elmstone knew that if *Sea Bride* were taken into Cape Town or some other civilized port, the ship would be subject to seizure and return to her original owners. *Sea Bride* was painted black and her name changed to *Helen,* with a Hamburg registry, and she sailed between Foulepointe, Madagascar (now Malagasy Republic) and Mauritius in the Indian Ocean east of Madagascar. *Helen* was finally wrecked off St. Mary's, Madagascar.

Since our departure from Simons Bay the condensing apparatus was found to be out of order. Compelled to take 12 casks of water from a schooner.

All the drinking water used aboard the cruiser was condensed by *Alabama's* engine from the vapor of sea water. Each week enough water was condensed to last through the week. During this part of the cruise, the joints of the pipes had become loose and the condenser had broken down, with only a week's supply of water on hand. Since the harbor at Angra Pequeña was surrounded by rocks and desert, water was very scarce and it became necessary to secure some from an English vessel, possibly from Capt. Loete, until the condenser could be repaired.

30th. Strong southerly wind. Put a man on shore at his own request, in accordance with sentence of Court Martial.

The man put ashore was James Adams, ordinary seaman, who was court martialed 30 August 1863. Adams was put ashore at Luderitz Bay at his own request. The sentence of the court martial had been merely forfeiture of all pay ($19.36 per month) and all prize money. The amount of prize money which would have been due Adams was to be calculated at the end of the cruise, or at the end of the Civil War. Adams had been in the Confederate States Navy only seven months when he was put ashore at Luderitz Bay.

31st. Got under way and stood out to sea. Strong southerly wind.
2nd. Sept. [1863] 6.30 a.m. Saw a large sail to windward.
10. Hove her to by signal. On boarding I found her to be the "Punjaub" of and to London from Kurrache, laden with salt petre and cotton.

This was the second time *Punjaub* had been seized by *Alabama*. The first time was 15 March 1863, as earlier noted in Fullam's Journal. At that time Captain Lewis F. Miller had signed a ransom bond for $55,000 obligating Thomas B. Wales, Thomas B. Wales, Jr., and other owners of *Punjaub* to pay the ransom bond within 30 days after the end of the Civil War. *Punjaub* was released the second time without an additional bond. The first ransom bond had the ship and tackle as security. This was doubtless the reason for her release the second time without a new ransom bond. It may be that on the second seizure the cargo of saltpeter and cotton, which was being sent from Karachi to London, was of neutral ownership.

5 p.m. Made a sail on weather bow.

3rd. 2.15 a.m. Saw a sail one point on weather bow. Made all sail in chase. At 3.15 hove chase to with blank cartridge. On boarding found to be the "Isle O'May" of and to London, from Colombo, with coffee.

The newspaper *Cape Argus,* 18 September 1863, confirmed Fullam's data, and added the information that *Isle of May* was boarded 4 September 1863.

Short allowance of water.

5th. 7.30 p.m. A steamer passed us on weather beam. Supposed to be the Cape Mail Steamer.

8th. Strong S. E. wind. Two sails in sight. By signal found her to be an English ship from Bombay to Liverpool. [We passed as the] U. S. Str. "Dacotah."

9th. Moderate wind. Eight vessels in sight, all English and principally from Calcutta to London. Hove one to. Boarding I found her to be the "Cameronian" of Liverpool, Calcutta to London, with a general cargo.

Cape Argus contradicted Fullam in saying that *Cameronian* was not boarded, a subject on which Fullam was the more credible source.

10th. 10.15 Made a sail on weather bow. Found her, by signals, to be an English barque, Calcutta to London. 8.30 p.m. Sail in sight on weather bow. At 10.35 after hailing three times, and firing a blank cartridge, chase hove to. On boarding I found her to be the ship "Flora" of Liverpool from Manilla, with a general cargo.

Cape Argus, 18 September 1863. Fullam had an amusing experience in boarding *Flora. Flora* had run into vexatious delays during her long passage from Manila to the point where Fullam boarded her (33.16 south and 16.20 east). She had fought baffling winds and then, two days before being boarded by Fullam, she encountered a two-masted, long-funneled steam warship which sent a boarding party to *Flora.* The warship wore the Stars and Stripes, but was in fact the CSS *Georgia.* Then Fullam boarded *Flora* while the CSS *Alabama* also wore the United States flag. Fullam told the captain that *Flora* was being boarded by the USS *Ticonderoga,* and the merchant captain believed that successive Union warships had boarded his vessel. *(Ticonderoga* was a screw steamer considerably larger and more heavily armed than *Alabama*.) When Fullam reported to Semmes the neutral character of *Flora*, he described the extreme anger that the Liverpool skipper directed toward all Yankees in general and those in particular who had further delayed his voyage from Manila.

11th. At 5 a.m. made a barque on weather bow. Made sail in chase. 6 a.m. Chase showed English colours.

Sunday. 13th [September 1863]. At 6.17 a.m. saw high land right ahead. Found it to be Table Mountain.

HO 156, p. 55 and map facing p. 54, shows Table Mountain. It is on the rocky Cape Peninsula and rises to a height of 3,550 feet.

Cruising. Land still in sight until the

16th. At 7.15 a.m. lowered propellor. 8. Under weigh, steaming towards Simons Bay. At 4.25 p.m. anchored in Simons Bay. Learnt of the visit of the C. S. Str. "Georgia," and also of the visit of the U. S. Str. "Vanderbilt," the latter leaving on the 11th inst. Simons Bay is a good anchorage, but not protected from S. Easters. Cape Town is pretty large with some thoroughfares second to none out of England (that is, in any of the places we have visited). The Cape people we found to be both kind, courteous and hospitable. It was with feelings of deep regret we took our departure from that place.

24th. 11.55 p.m. Got under weigh and proceeded out of the harbour.

The sequence of *Alabama's* visits to land areas in and near South Africa was: 1. Saldanha Bay 2. Cape Town 3. Simon's Bay 4. Luderitz Bay 5. Simon's Bay again.

The CSS *Georgia* arrived at Cape of Good Hope 16 August 1863, and the same day moved to Simon's Bay. She departed South Africa 29 August 1863. Apparently *Alabama* was in Simon's Bay 14 August and departed 15 August. With *Georgia, Tuscaloosa,* and *Alabama* going and coming in South Africa, the situation seemed much like the meeting of *Georgia* and *Alabama* in Brazil, but this time the two Confederate cruisers were not in the port at the same moment. The USS *Vanderbilt,* in pursuit of Confederate ships, bobbed back and forth between Cape Town and Simon's Bay, and missed each of the cruisers.

About 3 p.m. on 16 September 1863, *Alabama* doubled the Cape of Good Hope and continued along the coast southward and eastward until she came to anchor in Simonstown. The people ashore had the interesting news for Semmes that the USS *Vanderbilt,* under Commander Charles H. Baldwin, had departed Simonstown the preceding Friday, after

[145]

having hovered around for a day or two, but no news had been heard of her for the last two days preceding the arrival of *Alabama*. Baldwin had a ship that could out-shoot the rebel raider and also one that was faster. Alone among the pursuers who never caught her, Baldwin had been able to guess that *Alabama* was headed for South Africa. When he missed *Alabama, Tuscaloosa,* and *Georgia* in the Cape of Good Hope area, Baldwin correctly guessed that *Alabama* would head in the direction of the Indian Ocean, including Madagascar and Mauritius. Although Baldwin made many nearly correct guesses, he never zeroed in to the point of being in sight of *Alabama*. Indeed, the sidewheeler, which had been presented as a gift to the United States government by Commodore Cornelius Vanderbilt, was such a great consumer of coal that Baldwin spent much time in neutral ports persuading authorities that he really needed coal and was not just violating international law. In some ways, Baldwin's struggles with colonial officials over international law resembled those of Semmes himself. It is quite likely that *Alabama* could have defeated *Vanderbilt* in a ship duel had they met because the vulnerability of the paddlewheel probably more than offset *Vanderbilt's* advantage in size, firepower, and speed. It was a test that never came, however.

Alabama was delayed in Simonstown because there was no coal in the market, *Vanderbilt* having bought it all. On 19 September the steamer *Kadie* arrived in Simon's Bay, having brought coal for *Alabama* from Cape Town. After further refitting, *Alabama* departed 24 September to avoid being blockaded in Simon's Bay by the USS *Vanderbilt*.

25th. Saw six vessels. Chased one. Showed English colours to us. 7.50 a.m. Hoisted propellor. The previous day Ex-boatswains Mate Johnston was released and rated as seaman, Capt. Semmes promising to lay his case before Congress, with a view to restoration of the pay & prize-money forfeited by sentence of Court-Martial. The previous good conduct and services of Johnston inducing Capt. Semmes so to act.

The reference is to Brent Johnson, the former chief boatswain's mate.

The inducements held out by the American Consul caused us to lose 16 hands here. Shipped 13 more.

The 16 hands who deserted have been referred to by Fullam. The energetic consul who induced the men to desert was Walter Graham. The 13 hands shipped were: John Smith, Henry Angell, John Mehan, R. Evans, John Welham, Andres Pheiffer, Thomas Kehoe, Richard Hambly, Thomas Brandon, George Conroy, George White, James Hart, and John Wilson. All of these men were ordinary seamen.

U. St. Str. "Vanderbilt" still off the coast.

27th. 10.15 p.m. Passed a brig steering S. E.

28th. Fresh breeze, varying from N. to Wly.

2nd. Oct [1863]. Very cold. Southerly wind. Fair.

3rd. Moderate S. W. wind. 5.45 a.m. Sail reported ½ point on lee bow. Made all sail in chase. 8.40 Found her to be a brig rigged steamer under sail. Got up steam and lowered pro-pellor, making all plain sail in chase. Everybody calculating the chances of a brush with the fancied enemy, all apparently certain we should whip her. 11.20 a.m. Hove her to by signal. On boarding I found her to be the Str. "Mona" of and from London to Shanghai with coals, 60 days out. Passed as the U. S. Str. "Dacotah," bound to Mauritius. 1 p.m. Hoisted propellor and stood on course.

12th. Have had strong winds with heavy seas; varying between N. W. and S. W. Wind always shifting to the S. & W. with a squall. 12.20 p.m. Saw high land; found it to be St. Pauls' Island; sailed round the northern part of it.

16th. Still blowing fresh westerly gales with a heavy sea. 5.50 a.m. A heavy sea struck the port quarter, filling the gig, rendering it necessary to cut it away.

18th. Slight improvement in the weather to day, it being less cold. 10.35 p.m. A most brilliant lunar rainbow observed to the E. S. E.

20th [October 1863]. Jolly weather. Wind falling light.

22nd. Fine and warm. Got hold of the S. E. trade winds.

23rd. Fresh breeze, cloudy towards evening. 5.30 p.m. Whilst at general quarters the cry of "Sail ho" was heard from the mast head. She was observed to be a ship standing westerly. Did not chase.

26th. Light warm winds. 10.15 a.m. Sail descried right ahead. Hove her to by signal. On boarding I found her to be the English ship "Alma" of Aberdeen, Surabaya to Amsterdam, laden with sugar and rice.

Surabaja is variously spelled, including the spelling used by Fullam. This port is located on the northeast coast of Java near Bali. In addition to *Alma*, numerous other vessels boarded by Fullam were trading with Surabaja, carrying cargoes of sugar and rice.

Reports, having passed a U. S. Str. of War in the Straits of

Sunda on the 22nd inst. We suppose her to be the "Wyoming." [We] Passed as the U. S. Str. "Mohican" sent to relieve the "Wyoming."

The USS *Wyoming* was indeed in the East Indies at this time, near the Strait of Sunda. This screw steamer would probably have been no match alone for *Alabama. Wyoming's* speed was less and her armament less, but it is possible that the two ships could have met under circumstances where the slight differences in speed and armament would have been overcome. A few months before this, *Wyoming* had had a remarkable adventure in Japan. Under command of David McDougal, in July 1863, *Wyoming* had battled the Japanese in the Straits of Shimonoseki. In the engagement, four Americans were killed and seven wounded. The *Wyoming* attack was in reprisal for the earlier shooting by the Japanese at the American steamer *Pembroke.* Some three months after the Shimonoseki incident, Commander McDougal wrote Secretary Welles in Washington informing him of the movements of the CSS *Alabama* in and out of South Africa. These reports were based upon Hong Kong newspapers citing Cape Town newspapers, and appeared to have been reasonably accurate. To the factual report, McDougal added his own inaccurate opinion that *Alabama* would not sail into the Far East. McDougal said that nearly all of the American vessels in the China Seas had changed flags because they could get no cargo. McDougal continued with the following doubtless correct statement, "While at Macao three fine American vessels were put under Portuguese colors, and since leaving that port I have seen but three American vessels, one at Batavia and two in the Strait Strait of Sunda, one of which will change her flag on her arrival at Bankok." McDougal, writing from Anjer, Java, gave the further opinion to Welles that when *Alabama* left South Africa she would return to cruising northward in the Atlantic instead of heading for Sunda Strait. At the time that McDougal was writing from Anjer, Java, *Alabama* was on that date in position 21.14 south and 100.15 east, not far from McDougal in Java. Thus *Wyoming* became the fifth Union warship that came very close to the CSS *Alabama.* The others were *San Jacinto, Hatteras, Vanderbilt,* and *Kearsarge.* But *Wyoming* and *Alabama* never met.

A little sidelight on this pursuit occurred a few years before World War II when Charles Brooke, continuing his uncle's romantic tradition as Rajah of Sarawak, received an official visit from some half a dozen American submarines. Admiral Creed Burlingame, USN, of *Silversides* fame in World War II, told the writer about this official visit by the S-boats. When Rajah Brooke entertained the skippers of the submarines, one of the Americans asked Brooke how long it had been since an American warship had visited Sarawak. Brooke replied that he had expected the question and had had the answer looked up ahead of time.

[148]

The last American warship to visit there before the S-boats was the USS *Wyoming* when in pursuit of the CSS *Alabama*.

27th. Light airs and calms. Hot as blazes.

28th. Upon the application of Mr. Smith and myself, the following officers agreeing and volunteering, viz;–Messrs. Howell, Mecaskey, Evans, Mulnier and Schroeder, another guns crew was raised (three men and a powderboy from the other guns also being sent) and one of the after thirty twos was transported to the opposite side of the deck to the after broadside pivot port. Thus making seven guns on a broadside.

William Breedlove Smith, the captain's clerk, was a very busy man with the paper work of the CSS *Alabama*. Before the Civil War, Smith was a fledgling lawyer in the office of Thomas J. Semmes, a cousin of Raphael Semmes. Smith assisted Captain Semmes with the admiralty work in the CSS *Sumter* and then in *Alabama*. Later Smith had a similar role in the CSS *Shenandoah*. Although Smith and Fullam were not in the chain of command aboard *Alabama*, it is interesting that they engineered the setting up of the additional gun crew which consisted of Fullam, Beckett K. Howell (lieutenant of marines), Benjamin P. Mecaskey (boatswain), Baron Max von Meulnier (master's mate), James Evans (master's mate), and Julius Schroeder (master's mate) as the officers involved.

Wind and weather the same until 10 p.m. when it became squally until the mid watch. 5.50 p.m. Sail seen on port bow.

29th. 5.50 a.m. Fired a blank cartridge, showing U. S. colours, to which chase replied by showing Dutch colours. Taking Mr. Meulnier with me to interpret, I found her to be on boarding the Dutch ship "Anna," Batavia to Amsterdam, with sugar and rice. Reported, that on the evening of the 23rd inst., whilst at anchor off Anger, she was boarded by the U. S. Str. "Wyoming," 8 guns.

Anna was boarded by Fullam just six days after David McDougal had sent on her a boarding party from the USS *Wyoming*. *Anna* was boarded by *Alabama* in the East Indies in position 9.19 south and 101.52 east.

All hands ready for an exchange, that is, of shots. Expect to be roughly received, but nevertheless determined to whip her.

31st. A.M. Fine, light westerly airs. At 5.20 a.m., 6 vessels reported in sight. 7.30 Furled all sail and lowered propellor. Chased a large ship which on boarding I found to be the English ship "Jubilee" from Shanghai, 60 days to London, with tea, &c.

[149]

Fullam boarded *Jubilee* two days after *Anna*. The boarding of *Jubilee* at 8.56 south and 102.52 east showed that *Alabama* was continuing on her northeasterly course close to Sunda Strait, headed for the Java Sea and South China Sea.

Did not see the "Wyoming" in the Straits on the 26th inst. In chase of another which on boarding proved to be the Dutch barque "Jacob & Cornelia," Batavia to Amsterdam.

Batavia is located on the northwest coast of Java at approximately 5.56 south and 107.00 east.

In chase of another ship showing English colours. Found her to be the "Tamana," Canton to London.

Tamana was typical of the China trade which, at that time, still flourished for the British.

Had not seen the "Wyoming." Chased another, but, nary a Yank. On boarding I found her to be the English ship "Moneta," Shanghai to London, with teas, &c. To all these we passed as the U. S. Str. "Mohican" going out to relieve the "Wyoming."

When Fullam boarded *Moneta*, he could not have been surprised that she was English or that she carried a cargo of tea. Using the name USS *Mohican* as *Alabama's* alias was a good cover story for Fullam to give these neutral ships, and particularly convincing to say that *Mohican* was going out to relieve the USS *Wyoming*. A useful purpose in the apparently vain boarding of neutral ships was to find out what news there might be of the whereabouts of the USS *Wyoming*.

Nov. 1st [1863] Fine. 2.45 a.m. A sail reported; gave up chase; after another who at 10 a.m. showed English colours. 11.50 a.m. Another vessel in sight. Still in sight on the
2nd at 6.10 a.m. Saw another vessel, gave chase, and at 11.45 hove her to by signal. On boarding I found her to be the English ship "Janet Mitchell," Foo Chow to London, with a general cargo. (Received). Passed as H. M. Str. "Petrel."

Janet Mitchell was boarded by Fullam in position 8.56 south and 103.48 east. Foochow (Fuzhou) is a major Chinese port, as it was also in Fullam's day.

3rd. Light variable airs with occasional rain squalls. Hot, as hell. 5.30 p.m. Sail reported dead ahead. Went to general quarters for exercise.

[150]

4th. Moderate easterly wind. Fine. 9.20 a.m. Sail reported on starboard beam. Wore ship in chase. Hove chase to by signal. On boarding she was found to be the French ship "Jules Cezard" from Batavia to Nantes. Reported the U. S. Str. "Wyoming" at anchor in Batavia harbour on the 28th ult. Filled away again on course.

The bark *Jules Cezard* was boarded by Fullam in position 8.31 south and 103.12 east. From this it is apparent that *Alabama* was continuing to move northward and eastward in the Indian Ocean toward Sunda Strait between Sumatra and Java.

2 p.m. Sail made right ahead. 2.40 Overhauled chase, who showed Dutch colours. On boarding she was found to be the Dutch bark "Frans & Elise," Batavia to Amsterdam. Received Java papers containing very interesting news.

The bark *Frans and Elise* was the type of trading vessel most often seen in these waters, being Dutch owned and proceeding from Batavia to Amsterdam.

5th. 9.30 a.m. Sail reported on starboard beam. 10.30 Saw another, both proved to be brigs. Light variable airs.
6th. At daylight made sail in chase of a vessel on port bow. She proved on boarding to be the English ship "Burmah" of Liverpool, Foo Chow Foo to London.

This ship was boarded at 6.59 south and 103.30 east in the Indian Ocean at the entrance to Sunda Strait, the narrow channel through which most of the British China trade passed.

Sail reported on port quarter at 7.30. Stood in chase. 8.45 Hauled by the wind on port tack. 10 Wore ship to the S. S. W. in chase, giving it up at 11. Noon, sail reported 3 points on lee bow. 12.30 p.m. Two vessels reported to windward. 1.30 Three more in sight. Wind being light W. N. W., started fires and backed main topsails, lowered propellor and went ahead under steam. Five more vessels in sight. In chase of a bark. Fired two blank cartridges and hove her to. (Captured this vessel under the new flag of the C. States.) On boarding with Mr. Evans, I found her to be the bark "Amanda" of Bangor, from Manilla to Cork, laden with sugar and manilla [hemp]. Engaged transferring stores from the prize until 11.30, when we fired her and regained our ship.

The bark *Amanda* proved to be the first prize actually destroyed by *Ala-*

bama in four months. It is true that *Alabama* had captured *Conrad* and commissioned her as the CSS *Tuscaloosa*. Also, *Martha Wenzell* had been captured but released without ransom bond because she had been taken illegally within the marine league. Therefore, when *Alabama* destroyed *Amanda* on 6 November this was the first prize destroyed since the ship *Express,* which was on 6 July 1863.

Amanda was a 598-ton bark of Bangor, Maine, owned by various members of the Crosby family and by other shipowners of Bangor. There was one owner who lived in Searsport. Under command of Isaiah Larrabee of Franklin, Maine, with Hiram E. Swain as mate, also of Franklin, *Amanda* departed Manila 18 September 1863 bound for Queenstown with a cargo of sugar and hemp. At the time of her capture by *Alabama, Amanda* had just passed through Sunda Strait and was about 125 miles off Java Head (6.59 south and 103.23 east) when Fullam and Evans jointly boarded this American in the China trade. *Amanda* had various documents showing that her cargo was neutral, including a certificate from the British vice-consul in Manila. There was evidence that the owners of the cargo of sugar and hemp were British subjects, Ker and Company of Manila. The cargo was consigned to Halliday, Fox and Company of London. Semmes condemned *Amanda* despite her neutral cargo on the ground that evidence of neutral ownership had not been attested by oath. Whatever technical merit his position may have had, there is now an explanation as to why there was so much difference between the Confederate estimate of the value of the ship and cargo ($104,442) and the actual claims by the owners ($69,853.01). The difference ($34,588.99) represented the value of the cargo. Of course, the British owners of the cargo were unable to claim compensation from the American court. It is true that this calculation involves using both Union and Confederate figures, which were not necessarily consistent, but they were usually fairly close, except in a few cases like this one when neutral cargo was actually destroyed. It should be noted that there never was a case of a neutral ship being destroyed by the CSS *Alabama.* The nature of a ship's register was such that it was easier to determine the proper nationality of the owner of the ship than it was for the owner of the cargo. *Amanda* was number 47 of the ships destroyed by *Alabama,* making the total value of ships destroyed $3,610,660. It is interesting that *Alabama* not only destroyed this Maine vessel of the China trade in distant Sunda Strait, but on the occasion displayed for the first time the new Confederate flag at the entrance to Sunda Strait and Java Sea.

7th. 12.30 a.m. Stood on course under steam. 1.10 Let steam go down and made sail. Several vessels lights seen around the burning prize. Spite of the rain (heavy) the prize burnt with an awful brilliancy.

8th. Moderate N. W. wind. 3.25 a.m. Took a cast of the deep sea lead but no bottom at 75 fthms. 7 a.m. Land reported right ahead.

[152]

The S. E. part of Sumatra. Bent cables. 3.20 p.m. Made a bark on starboard bow. Found sandy bottom in 16 fthms. 5 p.m. Came to and anchored in 17 fthms. in Tampang Bay, S. E. part of Sumatra.

The war against the Dutch by the people of Sumatra did not begin until about a decade after the visit of the CSS *Alabama* to the Java Sea. BR 518a, p. 19. Tampang Bay is situated 5.51 south and 104.51 east, an indentation in Sunda Strait. The shore of the bay had a sandy beach with coconut trees standing close by like sentries. The anchorage, recommended by mariners today, is in 14 fathoms over a sandy bottom. This is mentioned because of Fullam's statement that *Alabama* anchored in 17 fathoms. The holding ground is good, but Tampang Bay is quite open to southeasterly winds.

Lowered propellors and started fires. Dutch bark standing in. 7 p.m. I boarded the bark and found her to be the "Java Whistle" (native), from Batavia to Redang, 11 days out.

Java Whistle was boarded by Fullam in Sunda Strait, more precisely at 5.57 south and 104.10 east. It could be wished that Fullam had elaborated on his few words concerning this "native" bark with the fascinating name. Redang is a small island off the coast of Malaya at position 5.47 north and 103.00 east.

Reported the U. S. Str. "Wyoming" at Batavia.

9th [November 1863]. Variable weather. 6 a.m. With Mr. Schroeder, I went in search of fresh provisions, &c; returned at 12 unsuccessful altho' I had called at three villages.

Julius Schroeder was a master's mate, one of the two officers from the Prussian Navy recruited in South Africa. Schroeder, born in Hanover, was probably able to speak other languages in addition to English and German.

4.30 Hoisted propellor.

10th. 3 a.m. Called all hands up anchor and hove in to a short stay. 4.30 Hove up and stood out through the Straits under all sail. 8.30 Started fires on all the boilers. 10.30 Backed main topsail and lowered propellor. Steamed ahead, all draw sail set. Noon. The western end of Beegee Island bore south, dist. one mile.

Fullam's Beegee should be spelled Sebesi. This island is in the northeastern part of Sunda Strait, 5.58 south and 105.29 east. It is about three miles in diameter and circular in shape. *HO 126* and *HO Chart 1142. Alabama* passed between the islands of Sebesi and Sebuko.

All the day, especially as each sail was reported (seven being in sight up to 4 o'clock), we expected to hear "She's a steamer, Sir" sung out by the masthead man. The quarter boats had been swung inboard and every precautionary measure taken with the battery so as to be ready in case the "Wyoming" should heave in sight.

Alabama was moving fast through Sunda Strait and into the Java Sea under sail and steam to avoid, if possible, battle with Wyoming.

Altho' all were aware that the enemy battery was considerably heavier than ours and a greater number of men manned her, yet we did not despair of whipping her, expecting however, that we should receive a terrible casting up before we had done so. We passed through without any signs of her. At 3.15 stood in chase of a ship on port bow. 4. Fired a blank cartridge and hove her to. On boarding her she proved to be the ship "Winged Racer" of and to New York from Manilla, sugar and manilla laden. I was sent on board with a prize crew. At 5 both vessels anchored in 17 fthms. abreast of North Island. Several vessels at anchor around us. Engaged in transferring stores and paroling prisoners until 3.35 a.m. of the 11th. All prisoners being sent away in their own boats to North Island, then set fire to prize and returned on board.

Alabama had just passed through the Strait of Sunda into a rain squall on 10 November about 2 p.m., running along Sumatra in the Java Sea, when an apparently American clipper ship appeared over the horizon under topsails moving toward North Island. The lookout told the officer of the deck and the officer of the deck gave the alarm, which must have made many of the crew think that Alabama was about to battle the USS Wyoming. After some 15 or 20 minutes, Alabama was close enough to make the clipper lie to, and the boarding party under Fullam went out to the ship and learned her identity. She was Winged Racer of New York, 1,768 tons, owned by Henry W. Hubbell, Robert L. Taylor, Edward H. Gillilan, and George H. Ashton. Winged Racer, with a cargo of the sugar which was usual in this trade, and with a general cargo besides, was bound for New York. In addition to sugar, the cargo included China camphor, Manila hide-cuttings, and 5,810 bales of Manila hemp. Winged Racer had departed Manila 8 October 1863. A month and two days later the tall Yankee clipper was suddenly confronted by the CSS Alabama. She was pursued for about 15 minutes before being brought to by a blank shot. Soon Fullam's boarding party came into view. Fullam boarded the prize and took Captain George Cumming and his ship's papers to Alabama for the admiralty proceedings. There was no claim that the cargo was neutral. The ship's register was American and she was even flying the Stars and Stripes when captured. Ship and cargo were condemned, but not so speedily burned. Captain Semmes studied the manifest of Winged Racer and saw thereon many articles which were needed in various departments of *Alabama*, particularly sugar and coffee, and especially tobacco. The autumn of 1863 had yielded only two prizes from which to replenish the supplies of the raider, and *Alabama* quickly commenced transferring needed articles. This operation started about 3:00 p.m. and lasted until approximately 2:00 a.m. When the transfer was completed, *Winged Racer* was burned.

This caused great excitement among the many Malay bumboatmen who had come out to sell fruits, vegetables, squalling pigs and chickens to the stewards. The boatmen were hanging onto lines attached from their boats to the big vessels to steady themselves in the midst of the trading activities, when they were suddenly aware of flames leaping up in the clipper, as Fullam, the boarding officer, put the torch to the beautiful ship. The Malay boatmen were seized with panic and hurriedly cut lines and pulled away from the doomed clipper. With the burning ship to advertise *Alabama's* presence in these waters, it was best for the Confederate to seek other paths, and *Alabama* steamed toward the China Sea, lighted by the glare from the blazing Yankee.

The Confederate estimate of the value of *Winged Racer* amounted to $150,000 of which $87,000 was for the ship and $63,000 for cargo. The clipper was number 48 of the ships destroyed by *Alabama,* but only the second destroyed in four months. Even so, the total value of vessels destroyed by the raider, according to the Confederate statistics, amounted to $3,760,660. The total claims filed by the owners of the clipper amounted to $341,823.54. *Winged Racer* produced several notable cases before the Court of Commissioners of the *Alabama* Claims: *Hubbell* v. *United States* (Case 278), *Sherman* v. *United States* (Case 279), and *Gillilan* v. *United States* (Case 1131). Together these cases brought out important principles in determining a formula for the measure of damage of goods destroyed by the CSS *Alabama* and other Confederate cruisers.

Captain George Cumming called Captain Semmes' attention to the fact that the Java Sea at the time of the capture of *Winged Racer* was smooth as usual and that land was near. Therefore, Cumming requested Semmes to allow him and the crew of *Winged Racer,* and also the captain and crew of *Amanda* who were still aboard *Alabama,* to be provided with *Winged Racer's* boats and some provisions so that they could go ashore. This was agreed to. Captain Cumming, Captain Isaiah Larrabee, and their ships' crews safely arrived in Batavia where they had opportunity to see the United States consul and also Captain David McDougal, commanding officer of the USS *Wyoming.*

Fullam's log entry for 11 November 1863 at North Island was: 4.48 south and 106.40 east. This was the approximate position where Captain Cumming and the seamen went ashore and where a short while later Fullam set fire to *Winged Racer.*

At 3.55 got the anchor up and steamed ahead. 4.10 Made sail. 6.30 Made two islands on weather bow. Moderate S. W. wind. Steering

[155]

N. Ely. 7. Made a small island on bow. 9.45 A ship reported two points on port bow. Stood in chase. Hoisted U. S. colours, to which (at 11.30) chase answered with U. S. colours; fired a blank cartridge, hoisting our own colours. She then made sail and kept away. More steam was got up and a most exciting chase commenced, a fresh westerly breeze blowing all the time. 12.15 Fired a shot from rifle gun, which fell to leeward. All hands were called aft to trim ship, and another blank cartridge fired. Still she kept on her course altho' we were rapidly overhauling her. Being pretty near her, another shot was fired from the bow gun, just over her main royal stay. She then hove to and a boat was sent on board to take possession. On boarding she proved to be the ship "Contest" of and to New York from Yokohama (Japan) with rice, &c. &c.

By this time the pursuit of a ship was a routine performance for *Alabama's* people who had chased so many. But when the lookout cried "Sail ho!" it was soon discerned that another clipper had loomed on the horizon, and excitement mounted. She had "the tall raking masts, square yards, and white canvas" of a clipper, and *Alabama* moved toward the prize with Union colors flying. This pursuit soon had all hands eagerly watching what Sinclair called "the derby of Gaspar Strait." *Alabama* had been running under sail but soon got up steam, yet even so seemed to be falling behind. Semmes asked for more steam from the engine room watch, then under Mathew O'Brien, only to receive the answer, "The tea-kettle will stand no more; if we attempt it we shall scatter the pieces for the chase to pick up." Officers and men whose duties did not keep them elsewhere were ordered to the after end and even some of the forward guns were moved aft, but *Alabama* seemed to be barely holding her own under a stiff breeze. When the raider was finally within range, about four miles of the target, a shell was fired by Lt. Armstrong's gun crew, striking close enough to throw spray over the target's quarter-deck, and at the same time the Confederate flag was flung to the breeze. The Yankee added more canvas and by skilful handling kept up the race until the wind began to subside and *Alabama* at last was able to close the range with the use of steam. When a second shot was fired, the chase decided the race was over and hove to. She was the clipper ship *Contest*. Pursuer and pursued were then anchored in the open sea (in 14 fathoms) with no land in sight in any direction while the crew of *Contest* was moved to the CSS *Alabama*.

2.35 Came to with port anchor in 14 fthms., prize anchoring near us. Engaged receiving stores from prize. 3.50 Saw a sail to the N. E. 7.35 All hands returned from prize. At 7.45 noticed that the prize was dragging. I was sent to let go another anchor. Owing to the

[156]

fresh breeze and current causing her to drag so quickly and losing sight of the Alabama, I returned without accomplishing the desired object. 9 p.m. Hove up anchor and steamed after prize. Coming up with her I boarded, set her on fire and returned to the Alabama.

Sinclair said that *Contest* was the most beautiful ship ever captured by the CSS *Alabama*. Impressed with her beauty as much as with her speed, many of *Alabama's* wardroom officers paid her the unusual compliment of crowding aboard to look over the handsome vessel. Captain Semmes regretted that he did not have enough spare guns to turn this speedy clipper into another Confederate commerce raider like the CSS *Tuscaloosa*.

The clipper ship *Contest* was one of the most famous clippers out of New York, a 1,098-ton vessel, which had been built only ten years earlier in New York by J. Westervelt. At the time of her seizure, she was owned by A. A. Low and Brothers and nine others. Her commanding officer was Frederick George Lucas and her first mate was James Delano Babcock. *Contest* had sailed 14 October 1863 from Kanagawa, Japan, bound for New York with a cargo of tea, silk, Japanese curios, and a general return cargo of the China trade. There was no question that this was an American ship and no evidence that the cargo was neutral. Not much time was required in admiralty proceedings.

Alabama's boarding party under Fullam freely helped themselves to the cargo as needed, and then Fullam applied the torch. Fullam noted that it was 9:00 p.m. when he set fire to *Contest*. Sinclair saw Captain Lucas leaning against *Alabama's* rail and watching his gallant ship as the fires lit up sky and water. Sinclair wrote of Lucas, "His brow is unruffled, and face calm. We will not inquire into his thoughts. He has merited our respect by his pluck, and we know how he must feel to lose such a ship. But he admits no personal grudges. We found the skipper of the *Contest* a frank, clever fellow." Captain Lucas, First Mate Babcock, and other *Contest* personnel remained in *Alabama* for nine days. When the raider met *Avalanche*, the Confederates obtained passage for Lucas, Babcock, and the others, in that British ship, which transported the mariners to Batavia. After about 17 days in Batavia, Babcock and his shipmates raised money with the help of several residents and proceeded from Batavia to Singapore, about 10 December 1863. After a month in Singapore, Babcock obtained passage in *Atlantic,* a whaling ship, which reached New Bedford, Massachusetts on 1 May 1864.

Captain Lucas filed statements of personal property losses in *Contest* of $4,638 before the Court of Commissioners of the *Alabama* Claims. To the same tribunal the first mate of *Contest,* James Delano Babcock of New Bedford, had the distinction of submitting Case Number One. The claim was filed by Babcock through his attorney John A. Weeks on 28 July 1874. At the time the claim was filed, as a coincidence, Babcock was first mate of another one-time prize of the CSS *Alabama*, the Pacific Mail Steamship Com-

[157]

pany's *Ariel*. The name of Babcock's Case Number One was *James D. Babcock* v. *United States*. In it Babcock testified that more than a decade earlier he had signed on *Contest* while she was tied up at the docks in New York City for a voyage to China, Japan, and return. The outward-bound voyage, according to Babcock, was routine and *Contest* had gone through the usual procedures in the China trade until her losing race with *Alabama*. Babcock described his encounter with *Alabama* in a manner which throws light upon Fullam's boarding operations. Babcock said:

> ...We started for New York about the 17th October, 1863. Nothing worthy of note took place until, about 10 a. m., November 11, 1863, we sighted a vessel steering across our course; as she drew near to us, we made out the American ensign at her "gaff;" at the same time she fired a lee gun for us to "heave to." Not knowing of any reason to stop for a vessel unless in distress, we kept on our course. She then fired a shot at us, hauled down the American, and set the confederate flag; we then realized our danger, and made every possible effort to escape. She chased us three hours, firing both shot and shell, and gradually closing upon us, until about 1 p.m., when finding ourselves at her mercy, and in order to avoid bloodshed, we "hove the ship to." We were immediately boarded by an armed crew, and the officer in command ordered us to haul down our flag, as we were a prize to the Confederate States ship "Alabama." They then anchored the ship in 18 fathoms of water, our position, by account, at that time being latitude 5° 16' south, longitude 106° 46' east, Batavia being about seventy miles south. After plundering the "Contest," we were taken on board the "Alabama" as prisoners of war, and not being allowed to secure any of our personal effects or property.

Babcock added that *Alabama* sent over two boatloads of men to set numerous fires in *Contest,* and the ship was burned nearly to the water's edge before sinking. Babcock and other members of the crew of *Contest* were put aboard the British ship *Avalanche,* and in her traveled to Batavia. Later Babcock returned to the United States, became an ensign in the United States Navy, and subsequently returned to the merchant marine and the China trade. With the end of the Civil War, the *Alabama* Claims tortured the diplomatic relations between the United States and Great Britain until the Treaty of Washington was signed and the Geneva Arbitration was completed; then the United States government, on 23 June 1874, set up the Court of Commissioners of the *Alabama* Claims, described in Statutes at Large of the United States, 43rd Congress, First Session. So it came to pass that under this act Babcock, through his attorney, filed the first case under the *Alabama* Claims Commission. It is of interest to note that Babcock was once more in the China trade 11 years after his adventure with Fullam and the CSS *Alabama*. Indeed, Babcock's claim for $2,384 before the *Alabama* Claims Commission was originally filed before the United States consul in Yokohama. Babcock's testimony gave incidental information concerning the China trade, such as the kind of money used in the China trade during the Civil

War: gold dollars, Mexican silver dollars, and gold drafts, among others. The Civil War caused United States paper money to be depreciated in Japan, as well as in Europe, and this was developed in Babcock's testimony.

In addition to Babcock's case, there were nine other cases before the *Alabama* Claims Commission arising from *Contest*. All of the owners were represented in one case, *Abiel A. Low,* et al. v. *United States,* Case 618½. The ten owners collectively filed claims amounting to $26,500. This did not include $18,500 which they had already received in insurance payments on the ship. The total cargo was valued by claimants at $30,522.38. When the insurance of $20,000 for the cargo was subtracted from this, the net loss represented $10,522.38 on the cargo. When these losses were added to the claims of Captain F. G. Lucas and two other claimants, the total claims filed in the case of *Contest* amounted to $42,865.97.

The Confederates valued *Contest* at $72,815, and her cargo at $50,000, for a total of $122,815. This brought the total Confederate evaluation of prizes destroyed by *Alabama* to $3,883,475. *Contest* was number 49 among the prizes destroyed.

10.15 Hoisted propellor and banked fires. Under topsails. Steering E. N. Ely.

12th. Fine, moderate W. S. W. wind. 11.30 a.m. Sail reported on port bow. Made more sail and hauled by the wind on starboard tack. Hove the lead each hour.

13th. Moderate West'ly winds. At 7 p.m. came to with port anchor in 17 fthms. water.

14th. 6.30 a.m. Got under weigh. Took a cast of the lead each hour. 1 p.m. Court Martial assembled to try F. Townshend, seaman, for mutinous conduct. Adjourned 6.15 p.m.

Frank Townshend was the seaman who wrote the poem entitled, ''The Fight of the 'Hatteras' and 'Alabama'.'' This poem was published in 1889 in Frank Moore, *The Civil War in Song and Story.*

East Discovery bank bore W. N. W. 3 miles distant.

Also known as Discovery East Bank and Discovery Oostbank, it is a coral reef with an area of sand in the center. *HO 126,* p. 214, and *HO Chart 3117.*

Sunday, 15th [November 1863]. 5.40 a.m. Saw what appeared to be a rock. Clewed up all sail and let go the port anchor, in 25 fthms. Lowered a boat and found it to be a collection of logs. 8.25 Got under weigh. 5 vessels reported during the day. 7.15 p.m. Came to with port anchor in 30 fthms.

16th. 4.15 a.m. Got under weigh. Two small vessels in sight on port bow. The sentence of F. Townshend and A. Hyer (sea.) who were found by the gen'l court martial guilty of mutinous and seditious conduct, were read to them and was as follows, viz;—that they be reduced to the grade of ordinary seamen, forfeit three months pay, and be placed in solitary confinement in double irons on bread and water for thirty days.

Albert Hyer was recruited as an ordianary seaman 26 March 1863. Hyer was undoubtedly a mariner from a Union merchantman, very likely from *Kingfisher, Nora,* or *Charles Hill,* to judge from the date of his enlistment. Within eight months he was promoted from ordinary seaman to seaman. After the court martial mentioned by Fullam, *Alabama's* next port of call was Singapore, and there Albert Hyer deserted on Christmas Day, 1863. Frank Townshend was discussed earlier.

9.30 p.m. Wind falling light, took in sail and at 9.45 let go the port anchor in 25 fthms.
   17th. Caramata Island in sight 50 miles distant.

Karimata Archipelago is framed by the land masses of Sumatra, Java, and Borneo. It is on Karimata Strait which connects the Java Sea with the South China Sea. *HO, 126,* pp. 216–217; *HO Chart 3032; BR 518a; Britannica Atlas,* Chart 102.

Court Martial sentenced Michael Mars (sea.) to lose one months pay, to do police duty 3 months, and to be triced up three hours daily for one week.

Michael Mars was adventurous to the point of being foolhardy. Just what Mars did to attract the court martial verdict and punishment explained by Fullam is by no means clear, but a number of other facts are known about this English sailor. Mars belonged to the Royal Naval Reserves in Bristol. He joined the Confederate States Navy at Terceira and was coxswain of *Alabama's* cutter. When *Alabama* was at Arcas, Mars jumped in the water and attacked and killed a large shark in full view of many shipmates, doubtless the principal reason for the act of showmanship. The police duty mentioned by Fullam was cleaning ship.

Light N. W. wind with a two knot (N. Wly.) current running, so remained at anchor. In the Caramata pass. Have had light winds and fine weather lately.
   18th. Fresh westerly breeze. 6.30 a.m. Got under weigh. Land reported at 7.15, half point on weather bow. Found it to be the islands of Sourouton & Caramata.

Sourouton is south and west of Karimata Archipelago. It is also spelled Serutu and Seroetoe, and its location includes the point 1.43 south and 108.44 east. See *HO 126,* pp. 216–217; *HO Chart 3032;* and *BR 518a.*

[160]

Not being able to reach to windward of Sourouton on account of the strong S. Ely. current, anchored in 20 fthms at 3.30 p.m. 9 p.m. Showed a light to a passing bark.

19th. Wind westerly. Moderate with occasional rain squalls. 10.30 a.m. Made a sail right ahead standing towards us. Sent a boat on board, passing ourselves off as a Dutch surveying vessel. I then went on board and made arrangements for the transfer of prisoners of the prize ship "Contest." By 7 p.m. had transferred all prisoners, and hoisted up boats. The vessel proved to be the (late Yankee) ship "Avalanche" of Liverpool, Singapore to London. Obtained papers conveying the most gratifying news.

Captain F. G. Lucas of *Contest,* his first officer James Delano Babcock, and other members of the crew were transported in *Avalanche* to Batavia. The "gratifying news" from the English captain was that American maritime commerce was declining toward the vanishing point.

(Chronometers)

20th. Moderate westerly winds with occasional squalls. Noon, a sail in sight. At 1.25 p.m. I took the cutter and sailed in chase of a bark to windward. 2.30 I boarded and found her to be the bark "Amy Douglas" of and from Bangkok to Hong-Kong.

Fullam boarded *Amy Douglas* in the approximate position 1.47 south and 108.66 east. This area of Karimata Strait is one of the most difficult in the world to navigate. Sinclair described in detail the haggard sleeplessness of Captain Semmes who constantly checked navigational data while going through Karimata Strait. Navigators in the Karimata area contended with inaccurate charts, tricky currents, and coral reefs.

Saw another vessel, so tacked in chase. At 3.30 I boarded and found her to be the "Aloinir" of Nantes, from Manilla to Valparaiso, 9 days out. At 6 regained the Alabama. Passed as the U. S. Str. "Wyoming."

The USS *Wyoming* was not far away at this time.

21st. Made a sail on starboard bow. 9.30 Showed English White to a bark showing Norwegian colours. Wind hauling to the S. W. 3 p.m. Got under weigh. Got a [lead] cast as usual each hour. 11.50 Called all hands and lowered propellor.

22nd. Light westerly airs with some heavy rain. 12.30 a.m. Took in all sail and went ahead under steam. 2.30 Saw two vessels, one of which showed English to our St. Georges colours. 2.40 p.m. Abreast of Direction Islands.

Direction Island is the northeasternmost of some 20 coral islands, collectively known as South Keeling—a division of the Cocos Islands. The South Keeling group form a horseshoe around a central lagoon. *HO 126*, p. 40, and *Ho Chart 3109*. Other islands in the vicinity have interesting names, such as Home Island and Prison Island. Direction Island, and only one other island in the group, was (1949) permanently inhabited. *Alabama* crossed the equator at 108.02 east.

3.45 p.m. Crossed the Equator.

23rd. Passed West Island. 11.45 a.m. Sail in sight on starboard bow. Noon. Fresh N. N. E. breeze. 12.45 Showed St. Georges ensign and "Greyhound" to the ship "Maiden Queen," Foo Chow Foo [Foo Chow] to Londonderry. 1.30 Made Flat Island on starboard bow. 3. Sail reported broad off the lee bow, and one right ahead. 3.30 Showed English White to the British bark "Roy O'More" from B. R. 5.30 p.m. Hoisted propellor and made sail. 6. Wind shifted (Nwly.) to the S. W. Occasional rain. 2 knots of current E. S. E.

25th. Light variable winds with disagreeable rain. As usual, hove the lead.

26th. Calm with heavy northerly seas. A strong current setting us toward the N. E. in close proximity to shore. 2.30 p.m. Bent a hawser to the largest kedge and came to in 50 fthms.

Alabama was in position 3.38 north and 110.24 east. The kedge was a small anchor which could be planted ahead of the ship by means of a small boat. When working the capstan and thereby pulling the ship up to the kedge anchor and repeating the operation, the procedure was known as kedging. This was a very slow process, and was used when the ship was becalmed.

27th. A fine fresh breeze springing up, got under weigh at 7.15 a.m., but in an hour's time it fell calm again. So at 12.30 came to again in 55 fthms. water. Current setting to the N. E. at the rate of 2 knots per hour.

28th. Still at anchor, with light variable airs, sometimes raining for hours. Slow work this, very.

29th. Light N. E. wind, freshening toward daybreak. 9 a.m. Called all hands and hove up the kedge. Set every stitch of canvas.

Here Fullam noted that the kedging had ended because the wind had freshened, and *Alabama* again moved northward under all canvas.

30th. Breeze gradually increasing. Heavy squall at 2.30. Took a reef in topsail. Sea rising.

2nd. Dec. [1863]. Strong breeze. Still under reefed topsails.
11.30 a.m. Saw a bark to leeward, standing southerly. 7 p.m.
Anchored in 18 fthms., to leeward of Pulo Condore.

Alabama was cruising along the coast of Cochin, China, as Viet Nam
was then called. When the ship came to anchor in the welcome 18 fathoms
of one of the bays of Pulo Condore on 2 December 1863, the CSS *Alabama*
had reached the most northerly point of her cruise in the South China
Sea. Her position was 8.30 north and 107.16 east. Pulo Condore is a
group of 12 islands lying about 45 miles from the coast of Viet Nam.
These mountainous islands are on the sea route between Saigon and
Singapore. *HO 125,* map facing p. 70, also pp. 120–123; *HO Chart 3147;*
BR 510, p. 210.

3rd. 9 a.m. Sent a boat to examine the anchorage further in
shore. Saw a junk close in. Boat returned at 1 p.m. Reported
good anchorage, and brought off an officer belonging [to]
the French transport junk at anchor.

Pulo Condore, a short while before *Alabama's* visit, had been acquired
by the French and was governed by a French naval officer from his head-
quarters on the mainland. The junk, mentioned by Fullam, was officially
designated as a French man-of-war.

A very capacious harbour and well sheltered. 1.30 Got under
weigh. At 2.30 anchored in 9 fthms. 5 p.m. Let go a kedge
from port quarter and swung ship broadside to the entrance,
in order to command the harbour.

Alabama was put in this broadside position so that her guns would be
well situated if the USS *Wyoming* suddenly entered the harbor. The
commerce raider was in need of minor repairs and this was a snug refuge.

Wind N. E., coming down the hills in heavy gusts.
5th. Light N. E. breezes. Pulo Condore proper is a moun-
tainous island of considerable extent.

At Pulo Condore, Governor Bizot made the Confederates feel most
welcome. Shore leave was freely granted, and *Alabama's* officers had
several conversations with the governor. While it was disappointing that
there was no rum ashore, the crew members were otherwise free to amuse
themselves as they wished. Sinclair said, "The boat's crew are a picture for
the artist, dressed in their summer uniforms of white linen duck and straw
hats. . . ." Meantime, the heads of *Alabama's* four departments were busy
with repairs: sailmaker, gunner, boatswain, and carpenter. The decks of
the ship were cluttered with tools, paint, tar buckets, canvas, and repair
materials. Thus *Alabama* spent two weeks. The copper covering of her hull

[163]

had so deteriorated that teredos were getting into the ship's planking and timbers. The ingenuity of Lt. Kell and of the ship's carpenter, William Robinson, contrived an hydraulic caisson which was a kind of diving bell permitting men to work under the ship's hull.

It is surrounded by smaller islands. The French authorities in Cochin, China have taken possession of it and use it as a penal settlement. A small number of troops are kept here. The village, to the S. E., is a mere collection of huts; the natives, still in their original degraded condition, subsist chiefly upon yams, fish &c. The soil being very unproductive and the soldiers staying ashore, rendered it impossible to obtain any fresh provisions. The harbour is well stocked with fish, but I suppose their natural bashfulness prevented us making their acquaintance to the extent desired. Game of any kind is not plentiful.

However limited the diet of the natives may have been, Sinclair made it clear that *Alabama's* officers and men had a better diet than usual while they were in Pulo Condore.

8th. Alternate calms and breezes. The Commandant of the post paid us a visit this morn.

9th. Calm and clear. 2.30 p.m. Saw a barque rigged steamer standing in toward the anchorage on the other side of the island. All hands scraping, painting and renovating generally.

10th. 12.25 p.m. Saw a steamer standing southerly. Found her to be (as we had learned previously) an American steamer in the service of the French Marine, from Saigon to Singapore.

Saigon was known as "the Pearl of the Far East." The distance from Saigon to Singapore is 649 miles. Saigon, unhappily, became better known in the twentieth century than in the nineteenth, but in 1863 few Americans and not many Europeans had been there because Saigon was first opened to international commerce just two years before *Alabama* visited there. *BR 510,* p. 377.

12th. Saw a large ship bound southerly. Strong E'ly breezes. Finished painting ship. Hands on shore washing clothing, &c.

13th. Sunday. Strong gusts. 5 p.m. Let go the starboard anchor.

14th. Moderate N. E. breeze. 5 p.m. Hove up the kedge.

15th. Light variable winds. Called all hands at 4 a.m. and got under weigh, standing southerly under two topsails and topmast staysail.

[164]

On this 15 December 1863, *Alabama* commenced her return voyage from the Far East.

16th. Moderate N. W. wind. 8.30 Made a brig standing to the eastward.

17th. Fresh N. Wly. wind with occasional showers. 4.30 p.m. Hoisted colours in return to a French mail steamer steering northerly.

18th. Fresh N. E. wind with heavy rain.

19th. Fresh N. E. wind, alternately fine and showery. 10.30 a.m. Land descried on starboard bow. 4.30 p.m. Anchored S. W. off Pulo Aor.

Pulo Aor (located 2.27 north and 104.31 east) had already become the stopping-off place for ships bound to and from China. It is only one island, but from the distance looks like two because it is crested by two hills (one is 1,792 feet high and the other is 1,484 feet). This thickly wooded, reef-enclosed island is about three miles long and 1½ miles wide.

20th. Sunday [December 1863]. To the S. W. of the island is the anchorage and where also are the dwellings of the Malayan inhabitants who are governed by a Rajah on a small scale, who affords assistance in the shape of wood and water, cocoa nuts and perhaps a few fowls. The natives, apparently inoffensive are not to be tricked. Rings, printed goods, &c. are better exchanged than money. Saw a grave on shore, evidently that of a European.

21st. 3.25 a.m. Got under weigh and stood on course under steam. 5.50 Made a ship rigged steamer under sail and steam, steering S. S. W. Saw high land ahead and a heavy rain squall coming on,—let go the anchor in 10¼ ftms.

Under the best of circumstances, navigation was difficult in these waters. Because of the rain squall, *Alabama* came to anchor for the purpose of waiting for visibility to improve.

Observing the steamer astern, went to quarters and prepared for action. Steamer passed within point blank range, showing British colours. [We] hoisted French colours in return. Beat the retreat. 12.15 Got under weigh and stood towards Singapore.

At this time *Alabama* was being navigated by a Malay pilot. Singapore was a British colony in December 1863. Having been destroyed by the Javanese c. 1365, Singapore was re-established 30 January 1819 by Sir

[165]

Stamford Raffles, an official of the East India Company. In time, Singapore became capital of the Straits Settlements. At the time of *Alabama's* visit, the colony had a population of about 120,000 of whom about half were Chinese and the remainder Indians, Malays, Japanese, and widespread samplings of other Orientals, in addition to the British and some other Europeans. The island of Singapore embraces some 217 square miles, being 27 miles long and 13 miles wide. The city of Singapore was one of the principal seaports of the Far East, commanding Malacca Strait which was an important funnel of shipping between Europe and the Orient. A ship would have to travel a long way to find equal harbor and docking facilities. In Fullam's day, Singapore was a stopping place for American and other vessels in the China trade. In Singapore, *Alabama* was brought up to date on the movements of the USS *Wyoming*. *Wyoming* had preceded *Alabama*, or followed her, all over the South China Sea and nearby waters.

At 6 [p.m.], came to with port anchor in 7 ftms. Shortly after,
I went on shore, making arrangements respecting coaling.
22nd. 11 a.m. Hove up anchor, went alongside the wharf,
and commenced coaling, and receiving stores. By 10.30 we
finished coaling.
23rd. As usual, we received a cordial reception from the
inhabitants. This day was set apart for receiving visitors. 10
men absent without leave.
24th. 9 a.m. Got under weigh and 10 a.m. left here. Shipped 4.

The ten deserters included Richard Hambly, F. Mahoney, John Allan, John Doyle, John Grady, James Smith, James Williams, Henry Cosgrove, and Albert Hyer. Albert Hyer, a short while before, had been convicted by court martial. The name of the tenth man is unknown. It may have been Frank Townshend, who had been convicted by court martial at the same time as Hyer.

The newly enlisted Confederates from Singapore were: Thomas Watson, Robert Devine, James King (second of this name), and H. Higgins.

Went ahead under steam up the Straits of Malacca. 9.30 Passed
the steamer "Kwangtung."

This gunboat of the Royal Navy was named *Kwantung* for Kwantung Bay. The vessel *Kwantung* was visited by some of *Alabama's* officers on 11 August 1863 when both ships were at Simon's Bay and *Kwantung* was the flagship of Sir Baldwin W. Walker.

10 [a.m.]. Discharged harbour pilot. 3 p.m. Hove to with a gun
a large suspicious looking bark under English colours. Upon

[166]

boarding, I examined her papers, which barque proving to be irregular I took possession, Capt. Semmes coming on board himself and condemning her. She was an American-built vessel, with the original American Captain and mate. Her papers certified her to be the "Martaban" of Moulmain. From information we proved her to be the "Texian Star" of Galveston. Removed prisoners and returned at 5.20 on board [Alabama], having fired prize and stood for Malacca.

The CSS *Alabama* left Singapore very early and was steaming through the Strait of Malacca when, about 11 o'clock, the cry "Sail ho!" sounded from the rigging. A couple of hours chase brought under the guns of the rebel raider a vessel which had a decidedly American appearance. *Alabama* hove her to with a shot, and she hoisted English colors. A boat was lowered and Fullam, as Semmes described him, "one of the most intelligent of my boarding-officers, and who was himself an Englishman," was sent on board. Fullam ascertained that she was the British ship *Martaban* and that her register confirmed her as British. However, he also learned that this 799-ton bark had been built in Boston in 1858 and was then named *Texan Star*. Fullam requested the captain of *Martaban,* Samuel B. Pike, to go aboard *Alabama* and have his papers inspected, but the skipper said that he stood on his rights as a British subject and refused to go. Fullam reported this situation to Captain Semmes. Semmes was so much perplexed by the alleged transfer of flag from American to British registry and the supporting complexities which Fullam presented to him, that Old Beezwax himself violated his own precedents and boarded *Martaban*. Semmes later stated that this was the only ship he ever personally boarded before or after this event. As Semmes went on board *Martaban*, his shrewd and watchful eye took in all the tell-tale evidence of her recent transfer of ownership: the bright new English flag, her American lines, long graceful hull, flaring bow, rounded stern and taut masts, the sky-sail poles and square yards that would spread the greatest amount of canvas to catch the breeze. Even the food being prepared in the galley was as American as could be, potatoes and codfish. As Semmes passed into the cabin, he saw the anxious faces of the mates and realized that they had doubts as to the reception of their newly acquired British status. The captain of *Martaban* was in every respect a typical Yankee skipper and he spoke with a New England tone. There was no bill of sale among the papers, the paint was scarcely dry that carried her new name, and the crew list had been made out in the same handwriting. Weighing all these facts, Semmes announced to the captain that he intended to burn the ship. The captain was aghast and shouted that he dare not do it under an English flag. But Semmes was not deterred and soon transferred the crew and their belongings to *Alabama*. In half an hour *Martaban* was in flames. As was always done, the flag of the burning vessel was taken by

[167]

the signal-quartermaster, marked with the day, the latitude and longitude of capture, and stowed in the bags which held all of the flags captured by *Alabama*. There was no doubt that the cargo was British, and Semmes commented that if the owner had left the ship under American registry with the cargo properly documented as British, the ship probably would have been released on ransom bond. Later Semmes shrewdly figured that, since by this time the ship had been burned, Captain Pike probably would feel that he had nothing to hide. Semmes asked the captain under oath if the transfer had been *bona fide*. The captain then admitted that in his alarm over rumors of the raider's presence in the East Indies, the ship had been transferred under a sham sale. With this admission, Semmes seemed satisfied that his course had been the correct one.

Prior to the capture of *Martaban,* she was under command of Pike and operating in the East India trade. Later information from Captain Pike's testimony revealed that, while *Texan Star* was in the East Indies, a letter was received from the ship's owners, Samuel Stevens and Company of Boston, dated 3 July 1863, warning Pike that the CSS *Alabama* was threatening the East Indian trade. Pike was further advised to execute a sale transferring *Texan Star* to British registry and changing her name. Pike received this letter while *Texan Star* was moored at Moulmein, Burma, not far from the Gulf of Martaban which is south of Rangoon. On 13 November 1863, two days after Pike received the letter, he wrote to Stevens and Company saying that he would like to avoid making a fake transfer unless he knew more about the persons who were supposed to become the new owners. Meantime, *Texan Star* was taking aboard a cargo of 12,556 bags of rice (each weighing 164 pounds) consigned to Singapore. After all the cargo was taken aboard and Captain Pike was nearly ready to get his clearance papers from the customs house, the mail steamship from Singapore arrived in Moulmein bringing the doleful news that various American ships had been destroyed by the CSS *Alabama* in and near the Strait of Sunda. Then Captain Pike wrote his owners on 9 December saying that he was making a fake transfer of title to M. R. Currie and Company, changing the name of *Texan Star* to *Martaban,* and above all, changing the registry from American to British. The temporary transfer of title to Currie was balanced by a mortgage of 80,000 rupees to the American owners with the further stipulation that Captain Pike would remain in command of the ship. Currie and Company received one percent commission for the service.

Martaban sailed on 12 December 1863 from Moulmein bound for Singapore. Twelve days later, not far from Singapore, *Martaban* was sighted by *Alabama,* boarded by Fullam, then by Semmes, condemned as a legitimate prize, and burned. When the case was litigated before the *Alabama* Claims Commission, the decision that this ship was really American was upheld. The claims filed for the loss of the ship amounted to $35,600, or 80,000 rupees. The loss on the cargo was $15,000, and claims for personal property $2,322.25. Thus the total claims came to $52,922.25. (The Confederates valued the ship at $97,628.) When this case was adjudicated before the Court of Commissioners of the *Alabama* Claims in *Samuel Stevens, et al,* v. *United States,* it would not have been possible to win a judgment had the owners of the ship been British. See also, Donald Davis, "Visit of the Fighting Alabama," in Singapore *Times,* 19 January 1956.

25th. Christmas Day. Sent all prisoners on shore this morning, having anchored off Malacca last night. Returned on board at 9.45. 10 a.m. Hove up and stood on course. Chased a bark which on boarding I found to be the "Gallant Neill" of and to Madras from Singapore. Hoisted French colours to many ships during the day. P.M. Spliced main brace and drank to sweethearts and wives. 5.45 p.m. Came to in 25 fthms. Several vessels anchored around us. 7 p.m. I boarded a ship ahead of us and found her to be the "Puget" of Marseilles, Singapore to Madras. Calm with steady rain.

Of all the splices of lines and braces so necessary aboard a sailing ship, the most welcome activity of all was here referred to by Fullam because splicing the main brace meant having drinks. The CSS *Alabama* had a generous and popular policy regarding liquor (and probably would have found a different policy impossible), but it was a constant worry to the officers lest the men get liquored up and mutiny. In any case, Fullam was here speaking of Christmas Day, a special occasion for drinks, but really just another working day in a fighting ship at sea. Even on this day, Fullam had to take his boarding party to discover the nationality of the ship *Puget,* which proved to be French.

26th. 2.30 a.m. Observed a steamer to the northward. 6.10 Got under weigh and steamed ahead. Six vessels and a steamer in sight. Chased a ship which, on boarding, I found to be the "Sonora" of Newburyport, Singapore to Akyab.

Sonora was a 708-ton ship of Newburyport, Massachusetts, under command of Lawrence W. Brown and owned by William Cushing, John N. Cushing, and five other persons, all of Newburyport. *Sonora* departed New York 26 March 1863, bound for Melbourne, Australia, with 48 passengers on board. After two days at sea, three stowaways were discovered. They were deserting soldiers who were found hiding in the ship while still in their military uniforms. They were added to the seamen aboard *Sonora.* Despite anxiety concerning the Confederate cruisers, *Sonora* arrived safely in Melbourne, discharging cargo and passengers. She was then ordered by her owners to proceed to Akyab, Burma, and there pick up a cargo of rice not later than 15 June 1864. The rice was to be transported from Akyab to Europe. In Melbourne, *Sonora* took on about 1,000 tons of cargo and 290 Chinese passengers bound for Hong Kong. The Chinese had come from the gold fields of Australia and some of them had enough gold to gamble day and night aboard *Sonora*. After 48 days at sea, *Sonora* arrived in Hong Kong and made ready for the planned journey from Hong Kong to Akyab, Burma, with a cargo and some 200 Chinese passengers, including 15 women. Because *Sonora* had to travel close to Singapore to reach the contracted destination in Akyab, the extra freight and passenger fares seemed pure bonus in an era when turn-around time for ships meant less than it does today. In Singapore, *Sonora* discharged the crew who had brought the ship from Australia and replaced them with seamen who were looking for jobs, including 14 men who had served in *Contest,* a recent prize of the CSS *Alabama.* A favorite topic of discussion in Singapore at the time, according to Captain Brown, was the American Civil War and the question as to whether the British government would eventually intervene and destroy the North or whether the North would eventually be able to collect damages for ships destroyed by cruisers like the CSS *Alabama* which had been fitted out in Great Britain. Despite forebodings, *Sonora* became the first American ship to depart Singapore in two months. On 26 December about 6 a.m., *Sonora* was lying becalmed and helpless while her crew busily washed down the decks. Thus engaged, Captain Brown through his glasses spied a steam-ship rapidly approaching and flying the blue British ensign. Captain Brown asked several of his seamen who had worked aboard *Alabama* whether they recognized the strange steamer. One of them said that undoubtedly she was the Confederate raider because he recognized a boat hanging at *Alabama's* rails which had been taken from *Contest.* In a short time the CSS *Alabama,* under steam and flying the new white flag with the Stars and Cross of the Confederacy, pulled alongside *Sonora* which was a large and splendid clipper ship. She was boarded by Fullam, tried and condemned by Semmes, and burned. Captain Brown was most vehement in telling Lt. Sinclair that the USS *Wyoming* should have been patrolling the Straits of Malacca rather than going off after coal at the time *Alabama* captured *Sonora.* Total claims filed as a result of the burning of this ship amounted to $89,044.44. The Confederates valued this 51st prize at $46,545.

Light. Chased another, which proved to be the Yankee ship "Highlander" of Boston, from Singapore to Akyab, in ballast. Made prizes of both and set fire to them, the crews of each being placed in boats with provisions, &c.

Highlander was a beautiful clipper of 1,050 tons, commanded by Jabez H. Snow. When Captain Snow with his ship's papers in hand reached

Alabama's deck, he said to Semmes, "Well, Captain Semmes, I have been expecting every day for the last three years, to fall in with you, and here I am at last! . . . I have had constant visions of the *Alabama* by night and by day; she has been chasing me in my sleep, and riding me like a night-mare, and now that it is all over, I feel quite relieved."

On 7 March 1863, Captain Snow had contracted with Hyde and Jones of London for a charter party under which *Highlander* would sail to Akyab, or another port in Burma, and there pick up a cargo of rice and transport it to Cork or Falmouth. *Highlander* was permitted under the charter party to make an intermediate voyage. This explains the fact that *Highlander* was still en route to Akyab on 26 December 1863, when she had the bad fortune to cross the path of the CSS *Alabama* in the Straits of Malacca. On these facts turned the decision of the first *Alabama* Claims Court that ships like *Highlander* and the earlier *Jabez Snow,* sailing under charter parties, could claim net freight on cargo which was soon to be loaded in the ship even though the ship was traveling in ballast at the time. Moore, 4287. Total claims filed for *Highlander* were $191,171, including $84,000 for loss of the vessel and $62,402 for the loss of freight. The Confederate estimate of this prize number 52 was $75,965.

11.30 Discharged the Straits pilot. Noon. The Light Ship bore S. E., distant eight miles.

This was the North Sand light-ship in the Straits of Malacca.

Gave chase to a suspicious looking vessel, who, on our firing a gun, hove to, showing Bremen colours. Boarding with Mr. Meulnier,

Baron Max. von Meulnier was the Prussian master's mate who spoke many languages.

I found her to be the (late Yankee) ship "Ottone" of Bremen, Singapore to Rangoon. 3.30 Blew off steam, made all sail, and hoisted the propellor up.

27th. Sunday. Light westerly breeze with heavy rain. 6 a.m. Java Island in sight on port bow. Saw 4 vessels, one showing Dutch colours. 6 p.m. Java Island, bore S. by E. ¼ E. dist. 20 miles.

28th. Variable winds with heavy rain. Occasionally got casts of the lead. 2.30 p.m. Made a sail to windward.

30th. Moderate E'ly wind. Fine. Court martial sentenced Jno. Smith O. S. [ordinary seaman] to 30 days solitary confinement, and loss of three months pay &c. 3.50 Sail in sight.

[171]

Boarding I found her to be the ship "Thomas Blythe" of and from Liverpool to Singapore with a general cargo. Passed as the U. S. Str. "Wyoming."

31st. A. M. Moderate Easterly breeze. P.M. Cloudy with occasional showers. Out of the Straits of Malacca. At noon Pulo Bay bore S. E. ½ S. dist. 40 miles. Last day of this most (to us) eventful year. We Alabamians have exceeding cause to be grateful for our almost miraculous preservation during the past year.

Fullam's enthusiasm for the Confederate cause mounted as he surpassed all other officers in the number of prizes boarded.

1864. January 1st commences with a light S. Wly breeze which gradually increases toward night, until 7.30 p.m. when a tremendous squall struck us, rendering it necessary to reef. Saw a sail during the afternoon. Evening "All hands spliced the main brace."

Fullam recorded *Alabama's* position on this New Year's Day as 6.24 north and 93.30 east.

2nd. Fine. Moderate westerly winds.

Sunday, 3rd. This being the first Sunday in the month the Articles of War were read.

This was the first date that Fullam had mentioned reading the Articles of War for some time. The significance may have been the desertion of the ten men in Singapore on 24 December.

Two sails in sight to windward in the afternoon. Light westerly wind.

4th. Moderate and light westerly wind. 6.20 A sail hove in sight. Nearing her, she proved to be foreign. Two more vessels in sight in the afternoon. Gave chase to one, who by signal proved to be the English ship "Glennalice," Singapore to Jeddo.

The position of contact was 6.00 north and 91.40 east. *Glennalice* was bound to Jedo, an earlier name for Tokyo.

5th. Light variable southerly winds until evening, when a fresh S. S. E. wind blew. Chased a vessel to windward that showed French colours.

8th. Moderate easterly winds. Cloudy. 3.00 p.m. Made a sail on port bow, standing northerly. On boarding she proved to be the English bark "Lady Harriet" from Mauritius.

The chief port of Mauritius was and still is Port Louis. Port Louis is situated at 20.10 south and 57.30 east.

9th. Fresh N. E. wind. 8 p.m. In chase of a sail but gave it up having lost her in the darkness. Midnight. Hove to off Point de Galle.

Galle is on the southwest extremity of Ceylon, 6.02 north and 80.13 east.

10th. 5.30 a.m. Filled away again and stood on course. Two sails reported, one evidently foreign. It fell calm towards evening.
11th. Calm until daylight when it blew strong from the N. E. Had to take a reef in the topsails. 6.35 p.m. This being the anniversary of our engagment with the "Hatteras" (the first yard-arm engagement between two steamers), the main brace was spliced with a very long splice indeed!

It was on 11 January 1863 that *Alabama* spent very few minutes in sinking the USS *Hatteras,* an adventure which occupied more of Fullam's space than any other during the cruise of *Alabama.*

12th. Fresh N. E. breeze until evening when it became calm.
13th. Light variable easterly winds. P.M. Went to general quarters.
14th. Light easterly breeze from noon. Daylight observed a bark to the S'd. [southward]. 12.20 Hauled by the·wind in chase of a ship to windward. 3. Fired a blank cartridge and hove chase to. On boarding I took possession,–the ship "Emma Jane" of Bath, Bombay in ballast to Moulmein. Trans-ferred prisoners, stores, &c. and set fire to her. The Captain having his wife with him was accommodated in the ward room.

Emma Jane proved to be the first ship burned by *Alabama* in the Indian Ocean. *Emma Jane* was in ballast to Moulmein, Burma, and therefore no admiralty court proceedings were necessary because there was no problem concerning claims of a neutral cargo and the ship herself was of American registry. *Emma Jane* was a ship of 1,097 tons, of Bath, Maine. She was built in Bath in 1854 and was owned by David C. Magoun and others, and operated under the command of Francis C. Jordan. *Emma Jane* sailed from Bombay on 6 January 1864 in ballast because she could get no cargo in an area where the CSS *Alabama* was threatening, but she was proceeding under charter. Eight days after leaving Bombay, *Emma Jane* was in position 7.59 north and 76.04 east when she fell into the clutches of *Alabama* and

[173]

was burned. Total claims filed for *Emma Jane* were $95,557.34. Of this amount, $58,103.25 was for the ship alone. The Confederate evaluation of this prize, number 53 of the vessels destroyed, was $40,000.

Two more vessels in sight, one showing English colours.

15th. Light breeze with a couple of heavy showers until noon, from the ed. [eastward]. P.M. Light N. W. wind. 6 a.m. Sail in sight.

16th. Light northerly winds. Several vessels in sight during the day. 5.20 a.m. Made land ahead. Stood in towards it. 4.30 p.m. Came to in 12 ftms. off Anjengo, Malabar. Communicated with the authorities.

Anjengo, Malabar, has declined in importance since Fullam's day. This is a rocky area marked by coconut palms growing close to the water's edge. The old province of Malabar is situated between the lines 10.15 and 12.18 north, but mariners then and later often referred to the whole seacoast from Cape Comorin to Bombay as the Malabar Coast. Anjengo is actually located somewhat south of the province, being at 8.53 north and 76.34 east.

17th. Light westerly wind. 6 a.m. Sent on shore Captain and crew of prize ship "Emma Jane." 9.30 Got under weigh. Mustered crew. Saw several vessels, all English. Signalled the bark "Nerbudda," Siam to Bombay.

For Siam, see *BR 510*, pp. 162–188. French power was being extended in Cochin, China (1858–1867), and into Cambodia (1863 –1864) about the time of *Alabama's* cruise in neighboring waters.

Passed as H. M. Str. "Tartar." Hoisted English blue to the rest. Shipped 2 men.

These two men were Charles Colson and John Johnson, both of whom were ordinary seamen who enlisted 16 January 1864. As events proved, Colson and Johnson were two of the last eight men recruited aboard *Alabama*. The men, enlisted throughout the cruise, totaled 186 plus 30 officers.

18th. Light westerly breeze. Two sails in sight, one showing Portuguese colors. I boarded, proving to be the "Alexandra & Herculano," Rio Janeiro, 70 days to Goa.

Blunt, 537, used the same spelling as Fullam for Rio de Janeiro. The Portuguese colony of Goa (now part of India), including the old city of that name, was described in *HO 159*, pp. 208, 215, 217. When Fullam boarded *Alexandra and Herculano,* he found that this vessel was Portuguese and was proceeding from one Portuguese port to another.

[174]

Called ourselves the "Tartar."

19th. Light variable northerly winds. 9.30 a.m. Sail in sight right ahead. 4.40 p.m. Got up steam on two boilers, reduced sail to topsails, lowered propellor and steamed in chase. Fired two blank cartridges. 8 p.m. I boarded and found her to the ship "Ally" of and from Bombay to Mauritius, with coolies. Told them we were the "Wyoming." 8.30 Hoisted propellor and made sail.

20th. Light N. E. winds; daylight, sail in sight.

21st. Fresh E. N. E. wind. 8.52 a.m. Minicoy Island in sight on starboard bow. 11.30 Hove to off the island. Several boats sailing round us but none coming on board.

The closest land to Fullam's celestial observation on 21 January 1864 was Minikoi Island (also spelled Minicoy), situated 8.16 north and 73.01 east. *HO 159,* pp. 384–385; *HO Chart 1591.* This is one of the Laccadive Islands which are north of the Maldive Islands.

At this point in Fullam's Journal the manuscript has the following footnote which was crossed out: "This evening (29th) a curious phenomena was observed in the sea. A remarkable whiteness; caused I believe by the rising of the moon behind a cloud, its light traveling through a humid atmosphere reflecting its rays on a sea of phosphorous nature,—Took cast of lead. Bottom in 100 fthms."

Filled away again, and stood on course.

22nd. Fresh N. N. E. wind. Fine.

30th. Fresh breezes varying from N. to N. E., chiefly N. N. E. 11 p.m. Crossed the Equator.

Fullam's observation, a few hours before crossing the Equator, was 0.51 north and 48.43 east.

Feb. 2nd [1864]. Fine. Wind changed to N. W. Moderate.

6th. Light northerly airs. Hot. Very.

9th. Light airs and calms with oppressive heat. 12 a.m. Lowered propellor and at 1.30 went ahead under steam. Johanna Island in sight at 6.30 a.m. Mohilla on starboard bow, and Comoro on starboard beam.

The islands were dependencies of Madagascar. It was not until 1885 that the French declared Madagascar a protectorate and not until 1896 that the French annexed this fourth largest island in the world. The Malagasy Republic was created in 1958 and two years later declared completely independent.

10.30 a.m. Sail reported on starboard bow about 2½ points.

*At 1.35 p.m. anchored off Johanna. Engaged in supply of fresh
provisions for all hands, who were much in need of it.*

*Johanna is, especially on its northern side, very high; not
however so much so as Comoro is. It is very hilly. The soil
is very rich and capable of cultivation. Some of it indeed is
under the direction of an English resident on the southern side
of the island, been made to produce sugar cane much superior
to Mauritius. A steam engine of about thirty horse power is
about to be started to make sugar. The island is under the
authority of a King or Sultan. Four is the orthodox number of
wives, exclusive of concubines, who form an indispensable
part of a household. The people are hospitably inclined, but
full of low cunning. Though of course superior to theft, and
most ready to swear to their honesty, they should not be
trusted. Slavery in its domestic relations, and the slave trade
is carried on. Mahometanism is the religion of the people. The
town is a miserable collection of rough stone houses and
matted huts. There are five or six houses of larger dimensions
than the rest, which are occupied by the principal dignitaries.
Fresh meat, pumpkins, limes, oranges, plantains, and a variety
of tropical fruit are obtained. There is good water, but no
liquor or spirits can be procured. The anchorage is good but
is not to be recommended during the northerly monsoons as
it is open to those winds.*

For three consecutive years the northeast monsoon struck Johanna on 25
December. January is reported by *HO 161* to be the worst month for exposure
to monsoons on the north side of the island. *Alabama* was at Johanna and
other neighboring islands from 9 February 1864 to 15 February.

*15th [February 1864]. Fine, light northerly airs, receiving
fresh provisions, &c. for sea use until 11.30 when we called
all hands up anchor. 12 Stood out to sea under steam. P.M.
Hoisted propellor, making all plain sail.*

*16th. Light northerly airs. Fine. P.M. Court-martial sentenced
four men to be reduced to the grade of landsmen, forfeit one
months pay, and be blacklisted two weeks, charge: desertion.*

*19th. Toward 2 a.m. a strong breeze blew from the Nd & Wd
[northward and westward], fell calm however soon after. Saw
a ship, steering northeasterly. Night coming on gave up chase.
P.M. Light N. E. wind.*

20th. Commenced with a light N. E. wind, which soon merged into a stiff N Wester [northwester]. Had to double reef the topsails. Throughout the remainder of the day, light N Westerly winds.

22nd. Fine. Easterly winds. P.M. Wind S. E.

24th. Strong gale, varying between S. E. and S. W. Close reefed. Cloudy with occasional rain.

25th. Moderated towards noon. Wind from N. N. E. to S. E. P.M. Made all plain sail. 12.45 Sail reported about a point on starboard bow; hauled up for chase, hoisted English colours, and signalled her name (ship) "Caspatrick." Hoisted French flag, and "L'Invincible" as our name. Between 8 p.m. and 2 a.m. of the

26th. we had most vivid, incessant lightning, heavy peals of thunder, and continuous rain. Fresh breeze from the S. S. E. to N. E.

27th. Fresh S. E. breeze. Heavy sea. Fine. 4.55 p.m. Owing to the vessel pitching, an O. S. [ordinary seaman] washed overboard from the head. An alarm was immediately made, and a couple of gratings thrown overboard with one of which, Michael Mars jumped over the taffrail into the sea and succeeded in succouring the man, whose strength was well nigh exhausted. Altho' the ship was immediately brought by the wind, the mainyard backed, and a boat lowered, yet, but for the gallant conduct and timely assistance of Mars, Godson must have become food for fishes.

The ordinary seaman was Henry Godson who had enlisted in November 1862. Before Godson fell overboard, he had been on the sick list for a long time, but in February 1864 he was convalescent and ordered by the ship's surgeon to be carried on deck for fresh air and sunshine. He was on the topgallant forecastle when the pitching ship threw him overboard on the leeward side. The officer of the deck, Lt. Joseph D. Wilson, quickly gave orders to bring *Alabama* to a standstill and to put a lifeboat over the side. Meantime, however, Michael Mars sprang to action. Mars was coxswain of the cutter. (Fullam earlier described Mars' attack on the shark at Arcas and his cracking the whip with snakes at Pulo Condore.) When Godson fell overboard, Mars, immediately seized a couple of gratings and threw them into the rough sea. By then Kell had reached the scene and ordered Mars not to risk his life trying to reach the struggling man. Sinclair later said that Mars replied, "Keep cool, Mr. Kell, I will save the poor fellow." Mars then

[177]

plunged into the water, swam to Godson's side, and put the exhausted man on a grating. Soon the lifeboat picked up both Godson and Mars and took them back aboard the cruiser amidst the yells of approval from their shipmates.

Hoisted boat and filled mainyard.

2nd. March [1864]. Moderate and fresh S. E. winds until noon of today when it blew freshly from the E. N. E. with rather a heavy sea.

3rd. Commenced with a fresh N. E. wind, with a heavy sea. Toward evening it hauled more to the northward, and by 8 p.m. blowing a gale from the W. N. W. with a tremendous sea. Close reefed everything and hove to.

4th. Opened with a W. S. Wly. gale and fearful sea. Moderated towards daybreak. Had two ports stove during the previous night. Moderated, so that by 1.30 p.m. we had shaken out all reefs. The sea still running high; the ship labouring and straining heavily. Evening, light S. E. wind.

5th. Fine. Variable easterly winds.

6th. Sunday. Read Articles of War &c., after which, in a General Order, the Commander publicly expressed his approbation of the gallant conduct of Michael Mars, A. B. [able bodied seaman] in jumping overboard to rescue a shipmate a few days ago. Strong N. Wly. winds. Four vessels in sight to windward. 3.30 p.m. Blowing fresh, the sea rising rapidly. Close reefed topsails and trysails. Occasionally rain.

7th. Variable Wly. winds with heavy swell. Two vessels in sight. Exchanged English colours with one.

8th. Moderate easterly winds. Fine. Three vessels in sight.

9th. Bright and clear. Wind westerly. 8 vessels reported in sight. Showed English Red and "Peterel" to the Dutch bark "Van der Palau." 10 p.m. Light breeze. Shortened sail to topsails and wore ship to the southward.

10th. Fine. Light westerly wind.

11th. Fine. Light southerly wind. 8 a.m. Land reported 3 points on starboard bow. Noon. Cape of Good Hope bore north (true), dist 46 miles. Wind freshening. 3 p.m. Made a ship on starboard beam, showed Dutch to our English colours. 5.15 Made a three masted steamer to the west'd., standing S. E. 5.50 Made a brig under easy sail to the northward. 6 p.m. Cape lighthouse bore (per con.) E. S. E., dist 20 miles.

12th. Fresh southerly wind. By the wind on port tack, under close reefed topsails and fore staysail. 4.10 p.m. Made a barque rigged steamer ahead, standing S. Ely. Supposed to be the English mail steamer for the Cape. Turned out one reef and set trysails, keeping off N. N. W. 4.50 The steamer having passed out of sight, took in trysails. 6 p.m. Under close reef. 5.50 Made a sail to the south'd and eastward; made sail to work ship in chase. Supposed her to be English.

13th. Sunday. Fresh southerly wind. Daylight, bore ship to the west'd. Turned reefs out of topsails, and set topmast staysail and trysails. 8.40 a.m. Made a large ship to windward. 9.30 Wore ship and hove chase to by signal. On boarding I found her to be the "Scottish Chief" of St. John, N. B., Calcutta to London, with a general cargo. Passed as the U. S. Str. "Dacotah." 3 o'clock. Made a sail on weather bow, chased; altered course at 3.30 as another vessel was descried. 5.30. Hove vessel to by signal. On boarding I found her to be the barque "Orion" of and bound to Hamburg, 45 days from Macao. Passed as the "Dacotah." Reefed and stood on port tack.

14th. Strong, southerly breeze. Daylight. Wore round to the eastward. 11 a.m. Sail reported a point abaft the weather beam; wore ship and stood in chase. Proved to be a large, double topsailyard ship. 4 p.m. Gave up chase. Sundown. Took off bonnets off trysails and reefed topsails.

15th. Strong southerly breeze with heavy sea.

16th. Moderate southerly wind. Turned out all reefs. Still cruising in the homeward bound track. Evening. Reefed again.

17th. [March] Light variable southerly wind. Being St. Patrick's Day, the main-brace was spliced.

18th. At daylight wore round to the westward. Made sail in chase of a vessel to windward.

17th and 18th. Each evening lightning (forked) and thunder. 6 a.m. To our English, chase replied with Spanish colours. On boarding I found her to be the barque "Manilla" from Manilla to Cowes. [Manila] Reported having been boarded off the Straits of Sunda by H. M. Str. "Scots" (query "Centaur") [on] Feb. 11th. [Manila] Had experienced dreadful weather in 29.30 S. long. of Mauritius, losing every stitch of canvas. Called ourselves H. M. Str. "Fawn," Capt. Townley. 10.30 a.m. Made a bark on port bow, kept off in chase. A *thick fog set in at 10.40. Lost sight of chase. 1.25 p.m. Gave up the chase. Evening. Wind chopped round to the westward, blew fresh with rain squalls, thunder and lightning. 8.10 Wind N. E. changed in a squall to south.*

19th. [March] Light variable airs. 6 a.m. Made a sail to the northward. 9.30 Got up steam and lowered propellor. 10 Clewed up and furled topsails and went ahead under steam.

Sunday. 20th [March 1864]. Commenced with a light S. W. breeze and hazy sky. 6 a.m. Made a ship on weather bow, and a schooner on weather beam. Chased the ship, hove her to with a blank cartridge. On boarding I found her to be the ship "Sardinia" of and to Liverpool, 64 [days] from Bombay. 9.30 Schooner showed English colours, and: by signal [identified herself as] from Rio Janeiro to Algoa Bay. Mustered crew &c. Exchanged English red with a Dutch ship. Noon. Cape Town about 40 miles dist. Took in all sail. 1.30 Made Table Mountain half a point on starboard bow. 5.15 Came to in 6½ fthms. with starboard anchor out 60 fthms. cable. Signal Station on Lions Rump W. ½ N., and lighthouse on point N. W. by W. Went on shore to [see] the Governor.

Fullam noted *Alabama's* position on 20 March 1864 as 33.50 south and 14.32 east, very close to Table Bay. For Algoa Bay, see *HO 156*, p. 91. Table Mountain rises to an altitude of 3,550 feet. See *HO 105*, p. 347; *BA Chart 2091*. From Lion's Rump to Lion's Head is a ridge that runs about 1¼ miles and rises to 1,145 feet.

21st. Strong S. E. gale. Veered cable to 90 fthms. and let go port anchor.

22nd. Strong S. E. breeze with clear weather. 10.30 a.m. A schooner flying U. S. colours, came in from sea.

23rd. Strong southerly wind. Noon. Commenced coaling.

24th. Fine light breeze. Receiving provisions, coals &c &c. Receiving a most cordial reception.

More than a cordial reception awaited *Alabama* at Cape Town. The proceeds from the sale of *Sea Bride* and the wool cargo of the CSS *Tuscaloosa* (ex-*Conrad*) were taken aboard *Alabama*. *Alabama* also took on board 207 tons of coal. This was the last coal taken aboard. When sunk by *Kearsarge* in June 1864, *Alabama* had 133 tons of coal. Subtracting this from the total number of tons obtained with each coaling operation, the coal used on the entire cruise was 1,786 tons.

*25th. Good Friday. Light moderate wind N. W'ly. Made
preparations for sea. Whilst getting under weigh a steamer
was reported showing U. S. colours. He got inside the harbour
before we got under weigh. The unkindest cut of all. 10.30
a.m. Left Cape Town. Steered W. by S. until noon. Hauled
up more to the northward. 3 p.m. Made a ship on the port
tack. 4 p.m. Sail reported on the port beam. Saw several
sails toward evening. 6.20 Made sail to t'gallantsails. 6.30
Hoisted propellor; filled away and blew off steam. Shipped 4
hands.*

The four new hands were John Buckley, Fred Lennen, H. Micoy, and
Nicholas Adams. All four were ordinary seamen and they were badly needed
as replacements for men who had deserted, particularly at Singapore.
While cruising, *Alabama's* chief supply of recruits in the Confederate States
Navy was from Union merchant vessels. The cruise to the East Indies and
the South China Sea, however, had yielded few prizes and limited opportu-
nities to recruit.

During the whole cruise of *Alabama* approximately 2,000 Union merchant
seamen were captured, along with their ships. The number of men enlisted
during the cruise was 99, for the most part from Union prizes. This compares
with the number of enlisted men who joined *Alabama* at Terceira (nearly
all Britishers) and totaled 87. In other words, the commerce raiding seamen
in the CSS *Alabama* were approximately one-half from Yankee ships and
one-half Britishers, as far as can be judged from their point of origin. Of
course, not all mariners in Union vessels were born under the Stars and
Stripes. In contrast, few indeed were the Southerners who served in that
Confederate ship.

*26th. Moderate northerly wind. Wind shifted in a squall to
the S. W. Sky overcast all day. A.M. Two sails in sight.
Easter Sunday. 27th. Fresh S. S. E. wind. Cloudy.*

On this Easter Sunday, Fullam reckoned his position at 31.52 south and
12.39 east. During the following week, when Fullam made no entries in
his journal, he made daily entries in his log of the CSS *Alabama*, recording
on 2 April the position at 24.13 south and 0.23 east. Later that day *Alabama*
crossed the Greenwich Meridian. Fullam noted for 3 April the ship's position
at 1.34 west.

*Sunday. April 3rd [1864]. Moderate S. S. E. wind during the
past week. Mustered crew and read Articles of War.
4th. Variable easterly wind.*

[181]

5th. Fine S. E. breeze. 1 p.m. Hauled by the wind on star-
board tack to cruise across the homeward Indian track [from
India and the East Indies]. Under short sail.
7th. Made sail and at noon steered W. N. W. Fresh southerly
breeze. Sky overcast. St. Helena bearing N. W. by W. true
dist. 140 miles.

Napoleon's place of exile, Saint Helena, is an island of only 47 square miles, characterized by bare cliffs, mountains, and volcanic waste. Situated some 1,200 miles off the coast of Africa, it is 700 miles from the nearest land. The CSS *Alabama* lingered some days in the vicinity of Saint Helena because this island was in the path of South Atlantic shipping. The fact that at this stage of the cruise *Alabama* went so long without a prize was not due to lack of ships but only due to the fact that the Union carrying trade had fled to foreign registry.

7 p.m. Shortened sail to topsail and hauled by the wind on port
tack.
8th. Daylight, squared away again. Fresh S. E. wind. P.M.
No signs of ships, so steered W. N. W. for the coast of Brazil.
Until the
17th. Sunday, had light southeast winds. 10 a.m. Made a sail
on port beam, kept away in chase. At 1.15 p.m. hove chase
to by signal, and sent a boat on board, when she proved to
be the Italian bark "Carlo," Buenos Ayres to Antwerp, with
wool, tallow, &c. 1.30 Sail reported bearing S. by E. Kept off
for her. 4.50 Overhauled chase. Boarding I found her to be the
French ship "Formose" of and to Bordeaux from Callao. To
each of these we called ourselves the U. S. Str Dacotah.
Filled away on course.
18th. Alternate sunshine and showers. Light variable winds.
Daylight made a sail two points on lee bow. Stood in chase.
8.10 a.m. Bark showed Hamburg colours. Hove her to by
signal. On boarding she proved to be the bark "Alster," Apia
Island to Falmouth, with palm oil.

The Hamburg bark *Alster* bore the name of a lake in Sweden in the Varmland area.

Have experienced a succession of light variable winds and
calms until the
22nd, when a light breeze gradually freshened into a
moderate E. S. E. wind. At 11.25 a.m. made a sail on lee bow.

[182]

Noon. Wind, light easterly. 8 p.m. Still in chase of a suspicious looking ship.

23rd. Moderate east wind. 6 a.m. To our U. S. colours, chase replied by hoisting the same. 6.30 Hove her to by signal and sent a boat on board; she proved to be the ship "Rockingham" of Portsmouth, from Callao to Queenstown, with guano. Of course, made a prize of her. Transferred Captain, his wife, and stewardess, mates and crew, with some provisions, &c. 2.30 Went to general quarters, and fired two shots and two shells from the starboard battery at prize. After some excellent firing, boarded and set fire to prize.

Rockingham was a 976-ton ship, built in Portsmouth, New Hampshire in 1858 and operated out of Portsmouth by two brothers, William P. Jones and Albert L. Jones, sole owners. Under command of Edward A. Gerrish, *Rockingham* was in the guano trade. As Fullam noted, *Rockingham* came over the horizon into *Alabama's* view about 11.25 a.m. on 22 April 1864. There followed a stern chase, as *Alabama* slowly gained on the suspicious-looking square-rigger. By nightfall the prize was in the distance, as she continued to be at 8 p.m. Boarding at night was particularly difficult and therefore no special effort was made to overtake the craft until the next morning at 6.30 when *Alabama* signaled *Rockingham* to heave to. *Rockingham* was carrying a load of guano from the Chincha Islands, the west coast of South America, and was bound for Queenstown at the time of her capture in position 15.53 south and 31.44 west. *Rockingham* was the first prize taken by *Alabama* since *Emma Jane,* more than three months before. This was a welcome opportunity for Captain Semmes' prize court to pronounce spurious the claims of neutral ownership of the cargo.

The sea was smooth and the weather conducive to exercising the gun divisions. This proved to be *Alabama's* last target practice before the engagement with the USS *Kearsarge. Alabama's* gunnery was very effective against *Rockingham,* the hull being damaged considerably and the cabin nearly demolished. Later, the gunfire against the USS *Kearsarge* was notably less effective. After the gun exercises, *Rockingham* was again boarded and this time set on fire. This prize, number 54, resulted in claims filed with the United States State Department totaling $216,955.55, of which $90,000 was for the ship alone. The value set by the Confederates on *Rockingham* was $97,878. This brought the total of Confederate evaluations to $4,241,491.

4 o'clock filled away again on course. 9.20 p.m. made a ship on lee beam; wore ship and stood in chase. Fired a blank cartridge and a shell from No. 1 gun. On boarding I found her to be the ship "Robert McKensie" of and from Liverpool to Calcutta, 38 days out.

[183]

24th. Sunday [April 1864]. Light wind varying from E. N. E.
9 a.m. Made a sail ahead. 10.30 Hove her to by signal. On
boarding I found her to be the ship "Kent" of and to London,
48 days from Melbourne.

The position of *Kent* when boarded by Fullam was 15.19 south and 32.06 west, off the South Atlantic coast of South America in the track of vessels trading to and from the Pacific Ocean.

11.30 Stood on course, to the northward again. 3.30 p.m. Sail
reported on starboard beam. 6 p.m. Another vessel in sight.
    25th. Light variable easterly wind. 6.15 a.m. Made a sail to
windward. Tacked in chase. Hoisted Yankee colours and
signalled chase to heave to. At 8.15 I boarded and found her
to be the bark "Bertha Martha" of Liverpool, Sunderland to
Arica.

Bertha Martha was in the guano trade to the West Coast of South America.

Filled away again. 11.35 Another vessel in sight. Set all sail
in chase. 5.15 Chase showed English colours.
    26th. Light E. N. E. wind. At daylight made a sail on weather
bow. Gave chase. On boarding I found her to be the bark
"La Flor del Plata" of Mayport, Liverpool to Monte Video.
10.30 Saw a brig standing southerly. Wind moderate E. S. E.
    27th. A.M. Barque in sight to windward, steering southerly.
1.10 p.m. Sail reported. 5. Made a sail right ahead. 5.30
Hoisted Yankee colours and hove her to by signal. Boarding
I found her to be the barque "Tycoon" of and from New York
to San Francisco, with a valuable cargo (general). Of course,
took possession. Engaged transferring prisoners and stores
until
    28th. 2.50 a.m. when we set fire to prize.

Alabama was moving northward and nearing the equator when a ship loomed over the horizon and slowly approached. It was late in the afternoon when the two ships were close enough for Fullam to board the merchantman. She was the clipper ship *Tycoon* of New York, 717 tons, owned by William W. Wakeman and eight others. *Tycoon*, under command of Edward Ayres, departed New York 19 March 1864 bound for San Francisco with a large and valuable general cargo, and passengers as well. Crew and passengers were taken aboard *Alabama*. No claim was made that the cargo was neutral, and ship and cargo were speedily condemned. Generous supplies of merchandise needed by various departments of the raider were moved from ship to ship.

[184]

The value placed by the Confederates on *Tycoon* and her cargo (55th and last prize) was $390,000, making a grand total of Confederate evaluation of prizes destroyed by *Alabama* at $4,631,491. On the Union side, total claims filed for loss of *Tycoon* amounted to $424,551.63. One of the owners of the cargo, J. K. Prior, asked $541.75 for merchandise lost aboard *Tycoon* (Case 1123 before the Court of Commissioners of the *Alabama* Claims), and also requested $774.62 for merchandise lost when *Alabama* burned *Sea Lark* on 3 May 1863. Prior was a three-time loser because he lost merchandise valued at $2,772.38 when the CSS *Florida* burned *Commonwealth*.

After *Tycoon* was burned, her passengers and crew were carried as prisoners of war aboard *Alabama* to Cherbourg and there turned over to the United States consul. The third mate and carpenter of *Tycoon*, John H. Little, later testified that he was a prisoner aboard the CSS *Alabama* for 45 days, of which he was kept in irons for 44 days. He was, he said, "without shelter or clothing." On 11 June 1864, Little was released from *Alabama* and proceeded from Cherbourg to Havre in care of the American consul. He remained in Havre about two weeks, when the consul sent him to London. After five days in London, Little signed on the American vessel *Adriatic*, working his passage to New York. On 12 August, *Adriatic* was captured by the CSS *Tallahassee*. This time, Little did not remain a prisoner long. With other prisoners from *Adriatic*, he was put aboard the bark *Suliotte* and arrived in New York only five days after his capture by the Confederate cruiser.

2 a.m. Set all plain sail and stood on course. 6 a.m. Saw a vessel on weather quarter. Variable wind from E. to E. S. E. Evening, heavy rain squalls.

29th. Commenced with moderate E. S. E. wind. Fine. 10.30 a.m. Made a sail on weather beam standing southerly. Evening, increased to a fresh S. E. wind.

30th. Fine. Fresh E. S. E. breeze. 8.15 a.m. Sail reported on weather beam. Found it to be a bark standing southerly.

1st May [1864]. Fresh E. S. E. breeze with heavy rain squalls.

2nd. Moderate E. S. E. breeze with heavy squalls. 1 p.m. Made a barkentine on weather bow, standing southerly. 3.15 Crossed the Equator. In the North Atlantic again, at which, all hands are delighted.

Alabama crossed the equator for the last time at 3.15 p.m. in longitude 30.38 west, cruising off the coast of Brazil. Almost hourly the rain came in torrents. Fullam said, however, that "all hands are delighted," because everybody knew that *Alabama* was now on the last leg of the cruise. Sinclair stated that this was the only time when *Alabama's* ship's company knew what the destination would be.

3rd. 7 a.m. Wind shifted suddenly from S. E. to E. N. E. Moderate with occasional squalls.

4th. Variable weather. Wind moderate from E. to N. E.

5th. Fresh breeze E. N. E. to N. E. Fine.

8th. Sunday. Fresh E. by N. to N. E. by E. breeze up to today.

11th. Wind lighter, E. S. E. to N. E. by E. P.M. Sail in sight on weather bow. Hove her to by signal. Boarding I found she was the Hamburg brig "Margarite," Liverpool, 27 days to Puerto Cabello. Told them we were the "Wyoming."

12th. Light S. easterly wind. 9 a.m. Saw a brig on lee bow. Chased until 1 p.m. when we gave it up. Towards evening it fell calm.

13th. Light airs. South to N. W. Calm.

14th. Daylight, saw a vessel to the N. W. Calm. Occasionally light airs. 6 a.m. Another vessel in sight to the northward.

15th. Variable light winds and calms during the early part of the day. 9 a.m. Made a sail two points abaft weather beam. Proved to be a Portuguese brig. Evening. Four more in sight. Chased, fired two guns, hove to and, at 10.30 p.m., boarded the Spanish brig "Tores Eliza," Santander to Porto Rico, 19 days out.

16th. Light breeze N. E. by E. to E. by N.

17th. Light variable northeasterly.

19th. Moderate and light easterly winds. 2 p.m. Sail descried on weather quarter.

Tacked ship in chase. To our Yankee colours, chase replied with French. Boarding I found her to be the barque "Mere de Famille," Monte Video, 42 days to Havre. Passed as the "Dacotah."

When Fullam earlier boarded *Margarite,* the brig was in position 18.37 north and 41.01 west. When he boarded *Mere de Famille,* the position was 26.32 north and 41.44 west, so the Confederate cruiser was making 60 miles per day average speed.

20th. Moderate breeze varying from east to S. E. 9.10 a.m. Made a large sail to windward. 11 Chase showed English colours; [we] hoisted U. S. colours in return. 4.30 p.m. Another sail in sight to windward.

21st. Light from E. S. E. to daylight. 4 vessels in sight; one hull up on weather bow. 10 a.m. Set mainsail. 11.25 Fired a blank cartridge from rifle pivot, when chase showed English colours.

22nd. Sunday. Light southerly to west wind. A.M. Three vessels in sight. 4.30 p.m. A sail in sight on starboard beam.

23rd. Moderate westerly wind. 6.15 a.m. Two vessels in sight to the S. E. 12.45 Sail in sight to windward. Chased. 5 p.m. Hove chase to by signal. Boarding I found her to be the barque "Cymbeline" of and to London, 105 days [from] Yokohama. Told them we were the "Dacotah."

24th. Fresh west wind. 9.30 p.m. Reduced sail to topgallant-sails. Saw a schooner steering southerly. Chased; fired a blank cartridge. Hove her to with a shell. 11.30 Boarded and found her to be the Nova Scotia schooner "Maria Louisa," Philadelphia, 19 days to Rio Janeiro.

25th. Fresh gale. Wind varying from W. to N. W. 12.30 p.m. Sail in sight on weather quarter. 2. Single-reefed topsails. 4 p.m. Close reefed, and took bonnets off topsails. Strong gales. Sent down royal yards. 9 p.m. Took in fore topsails. Midnight. Heavy squalls.

26th. Commenced with a fresh N. W. gale. 8 a.m. Showed English colours to French barque. Strong gales with heavy sea.

27. Strong N. W. gale with fearful sea. Moderated towards evening. A.M. Made a ship on starboard beam, on starboard tack. 2.20 p.m. Wore ship to westward. Saw a ship to the southward at 7 o'clock. 7.30 Set foretopsail.

28th. Strong gales with heavy squalls and rain. 2 a.m. Furled foretopsail. Weather moderating at daylight. Set close reefed topsails and staysails. 10 Made sail to topsails and foresail. 10.25 Showed French colours to an English barquentine. By midnight—calm.

29th. Sunday. Commenced with a calm; which at 2 a.m. changed to a N. E. breeze—strong. Close reefed. 5.30 Sail reported 3½ points on weather bow. 10. Wind changed to N. N. W. Towards evening wind moderated.

30th. Variable winds between N. E. and N. Fresh. Sail in sight on weather quarter, at daylight another on weather bow. 6 a.m. Sail on lee bow. Three more vessels in sight by evening.

31st. Moderate and fresh breezes from N. to N. E. 12.10 a.m. Made a sail on lee bow. Daylight, hoisted French colours–7 vessels in sight. Crossed royal yards. 11 a.m. Signalled Eng. brig "Eleanor," Natal to London. Told him we were H. M. Str. "Greyhound." Learnt that a large ship ahead was English, from Calcutta to London; that a barque ahead was English, from Monte Video to England.

1st June [1864]. Moderate breeze N. E. to Nly. Daylight, 4 vessels in sight.

4th. Fresh N. E. wind. 4.15 p.m. Sail hove in sight on port bow. 5.15 Hove her to by signal. Boarding I found her to be the Hamburg brig "Julie Caroline" (418), Liverpool, 9 days to Puerto Cabello. Told them we were H. M. Str. "Scourge."

When Fullam boarded *Julie Caroline,* the position was 42.10 north and 17.58 west. With *Alabama* returning to Europe, expectations were high that it would not be long before the men could be discharged from their arduous duties in many months at sea.

5th. Sunday. Moderate and light N. E. wind. Being the first Sunday in the month, the Articles of War were read. 6.30 a.m. Sail in sight 3 points on port bow. 7.15 Another, a point on starboard bow. 10.20 Boarded the Bremen brig "Koenigsmunde," Liverpool to Cien-Fuegos. 10.30 Sail in sight on starboard bow. 1 p.m. Hove chase to by signal. Boarding I found her to be the brig "Ben-gairne," Glasgow to Santos. Received papers up to May 26th, having news of the dreadful fighting in Virginia, and of the Florida's doings, also various other interesting news.

The CSS *Florida,* under Commander John Newland Maffitt, departed Brest, France, 10 February 1864 on her second cruise and was still at sea when Fullam received news of her in June 1864. Eventually, *Florida* and the ships she outfitted proved to be among the most successful of the Confederate commerce raiders, burning 46 prizes, bonding 13 more, and losing one through recapture. Owsley, *Florida,* 161, placed the damage inflicted by the CSS *Florida* and her tenders at $4,051,000.

Sinclair said that on this last lap of *Alabama's* cruise the ship's company was getting so many newspapers from the numerous neutral ships boarded, as well as from the occasional prizes, that the men were generally aware that the cause of the Confederacy was already lost. To some at least, it seemed a shame to have burned so beautiful a ship as the last prize, *Tycoon.*

6th. Light and moderate N. west'ly breeze. 5.30 a.m. Brig reported in sight. Exercised at general quarters. 6.30 p.m. Barque in sight to windward.

7th. Variable light and fresh N. W. winds and heavy swells.

[188]

8th. Strong N. Wly winds with occasional squalls. 4.45 a.m. Made a sail on weather bow. Chased a vessel that hove in sight at 1 o'clock. 5 p.m. To our English red, chase showed Spanish colours. 6 p.m. Hailed and found her to be the ship "Iberica," Singapore to Liverpool.

Iberica was encountered at 45.45 north and 12.04 west, as Alabama made her way toward the coast of France. Iberica was next to last among the vessels mentioned by Fullam as overhauled by the CSS Alabama.

Two square rigged vessels in sight just before dark.
9th. Commenced with a fresh N. Wly. breeze. By 8 a.m. 4 vessels in sight. Boarded the Genoese barkentine "Raffaeline" from Genoa to Cardiff.

The barkentine Raffaeline was boarded by Fullam at 47.35 north and 9.01 west. This was the last vessel which Fullam reported boarding while he was in the CSS Alabama and the last vessel reported by him as being overhauled by Alabama. ORN, 1, III, 681, indicated that, in addition to the Italian barkentine met on 9 June, Alabama encountered on the same day a Dutch bark. Fullam gave the number of vessels "seen, spoken and boarded" during the entire cruise of Alabama as 447.

Three more sails in sight by noon. This afternoon was spent in converting our vessel into a full rigged ship. A cross-jack and mizen-topsail yards, previously taken from prizes and rigged up; and a mizen topgallant yard improvised for the occasion, its being the main royal yard. The preceding was effected for purposes of disguise.

Another camouflage device often used by Alabama was to add a false smokestack to the one genuine stack.

Two more vessels in sight by sundown.
10th. Commenced with a moderate N. W. wind which gradually hauled to the W. S. W. At 1.30 a.m. lowered pro-pellor and furled all square sails. 2.30 Went ahead under steam. By noon, in the Channel. 11 vessels seen. S. Wester [southwester] with fog. 5 p.m. Took a Channel pilot on board. Cleared up with the wind Northerly. Many vessels seen. 10.45 p.m. Made the Start Light on port bow.
11th. 5 a.m. Made Portland Bill.

The Start Light was located on Start Point. Start Point, Cherbourg, and the Bill of Portland were commonly used by mariners as a triangle useful for navigation. *HO 132* describes the Bill of Portland. It is on the south coast of England and is the southern extremity of the Isle of Portland, south of Weymouth, and more precisely at 50.31 north and 2.27 west. In other words, the Bill of Portland is on the British side of the English Channel, directly opposite Cherbourg.

Moderate easterly wind. Steering toward Cherbourg. Noon. Took Cherbourg pilot on board. 12.40 Came to in 6½ fathoms inside the harbour.

For Cherbourg harbor, see *HO 132* and *BR 503-c. Alabama* put into Cherbourg because the ship was much in need of repairs and the French naval base there had been completed in 1858. The Confederates obviously hoped to use the facilities for repair without involving legal questions that might have come up regarding the Foreign Enlistment Act if *Alabama* had put back to England where the ship had been built.

Several French vessels of war, amongst which, the ironclad frigate "Couronne" and a Brazillian frigate at anchor. Evening. Paroled all prisoners and sent them on shore.

12th. Sunday [June 1864]. Received many official visits.

14th. Southerly wind. Overcast sky. A.M. Steamer descried in sight standing in for the harbour. Later, according as we expected, she hoisted Yankee colours. Proving to be the U. S. Str. "Kearsarge," Capt. Winslow.

All hands expecting an opportunity to exchange civilities with her [Kearsarge]. P.M. Sent down yards off mizen mast and halyards. This afternoon our commander

Thus Fullam faced the crisis of his life. This was also a major event of the Confederate States Navy.

The last entry in the Log was made 11 June and did not give a celestial observation but noted that *Alabama* was "anchored in Cherbourg harbour." The Log ended four days earlier than the Journal. The last entry in the Journal was on 14 June 1864. There were two or three additional words at the end, but they were illegible, as the pen ran dry. Although Fullam's Journal ended before the *Kearsarge* engagement, a short account of the battle should be added as a vehicle to round out the narrative of *Alabama's* boarding officer. This is especially appropriate because of Fullam's actions during the battle.

The surgeon on board the USS *Kearsarge*, John M. Browne, later wrote that on Tuesday the Union warship arrived off Cherbourg and there, inside the breakwater, the Confederate flag was observed flying. The Yankee officers and crew from the deck of *Kearsarge* gazed intently at the "daring rover" that for two years had escaped her foes and managed to inflict tremendous damage on Union commerce. As he looked upon her, Browne wrote, "She was a beautiful specimen of naval architecture." [John M. Browne, "The Duel Between the 'Alabama' and the 'Kearsarge'," in *Battles and Leaders of the Civil War*.]

The arrival of *Kearsarge* at Cherbourg on 14 June was the result of careful planning, since the Union warship was at Flushing, the Netherlands, just three days earlier when *Alabama* first came into the French harbor. Indeed, a letter from Thomas H. Dudley, the consul at Liverpool, to Seward told the secretary of state that *Alabama* was to arrive in a French port for repairs "very soon," and the date of the communication was 3 June, eight days before *Alabama* actually arrived in Cherbourg. Dudley said that he had this information from several sources. It is evident from this circumstance that *Alabama's* usually tight security had been breached, either by accident or possibly by design. The last leg of the voyage of the Confederate cruiser was the only one during which Semmes made his next destination generally known to the ship's company.

One of the most famous names in the entire history of the United States Navy is *Kearsarge*. There is a *Kearsarge* even now in commission, an aircraft carrier (CV-33) which has served in Vietnam and in the recovery of astronauts. What made the name famous, however, was the first USS *Kearsarge*, whose name appears in Fullam's Journal. This *Kearsarge* was an approximate match for the CSS *Alabama*. Built in the Portsmouth Navy Yard in Portsmouth, New Hampshire, launched 11 September 1861, and commissioned 24 January 1862, the USS *Kearsarge* under command of Captain Charles W. Pickering left the United States on 5 February 1862 for her first foreign duty in the Civil War. This called for her to proceed to Gibraltar and there join other Union vessels which were successfully blockading the Confederate States cruiser *Sumter*. Although Fullam never served in *Sumter*, most of the officers in *Alabama*, of course including Semmes, had served in that first Confederate cruiser. Now in June 1864, *Kearsarge* was about to have another opportunity at another Confederate commerce raider, the most successful and famous of them all, *Alabama*.

Kearsarge's commanding officer at this time, John A. Winslow, was born in Wilmington, North Carolina, and became a midshipman in the United States Navy at an early age, a contemporary of Semmes. In his book, *The Life of John Ancrum Winslow*, John M. Ellicott pointed out that this was a dramatic time in the lives of these two commanders, Winslow and Semmes. They had both engaged in the Mexican War as young men, had been shipmates, and had roomed together. Indeed, both had commanded ships and had lost their ships (without ending their naval careers), and both had received commendations for bravery. Now after years of trial and sometimes bitter, sometimes exciting experiences, after a period of chase by one and evasion by the other, they

[191]

met again as grim opponents. Semmes knew that Winslow was a man of a singular intentness of purpose and that he would be vigilant and determined. Winslow knew Semmes' genius for escape and his aversion to being caught in a trap, and no doubt expected the daring Confederate to come out and fight. There is much to indicate that Semmes, once he had decided to go out and fight, looked forward to a duel with a Union warship which he hoped would repeat *Alabama's* victory over *Hatteras*. In any case, *Kearsarge* had scarcely arrived in Cherbourg when Semmes, via the Confederate agent in that seaport, announced a challenge to battle. Such a challenge from Winslow would have implied recognition of *Alabama* as a warship of a *de facto* government, but *Kearsarge's* entrance into the harbor and exit while the Confederate lay nearby was an implied challenge in military circles.

Semmes carefully weighed his chances. Surely he knew that for the dying Confederacy the contest was drawing to a close, and if sunk, his cruiser would be irreplaceable. *Alabama* desperately needed innumerable repairs. Kell later wrote that Captain Semmes called him in to discuss *Alabama's* position. The cruiser was showing the terrible strain of her long voyage, both on the ship and the ship's company. Her machinery needed repairs, her boilers were worn out, and her seams were opening, joints loose and copper bottoms in rolls. Kell pointed out that *Kearsarge* was staunchly built as a man-of-war and *Alabama* designed more lightly for flight and speed; *Alabama's* heavy guns were better at long range, *Kearsarge's* better at close range. Probably Semmes realized that if the crew were allowed shore leave in Cherbourg they might never be reshipped, and if not allowed leave they might soon desert. On the other hand, the men were in better fighting condition, having practiced firing at the prize *Rockingham,* and they seemed to be enthusiastic about meeting *Kearsarge*. Semmes evidently had other reasons to fight. He was reported to have said that he would "prove to the world that his ship was not a privateer, intended only for attack upon merchant vessels, but a true man-of-war...."

Alabama and *Kearsarge* were closely matched as to tonnage, length, beam, depth, draft, speed, and engines. Even the batteries might appear at a glance to be evenly matched, with more guns aboard *Alabama* and greater weight of metal listed for *Kearsarge's* guns. Actually, *Kearsarge* had several advantages over the raider. Although *Alabama* was officially listed as the faster vessel (with 12.8 knots on her trial trip and some 13 knots maximum speed) while *Kearsarge* was listed with 11 knots maximum speed, the Union vessel proved speedier during the battle. *Alabama's* speed (only some 10 knots at the time) was doubtless reduced by the presence of barnacles on her hull and possibly also by the full load of coal (taken on in Cherbourg) which minimized the area exposed above the water line. During the battle, *Alabama's* guns were shooting high, and this could have been due to failure to allow for the full load of coal. A big advantage of *Kearsarge* was the anchor chain which partially protected her amidships. In so using the anchor chain, Winslow was following an armorclad device earlier used by David G. Farragut in his Mississippi River campaign, and suggested to Winslow by the executive officer of *Kearsarge*, Lieutenant Commander James S. Thornton who had served with Farragut at Mobile. There has been much written about the chain armor, and it is often alleged that Semmes knew about it before the fight. It was also said that the coal protected *Alabama* as much as the chain protected *Kearsarge*.

On that Sunday morning of the impending battle the scene aboard *Kearsarge* was recorded by Ellicott in his book on Winslow:

> ... Inspection over, the quarterdeck was equipped for church, and services began, conducted by the captain. ... the quartermaster continued to gaze ... and levelled his glass over the rail toward Cherbourg. Almost immediately he cried out: "She's coming!"
>
> Winslow closed his service without ceremony, went quietly to the rail and took the glass. There indeed, was the *Alabama*, steaming rapidly toward him, accompanied by a French ironclad.
>
> *After more than a year of tempestuous cruising and blockade, of super-irritating diplomatic wrangle, of physical wear and tear, and of bitter disappointment, a reward for his* indomitable perserverance was at last in sight, greater than he had ever anticipated. The greatest of Confederate commerce destroyers had been brought to bay, and forced to an open fight. ... She had been sought in vain by twenty-five United States warships, and her pursuit had cost over seven millions of dollars. Besides this, there was a personality in the coming encounter: her captain had been Winslow's shipmate, messmate and roommate during a previous war, and his daring, skill and bravery then had well-nigh made him a hero in the eyes of the more modest man. Can it be doubted that, when Winslow focused his glass upon the oncoming *Alabama*, he realized that the supreme moment of his life was at hand? Returning his glass to the quartermaster, he quietly directed his executive to beat to quarters.

As *Alabama* steamed out to meet *Kearsarge* in battle, there was one genuine armorclad on hand, the French warship *Couronne*. The Frenchman came out to guarantee that the combatants would respect the French three-mile limit. Watching also from the shore was a vast crowd of people gathered from the surrounding countryside and many down by excursion train from Paris to witness the scene. The engagement between *Alabama* and *Kearsarge* proved to be one of the great spectacles of the Civil War, a duel viewed by more than 15,000 people lining the French shore while others watched from vessels in the area, a scene painted at the time by many artists, including the famous Edouard Manet.

Alabama and *Kearsarge* circled each other like aroused gamecocks, gradually moving nearer at every circle, testing their speed. It became clear that *Kearsarge* was the speedier. Seven times they described nearly complete circles, maintaining continuous fire. The Confederates fired more rapidly (370 shots) and the Union vessel more effectively (173 shots). About 15 minutes after the action began, *Alabama* lodged a shell in the sternpost of the Yankee. Had it exploded, the outcome of the battle probably would have been quite different. Such damage at least would have slowed down *Kearsarge*. Many of *Alabama's* shells failed to explode due to defective powder or fuses, doubtless caused by much time at sea and little opportunity for refitting. Sinclair said that boarding was to be the battle plan of the Confederates. The statement was based upon the assumption (of course proven false) that *Alabama* was the speedier ship and would be able to close the range. This idea of boarding in the days of steam was ridiculed by Frederick Milnes Edge in his article about the battle.

As the action became hot, the air was filled with flying debris. The Confederate colors were shot away with the spanker gaff, but another ensign was quickly hoisted at the mizzenmast head. *Alabama* was suffering severely from *Kearsarge's* gunfire. Her bulwarks were torn and her decks shot up, and men were dying at their guns. A desperate but forlorn attempt was made to keep the raider afloat, but her engines were slowing down. When one 11-inch shell from *Kearsarge* hit at the water line and exploded in the engine room, *Alabama's* whole frame trembled, the fires of the engines were drowned, and water entered rapidly.

When it became apparent that *Alabama* was losing the battle, the Confederates would have headed back toward neutral waters but could not do so because *Kearsarge,* with the advantage of speed, had the option of moving between the raider and the land. Captain Semmes had ordered Kell to prepare the ship to run for the shore, and Kell had made every effort to do so. He had cleared the decks of some of the dead and torn bodies of the gallant gun crew who had perished at their post. Michael Mars used a shovel to cast overboard the human remnants. Kell checked on the engines below and the chief engineer reported that the furnace fires were out. As Kell inspected the ship, he found Assistant Surgeon Llewellyn still beside the operating table, but before his horrified eyes the patient was swept away by the explosion of the 11-inch shell that went through the vessel's side, leaving water pouring in. Fullam, Beckett Howell, and Dr. Llewellyn had been attending the wounded.

When Kell reported to Captain Semmes that *Alabama* might float ten minutes, Semmes ordered the firing to cease and the colors to be struck. The white flag was shown from the stern. The command was then given by Semmes for every man to save himself. There was some confusion aboard *Kearsarge* as to the actual surrender time of the raider. Concern for the wounded was a compelling reason for Semmes' decision to surrender, and he ordered Kell to dispatch an officer to *Kearsarge* with a request for boats to save the wounded and those who could not swim. Kell immediately sent Fullam, Wilson, and Howell in the smallest of *Alabama's* boats (one of only two which had not already been destroyed by battle damage) to take wounded men to *Kearsarge* and request that warship to send her boats to pick up survivors. When Fullam's boat carrying the wounded reached *Kearsarge*, Lt. Wilson climbed on board and surrendered his sword, but Fullam and Howell were permitted to leave the Union warship in order to pick up more survivors still struggling in the water. Later, two boats from *Kearsarge* appeared, along with two French pilot boats and the English yacht *Deerhound*. *Deerhound* was a steam yacht commanded by Captain Evan P. Jones. The vessel's owner, John Lancaster, was aboard also and ready to make quick decisions regarding rescue work. The Lancaster family, one maid, the captain and crew brought the number on the yacht to 20. *Deerhound* played an important part in the rescue of survivors. Surprisingly, *Deerhound*, which was in attendance at the death of *Alabama*, was built by Laird's at the same shipyard and time as *Alabama*.

After Fullam carried his first load of wounded men to *Kearsarge*, he made other trips in the dinghy picking up survivors, but these he took to *Deerhound*, apparently recognizing that it would be better to be in the yacht than in the Union warship. Later Fullam was roundly criticized by Browne, Edge, and some other writers. Many authors have discussed pro and con the dramatic battle.

Captain Jones of *Deerhound* was operating directly under the instructions of the steam yacht's owner, John Lancaster, in rescuing the men from the water. *Deerhound's* two small boats were also picking up survivors. Altogether, *Deerhound* rescued 42 Confederates, including 12 officers. In contrast, the two boats from *Kearsarge* picked up only four officers (in addition to Lt. Wilson who had already been taken to *Kearsarge* by Fullam). These were: Miles J. Freeman (engineer), John W. Pundt (assistant engineer), Dr. Francis L. Galt (paymaster and surgeon), and Benjamin P. Mecaskey (boatswain). There was no doubt that *Alabama's* senior officers preferred to be passengers in *Deerhound* rather than prisoners of war aboard *Kearsarge*, and this fact influenced the pattern of rescue.

From the CSS *Alabama*, nine men were killed in action and 12 were drowned. Of these 21 men, at least 13 had served from the start of the cruise and at least 11 were foreigners (Englishmen, Welshmen, Germans, or Portuguese). Among those who lost their lives were three officers: William Robinson, the ship's carpenter, William Robertson, an assistant engineer, and Dr. Herbert Llewellyn, the ship's surgeon.

All three officers were drowned. Robinson had served throughout the cruise of *Sumter* as well as of *Alabama,* and was presumably the only American among those killed. Robertson was a Britisher who had left an English vessel at Cape Town and joined *Alabama.* Dr. Llewellyn was the son of an English clergyman and a godson of Lord Herbert of Lea. He was educated at Marlborough College and studied at Charing-Cross Hospital. Among the dead were several who were prominent in Fullam's narrative of the cruise, for example, A. G. Bartelli (a Portuguese who was the personal steward of Captain Semmes), David White (the Delaware slave emancipated by *Alabama),* and James King (second of that name, who was master-at-arms aboard the cruiser and a former Savannah pilot). Of *Alabama's* personnel 21 were wounded, including Armstrong, Anderson, and Semmes, but none of the wounded were drowned. Semmes was so badly wounded in his right hand by shrapnel that he could not use one arm in swimming. One of Semmes last acts before *Alabama* sank, stern first, was to summon the fabled Michael Mars and the stalwart George Freemantle. To these two men, Semmes entrusted the ship's official papers which were still on board (earlier off-loaded at Cherbourg were other papers as well as the captured chronometers whence they were taken to England in the English yacht *Hornet,* Captain Hewitt). Mars was instructed to take the papers to *Deerhound.* This he did, holding the package over his head with one hand while he skillfully swam with the other. George Freemantle with the second set of papers similarly made it to safety.

Kearsarge had no men killed in action. However, William Gowin, an ordinary seaman, died of his wounds shortly after the battle, and two other Union sailors were wounded: James McBeth, an ordinary seaman, and John W. Dempsey, a quarter-gunner.

For *Kearsarge* the victory over *Alabama* was pyrrhic. In a sense Semmes and the CSS *Alabama* in defeat won so much admiration in Great Britain and France as to constitute a propaganda victory. This fact stands out the more boldly when it is considered that the South generally lost the propaganda war.

The psychology of victory in defeat is understandable in the light of the high morale aboard the raider. Of this intangible, Sinclair wrote: "... no reward was ours in the way of promotion out of the regular plod, with perhaps the exception in our commander's case; and nothing in the way of 'orders' or crosses of merit to be looked for even in that. And our selection for the work ... was considered by our government and also by our brother officers a substantial reward in advance, passing expression, and the part we were filling the envy of our compeers."

APPENDICES AND LOG
AS PRESENTED IN THE FULLAM MANUSCRIPT

Tabular View of Captures,&c.

	Sunk	Burnt	Ransomed	Released	Sold	Commis-sioned	Total
Vessels of War. Steamer	1						1
Merchant Steamer			1				1
Ships		25	5	1			31
Barques		17	1	1	1	1	21
Brigantines		4	1				5
Schooners		6	1				7
Total	1	52	9	2	1	1	66

Values of Vessels Burnt &c. &c. &c.　　　　　　　　　　*Values of Vessels destroyed &c. &c.*

	Sunk	Ransomed	Released Estimated	Sold	Commis-sioned	Total
Vessels of War	$160,000					$160,000
	Burnt					
Steamers		261,000				261,000
Ships	2,910,850	286,750	(80,000)			3,197,600
Barques	1,318,458	7,000	(70,000)	17,500	100,936	1,443,894
Brigantines	48,568	6,000				54,568
Schooners	75,699	1,500				77,199
Total				17,500	100,936	

Grand Total Exclusive of released vessels　　$5,194,261

[Disposition of Prizes]

Nature	Number	Values &c.
Commissioned	1	$ 100,936
Sold	1	17,500
Ransomed		562,250
Burnt		4,353,575
Sunk		160,000
Grand Total		$5,194,261

Stores, Values of, Received in Various Departments	$28,093
Values of Vessels, & c.	$5,194,261
	$5,222,354
	150,000*
	5,372,354
	$1,074,470 8/10

*Fullam subtracted the values of the two ships which were released without ransom bonds. Fullam's figures, as shown here, are correct, but the sub-totals could be misunderstood. (Editor's Note)

Values of Stores Received in Various Departments

Purser's	$16,848
Engineer's	1,496
Gunner's	4,000
	(Estimated)
Boatswain's	905
Carpenter's	1,250
Sailmaker's	3,594
Total	28,093

The Number of vessels spoken and boarded.

From date of Commission to 30th. May, 1864. 386
11th. June, 1864 61

Total   447

Quantities of Coal Received on Board During the Cruise

Liverpool	340 tons
Terceira	200 tons
Blanquilla	280 tons
Las Arcas	89 tons
Kingston	158 tons
Fernando de Noronha	180 tons
Bahia	35 tons
Simons Town	180 tons
Singapore	250 tons
Cape Town	207 tons
	1,919 tons
[On arrival at Cherbourg]	133*
Total Used	1,786

*Estimated quantity on board when sunk, subtracted to show fuel actually consumed. (Editor's Note)

From Liverpool to Terceira, or rather Moelfra Bay to Terceira. 31st July to 10th. Aug. 1862. 1504 miles. 10 days at sea. 14 [days] in harbour to 24. Aug. 1862. Date of Commission to first seeing an enemys vessel of war 18th. Nov. 86 days.

7871 miles 1504
24th. Aug. 1862 to 9th. Sep. 1863 [35,124] 36,628
Days: 305 at sea. 76 Harbour
16th. Sept. [1863] 312 Sea. 76 Harbour [548] 37,175
17th. Jan. 1864 [9,668] 46,843
15th. Feb. " 422 Sea. 118 Anchor [2,662] 49,505
25th. March " 456 Sea. 123 " [3,261] 52,766
6th. May " 498 " 123 " [5,021] 57,787
*31st. " " 523 " 123 " [6,780] . . . . .6,780 [64,567]
11th June " 534 " 123 " [2,800] . . . . .2,800 [67,367]

67,367

*Beginning with the entry of 31 May, the figure is no longer cumulative, but the total mileage is easily reckoned at 67,367. (Editor's Note)

Under Steam, whether going in or out of port, or in chase.

15th Feb. 1864		30 days 3 h. 30 m.
		9.00
25th. Mar.	30 "	12. 30.
		19.00
	31 "	9. 30
		34. 30
*Total under Steam	32 "	20. 00

*This cumulative total in the manuscript has an error in addition. The corrected total is 32 days and 18 hours. (Editor's Note)

The Number of Prisoners captured during the cruise amounted to above [more than].	2000.
The Number Paroled	978
	32
Total Paroled	1,010

U.S. Str. "Hatteras" 9 Guns. 129 men. 11th Jan. 1863. Lat. 28. 53 N. Long. 94. 22 W. 4 Thirty-twos. 2 rifled Thirty pdrs. carrying 68 lbs. shot. 1 Rifled Twenty pdr. 1 Twelve and 1 sixpounders. $160,000 [Value of ship for prize purposes.]

Lat's. and Long's. at Noon of Dates
Ship "Ocmulgee" Nantucket. 5th Sep. 1862. Lat. 38.27. N. Long. 29.35. W. Whaling. Whale oil. $50,000.
Schr. "Starlight" Boston. 7th. Sep. 39.08 N. 30.57 W. Fayal to Flores. Passengers. $4,000.
Bar. "Ocean Rover" Mattapoisett. 8th. Sep. 39.26 N. 31.06 W. Whaling. Whale Oil. $70,000.
Bar. "Alert" New Bedford. 9th Sep. 39.37 N. 31.05 W. Whaling. Whale Oil. $20,000.
Schr. "Weather Gage" [Weathergauge] Provincetown. 9th. Sep. 39.37 N. 31.05 W. Whaling. Whale oil. $10,000.
Brgt. "Altamaha" Sippican. 13th. Sep. 40.34 N. 35.09 W. Whaling. Light. $3,000.
Ship "Benj. Tucker" New Bedford. 14th. Sep. 40.34 N. 34.09 W. Whaling. Light. $18,000.
Schr. "Courser" Provincetown. 16th. Sep. 39.30 N. 31.10 W. Whaling. Oil $7,000
Bar. "Virginia" New Bedford. 17th. Sep. 39.29 N. 33.20 W. Whaling. Light. $25,000.
Bar. "Elisha Dunbar" New Bedford. 18th. Sep. 39.46 N. 35.24 W. Whaling. Light. $25,000.
Ship "Emily Farnum" Portsmouth. 3rd. Oct. 39.08 N. 50.36 W. New York to Liverpool. General. Released.

Ship "Brilliant" New York. 3rd. Oct. 39.08 N. 50.36 W. New York to Liverpool. Grain & Flour. $164,000.
Bar. "Wave Crest" New York. 7th. Oct. 40.14 N. 54.05 W. New York to Cardiff. Grain & Flour. $44,000.
Brgt. "Dunkirk" New York. 7th Oct. 40.14 N. 54.05 W. New York to Lisbon. Grain & Flour. $25,000.
Ship "Tonawanda" Philadelphia. 9th. Oct. 40.04 N. 54.36 W. Philadelphia to Liverpool. General & Passengers. Ransomed $80,000.
Ship "Manchester" New York. 11th. Oct. 41.07 N. 55.29 W. New York to Liverpool. Grain. $164,000.
Bar. "Lamplighter" Boston. 15th. Oct. 41.31 N. 59.17 W. New York to Gibralter [Gibraltar]. Tobacco. $117,600.
Ship "Lafayette" New Haven. 23rd. Oct. 39.34 N. 62.11 W. New York to Belfast. Grain. $100,337.
Schr. "Crenshaw" New York. 26th. Oct. 40.10 N. 64.24 W. New York to Glasgow. Grain. $33,869.
Bar. "Laurietta" [Lauretta] Boston. 28th. Oct. 39.16 N. 67.39 W. New York to Gibralter [Gibraltar]. Grain. $32,880.
Brig. "Baron de Castine" Castine [Maine] 29th. Oct. 39.00 N. 68.30 W. Castine to Cuba. Lumber. Ransomed $6,000.
Ship "Levi Starbuck" New Bedford. 2nd. Nov. 36.13 N. 66.13 W. Whaling. Light. $25,000.
Ship. "T.B. Wales" Boston. 8th. Nov. 29.14 N. 57.57 W. Calcutta to New York. General. $245,625.
Bar. "Parker Cook" Boston. 30th. Nov. 19.00 N. 68.45 W. Boston to Hayti General. $10,000.
Schr. "Union" Baltimore. 5th. Dec. 19.59 N. 74.10 W. Baltimore to Jamaica. General. Ransomed. $1,500.
P.S. [Postal Steamer] "Ariel" New York. 7th. Dec. 19.08 N. 74.10 W. General & Passengers. New York to Aspinwall. Ransomed. $261,000.
Bar. "Golden Rule" New York. 26th. Jan. 1863. 17.47 N. 75.00 W. New York to Aspinwall. General. $112,000.
Brgt. "Chastelain" Boston. 27th. Jan. 17.20 N. 72.15 W. Guadalupe to Cuba. Light. $10,000.
Schr. "Palmetto" Trenton. 3rd. Feb. 27.17 N. 66.09 W. New York to Porto Rico. General. $18,430
Ship "Golden Eagle" New Bedford. 21st. Feb. 29.28 N. 44.53 W. Chinchas to Cork. Guano. $61,000.
Bar. "Olive Jane" Boston. 21st. Feb. 29.28 N. 44.53 W. Bordeaux to New York. Wines & Spirits. $43,208.
Ship "Washington" New York. 27th. Feb. 30.19 N. 39.54 W. Callao to Cork. Guano. Ransomed. $50,000.
Ship "Bethiah Thayer." Rockland. 1st. Mar. 29.50 N. 38.13 W. Callao to Cork. Guano. Ransomed. $40,000.
Ship "John A. Parks" Hallowell. 2nd. Mar. 29.28 N. 37.51 W. New York to Buenos Ayres General. $66,157.
Ship "Punjaub" Boston. 15th. Mar. 8.37 N. 31.39 W. Calcutta to London. General. Ransomed. $55,000.
Ship "Morning Star" Boston. 23rd. Mar. 2.08 N. 26.04 W. Calcutta to London. General. Ransomed. $61,750.
Schr. "Kingfisher" New Bedford. 23rd. Mar. 2.08. N. 26.04 W. Whaling. Whale oil. $2,400.
Ship "Nora" Boston. 25th. Mar. 1.22. N. 26.04. W. Liverpool to Calcutta. Salt. $76,636.
Ship "Charles Hill" Boston. 25th. Mar. 1.22. N. 26.04. W. Liverpool to Montevideo. Salt. $28,450.
Ship "Louisa Hatch" Rockland. 4th. Apl. 3.12. S. 26.02. W. Cardiff to Point de Galle. Coal. $38,315.
Brgt. "Kate Cory" Westport. 15th. Apl. 4.10. S. 32.10. W. Whaling. Whale oil. $10,568.
Bar. "Lafayette" New Bedford. 15th. Apl. 4.10 S. 32.26 W. Whaling. Whale oil. $20,908.
Bar. "Nye" New Bedford. 24th. Apl. 5.45. S. 31.52. W. Whaling. Whale Oil. $31,127.
Ship. "Dorcas Prince" New York. 26th. Apl. 7.36. S. 31.37. W. New York to Shanghai. Coals &c. $44,108.
Bar. "Union Jack" New York. 3rd. May. 9.39 S. 32.35. W. New York to Shanghai. General. $77,000.
Ship "Sea Lark" Boston. 3rd. May. 9.39 S. 32.35. W. Boston to San Francisco. General. $550,000.
Ship "S. Gildersleeve" New York. 25th. May. 12.14. S. 35.11 W. Sunderland to Calcutta. Coals. $62,783.
Bar. "Justina" Baltimore. 25th. May. 12.14 S. 35.11. W. Rio Janeiro to Baltimore. Ballast. Ransomed. $7,000.
Ship "Jabez Snow" Bucksport. 29th. May. 12.35. S. 35.33. W. Cardiff to Calcutta. Coals. $72,781.
Bar. "Amazonian" Boston. 2nd. June, 15.0l S. 34.52. W. New York to Montevideo. General. $97,665.
Ship. "Talisman" New York. 5th. June. 15.00. S. 35.00. W. New York to Shanghai. Coals. &c. &c. $139,135.
Bar. "Conrad" Philadelphia. 20th. June. 25.07 S. 40.26. W. Buenos Ayres. to New York. Wool. $100,936.

Ship "Anna F. Schmidt" Boston. 2nd. July. 26.14 S. 37.40 W. Boston to St. Thomas, last to San Francisco. General. $350,000.

Ship "Express" Portsmouth. 6th. July. 28.28 S. 30.07 W. Valparaiso to Antwerp. Guano. $121,320.

Bar. "Sea Bride" Boston. 5th. Aug. Off Cape Town. Boston to Cape Town. General. *Sold.* $17,500. [$16,940 is the figure in *ORN* 1, III, 680. In the manuscript an attempt was made to erase this figure.]

*Bar. "Martha Wenzell" Boston. 9th. Aug. Off False Bay. C.G.H. [Cape of Good Hope.] Akyab to Falmouth. Rice. Released.

Bar. "Amanda" Bangor. 6th. Nov. 6.59 S. 103.23. E. Manilla to Cork. Manilla and Sugar. $104,442.

Ship "Winged Racer" New York. 10th. Nov. Off North Island. (Java Sea) Manilla to New York. Sugar and Manilla. $150,000.

Ship "Contest" New York. 11th. Nov. 4.48. S. 106.50. E. Yokohama to New York. General. $122,815.

Bar. "Martaban" of Moulmain alias "Texian Star" of Galveston. 24th. Dec. in Straits of Malacca 1.17 N. 103.21 E. Moulmain to Singapore. Rice. $97,628.29.

*All data on *Martha Wenzell* was crossed out but otherwise legible. This episode is discussed in Fullam's Journal. The Confederates admitted that the seizure was illegal. (Editor's Note)

Ship "Sonora" Newburyport. 26th. Dec. Straits of Malacca. 2.56 N. 100.48. E. Singapore to Akyab. in ballast. $46,545.

Ship "Highlander" Boston. 26th. Dec. Straits of Malacca. 2.56 N. 100.48. E. Singapore to Akyab. in ballast. $75,965.

Ship "Emma Jane" Bath. 14th. Jan. 1864. 7.59 N. 76.04 E. Bombay to Moulmain in ballast. $40,000.

Ship "Rockingham" Portsmouth. 23rd. April 15.53 S. 31.44 W. Callao to Queenstown. Guano. $97,878.

Barque "Tycoon" New York. 27th. April 11.16 S. 32.03 W. New York. to San Francisco. General. $390,000

Position each day at noon of the S. S. "290" "Enrica" "Barcelona" Liverpool to Terceira.*
Left the Mersey. 9.15 A.M. 29th July 1862.
Left Moelfra Bay 2 A. M. 31 st. July 1862.
Arrived at Porto Praya, Terceira. 10 August 1862.

Date	Lat	Long.	Con.	Dist.
1862	N	W	—	—
Aug 1	55.15	10.30.53		335
2	53.24	12.15.43		
3	51.28	14.52		
4	49.29	15.15		
		16.10	[corrected by Fullam to 16.10]	
5	47.32	15.54		
6	45.14	17.08		
7	42.57	18.39		
8	41.11	22.13		
		25.16	[corrected by Fullam to 25.16.]	
9	39.33	25.24		
10	Anchored 6 A. M.			

*It is interesting to compare the celestial observations in Fullam's Log, published in this Appendix for the first time, with the Log of Raphael Semmes, which was published in 1864 by Saunders, Otley and Company of London. (Raphael Semmes, *The Log of the Alabama and the Sumter. From* the *Private Journals and Other Papers of Commander R. Semmes, C.S.N., and Other Officers*. London: Saunders, Otley and Company, 1864.) Few indeed are the identical findings of latitude and longitude, as sextants read the stars, but the reckonings were so close as to support the conclusion that two good navigators made independent and reliable observations. For *Alabama*, the Saunders, Otley entries began 25 August 1862 in contrast with the Fullam entries which began 1 August 1862. Even before this, Saunders, Otley had observations for *Sumter*. (Editor's Note)

Position each day at noon during the Cruise of the C. S. Str. "Alabama."*
8 Guns. Capt. R. Semmes.
Aug. 24th. 12.30 P. M. Got under weigh.

Date	Lat.	Long.	Date	Lat.	Long.
1862	N	W	1862	N.	W.
Aug. 24	39.14	25.24	Sep 9	40.35	30.42
25	39.40	26.25	10	39.36	31.00
26	40.00	24.24	11	40.18	33.54
27	38.57	19.20	12	40.34	35.09
28	37.27	19.00	13	40.34	34.09
29	36.25	21.24	14	40.01	32.26
30	36.23	21.50	15	39.30	31.19
31	35.34	22.12	16	39.29	33.20
Sep. 1	35.27	24.20	17	39.46	35.24
2	36.17	25.54	18	38.30	34.55
3	37.22	27.57	19	37.19	36.16
4	38.27	29.35	20	36.33	36.49
5	38.27	30.40	21	35.20	37.19
6	39.08	30.57	22	34.41	38.38
7	39.26	31.06	23	34.52	40.20
8	39.37	31.05	24	34.57	41.06
9			25		

*At this point began the cruise of the warship *Alabama* as distinguished from the merchant vessel *290* or *Enrica*. Fullam skipped from 10 August to 24 August *because* the ship was at anchor and fitting out. (Editor's Note)

Date	Lat.	Long.	Date	Lat.	Long.
Sep. 26	35.34	41.38	20	40.26	62.30
27	37.11	43.13	21	40.17	62.32
28 [S]	37.38	42.00	22	40.0	63.11
29	37.09	43.13	23	39.34	62.11
30	38.35	45.00	24	40.01	62.05
Oct. 1	40.26	46.31	25	39.56	63.18
2	40.39	47.57	26 [S]	40.10	64.24
3	39.58	50.36	27	39.38	67.53
4	39.53	50.58	28	39.16	67.39
5 [S]	40.19	51.12	29	39.00	68.30
6	41.00	54.15	30	39.16	69.11
7	40.14	54.05	31	37.51	67.25
8	41.00	54.46	Nov. 1	36.14	65.45
9	40.04	54.36	2 [S]	36.13	66.13
10	41.12	53.40	3	35.16	67.00
11	41.07	55.29	4	34.26	63.13
12 [S]	41.34	56.38	5	31.32	61.12
13	40.32	59.38	6	29.04	61.05
14	41.21	59.30	7	29.02	59.00
15	41.31	59.17	Nov. 8	29.16	57.57
16	42.10	59.16	9 [S]	27.49	58.04
17	42.06	59.46	10	25.40	57.30
Oct. 18	41.25	59.10	11	24.04	57.10
19 [S]	40.20	62.00	12	22.56	57.26

*[S] means Sunday throughout the Log.

Date	Lat.	Long.	Date	Lat.	Long.
13	22.07	57.27	31	20.12 N	91.59 W.
14	21.10	57.29			
15	19.56	58.00	1863		
16 [S]	18.00	59.09	Jan. 1	"	"
17	15.50	60.13	2	"	"
18	9.30 A.M. anchored		3	"	"
	in Port Royal		4 [S]	"	"
19	7.15 P.M. Got under weigh		5	10.40 A.M. Got under weigh	
20	13.15	62.50		20.12 N.	91.49 W.
21	12.10	64.27	6	21.12	93.13
	4.30 P.M. Anchored off the		7	22.36	94.13
	Island of Blanquilla				
22	"	"	8	24.36	94.44
23 [S]	"	"	9	26.18	94.11
24	"	"	10	27.44	94.14
25	"	"	11 [S]	28.52	94.54
26	8.15 P.M. Got under weigh		12	28.04	93.07
27	13.13	63.35	13	27.05	90.29
28	15.56	65.58	Jan. 14	25.58	88.56
29	17.44	67.14	15	26.22	88.36
30 [S]	19.00	68.45	16	23.43	87.22
			17	21.34	85.26
Dec. 1	19.38	69.47	18 [S]	19.50	82.37
2	20.04	71.50	19	18.31	80.31
3	20.15	73.00	20	17.45	77.41
4	20.02	74.10	21	7.00 P.M. Anchored in	
5	19.59	74.10		Port Royal Harbor	
6	19.49	74.20	22	"	"
7 [S]	19.08	74.10	23	"	"
8	20.08	74.10	24	"	"
9	18.24	75.18	25 [S]	8.25 P.M. Got under weigh	
10	18.30	75.30	26	17.47	75.00
11	18.53	76.46	27	17.28	72.15
12	18.43	76.50	28	17.57	70.22
13	18.44	78.18		6.00 P.M. Anchored off	
				St. Domingo	
14 [S]	18.16	80.40	29	18.19	69.26
15	18.39	82.55		9.00 A.M. Got under weigh	
16	19.16	84.10	30	19.30	67.40
17	19.17	84.17	31	21.44	68.03
18	19.30	85.27			
19	20.00	85.26	Feb. 1 [S]	24.07	68.10
20	21.16	86.30	2	26.17	68.00
21 [S]	22.06	88.33	3	27.17	66.09
22	21.26	91.04	4	27.59	64.09
	9.30 P.M. Anchored in		Feb 5	27.08	61.32
	15 fthms.		6	25.41	60.28
	10.30 A.M. Got under weigh		7	26.36	60.07
Dec. 23	20.18	91.40	8 [S]	25.41	58.51
24	5.15 P.M. Anchored Arcas		9	24.50	57.32
	Islands. N. N. W.		10	24.33	56.38
25	1.45 P.M. got under weigh.		11	24.51	56.16
	Anchored in between		12	25.16	55.27
26	Position of islands		13	25.58	55.36
27	"	"	14	27.09	53.17
28 [S]	"	"	15 [S]	28.31	50.00
29	"	"	16	28.45	46.52
30	"	"	17	28.12	44.59

Date	Lat.	Long.
18	28.15	44.33
19	28.05	44.24
20	28.32	45.00
21	29.28	44.53
22 [S]	29.33	45.00
23	30.21	44.00
24	30.31	42.41
25	30.24	41.09
26	30.29	40.24
Feb. 27	30.19	39.54
28	30.09	32.20
Mar. 1 [S]	29.5	38.13
2	29.28	37.57
3	28.42	37.00
4	27.03	35.42
5	26.04	35.20
6	25.09	35.20
7	24.30	35.14
8 [S]	22.06	34.30
9	20.20	33.50
10	18.26	33.10
11	16.17	32.30
12	13.58	31.40
13	11.31	31.33
14	9.24	31.43
15 [S]	8.34	31.39
16	7.45	30.20
17	7.52	30.40
18	7.14	29.52
19	6.00	28.00
20	4.31	26.35
Mar. 21 [1863]	2.40	26.20
22 [S]	2.06	26.20
23	2.08	26.04
24	1.46	26.06
25	1.22	26.04
26	1.12	26.25
27	1.16	26.18
28	0.47	26.14
29 [S]	0.18	26.05
	5.30 P.M. Crossed the Equator	
30	0.32 S	25.30 W
31	0.39	25.14
Apl. 1	1.00	25.13
2	2.11	26.00
3	2.52	25.50
4	3.12	26.02
5 [S]	2.24	26.55
6	3.46	27.54
7	3.53	30.00
8	4.08	30.40
9	3.49	32.15

Date	Lat.	Long.
	2.45 P.M. Anchored in Fernando de Nha in 13 fthms.	
10	"	"
11	"	"
Apl. 12 [S]	At Anchor	
13	"	"
14	"	"
15	"	"
16	"	"
17	"	"
18	"	"
19 [S]	At Anchor	"
20	"	"
21	"	"
22	3.47	32.08
	9.30 A.M. Got under weigh	
23	4.41	31.48
24	5.45	31.52
25	6.21	31.41
26 [S]	7.38	31.37
27	8.15	32.19
28	8.19	31.41
29	8.21	31.06
30	9.02	31.40
May 1	9.17	32.18
2	9.37	32.10
3 [S]	9.39	32.35
May 4 [1863]	9.49	32.35
5	10.04	32.54
6	10.24	32.30
7	12.07	33.07
8	12.31	33.46
9	12.56	34.45
10 [S]	13.31	36.12
11	13.30	38.13
	5.30 P.M. Came to an Anchor off Bahia.	
12	"	"
13	"	"
14	"	"
15	"	"
16	"	"
17 [S]	"	"
18	"	"
19	"	"
20	"	"
21	Noon. Got under weigh	
22	13.03	37.40
23	12.34	36.40
24 [S]	11.33	35.35
25	12.14	35.11
May 26	11.39	34.46
27	12.16	35.08
28	12.55	35.15
29	13.25	35.33

[204]

Date	Lat.	Long.
30	13.30	35.34
31 [S]	14.13	35.35
June 1 [1863]	14.44	35.14
2	15.01	36.52
3	15.09	34.58
4	14.47	34.49
5	15.00	35.00
6	15.18	35.20
7 [S]	15.07	35.29
8	15.56	35.20
9	16.52	35.34
10	16.18	34.46
11	15.31	35.37
12	17.25	34.34
13	19.21	35.33
14 [S]	19.53	35.13
15	22.44	35.00
16	23.42	35.16
June 17 [1863]	23.55	35.43
18	24.16	37.03
19	24.58	38.51
20	25.07	40.26
21 [S]	25.46	40.04
22	25.55	40.09
23	25.23	38.32
24	25.17	36.23
25	25.57	33.30
26	26.40	29.58
27	26.01	28.28
28 [S]	25.57	30.19
29	26.36	32.47
30	25.57	34.59
July 1	25.37	36.34
2	26.14	37.40
3	26.31	37.16
4	27.27	34.24
5 [S]	27.59	31.30
6	28.28	30.07
7	29.46	27.23
8	30.00	23.59
July 9	29.57	20.57
10	29.16	17.35
11	28.00	14.52
12[S]	26.45	13.16
13	28.14	13.11
14	29.21	11.16
15	30.07	7.47
16	30.29	3.41
17	30.16	00.00
18	29.54	3.29
19 [S]	29.58	5.54
20	29.57	7.45
21	30.43	10.37
22	31.33	12.55

Date	Lat.	Long.
23	32.00	14.32
24	33.35	15.13
25	33.56	15.56
26 [S]	33.27	17.01
27	33.42	17.24
28	33.45	17.49
29	33.10	17.50
	2.45 P.M. Anchored in Saldanha Bay.	
30	"	"
July 31 [1863]	At Anchor Saldanha Bay	
Aug. 1	"	"
2 [S]	"	"
3	"	"
4	"	"
5	6 A.M. Got under weigh 2.30 P.M. Anchored in Table Bay.	
6	"	"
7	"	"
8	"	"
9 [S]	6 A.M. Got under weigh. 2.30 P.M. Anchored in Simons Bay.	
10	"	"
11	"	"
12	"	"
13	"	"
14	"	"
15	11 A.M. Got under weigh	
16 [S]	34.30	17.59
17	34.04	17.11
18	33.25	16.56
19	32.54	17.09
20	32.45	16.52
21	33.15	15.34
Aug. 22	32.12	16.06
23 [S]	31.44	15.30
24	31.25	14.27
25	31.17	13.37
26	27.56	14.19
27	27.06	15.00
28	26.40	15.05
	6 P.M. Anchored in Angra Pequena.	
29	"	"
30 [S]	"	"
31	26.51	13.57
	6 A.M. Got under weigh	
Sep. 1	27.59	12.19
2	28.38	10.16
3	29.40	9.03
4	30.04	8.53
5	30.24	9.34

Date		
7	31.17	11.15
8	31.41	11.24
9	32.27	12.57
10	33.17	15.20
11	33.09	16.45
12	33.44	16.12
Sep. 13 [1863]	33.52	17.45
14	34.28	17.55
15	34.26	17.40
16	34.30	18.08
	At 4.25 P.M. Anchored in Simon's Bay.	
17	"	"
18	"	"
19	"	"
20 [S]	"	"
21	"	"
22	"	"
23	"	"
24	11.55 P.M. Got under weigh	
25	35.26	18.15
26	37.28	17.56
27 [S]	37.51	19.03
Sep. 28	39.02	23.17
29	39.01	27.19
30	39.10	32.03
Oct. 1	39.15	35.45
2	38.25	39.03
3	38.45	43.00
4 [S]	38.43	46.57
Oct. 5	38.48	48.41
6	38.45	53.26
7	37.52	57.30
8	38.03	60.19
9	38.17	64.20
10	38.26	68.59
11 [S]	38.28	72.44
Oct. 12	38.46	77.10
13	38.16	80.31
14	37.46	83.42
15	36.50	87.36
16	35.23	90.10
17	33.00	93.31
18 [S]	30.59	96.21
Oct. 19	28.24	98.49
20	25.33	99.44
21	22.40	100.14
22	21.14	100.15
23	18.52	100.1
24	15.45	101.28
25 [S]	12.28	102.14
Oct. 26	10.27	102.15
Oct. 27	9.55	101.56
28	9.39	102.01
29	9.19	101.52

Date		
31	8.56	102.52
Nov. 1 [S]	8.56	103.48
2	9.31	103.43
3	9.17	103.36
4	8.31	103.12
5	7.23	103.19
6	6.59	103.23
7	6.55	103.30
8 [S]	5.57	104.10
	5 P.M. Anchored in Tampang Bay.	
9	"	"
10	3 A.M. Got under weigh 1 mile S of Beegee [Sebesi] Island. 4 P.M. Anchored off North Island	
11	4.48	106.40
	3.55 A.M. Got under weigh	
12	4.19	107.57
13	7 P.M. Anchored	
	3.58	108.26
14	6.30 A.M. Got under weigh	
	3.44	109.0
15 [S]	1.40 A.M. Anchored	
	8.25 A.M. Got under weigh	
	3.62	109.35
16	7.15 P.M. Anchored	
	2.45	109.13
17	4.15 A.M. Got under weigh	
	2.30	109.13
	At Anchor	
	2.15 P.M. Anchored in 14 fthms. 9 P.M. Got under weigh. 9.30 Anchored.	
Nov. 18	6.30 A.M. Got under weigh	
	2.02	108.54
	3.30 P.M. Anchored.	
19	1.47	108.44
	At Anchor	
20	"	"
21	2 P.M. Got under weigh	
22 [S]	2.34	108.42
	3.45 Crossed Equator	
23	2.48 N	108.29
24	3.38	110.24
25	3.56	110.30
26	4.38	111.40
	2.30 P.M. Anchored	
27	4.53	111.51
	7.15 A.M. Got under weigh	
	12.30 P.M. Anchored	
28	At Anchor	
29 [S]	9.30 A.M. Got under weigh	
	5.02	111.45
30	6.15	110.33

Date	Lat.	Long.
Dec. 1	7.35	109.00
2	8.30	107.16
	3 P.M. Anchored off	
	Pulo Condore	
3	"	"
4	"	"
5	"	"
6 [S]	"	"
7	"	"
8	"	"
9	"	"
Dec. 10 [1863]	At anchor	
11	"	"
12	"	"
13 [S]	"	"
14	4 A.M. Got under weigh	
15	8.25	106.31
16	7.18	106.22
17	6.29	106.24
18	4.48	105.09
19	2.39	104.40
	4.15 Anchored off Pulo Aor	
20 [S]	At anchor	
21	3.25 A.M. Got under weigh	
	3.00	104.40
	6 P.M. anchor Singapore	
22	At anchor	
23	"	"
24	9 A.M. Got under weigh	
	1.17	103.21
	11.50 P.M. anchored Malacca	
25	2.13	102.06
	10 A.M. Got under weigh	
	5.45 P.M. anchored	
26	2.56	100.48
	6.10 A.M. Got under weigh	
27 [S]	4.08	100.12
28	4.46	99.40
29	5.29	98.20
30	5.40	96.39
31	6.18	94.45
1864		
Jan. 1	6.24N	93.30 [E.]
2	5.40	93.62
3 [S]	5.30	92.31
4	6.00	91.30
5	6.30	90.33
6	6.08	88.31
7	5.41	87.21
8	5.23	84.41
9	5.05	81.59
10 [S]	5.14	79.40
11	5.49	78.20
12	7.27	76.01
13	7.34	75.51
14	7.59	76.04

Date	Lat.	Long.
15	8.25	75.50
16	8.41	76.24
	4.30 P.M. Anchored off	
	Anjengo.	
17 [S]	8.40	76.40
	9.30 A.M. got under weigh	
18	8.32	76.09
19	8.06	75.00
20	7.30	74.22
21	8.17	73.01
22	7.53	70.10
Jan. 23 [1864]	7.06 N	67.14 E.
24 [S]	7.03	64.23
25	6.27	61.45
26	5.30	59.12
27	5.02	56.31
28	4.01	53.37
29	2.43	50.59
30	0.51	48.43
	11 P.M. Crossed the Equator	
31 [S]	1.31 South	47.12
Feb. 1	3.15	46.04
2	4.49	45.32
3	6.46	44.35
4	8.23	44.17
5	10.18	43.40
6	10.42	43.52
7 [S]	10.46	43.41
8	10.46	43.32
9	12.08	44.20
	1.35 P.M. Anchored off	
	Johanna	
10	"	"
11	"	"
12	"	"
13	"	"
Feb. 14 [S]	At Anchor off Johanna	
15	Noon. Got under weigh	
16	13.02 S	43.44 E
17	13.42	43.03
18	14.16	42.45
19	15.03	42.24
20	16.00	41.46
21 [S]	17.03	41.30
22	18.45	41.23
23	19.48	40.41
24	20.28	41.20
25	21.17	41.50
26	23.35	41.16
27	25.32	40.02
28 [S]	27.12	37.54
29	29.17	36.18
Mar. 1	31.32	34.40
2	33.20	32.22

Date	Lat.	Long.
3	35.04	29.53
4	35.12	28.32
5	35.51	26.46
6 [S]	35.10	25.00
Mar. 7 [1864]	35.10 S	24.00 E
8	35.51	21.43
9	35.47	20.33
10	35.43	20.14
11	35.08	18.32
12	33.57	17.14
13 [S]	33.35	16.11
14	34.01	15.20
15	33.48	15.25
16	32.51	16.36
17	33.08	16.26
18	33.30	15.50
19	32.56	15.56
20 [S]	5.15 P.M. Anchored in Table Bay.	
	33.50	14.32
21	"	"
22	"	"
23	"	"
24	"	"
25	10.30 A.M. Got under Weigh	
26	33.42 S	15.32
27 [S]	31.52	12.39
28	31.37	10.03
Mar. 29	30.25 S	8.26 E
30	28.53	6.56
31	28.02	4.52
Apl. 1	26.14	2.45
2	24.13	0.23
[Crossed the International Date Line]		
3 [S]	22.35	1.34
4	21.01	3.15
5	19.38	4.47
6	18.42	4.22
7	17.15	3.43
8	17.40	5.49
9	17.42	9.05
10 [S]	18.12	11.47
11	18.26	14.40
12	18.47	17.12
13	18.54	19.43
14	18.58	22.34
15	19.08	25.00
16	19.19	26.40
17 [S]	19.12	27.33
18	19.22	28.48
19	19.14	29.33
Apl. 20 [1864]	18.49 S	30.02 W
21	18.19	30.25
22	17.23	30.53
23	15.53	31.44
24 [S]	15.19	32.06
25	13.59	32.02

Date	Lat.	Long.
26	13.06	32.18
27	11.16	32.03
28	10.05	31.43
29	8.10	31.27
30	5.27	30.10
May 1 [S]	2.35	30.33
2	0.12	30.38
3.15 P.M. Crossed the Equator		
3	1.44 N	31.20
4	3.31	32.38
5	5.08	34.16
6	7.17	36.01
7	9.39	37.36
8 [S]	11.54	38.37
9	14.11	39.40
10	16.44	40.28
11	18.37	41.01
May 12 [1864]	20.12 N	41.20 W
13	20.34	41.12
14	20.55	41.03
15 [S]	21.12	40.55
16	22.05	41.13
17	22.57	41.45
18	24.34	41.53
19	26.32	41.44
20	28.05	41.25
21	29.25	40.34
22 [S]	30.25	39.48
23	31.41	38.33
24	33.14	36.41
25	35.52	35.32
26	37.43	33.43
27	38.41	32.38
28	39.23	32.27
29 [S]	39.50	32.30
30	40.26	30.12
31	40.55	27.07
June 1	41.36	24.06
2	42.09	22.08
June 3 [1864]	42.17 N	20.33 W
4	42.10	17.58
5 [S]	41.59	16.24
6	42.32	15.34
7	43.49	14.04
8	45.45	12.04
9	47.35	9.01
10	49.19	6.08
11	12.40. [P.M.] Anchored in Cherbourg Harbour.	
12 [S]		
13		
14		
15		
16		
17		
18		

Date	Lat.	Long.	Date	Lat.	Long.
19 [S]	Sunk [This notation in a different handwriting and evidently written at a later time.]		22		
20			23		
21			24		

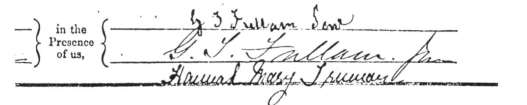

in the Presence of us,

The middle signature shown above is that of the author of this Journal. Along with his father's and another relative's, the signature of George Townley Fullam, Junior, appear on a marriage record in Hull dated 18 April 1878.

Ship "Brilliant" New York. 3rd. Oct. 39.08 N. 50.36 W. New York to Liverpool. Grain & Flour. $164,000.

Bar. "Wave Crest" New York. 7th. Oct. 40.14 N. 54.05 W. New York to Cardiff. Grain & Flour. $44,000.

Brgt. "Dunkirk" New York. 7th Oct. 40.14 N. 54.05 W. New York to Lisbon. Grain & Flour. $25,000.

Ship "Tonawanda" Philadelphia. 9th. Oct. 40.04 N. 54.36 W. Philadelphia to Liverpool. General & Passengers. Ransomed $80,000.

Ship "Manchester" New York. 11th. Oct. 41.07 N. 55.29 W. New York to Liverpool. Grain. $164,000.

Bar. "Lamplighter" Boston. 15th. Oct. 41.31 N. 59.17 W. New York to Gibralter [Gibraltar]. Tobacco. $117,600.

Ship "Lafayette" New Haven. 23rd. Oct. 39.34 N. 62.11 W. New York to Belfast. Grain. $100,337.

Schr. "Crenshaw" New York. 26th. Oct. 40.10 N. 64.24 W. New York to Glasgow. Grain. $33,869.

Bar. "Laurietta" [Lauretta] Boston. 28th. Oct. 39.16 N. 67.39 W. New York to Gibralter [Gibraltar]. Grain. $32,880.

Brig. "Baron de Castine" Castine [Maine] 29th. Oct. 39.00 N. 68.30 W. Castine to Cuba. Lumber. Ransomed $6,000.

Ship "Levi Starbuck" New Bedford. 2nd. Nov. 36.13 N. 66.13 W. Whaling. Light. $25,000.

Ship. "T.B. Wales" Boston. 8th. Nov. 29.14 N. 57.57 W. Calcutta to New York. General. $245,625.

Bar. "Parker Cook" Boston. 30th. Nov. 19.00 N. 68.45 W. Boston to Hayti General. $10,000.

Schr. "Union" Baltimore. 5th. Dec. 19.59 N. 74.10 W. Baltimore to Jamaica. General. Ransomed. $1,500.

P.S. [Postal Steamer] "Ariel" New York. 7th. Dec. 19.08 N. 74.10 W. General & Passengers. New York to Aspinwall. Ransomed. $261,000.

Bar. "Golden Rule" New York. 26th. Jan. 1863. 17.47 N. 75.00 W. New York to Aspinwall. General. $112,000.

Brgt. "Chastelain" Boston. 27th. Jan. 17.20 N. 72.15 W. Guadalupe to Cuba. Light. $10,000.

Schr. "Palmetto" Trenton. 3rd. Feb. 27.17 N. 66.09 W. New York to Porto Rico. General. $18,430

Ship "Golden Eagle" New Bedford. 21st. Feb. 29.28 N. 44.53 W. Chinchas to Cork. Guano. $61,000.

Bar. "Olive Jane" Boston. 21st. Feb. 29.28 N. 44.53 W. Bordeaux to New York. Wines & Spirits. $43,208.

Ship "Washington" New York. 27th. Feb. 30.19 N. 39.54 W. Callao to Cork. Guano. Ransomed. $50,000.

Ship "Bethiah Thayer." Rockland. 1st. Mar. 29.50 N. 38.13 W. Callao to Cork. Guano. Ransomed. $40,000.

Ship "John A. Parks" Hallowell. 2nd. Mar. 29.28 N. 37.51 W. New York to Buenos Ayres General. $66,157.

Ship "Punjaub" Boston. 15th. Mar. 8.37 N. 31.39 W. Calcutta to London. General. Ransomed. $55,000.

Ship "Morning Star" Boston. 23rd. Mar. 2.08 N. 26.04 W. Calcutta to London. General. Ransomed. $61,750.

Schr. "Kingfisher" New Bedford. 23rd. Mar. 2.08. N. 26.04 W. Whaling. Whale oil. $2,400.

Ship "Nora" Boston. 25th. Mar. 1.22. N. 26.04. W. Liverpool to Calcutta. Salt. $76,636.

Ship "Charles Hill" Boston. 25th. Mar. 1.22. N. 26.04. W. Liverpool to Montevideo. Salt. $28,450.

Ship "Louisa Hatch" Rockland. 4th. Apl. 3.12. S. 26.02. W. Cardiff to Point de Galle. Coal. $38,315.

Brgt. "Kate Cory" Westport. 15th. Apl. 4.10. S. 32.10. W. Whaling. Whale oil. $10,568.

Bar. "Lafayette" New Bedford. 15th. Apl. 4.10 S. 32.26 W. Whaling. Whale oil. $20,908.

Bar. "Nye" New Bedford. 24th. Apl. 5.45. S. 31.52. W. Whaling. Whale Oil. $31,127.

Ship. "Dorcas Prince" New York. 26th. Apl. 7.36. S. 31.37. W. New York to Shanghai. Coals &c. $44,108.

Bar. "Union Jack" New York. 3rd. May. 9.39 S. 32.35. W. New York to Shanghai. General. $77,000.

Ship "Sea Lark" Boston. 3rd. May. 9.39 S. 32.35. W. Boston to San Francisco. General. $550,000.

Ship "S. Gildersleeve" New York. 25th. May. 12.14. S. 35.11 W. Sunderland to Calcutta. Coals. $62,783.

Bar. "Justina" Baltimore. 25th. May. 12.14 S. 35.11. W. Rio Janeiro to Baltimore. Ballast. Ransomed. $7,000.

Ship "Jabez Snow" Bucksport. 29th. May. 12.35. S. 35.33. W. Cardiff to Calcutta. Coals. $72,781.

Bar. "Amazonian" Boston. 2nd. June, 15.0l S. 34.52. W. New York to Montevideo. General. $97,665.

Ship. "Talisman" New York. 5th. June. 15.00. S. 35.00. W. New York to Shanghai. Coals. &c. &c. $139,135.

Bar. "Conrad" Philadelphia. 20th. June. 25.07 S. 40.26. W. Buenos Ayres. to New York. Wool. $100,936.

[210]

BIBLIOGRAPHY

Collections of manuscripts and of published sources are discussed in the Introduction and in the annotations. Some authors and titles are made more readily available through the following list.

Adams, Charles F., *Before and After the Treaty of Washington*. New York: Printed for the New York Historical Society, 1902.

Adams, Ephraim D., *Great Britain and the American Civil War*. New York: Russell & Russell, 1925. Two volumes.

Albion, Robert G., and Jennie Barnes Pope, *Sea Lanes in Wartime The American Experience, 1775–1942*. New York: W. W. Norton and Company, 1942.

Allen, George W., Jr., The Confederate Steamer Nashville. Unpublished M. A. Thesis, University of Alabama, 1941.

American Lloyd's Registry of American and Foreign Shipping. New York: American Lloyd's, 1862–1864.

Anderson, Bern, *By Sea and By River. The Naval History of the Civil War*. New York: Alfred A. Knopf, 1962.

Badlam, William H., *Kearsarge and Alabama*. Providence: Soldiers' and Sailors' Historical Society of Rhode Island, 1894.

Balch, Thomas Willing, *The Alabama Arbitration*. Philadelphia: Allen, Allen, Lane & Scott, 1900.

Beaman, Charles C., *The National and Private "Alabama Claims."* Washington: W. H. Moore [1871].

Beaman, Charles C., *The Rights of Insurance Companies Under the Geneva Award*. New York: n.p., 1876.

Bemis, Samuel F., *A Short History of American Foreign Policy and Diplomacy*. New York: Holt, Rinehart, and Winston, 1959.

Bernard, Mountague, *A Historical Account of the Neutrality of Great Britain During the American Civil War*. London: Green, Reader, and Dyer, 1870.

Blunt, Edmund M., *The American Coast Pilot: Containing Directions for the . . .*

Coasts of North and South America. New York: Published by Edmund and George W. Blunt, 1850.

Bott, Elizabeth C., Admiral Semmes, CSN. Baton Rouge: Ortlieb's Printing House, 1911.

Boykin, Edward, Ghost Ship of the Confederacy. New York: Funk & Wagnalls, 1957.

Boynton, Charles B., The History of the Navy During the Rebellion. New York: D. Appleton and Co., 1868. Two volumes.

Bradford, Gamaliel, Confederate Portraits. Boston: Houghton Mifflin, 1914.

Bradlow, Edna and Frank, Here Comes the Alabama. Cape Town: A.A. Balkema, 1958.

Britannica Atlas. Chicago: Encyclopaedia Britannica, Inc., 1970.

British Admiralty, Geographical Handbook Series. London: The Admiralty, various dates. Indicated as a short title BR-510, and other numbers.

Brittin, Burdick H., and L. B. Watson, International Law for Seagoing Officers. Annapolis: U.S. Naval Institute, 1960.

Browne, Charles F., editor, Artemus Ward—His Travels. New York: Carleton, 1870.

Browne, John M., "The Duel Between the 'Alabama' and the 'Kearsarge'," in Battles and Leaders of the Civil War, vol. IV, pp. 615–625. New York: The Century Company, 1888.

Browne, John M., "The Duel Between the 'Alabama' and the 'Kearsarge' By the Surgeon of the 'Kearsarge'," in The Century Magazine, vol. 31 (April 1886), pp. 923–934.

Bulloch, James D., The Secret Service of the Confederate States in Europe or, How the Confederate Cruisers were Equipped. London: Richard Bentley and Son, 1883. Two volumes.

Callahan, James M., Diplomatic History of the Southern Confederacy. New York: F. Ungar, 1964.

Canfield, H. S., "Aboard a Semmes Prize," in Magazine of History, vol. 1 (1908), pp. 137–139.

The Career of the Alabama ("No. 290") from July 29, 1862 to June 19, 1864. London: Dorrell and Son, 1864.

Colton, George W., Colton's General Atlas. New York: G. W. and C. B. Colton and Company, 1866.

Commager, Henry S., editor, "Extracts from Lincoln's Messages to Congress Recommending Compensated Emancipation," in Documents of American History, 402–405. New York: F. S. Crofts and Company, 1943.

Commercial and Financial Chronicle. New York, 1864–1866.

Confederate States of America, Register of the Commissioned and Warrant Officers of the Navy of the Confederate States. Richmond: n.p., 1863.

Copplestone, Bennet, "Old Beeswax," in Blackwood's, vol. 219, pp. 330–344.

Correspondence Respecting the 'Alabama' Presented to Parliament 1863. London: n.p., 1863.

Coulter, E. Merton, The Confederate States of America, 1861–1865. Baton Rouge: Louisiana State University Press, 1950.

Cushing, Caleb, The Treaty of Washington. New York: Harper and Brothers, 1873.

Daly, Charles P., Are the Southern Privateersmen Pirates? New York: J. B. Kirker, 1862.

Dalzell, George W., *The Flight from the Flag*. Chapel Hill: The University of North Carolina Press, 1940.

Davis, Donald, "Visit of the Fighting Alabama," in Singapore *Times*, 19 January 1956.

Davis, George B., *The Elements of International Law*. New York: Harper and Brothers, 1915.

Davis, J. C. Bancroft, *The Case of the United States, to be Laid Before the Tribunal of Arbitration.* . . . Washington: G.P.O., 1872.

Davis, William W., *Civil War and Reconstruction in Florida*. New York: Columbia University Press, 1913.

Delaney, Norman C., *John McIntosh Kell of the Raider Alabama*. University, Alabama: The University of Alabama Press, 1973.

Delaney, Norman C., "The End of the Alabama," in *American Heritage*, vol. 23 (April 1972), pp. 58–69, 102.

Durkin, Joseph T., *Stephen R. Mallory: Confederate Navy Chief*. Chapel Hill: University of North Carolina Press, 1954.

Edge, Frederick M., *The Alabama and the Kearsarge*. London: William Ridgway, 1864.

Edge, Frederick M., *An Englishman's View of the Battle Between the Alabama and the Kearsarge*. New York: Anson D. F. Randolph, 1864.

Ellicott, John M., *The Life of John Ancrum Winslow Rear-Admiral, United States Navy*. New York: G. P. Putnam's Sons, 1905.

Emmons, George F., *The Navy of the United States, from the Commencement, 1775 to 1853*. Washington: Gideon and Co., 1853.

English Neutrality, Is the Alabama a British Pirate? Philadelphia: H. B. Ashmead, 1863.

Fay, Caleb T., *Geneva Award Fund. Statement of C. Fay of San Francisco, California, on the Atlantic and Pacific Coastwise Business, in Behalf of Coast War Premium Claimants*. Washington: McGill and Co., n.d.

Fenwick, Charles G., *International Law*. New York: The Century Co., 1924.

Formby, John, *The American Civil War*. London: John Murray, 1910. Two volumes.

Frank Leslie's Illustrated Newspaper, 1863.

Fullam, George T., Sr., *Hand Book to the Humber*. Hull: M. Harland and Son, n. d.

[Fullam, George T.] *The Cruise of the "Alabama," From Her Departure from Liverpool Until Her Arrival at the Cape of Good Hope By An Officer on Board*. Liverpool: Lee and Nightingale, 1863.

[Fullam, George T.] *The Cruise of the Alabama, Raphael Semmes, Commander. From Her Departure from Liverpool July 29, 1862. By an Officer on Board, with Gleanings from Other Sources*. n.p., 1864.

[Fullam, George T.] *Our Cruise in the Confederate States War Steamer "Alabama,"* from a Supplement to the *South African Advertiser and Mail*. Cape Town: *South African Advertiser and Mail*, 1863.

Geffcke, Friederich H., *Die Alabama—Fragt*. Stuttgart: Gott, 1872.

Goodrich, Albert M., *Cruise and Captures of the Alabama*. Minneapolis: H. W. Wilson Co., 1906.

Hackett, Frank W., *Reminiscences of the Geneva Tribunal of Arbitration*. Boston: Houghton, Mifflin and Company, 1911.

Hackett, Frank W., *The Geneva Awards Acts*. Boston: Little, Brown, 1882.

Hamersley, Thomas H. S., *Complete General Navy Register of the U.S.A., 1776–87*. New York: n.p., 1888.

Hamersley, Thomas H. S., editor, *General Register of the United States Navy and Marine Corps for One Hundred Years (1782–1882)*. Washington: Thomas Hamersley Publisher, 1882.

Hamersly, Lewis R., *The Records of Living Officers of the U. S. Navy and Marine Corps with a History of the Naval Operations During the Rebellion, 1861–1865*. Philadelphia: n.p., 1870.

Harbeck, Charles T., *A Contribution to the Bibliography of the History of the United States Navy*. Cambridge: privately printed, 1906.

Harper's Pictorial History of the Great Rebellion. New York: Harper and Brothers, 1866–1868.

Harper's Weekly, 1861–1865.

Hayward, Edwin J., The Confederate Cruiser *Georgia*. Unpublished M. A. Thesis, University of Alabama, 1940.

Haywood, Philip D., *Cruise of the Alabama, by One of Her Crew*. Boston: Houghton, Mifflin and Co., 1886.

Haywood, Philip D., "Life on the *Alabama*," in *The Century Magazine*, XXXI (April) 1886, pp. 901–910.

Heitman, Francis B., *Historical Register and Dictionary of the United States Army, from its Organization, September 29, 1789 to March 2, 1903*. Washington: G.P.O., 1903. Two volumes.

Heyl, Erik, *Early American Steamers*. Buffalo, New York: Published by the Author, 1953.

Hill, Frederick T., *Decisive Battles of the Law*. London: Harper and Brothers, 1907.

Hill, Jim D., "John Ancrum Winslow," in *The Dictionary of American Biography*, Volume XX. New York: Charles Scribner's Sons, 1936.

Hill, Jim D., *Sea Dogs of the Sixties*. Minneapolis: University of Minnesota Press, 1935.

Hobson, Henry S., *The Famous Cruise of the Kearsarge*. Bonds Village, Massachusetts: By the Author, 1894.

Hoole, William Stanley, *Four Years in the Confederate Navy: The Career of Captain John Low in the C.S.S. Fingal, Florida, Alabama, Tuscaloosa, and Ajax*. Athens: University of Georgia Press, 1964.

Horan, James D., editor, *CSS Shenandoah: The Memoir of Lieutenant Commanding James I. Waddell*. New York: Crown Publishers, 1960.

Huff, Grace C., The Confederate Cruiser *Shenandoah*. Unpublished M.A. Thesis, University of Alabama, 1940.

Hunt, Cornelius E., *The Shenandoah: or the Last Confederate Cruiser*. New York: G.W. Carleton and Company, 1867.

Hutchins, John G., *The American Maritime Industries and Public Policy, 1789–1914*. Cambridge: Harvard University Press, 1941.

Hydrographic Office (H.O. 105), *Sailing Directions for the Southwest Coast of Africa From Cape Palmas to Cape of Good Hope*. Washington: Government Printing Office, 1932.

    H.O. No. 145, *Sailing Directions for the West Coast of England and Wales*. Washington: Government Printing Office, 1939.

H.O. No. 150, *Sailing Directions for the East Coast of England.* Washington: Government Printing Office, 1943.

H.O. No. 161, *South Indian Ocean Pilot Islands Westward of Longitude 92°East Including Madagascar and the Comoro Islands.* Washington: Government Printing Office, 1917.

H.O. No. 162, *Sailing Directions for Malacca Strait and Sumatra.* Washington: Government Printing Office, 1933.

Illustrated London News, 1862–1864.

Johnson, Allen, Dumas Malone, and others, *Dictionary of American Biography.* New York: Charles Scribner's Sons, 1928–1940. 20 volumes.

Johnson, Reverdy, *A Reply to a Recent Speech of Sir Roundell Palmer on the Washington Treaty, and the Alabama Claims.* Baltimore: J. Murphy and Company, 1871.

Johnson, Robert E., *Thence Round Cape Horn, the Story of United States Naval Forces on Pacific Station, 1818–1923.* Annapolis, Maryland: U.S. Naval Institute, 1963.

Jones, Virgil C., *The Civil War at Sea.* New York: Holt, Rhinehart, Winston, 1960–1962. Three volumes.

Kell, John M., "Cruise and Combats of the 'Alabama' by Her Executive Officer, John McIntosh Kell," in *Battles and Leaders of the Civil War.* New York: The Century Company, 1888.

Kell, John M., "Cruise and Combats of the 'Alabama' By Her Executive Officer," in *The Century Magazine,* Volume 31 (April 1886), pp. 911–922.

Kell, John M., John McIntosh Kell Papers. Duke University Library.

Kell, John M., *Recollections of a Naval Life, Including the Cruises of the Confederate Steamers "Sumter" and "Alabama."* Washington: The Neale Company, 1900.

Kemble, John H., editor, *Two Years Before the Mast: A Personal Narrative of Life at Sea by Richard Henry Dana, Jr.* Los Angeles: The Ward Ritchie Press, 1964.

Khan, N. H., The *Alabama* Arbitration. Unpublished Ph. D. dissertation, University of Virginia, 1962.

Kirkaldy, Adam W., *British Shipping.* London: K. Paul, Trench, Trubner and Company, Ltd., 1914.

Kirkland, Charles P., *Liability of the Government of Great Britain for the Depredations of Rebel Privateers on the Commerce of the United States, Considered.* New York: Anson D. F. Randolph, 1863.

Knox, Dudley W., *History of the United States Navy.* New York: G. P. Putnam's Sons, 1936.

LaBree, Ben, *The Confederate Soldier in the Civil War, 1861–1865.* Louisville: The Courier-Journal Printing Company, 1895.

Lindsay, William S., *History of Merchant Shipping and Ancient Commerce.* New York: A M S Press, 1965.

List of Claims Filed with the Department of State, Growing Out of the Acts Committed By the Several Vessels Which Have Given Rise to the Claims Generically Known as The Alabama Claims. Washington: Government Printing Office, 1971.

Lloyd, Christopher, *The British Seaman 1200–1860.* London: Collins, 1968.

Lloyd, Christopher, *Ships and Seamen from Vikings to Present Day.* Cleveland: World Publishing Company, 1961.

Lloyd's of London, *Register of Shipping.*

Logan, F. A., "Activities of the Alabama in Asian Waters," in *Pacific Historical Review*, 31:143–150. May 1962.

London *Times*, 1861–1865.

Lossing, Benson J., *A History of the Civil War, 1861–1865*. New York: War Memorial Association, 1912.

Lossing, Benson J., *Pictorial Field Book of the Civil War*. Philadelphia: n. p., 1866. Three volumes.

Low, John, Log of the CSS *Alabama*, 28 July 1862 to 31 December 1863, and related Low Papers. These manuscripts are in the private library of Clarence B. Hanson, Jr., publisher of the Birmingham *News* and the Birmingham *Post-Herald*.

Lytle, William M., compiler, *Merchant Steam Vessels of the United States, 1807–1868*. Mystic, Connecticut: The Steamship Historical Society of America, 1952.

Macartney, Clarence E., *Mr. Lincoln's Admirals*. New York: Funk and Wagnalls, 1956.

Maclay, Edgar S., *A History of the United States Navy from 1775 to 1902*. New York: D. Appleton and Company, 1893. Three volumes.

McEwen, A. A. and A. H. Lewis, *Encyclopedia of Nautical Knowledge*. Cambridge, Maryland: Cornell Maritime Press, 1958.

Maffitt, Emma M., *The Life and Services of John Newland Maffitt*. New York: The Neale Publishing Company, 1906.

Malone, Dumas, editor, *Dictionary of American Biography*. New York: Charles Scribner's Sons, 1933.

Manning, J. F., *Epitome of the Geneva Award Contest in the Congress of the United States*. New York: Evening Post, 1882.

Manning, J. F., compiler, *Laws of Alabama Claims and Rules of Court*. New York: Evening Post, 1882.

Maps of the Society for the Diffusion of Useful Knowledge. London: Charles Knight and Company, 1846. Two volumes.

Marvin, Winthrop L., *The American Merchant Marine*. New York: Charles Scribner's Sons, 1902.

Maynard, Douglas H., "Plotting the Escape of the *Alabama*," in *The Journal of Southern History*, XX, 2 (May 1954), pp. 197–209.

Meriwether, Colyer, *Raphael Semmes*. Philadelphia: George W. Jacobs and Company, 1913.

Messages and Papers of Department of State. Washington: G. P. O., 1861–1866.

Miller, Francis T., editor, *The Photographic History of the Civil War in Ten Volumes*. New York: The Trow Press, 1911.

Moore, Frank, editor, *The Rebellion Record: A Diary of American Events*. New York: G. P. Putnam, 1861–1863, D. Van Nostrand, 1864–1868. Two volumes.

Moore, John B., *History and Digest of the International Arbitrations to Which the United States Has Been a Party*. Washington: G. P. O., 1898. Six volumes.

Morgan, James M., *Recollections of a Rebel Reefer*. Boston: Houghton, Mifflin and Company, 1917.

Morgan, Murray C., *Dixie Raider: The Saga of the CSS Shenandoah*. New York: E. P. Dutton and Company, 1948.

Navy Department, *Civil War Naval Chronology, 1861–1865.* Washington: G. P. O., 1971.

Navy Department, *Dictionary of American Naval Fighting Ships.* Washington: G. P. O., 1959–1968. Three volumes.

Navy Department, *Official Records of the Union and Confederate Navies.* Washington: G. P. O., 1894–1922. Index, 1927. 30 volumes, plus Index.

Navy Department, *Ordnance Instructions for the United States Navy.* Washington G. P. O., 1866.

Navy Department, *Register of Officers of the Confederate States Navy 1861–1865.* Washington: G. P. O., 1931.

Navy Department, *Report of the Secretary of the Navy, With an Appendix, Containing Reports from Officers.* Washington: G. P. O., 1864.

Neeser, Robert W., *Statistical and Chronological History of the United States Navy, 1775–1907.* New York: The Macmillan Company, 1909. Two volumes.

Nevins, Allan, *Hamilton Fish: The Inner History of the Grant Administration.* New York: Dodd, Mead and Company, 1936.

Newton, Lord, *Lord Lyons, A Record of British Diplomacy.* London: E. Arnold, 1913. Two volumes.

New York *Commercial Advertiser,* 1862–1864.

New York *Courier and Inquirer,* 1862–1864.

New York *Herald,* 1862–1864.

New York *Marine Register,* 1857.

New York *Shipping and Commercial List,* 1862.

Northcote, Sir Stafford, *Argument at Geneva.* New York: D. Appleton and Company, 1889.

Nye, Gideon, Jr., *Casual Papers on the "Alabama."* Hong Kong, China: Magazine Office, 1869.

O'Dowd, James, *Law and Facts of the Case of the Alabama, with Reference to the Geneva Arbitration.* London: n.p., 1873.

Osbon, Bradley S., *Hand Book of the United States Navy . . . from April 1861 to May 1864.* New York: D. Van Nostrand, 1864.

Owsley, Frank L., Jr., "The Capture of the CSS *Florida,*" in *American Neptune,* XXII, January 1962.

Owsley, Frank L., Jr., *The C.S.S. Florida: Her Building and Operations.* Philadelphia: University of Pennsylvania Press, 1965.

Owsley, Frank L., Sr., *King Cotton Diplomacy: Foreign Relations of the Confederate States of America.* Chicago: The University of Chicago Press, 1931 and 1959.

Owsley, Harriet C., "Henry Shelton Sanford and Federal Surveillance Abroad, 1861–1865," in *Mississippi Valley Historical Review,* vol. 48 (Sept. 1961), 211–228.

Palmer, Sir Roundell, *Speech Delivered in the House of Commons on the "Alabama" Question. March 11, 1863.* London: Macmillan and Company, 1863.

Papers Relating to Foreign Affairs, Accompanying the Annual Message of the President. Washington: G. P. O., 1861–1865.

Parker, William H., *Recollections of a Naval Officer, 1841–1865.* New York: Charles Scribner's Sons, 1883.

Porter, David D., *The Naval History of the Civil War.* New York: The Sherman Publishing Company, 1886.

Pradier-Fodere, Paul, *La Question de l'Alabama et le Droit des Gens.* Paris: Librairie Amyot, 1872.

Proceedings of the Chamber of Commerce of the State of New York, on the Burning of the Ship Brilliant, by the Rebel Pirate Alabama. New York: John W. Amerman, Printer, 1862.

Public Record Office. London. Manuscripts described in the Introduction of this book.

Rawley, James A., *Turning Points of the Civil War.* Lincoln: University of Nebraska Press, 1966.

R. (pseud.), *The Official Correspondence on the Claims of the United States in Respect to the Alabama.* London: Longmans, Green, and Company, 1867.

Read, George W., *A Pioneer of 1850 Adventures of George Willis Read 1819–1880.* Boston: Little, Brown, and Company, 1927.

Regulations for the Navy of the Confederate States. Richmond: Macfarlane and Ferguson, 1862.

Rhodes, H. T. F., and C. J. Smith, editors, *The International Year Book and Statesmen's Who's Who, 1962.* London: Burke's Peerage Limited, 1962.

Richardson, James D., *A Compilation of the Messages and Papers of the Confederacy, Including the Diplomatic Correspondence.* Nashville: U. S. Publishing Company, 1905.

Roberts, W. Adolphe, *Semmes of the Alabama.* Indianapolis: The Bobbs-Merrill Company, 1938.

Robinson, William M., Jr., *The Alabama-Kearsarge Battle: A Study in Original Sources.* Salem, Massachusetts: The Essex Institute, 1924.

Rodimon, William, *The Confederate Cruiser Florida.* Unpublished M. A. Thesis, University of Alabama, 1940.

Roe, F. A., *Naval Duties and Discipline.* New York: D. Van Nostrand, 1865.

Rowe, William H., *The Maritime History of Maine.* New York: W. W. Norton and Company, 1948.

Runciman, Sir Walter, Bart., *"Sunbeam II" in 1932 With Some Reminiscences of Sailing Ship Captains.* Newcastle Upon Tyne: Andrew Reid and Company, Limited, 1933. Volume 3.

Russell, John, Earl, *Recollections and Suggestions 1813–1873.* Boston: Roberts Brothers, 1875.

Scharf, J. Thomas, *History of the Confederate States Navy From Its Organization to the Surrender of Its Last Vessel.* New York: Rogers and Sherwood, 1887.

Semmes, Raphael, *Kruistogen van de Alabama en de Sumter.* Zwolle: Van Hoogstragen, 1865.

Semmes, Raphael, *Memoirs of Service Afloat During the War Between the States.* Baltimore: Kelly, Piet and Company, 1869.

Semmes, Raphael, *My Adventures Afloat: A Personal Memoir of My Cruises and Services in the "Sumter" and "Alabama."* London: R. Bentley, 1869.

Semmes, Raphael, *The Cruise of the Alabama and the Sumter. From the Private Journals and Other Papers of Commander R. Semmes, C.S.N., and Other Officers* New York: Carleton, Publisher, 1864.

Semmes, Raphael, *The Log of the Alabama and the Sumter*. London: Saunders, Otley and Company, 1864.

Seward, William H., *The Diplomatic History of the War For the Union*. Boston: Houghton, Mifflin and Company, 1884. George E. Baker, editor.

Ship Registers and Enrollments of Machias, Maine, 1780–1930. Rockland, Maine: The National Archives Project, 1942. Two volumes.

Ship Registers and Enrollments of New Orleans, Louisiana. University, Louisiana: Louisiana State University, 1941–1942.

Sinclair, Arthur, *Two Years on the Alabama*. Boston: Lee and Shepard, 1896.

Smith, Joseph A., *An Address Delivered Before the Union League of Philadelphia on Saturday Evening, January 20, 1906*. Philadelphia: J. B. Lippincott Company, 1906. Presenting a painting of the *Alabama-Kearsarge* Battle.

Soley, James R., *The Blockade and the Cruisers*. New York: Charles Scribner's Sons, 1890.

South African Advertiser and Mail, 19 Sept., 1863.

Spears, John R., *The History of Our Navy . . . 1775–1898*. New York: Charles Scribner's Sons, 1897–1899. Five volumes.

Standing, Percy C., "The Boarding Officer of the Alabama," in *Cornhill Magazine*, LXXV, May 1897.

Stanforth (Edward) Ltd. London, *Stanforth's Octavo Atlas of Modern Geography*. London: E. Stanforth, 1894, 2nd edition.

Stern, Philip V., editor, *The Confederate Raider Alabama: Selections from Memoirs of Service Afloat During the War Between the States*. Greenwich, Connecticut: Fawcett Publications, 1962.

Stowell, E., *Consular Cases and Opinions*. Washington: G. P. O., 1909.

Summersell, Charles G., *The Cruise of CSS Sumter*. Tuscaloosa, Alabama: Confederate Publishing Company, Inc., 1965.

Swanston, George H., *The Companion Atlas to the Gazeteer of the World*. Edinburgh: A. Fullerton and Company, 1860.

Tenney, W. J., *The Military and Naval History of the Rebellion*. New York: D. Appleton and Company, 1865.

The British Museum Catalogue of Printed Maps, Charts and Plans. London: The Trustees of the British Museum, 1967. 15 volumes.

The Times, London, *The Times Atlas. . . .* London: Office of *The Times*, 1867, 1895, 1897.

Todd, Herbert H., The Building of the Confederate States Navy in Europe. Ph. D. dissertation, Vanderbilt University, 1941.

Townshend, Frank, "The Fight of the 'Hatteras' and 'Alabama'," in *The Civil War in Song and Story 1861–1865*. New York: P. F. Collier, 1889.

Uniform and Dress of the Army and Navy of the Confederate States of America. Richmond: Charles H. Wynne, 1861.

U. S. Department of Commerce, Coast and Geodetic Survey, Serial No. 725, *United States Coast Pilot, Gulf Coast, Key West to Rio Grande*. Washington: G. P. O., 1949.

Vanity Fair. New York: Louis H. Stephens, 1861–1863.

Walker, Tillie, The Confederate Steamer *Alabama*. Unpublished M. A. thesis, University of Alabama, 1938.

Welles, Gideon, *Diary of Gideon Welles, Secretary of the Navy Under Lincoln and Johnson.* Boston: Houghton, Mifflin and Company, 1911.

Wells, Tom H., *The Confederate Navy.* University, Alabama: The University of Alabama Press, 1971.

West, Richard S., Jr., *Mr. Lincoln's Navy.* New York: Longmans, Green and Company, 1957.

Wheaton, Henry, *Elements of International Law.* Philadelphia: Lea and Blanchard, 1846.

Whipple, A. B. C., "The Hard-Luck Frigate," in *American Heritage,* II, 2.

Whitridge, Arnold, "The *Alabama* 1862–1864: A Crisis in Anglo-American Relations," in *History Today,* 5:174–185, March 1955.

Who's Who. London: C. and C. Black, 1849, 1909, 1945, 1963.

Young, James (see Philip D. Haywood).

INDEX

[222]

SPONSORS

The Friends of the Mobile Public Library gratefully acknowledge the generous contributions of the following listed Sponsors, who have made possible the publication of the Journal of George T. Fullam.

COMMERCIAL AND INSTITUTIONAL:

American National Bank and Trust Company of Mobile
The First National Bank of Mobile
The Merchants National Bank of Mobile
The Mitchell Foundation, Inc.
Mobile Federal Savings and Loan Association
Title Insurance Company

INDIVIDUAL:

Mrs. Clara Stone Collins
Mr. and Mrs. Stephens G. Croom
Dr. and Mrs. Samuel Eichold
Mr. and Mrs. A. Danner Frazer
Mr. Preston H. Haskell, Jr.
Mr. and Mrs. E. A. Hirs
Mr. and Mrs. Carl Hixon
Mr. and Mrs. Ralph G. Holberg, Jr.
Mr. and Mrs. John G. Janett
Mr. and Mrs. Julian F. McGowin
Mr. N. Floyd McGowin
Mrs. David B. Miller
Mr. Tom P. Ollinger

Mr. and Mrs. C. M. A. Rogers III
Mr. and Mrs. J. Craig Smith
Mr. and Mrs. Harry Sonneborn
Mr. R. J. Stockham
Mr. and Mrs. Frank Sturges III
Mr. and Mrs. James F. Sulzby, Jr.
Dr. and Mrs. Charles G. Summersell
Mr. and Mrs. John H. van Aken

We wish to acknowledge the unfailing cooperation of Mobile Public Library Director Donald J. Sager and all members of the library staff. Previous Directors Henry Blasick and Guenter Jansen were also very helpful.

DONORS TO BIDDING FUND

Altmayer, Mr. and Mrs. Jay P.
Barney, Mr. and Mrs. Howard
Bean, Mr. and Mrs. Robert L.
Betty, Mrs. Ellen M.
Betty, Mr. and Mrs. Sam
Brown, Dr. and Mrs. Claude L.
Burtu, Mrs. Cora M.
Butler, Mr. and Mrs. Charles
Cameron, Miss Connie
Cole, Mr. and Mrs. Frank
Coley, Mr. and Mrs. D. R., Jr.
Collins, Mrs. Clara Stone
Converse, J. B. & Company, Inc.
Crawford, Mrs. Cherry
Deasy, Mr. Edmund L.
Douglas, Mr. J. Andrew
Edington, Mr. and Mrs. Robert S.
Eichold, Dr. and Mrs. Samuel
First National Bank of Mobile
Fitzpatrick, Mr. and Mrs. H. T., Jr.
Fonde School, 4th Grade
  Mrs. Williamson, Teacher
Friend, Miss Ellen T.
Friends of Mobile Public Library
Gardberg, Mr. and Mrs. A.
Gidden, Mr. and Mrs. Kenneth
Gillies, Mrs. Alma B.
Gilroy, Mrs. Susie F.
Hamburger, Miss G. L.
Haskew, Capt. and Mrs. C. L.
Hines, Mr. H. C.
Hoell, Mr. and Mrs. Luther L. III
Holberg, Mr. and Mrs. Ralph
Hudson, Mrs. Cora M.
Hudson, Mrs. Victor
Ingate, Mr. and Mrs. Fred
Inge, Mrs. Francis Marion

Iverson, Mrs. Fred
Jernigan, Mr. and Mrs. W. H
Jones, Miss Lenore
Jones, Mr. and Mrs. Rupert S.
Kahn, Mr. Gordon
Kearley, Dr. and Mrs. Frank J.
Kennedy, Miss Sarah C.
Kilborn, Mr. and Mrs. Vincent
Lott, Mr. Wade
Lyle, Mrs. John F.
Mader, Mr. Charles
Mobile Public Library Board
McGehee, Dr. and Mrs. John
McGill, Mr. Max P.
Merchants National Bank of Mobile
Mobile, City of
  Commissioners: Joseph N. Langan
           George McNally
           Charles F. Trimmier
Mobile, County of
  Commissioners: Hugh Fort
           Will D. Hays
           Leroy Stevens
  Clerk: Ed Doody
Prichard, City of
  Major: V. O. Capps
  Councilmen: C. W. Dismukes
          L. C. Lassiter, Jr.
          H. W. Phillips
          N. J. Moulyet
          E. G. Sansom
  Clerk: Mrs. Berniece Centanne
Patrick, Mr. and Mrs. Frank
Parker, Mr. and Mrs. Jerry
Pearson, Mr. and Mrs. Joe
Richards, Miss Edith Horton
Scott, Mrs. W. H.

Sells, Mr. and Mrs. Raymond H.
Sledge, Mrs. E. S., Sr.
Smith's Bakery of Mobile
Smith, Mr. and Mrs. Carter
Southern Industries, Inc.
Stedman, Mrs. Lois R.
Thigpen, Mr. and Mrs. Roy M. Jr.
Thomas, Judge and Mrs. Dan
Tyson, Mr. and Mrs. John
Tyson, Mrs. Virginia Bragg
United Daughters of the Confederacy:
  Cradle of the Confederacy Chapter
    (Montgomery)

Mildred Rutherford Chapter (Mobile)
Alabama State Board
North Baldwin Chapter
Stars and Bars Chapter, Children of
  the Confederacy, (Mobile)
WKRG - RADIO
WKRG - TV
Walker, Dr. and Mrs. Howard
Waller, Miss Frances A.
Wharton, Dr. and Mrs. John
White-Spunner, Mr. and Mrs. Strat
Woodruff, Mr. Les
Yeatman, Mrs. Reaia

FULLAM JOURNAL COMMITTEE

B. L. Roberson, Chairman
Louis E. Braswell*
William E. Buckley, Jr.
Stephens G. Croom
M. N. Hardesty*

Gustavus O. Hamner
C. M. A. Rogers III
Mrs. Frank Sturges III*
Richard D. Wells
George M. Widney

*Presidents of the Friends of the Mobile Public Library during the period of publication.

Mrs. Harold S. Cohen, President of the Friends at the time the Journal was acquired, was active in the initial planning stages and also made useful comments to the Committee during publication.